Agonistic Democracy

This book delivers a systematic account of agonistic democracy, and a much-needed analysis of the core components of agonism: pluralism, tragedy, and the value of conflict. It also traces the history of these ideas, identifying the connections with republicanism and with Greek antiquity. Mark Wenman presents a critical appraisal of the leading contemporary proponents of agonism and, in a series of well-crafted and comprehensive discussions, brings these thinkers into debate with one another, as well as with the post-structuralist and continental theorists who influence them. Wenman draws extensively on Hannah Arendt, and stresses the creative power of human action as augmentation and revolution. He also reworks Arendt's discussion of reflective judgement to present an alternative style of agonism, one where the democratic contest is linked to the emergence of a militant form of cosmopolitanism, and to prospects for historical change in the context of neoliberal globalisation.

MARK WENMAN is Lecturer in Politics at the University of Nottingham, where he teaches contemporary political theory and the history of political thought. He has published articles on agonistic democracy and post-structuralism in leading academic journals, including *Contemporary Political Theory*, *Philosophy and Social Criticism*, and *Political Studies*. Mark is a founding member of CONCEPT, The Nottingham Centre for Normative Political Theory. He is also a Lead Editor of *Political Studies* and Editor in Chief of *Political Studies Review*.

Agonistic Democracy

Constituent Power in the Era of Globalisation

Mark Wenman
University of Nottingham

CAMBRIDGE
UNIVERSITY PRESS

CAMBRIDGE
UNIVERSITY PRESS

University Printing House, Cambridge CB2 8BS, United Kingdom

Cambridge University Press is part of the University of Cambridge.

It furthers the University's mission by disseminating knowledge in the pursuit of education, learning and research at the highest international levels of excellence.

www.cambridge.org
Information on this title: www.cambridge.org/9781316505380

© Mark Wenman 2013

First published 2013
First paperback edition 2015

A catalogue record for this publication is available from the British Library

Library of Congress Cataloguing in Publication data
Wenman, Mark, 1971–
Agonistic democracy : constituent power in the era of globalisation /
Mark Wenman.
    pages   cm
Includes bibliographical references and index.
ISBN 978-1-107-00372-9 (hardback)
1. Democracy – Philosophy.   2. Political science – Philosophy.   I. Title.
JC423.W369   2013
321.8 – dc23   2013017441

ISBN 978-1-107-00372-9 Hardback
ISBN 978-1-316-50538-0 Paperback

It is not in the least superstitious, it is even a council of realism . . . to be prepared for and to expect 'miracles' in the political realm

Hannah Arendt, 'What is Freedom?'

Tyranny does not endure, for it cannot root itself in the people; it cannot rely on their strength: it does not endure and cannot expand

Louis Althusser, *Machiavelli and Us*

Contents

Preface

Politics in a new century

The conceptual innovations explored in his book have been developed in the context of profound changes in liberal democratic societies, especially since the end of the Cold War. In this preface I outline these transformations under the headings of (i) the politics of diversity, (ii) the politics fundamentalism, and (iii) the politics of globalisation.

The politics of diversity

Contemporary western societies are characterised by a complex diversity of social and cultural identities, and the politics of diversity has become a predominant theme in Anglo-American normative political theory over the latter part of the twentieth and into the twenty-first century. The politics of diversity is rooted in the dynamics of social mobility. For example, the widespread migration of people since the end of the Second World War has altered considerably the demographics of former colonial powers such as Britain and France. Historically, these nations negotiated a degree of cultural diversity associated with internal regional and religious differences, but the politics of diversity has been greatly amplified by the influx of significant numbers of ethnically and culturally diverse groups, often from former colonies. Consequently, issues of 'race relations' have been at the forefront of political debate in Britain throughout the postwar period, and this led to the implementation of the Race Relations Acts in 1968 and 1976, which prohibited discrimination in areas such as employment and education. More recently, these debates have given way to discussions about 'multiculturalism', and whether formal parity of opportunity is sufficient to ensure equality or if 'positive discrimination' might be necessary to create meaningful equality in a diverse society.

In the United States, with its past experience of chattel slavery and a much longer history of immigration, issues of racial inequality have similarly been at the forefront of political debate. The violent reaction in the

x   Preface

southern states in the 1960s to the civil rights campaigns against racial segregation showed that, a century after the Reconstruction Amendments, American society remained deeply divided on the issue of *de facto* equality for African Americans. These campaigns resulted in the implementation of additional civil rights legislation, and, just like in the UK, subsequent debates have turned around the question of whether or not equality of opportunities legislation is sufficient, or if forms of 'affirmative action' may be necessary to create meaningful equality for ethnic minority groups in American society. In those former colonies where Europeans established permanent settlements, i.e. in the United States, Canada, Australia, New Zealand, South Africa, and South America, the politics of ethnic diversity is further compounded by the struggles of indigenous peoples for recognition of their traditional authorities and cultural practices. As we will see in Chapter 4, these struggles are especially emphasised by James Tully because they bring to the fore the complex forms of domination that still operate in contemporary pluralistic societies.

Other modes of diversity politics are both cause and effect of the radical changes in values characteristic of post-industrialised societies in the latter part of the twentieth century. This is apparent in the persistent manifestation of social movements from the late 1960s around issues of gender and lifestyle politics. For example, the emergence of second wave feminism has undermined the traditional hierarchical relationships between women and men in western societies and challenged the conventional understanding of gender roles in the family, the workplace, and in public institutions. These struggles have led to equality of opportunities legislation in the workplace, much greater participation of women in higher education and the professions, and to reformist legalisation on issues such as abortion, divorce, and child care provision. Similarly, the struggles of gay rights campaigners – initially for the legalisation of homosexuality and more recently for public recognition of same sex marriages, and for gay rights in institutions such as the armed forces and the Anglican Church – is testimony to a momentous transformation in social values since the 1960s.

Yet another source of the politics of diversity in the new century is the novel forms of risk associated with the ever-quickening pace of technological innovation. Citizens of post-industrial societies increasingly find themselves trying to make sense of a bewildering assortment of issues related to 'manufactured risks', from climate change and nuclear proliferation, to the possibilities of human cloning, stem cell research, genetically modified food, and a whole host of other issues associated with bio-technology. Often, these issues throw the deep diversity of values and opinions in contemporary societies into stark relief.

The politics of diversity has also unfolded in the context of the collapse of state socialism in Russia and Eastern Europe in the late 1980s and early 1990s, an ever-deepening crisis of the welfare state across Western Europe, the spread of neo-liberalism around the globe, and a massive expansion in material inequality both in the relatively affluent west and also in the 'developing' world. These tendencies have been hugely accelerated by the systemic economic crises that have followed the financial crisis of October 2008, and which threaten a global economic slump on the scale of the 1930s. In this conjuncture, it is important to note the concerns of authors as diverse as Nancy Fraser (1997), Richard Rorty (1999), Brian Barry (2001), and Slavoj Žižek (2006a) who have argued that the Left has become overly focused on questions of cultural diversity and has lost sight of its core priority, i.e. a collective struggle for a politics of redistribution and a reduction of material inequality. All of the thinkers examined in this book see themselves broadly on the Left, and so one of the themes explored here is whether and in what ways agonistic democracy can address the politics of diversity as well as struggles for economic equality.

The politics of fundamentalism

The politics of diversity routinely finds groups and individuals in dispute over issues that bring into play their most fundamental values, associated, for example, with religious doctrine or deep differences in moral norms or lifestyle choices. The issue of abortion and a woman's right to choose would be an obvious case in point, but so too would issues such as gay marriage, experiments with human cloning, and so on. It is perhaps not surprising, therefore, that cultural diversity often generates seemingly intractable forms of conflict and a polarisation of political debate, and it is significant that the new century has been marked by a rise in domestic and international conflict. Indeed, the optimism of the early 1990s – that the post–Cold War world might be one of a progressive coalescence around liberal values, encapsulated in Francis Fukuyama's notion of the 'end of history' – has given way to a world marked instead by what John Gray calls 'renascent particularisms, militant religions, and resurgent ethnicities' (Fukuyama, 1992; Gray, 2007, 2).

This rising tide of conflict is nowhere more evident than in the emergence of religious forms of fundamentalism around the globe as a backlash against western secular values, i.e. excessive consumerism and narrow forms of individualism. For example, this is apparent in the enormous prominence of evangelical Christianity throughout many parts of the developing world, and of course in the United States where evangelicalism has been brought directly into mainstream political debate, not just on issues such as abortion, but more generally in support of prominent conservative Christians for the Republican Party. It is also manifest in the intense controversies that have surrounded the campaigns of Islamists in Europe and elsewhere: for example, following the *fatwa* that was placed on Salmon Rushdie by the Ayatollah Khomeini for the publication of his *Satanic Verses* in 1988, and which led to a failed assassination attempt against Rushdie in 1989; in protest against the cartoon depictions of the Prophet Muhammad published in the Danish Newspaper *Jyllands-Posten* in 2005, which included the firebombing of Danish embassies in a number of Islamic states and the burning of Danish flags in Gaza City and elsewhere; and in opposition to the French Government's decision to ban the display of religious insignia in public institutions and more recently to outlaw face covering in any public arena.

Indeed, wherever we look today we see uncompromising conflict and clashes of reciprocal intolerance: from the ethnic conflicts which have raged in the former Yugoslavia and Rwanda, to the resurgence of far-Right populism in parts of Europe; to the acts of terrorism carried out by radical Islamists against the American embassies in Tanzania and Kenya in 1998, the World Trade Centre on September the 11th, 2001, and subsequently in Madrid (2004), London (2005), Mumbai (2008) and in many other cities around world; to the neo-conservative 'War or Terror' instigated by the Bush regime and the subsequent wars in Iraq and Afghanistan; to the heightening of the Israeli/Palestinian conflict following the electoral victory of Hamas in Gaza 2006. One might be forgiven for thinking that we have returned to something like the early modern wars of religion.

Moreover, the diffuse nature of these conflicts has played into the hands of neo-conservative ideologues in Washington, London and elsewhere who have consolidated the post–9/11 security state with its systematic use of extra-judicial executive power. This is evident, for example, in the restriction of civil liberties, increased surveillance, the use of indefinite detention in the Guantanamo confinement centre as well as of simulated torture techniques, special rendition, etc. Giorgio Agamben has brilliantly evaluated these developments in terms of a resurgent mode of 'sovereignty', which is propagated in the form of a 'permanent state of exception' and we return to this idea at several points in the book.

One of the strengths of agonistic democracy has been to address these challenges head on. Indeed, William Connolly and Chantal Mouffe in particular have sought to attend to questions of fundamentalism and uncompromising forms of conflict. Moreover, we will see that the agonistic theorists address the present climate of violence and intolerance in a manner that is distinct from the more mainstream approaches in contemporary political theory. Where liberals and deliberative democrats typically seek to overcome or transcend conflict by bringing it under a set of regulative principles (foundational principles of justice or context-transcending principles of communicative rationality), the agonists insist that these responses actually serve to exacerbate the problem. Instead, we should look to sublimate this hostility by transforming it into more constructive modes of rivalry. Paradoxically, perhaps this is the key to social cohesion in a world of diverse fundamentals. However, we will see that it is also crucial to properly understand the causes of these developments, and Mouffe and Connolly both explain the rise of the politics of fundamentalism in existential terms, i.e. as a manifestation of a human propensity for 'antagonism' or of an underlying politics of *ressentiment*. We will question these analyses in the course of this study, and draw attention instead to the specific socio-economic circumstances that condition the politics of fundamentalism, and this brings us to the politics of globalisation.

The politics of globalisation

Over the past few decades the processes of globalisation have intensified the politics of diversity and of fundamentalism. Globalisation is typically presented as a set of social and economic processes that have greatly accelerated the experience of 'interconnectedness' (Held and McGrew, 2002, 1). Driven by technological developments in the communications industry (especially the Internet and the commercial use of satellites), globalisation has drastically reduced the mediating effects of physical distance. Every day I am drawn into a whole series of issues, as graphic images of physically distant events – such as 9/11, the US Presidential election, or the latest tragedies in Gaza or the West Bank – are beamed into my living room as they unfold. In other words, in the era of globalisation the politics of diversity is not only propelled by the physical movement of peoples around the world, but also by the virtual proximity of culturally distinct groups and individuals in their networks of instantaneous electronic communication and in media-projected broadcasts of daily events in 'real time'. At the forefront of these processes has been the impact of economic globalisation, which is manifest particularly in the escalating volume and velocity of the movement of capital across state borders, and the increasing tendency of producers to relocate their operations to the global south where costs are low and where workers' rights are not adequately protected. These trends have been illustrated dramatically by the impact of the on-going financial crisis, which has confirmed what theorists of globalisation have long been saying, i.e. that the 'world is fast becoming a shared social and economic space' (Held and McGrew, 2002, 2).

However, drawing on radical social theorists such as Paul Virilio and Manuel Castells, Connolly and Tully have both argued that the processes of globalisation represent something more challenging than the idea of increasing interconnectedness. Whilst this captures part of what is going on, it fails to grasp the more profound transformations underway in the social experience of time and in the emergence of distinct forms of control associated with the network society. Tully's account of globalisation is additionally finessed by his concern with the impact of globalisation on indigenous peoples and, more generally, on the developing world. Indeed, we will see in Chapter 4 that he has developed a remarkable account of the impact of globalisation on the non-European world in the second volume of his *Public Philosophy in a New Key* (2008). Through an analysis of the deep continuities between contemporary processes of economic globalisation (such as structural adjustment programmes through the World Bank and the IMF) and the former experience of European colonisation (i.e. in the continued exploitation of peoples in the global south, and the gross levels of material, cultural, and political inequality that persist between the Great Powers and their former colonies and dependencies), Tully demonstrates why globalisation must be understood as a continuation of Euro-American imperialism by other means. He is, of course, not alone in this assessment. For example, the idea that globalisation represents a novel form of imperial rule has been popularised by the success of Michael Hardt and Antonio Negri's *Empire* in 2000. However, the detail of Tully's account of the operations of contemporary imperialism is highly pertinent, and I take much of what he says as the starting point of my own account of agonistic democracy in the era of globalisation, which is set out in Chapter 7.

Theorists who are broadly positive about the potential benefits inherent in globalisation – such as David Held and Anthony Giddens – nonetheless acknowledge that this is an uneven process, which has generally had a negative impact on democracy at the level of the nation-state. Indeed, it is clear that globalisation leads to a transfer of power away from the peoples' representatives in national parliaments, and towards unelected and unaccountable transnational elites in the World Bank, the IMF, and other powerful institutions (Giddens, 1999; Held and McGrew, 2002). For Held and other cosmopolitan democrats, the solution to these developments is to find ways to democratise international institutions in order to ensure more effective forms of transnational governance. This approach is just one of a variety of conceptions of cosmopolitan democracy which have emerged in recent years and which I outline briefly in Chapter 2. All of them can ultimately be traced to Immanuel Kant's arguments for a world federation of republican states governed by principles of 'cosmopolitan right' which he articulated at the end of the eighteenth century. For reasons we will see in Parts I and II of the book, each of the agonistic thinkers has explicitly rejected the Kantian conception of cosmopolitanism and the arguments of those who follow in this tradition. Indeed, Mouffe has rejected arguments for cosmopolitanism outright, suggesting instead that we should focus on renewing democracy at the national and the regional level as the best way to challenge the negative impact of the processes of globalisation. By way of contrast, Connolly, Tully, and Bonnie Honig have all sought to offer agonistic forms of cosmopolitanism – what Honig calls 'agonistic cosmopolitics' – as an alternative to the predominant Kantian perspectives, and as a necessary supplement to the regeneration of democracy at the level of the nation (Honig, 2006, 117).

I argue that Mouffe's outright rejection of cosmopolitanism fails to understand the potential in the novel social movements against the institutions which have been at the forefront of propagating market liberalisation and economic globalisation, manifest, for example, in the summit protests in Seattle, Genoa, and elsewhere. These demonstrations have also taken on a more constructive form, with the formation of the World Social Forum in Porto Alegre in Brazil in 2000, and subsequent World and Regional Forums which have been attended by large numbers of activists and campaign groups from around the world. In the past few years these struggles have become more intense with the emergence of the Occupy movement, and this escalation of democratic movements across state borders, made possible by the new digital technologies, has been nowhere more palpable than in the series of Arab uprisings that have spread across North Africa and the Middle East since December 2010. Connolly, Tully, and Honig are right to see in these kinds of developments the potential for forms of transnational democratic solidarity. However, I argue that none of them go far enough in the direction of a militant form of cosmopolitanism, one which is committed, above all, to the possibility of the emergence of radically new ideas and practices, and in order to address issues such as climate change, nuclear proliferation, and global inequality.

Acknowledgements

This book has been a long time in the making. During this time I have had the good fortune to discuss many of the themes examined here with numerous colleagues and in a range of different contexts: seminars, conferences, workshops, PhD supervision meetings, PhD examinations, via email, and in more social settings. Occasionally these discussions have been heated and polemical and at other times calm and collaborative. They have all been enriching, and in one way or another have helped to shape the views I have set out in the following pages.

In this respect, I'd like to thank the following interlocutors: Richard Bellamy, Jane Bennett, Andreas Bieler, Gary Browning, Terrell Carver, Simon Choat, Romand Coles, William Connolly, Diana Coole, Charles Devellennes, Mark Devenney, Torben Bech Dyrberg, Alan Finlayson, Philip Goodchild, Oliver Harrison, Bonnie Honig, David Howarth, Andreas Kalyvas, Alexandros Kioupkiolis, Andy Knott, Ernesto Laclau, Moya Lloyd, Oliver Marchart, James Martin, David Morrice, Adam Morton, Chantal Mouffe, Saul Newman, Aletta Norval, the late Joel Olson, David Owen, Emilia Palonen, Mark Philp, Vanessa Pupavac, Paul Rekret, Andrew Robinson, Quentin Skinner, Graham Smith, Yannis Stavrakakis, Marc Stears, Paulina Tambakaki, Lasse Thomassen, Simon Tormey, James Tully, Elif Uzgoren, Nathan Widder, Jonathon Willet, James Williams, Clare Woodford.

I'd also like to thank colleagues at The Nottingham Centre for Normative Political Theory (CONCEPT), both for a particularly helpful discussion of a previous draft of Chapter 1 and for many elevated debates over the years: Tony Burns, Ros Hague, Ben Holland, Mathew Humphrey, Ignas Kalpokas, Gulshan Ara Khan, Marie Paxton, Chris Pierson, Matthew Rendall, Frances Ryan, Lucy Sargisson, David Stevens, Chris Woodard.

Thanks are also due to the editorial team at Cambridge and to two anonymous referees.

My family has also been immensely supportive in seeing this project through to completion, and I would especially like to thank my mother,

Jennifer Wenman, who has been a resolute source of encouragement, and to acknowledge the inspiration I have drawn from my late grandmother, Ada Wainwright, and from my late uncle, Jonathan Wainwright.

Above all, I want to acknowledge my enormous gratitude to Gulshan Ara Khan.

Thoughts and ideas do not exist in isolation, and although you disagree profoundly with my commitment to the prospect of revolution, we agree on much else, and I have learnt an enormous amount over many years from our on-going discussions and dis/agreements. This would not have been possible without you, and the book is dedicated to you and to our own little miracle – Elizabeth Ara.

Part I

Introduction: agonism and the constituent power

Situating contemporary agonistic democracy

In the 1980s Anglo-American normative political theory was defined to a large extent by debates between liberals and communitarians about the essential features of moral personhood and the relative priority of the right or the good. Subsequently, this dispute has given way to the emergence of a proliferation of normative positions and to a renewed interest in democracy. Liberal conceptions of justice have retained a predominance, but are now challenged by multiculturalist arguments for the recognition of group rights, as well as a number of new and distinctive models of democracy including deliberative democracy, agonistic democracy, cosmopolitan democracy, and radical democracy.[1] Each of these approaches has marked out a standpoint in contemporary debates, and often in explicit rivalry with one another. Moreover, deliberative democracy, cosmopolitan democracy, and the various arguments for the recognition of group rights have a greater acceptance within the mainstream of the discipline than the agonistic model. This is not because the agonistic perspective is less coherent or well developed, despite what its critics might say. Instead, this is because agonism is less conventional, in terms of both the modes of argumentation typically invoked by agonistic democrats and the prescriptions they offer for the renewal of democracy. Indeed, one characteristic feature of agonistic democracy – which sets it apart from the other traditions – is its engagement with the strands of continental thought associated with post-structuralism and post-modernism. For this reason, agonism is frequently misunderstood by those working in the mainstream of the Anglo-American academy, and is sometimes dismissed as at best incoherent, or worse, as dangerous and nihilistic.[2] This book is written in part to put these misconceptions right: to bring the agonistic model into sharp focus, evaluate its basic concepts,

---

[1] For the idea that democratic theory can be organised into distinct models, see: Macpherson, 1979 and Held, 2006.

[2] See, for example: Young, 2000, 51; Blake, 2005, 231, 241; Stears, 2007.

and make the case that the leading theorists of agonism have developed some of the most important reflections on democracy in contemporary political thought.[3] It is also my objective, however, to further develop the agonistic perspective and in particular to move agonistic democracy in the direction of a more stringent critique of liberal democracy.

Part II of the book evaluates the contribution of four theorists who exemplify the agonistic perspective: William Connolly, Bonnie Honig, Chantal Mouffe, and James Tully. Over the past two decades each of these authors has developed their own distinctive theories of agonism, but they focus on related themes and concepts and have acknowledged their proximity to one another. At various points along the way I also engage the ideas of other notable contemporary agonists, and especially Patchen Markell, Aletta Norval, David Owen, and Linda Zerilli. One objective here is to present the work of this collection of authors as a distinct tradition within contemporary political theory. The four main thinkers are brought into a series of debates with one another, and with the post-structuralist and continental theorists who influence them, including: Friedrich Nietzsche, Carl Schmitt, Ludwig Wittgenstein, Hannah Arendt, Michel Foucault, Gilles Deleuze, and Jacques Derrida. The work of each of these thinkers is also engaged in some detail, and in my overall orchestration of these discussions I develop a position that draws extensively on Arendt. We will see that there are some not insignificant differences between these respective post-structuralist and continental thinkers. Indeed, the agonists and their corresponding influences differ among themselves – sometimes significantly and other times less so – and agonistic democracy takes a variety of forms as the following chapters show. Nevertheless, in the context of wider debates within contemporary political theory, the similarities between the agonistic theorists are also very significant, and set them apart especially from liberalism and deliberative democracy. In Chapter 1 we see that the term agonism comes from the Greek *agon*, meaning conflict or strife, and I make the case that, despite their differences, the theorists examined in this book coalesce around an acknowledgement of pluralism, tragedy, and the value of conflict.[4]

---

[3] The secondary literature on agonistic democracy is relatively sparse, certainly compared to the extensive commentary that has now grown up around the idea of deliberative democracy. However, there is a small – and growing – body of work that seeks to evaluate the impact of the agonistic approach, and to examine points of similarity and difference between the various theories of agonism, see: Deveaux, 1999; Wenman, 2003b; Fossen, 2008; Schaap, 2007, 2009; Wingenbach, 2011.

[4] In the emerging interpretive literature, there seems to be something of a penchant for developing typological classifications of different forms of agonism, with Andrew Schaap identifying three distinct kinds and Ed Wingenbach presenting a five-part categorisation,

It is also important to appreciate that in many respects, as Tully has said, agonistic democracy represents a contemporary adaptation of republican theory (Tully, 2003, 503). Indeed, with their stress on the exercise of democratic freedom as means to counter oppression, normalisation, and exploitation, as Gulshan Khan has argued, the agonistic theorists are best seen as part of a more general republican revival in contemporary political theory (Khan, 2013). The agonistic approach shares with thinkers such as Quentin Skinner, Philip Pettit, and Maurizio Viroli, the view that negative forms of liberty – as non-interference and the legal protection of individual rights – are insufficient to maintain political freedom (Khan, 2013). The more important objective is to struggle against domination, dependence, and arbitrary forms of power.[5]

Agonistic democracy also needs to be compared and contrasted to the contemporary tradition of radical democracy, associated with authors such as Alain Badiou, Ernesto Laclau, Jacques Rancière, and Slavoj Žižek. These theorists also draw extensively on continental and postmodern thought, and (I would argue) they similarly share a basic republican view of politics as a struggle against domination. However, we will see that the radical democrats differ from the agonistic democrats in some decisive respects, and most importantly in the way they envisage the emergence of the constituent power, which is the central theme of this book. Indeed, the tension between the constituent and the constituted powers, between power *qua* capacity (*potentia*) and power *qua* right (*potestas*), and the idea that the constituent power manifests in distinct modes, i.e. as augmentation and revolution, provide the key evaluative concepts underpinning this study. These concepts are explored in detail

see: Schaap, 2009, and Wingenbach, 2011, Chapter 3. These taxonomies have some validity. However, my sense is that there isn't a sufficient mass of agonistic theory to really warrant this approach. Whilst this method might make sense when analysing a large body of thought – liberalism, say, or western Marxism – the trouble here is that, on both Schaap's and Wingenbach's accounts, each distinctive type of agonism is actually only represented by one (or perhaps two at most) author(s). My analytical strategy is different. In Chapter 1 I identify something like the core of the agonistic matrix, by pulling together themes that underpin each of the contributions, past and present, and in the remainder of the book I scrutinise the detail of each of the major contemporary contributing authors.

[5] For the neo-republican revival in contemporary political theory, see: Pocock, 1975; Skinner, 1990, 1998, 2000, 2008; Pettit, 1997, 1999, 2002; Viroli, 2002, 2008; Laborde and Maynor, 2008. The connection between agonism and republican thought has been stressed by various commentators, see: Deveaux, 1999; Honig, 1993; Wenman, 2003b; Tully, 2008a. However, I am particularly grateful to Khan (2013) for pointing out the core connection between agonism and republicanism in the common emphasis on liberty as the absence of domination. This pivotal insight has been very helpful in enabling me to situate the agonistic theorists in relation to other traditions within contemporary political theory, and I return to this observation at various points in the book.

in Chapter 2, but we also need to give a little more account of these ideas from the outset.

Agonism and the relative priority of the constituent power

Unlike most normative political theory in the western canon, the theorists of agonistic democracy do not seek to ground their respective visions of politics in substantive accounts of human nature, in teleological assumptions about the good life or concerning the movement of history, or in consequentialist theories of morality; nor do they share the currently predominant liberal view that we can establish agreement on constitutional essentials via recourse to deontological procedures, or a 'public use of reason', that somehow brackets off fundamental disagreements between contending 'comprehensive doctrines' or conceptions of the good. Indeed, each of the thinkers examined in this study broadly shares Nietzsche's observation that 'since Copernicus', Man (with his concomitant notions of reason and rationality) has 'been . . . rolling faster and faster away from the centre' (Nietzsche, 1994b, 115; 1968, 8). As a consequence, the agonists are typically described as 'anti-essentialist' or 'anti-foundationalist' thinkers. However, these characterisations are too pronounced because they suggest that the agonists claim to operate without recourse to any underlying categories whatsoever, whereas, in fact, like all political theories, they offer a mixture of descriptive and prescriptive statements, forged through a complex amalgam of ontology, sociology, psychology, historical studies, and ethics. Instead, the agonistic theories are better understood as 'post-foundational' viewpoints, that do 'not attempt to erase completely' claims about essences and foundations, but to 'weaken their ontological status' (Marchart, 2007a, 2).[6] Indeed, these theories typically combine philosophical enquiry with a stress on the ultimate groundlessness of all claims to political legitimacy.

Moreover, this constitutive groundlessness is tied in an inherent way to the idea that human nature is incomplete and without foundation, i.e. to a conception of human *Dasein* as a mortal being who finds herself thrown into time and historicity, and this in turn gives rise to a certain precedence of human freedom. There are numerous ways to articulate this basic

[6] For a comparable reading, see Stephen White's discussion of 'weak ontology' (White, 2000). Wingenbach (2011, Chapters 1 and 2) also stresses the post-foundational status of contemporary agonistic theory, as well as the distinctions between agonistic and radical democracy.

assumption, i.e. that existence precedes essence, and one of those ways is to insist on the priority of the constituent power. The 'constituent power' nominates the human capacity for creation, to institute new forms of life, to bring new ways of being into the world, or perhaps even to create new worlds. As Arendt says, the constituent power manifests as an 'interruption' of an established state of affairs, and, as such, it is associated with the human capacity for initiative (Arendt, 1958, 9; 1977b, 166). She also likens the emergence of the constituent power to something like a miracle, because every new emergence 'seen from the perspective . . . of the process . . . it interrupts, is . . . something which could not be expected' (Arendt, 1958, 9, 178; 1977b, 166, 168). So, by Arendt's account, it is not God but 'men who perform . . . [miracles] . . . men who because they have received the twofold gift of freedom and action can establish a reality of their own' (Arendt, 1977b, 169).

In political theory this capacity for freedom is intrinsically related to democracy. Indeed, the idea of the primacy of the constituent power underpins Sheldon Wolin's claim that we should 'reject the classical and modern conception that ascribes to democracy "a" proper or settled form', because to do so is to tame the creative power of the *demos* by reducing democracy to a system or process of government (Wolin, 2004, 601). Democracy is better understood as an authorising or founding *moment*, rather than a *form*, i.e. as a moment of innovation that makes 'itself' felt by 'protesting actualities and revealing possibilities' (Wolin, 2004, 603). None of the four main thinkers examined in this book would be willing to go quite so far as Wolin in asserting the outright priority of the constituent power, for reasons I discuss in a moment. However, they all broadly share the idea of the irreducible quality of a pre-juridical moment of political freedom that initiates and composes concrete social and political forms. This does not mean that democratic subjects can remake the world at 'will', and, as we will see at various points in the book, the association of the constituent power with 'the will' is ill conceived and ignorant of the ways in which the emergence of the constituent power is always conditioned by human plurality. It does mean, however, that all extant political forms of state and civil society, all existing political identities and relations and forms of constituted authority, are ultimately products of the constituent power, and so they remain forever vulnerable to the (re-)emergence of the constituent power, as various corrupt bodies in the Arab world have recently found out.[7]

---

[7] For recent scholarly discussions of the constituent power, and of the tensions between the constituent power and constituted authority, see: Negri, 1999; Kalyvas 2005, 2008; Loughlin and Walker, 2007.

However, it is notoriously difficult to articulate this capacity for invention that is at the heart of democratic politics, and it is not possible to figure this element of creativity without first making some decisions about conceptual priorities. For example, the constituent power has been variously presented as 'freedom' and 'action' (Arendt), as revolutionary 'now time' (Walter Benjamin), as 'sovereign decision' (Schmitt), and as 'absolute process' (Antonio Negri). Each of these candidates contains conceptual and probably also ethical connotations, and I examine these alternatives at various points in this study. However, the most satisfactory, and consistently republican nominations of the constituent power are those offered by Arendt, and it is Arendt's presentation that shapes the general direction of this book. She says, 'men *are* free – as distinguished from their possessing the gift for freedom – as long as they act, neither before nor after; for to *be* free and to act are the same' (Arendt, 1977b, 151, emphasis in the original). Moreover, to the extent that this groundless capacity of/for action (mixed also, as we will see in the final chapter, with the faculty of judgement), is able to establish new social and political forms, this is the only source of (provisional) grounding in the context of modernity where all traditional forms of authority are increasingly undermined; so that, as Claude Lefort says, the story of modern democracy with its recurrent reconfigurations of power becomes an unprecedented adventure (Lefort, 1988, 19).

Wolin's formulations suggest an absolute priority of the constituent power vis-à-vis forms of constitutional government. Indeed, the contingency of constituted authorities becomes most apparent in times of crises; in revolutions, war, and insurrection, and, although the idea of the constituent power has always been implicit in the republican conception of freedom, it is not a coincidence that the first explicit formulation of the primacy of the constituent power was put forward by Emmanuel Joseph Sieyès in the context of the French Revolution. He said, it is not any 'ordinary legislature' that can give itself a constitution, but the Estates-General, as the embodiment of the *pouvoir constituant*, must not be bound by any 'extraneous authority', and the 'only rules to which is will be obliged to give credence will be those it has made for itself' (Sieyès, 2003b, 34). As we will see in Chapter 2, this stress on the absolute priority of the constituent power was reiterated by Schmitt in the context of the crisis of the Weimar Republic. However, the contemporary agonistic democrats do not share these formulations, Mouffe notwithstanding, and they stress instead a *relative* priority of the constituent power and the on-going imbrications of the constituent power and constituted authority. As Honig says, agonistic democracy is best understood as a form of constitutionalism, but one that is forever inhabited by 'the radically risky tumult of *a*constitutionalism' (Honig, 2001a, 799–800).[8] In order then to grasp the specificity of the contemporary agonistic viewpoint, and to see how the agonistic democrats position themselves, and especially with respect to the liberals and deliberative theorists on one side and the radical democrats on the other, we need to look more closely at this nuanced conception of the relationship between *potentia* and *potestas*. At this point, we also need to introduce a second set of categories, again taken from Arendt, which is the distinction she draws between distinct modalities of the constituent power, between augmentation and revolution. These ideas are explained in detail in Chapter 2, but again we need a preliminary discussion here because these concepts frame all else that is to follow.

The constituent power as augmentation and revolution

In order to understand the full significance of Arendt's presentation of the different modalities of the constituent power we need to look in detail at her account of the exercise of freedom as augmentation in ancient Rome, and how this differed from the distinctly modern experience of revolution. These ideas are laid out in full in Chapter 2. However, at this point we can say, in brief, that for Arendt the modern revolutionary mode of the constituent power is characterised by an absolute beginning – and consequently a moment of radical rupture – that brings a new principle or set of norms and values into the world, as it were *ex nihilo*. This reiterates Benjamin's conception of radical origin, or *Ur-sprung*, understood as an originary break or rupture, as a miraculous leap into being that shatters the historical continuum, one that gives birth to new processes but does not determine their subsequent generation (Benjamin, 1988, 45).[9] By way of contrast, the constituent power in the form of augmentation is a (re)foundation that simultaneously expands and preserves an existing system of authority. These formulations, of the absolute and relative priorities of the constituent power, are crucially important in this study and for several reasons. They are analytically important because they help us to better understand the contemporary tradition of agonistic democracy. Indeed, we will see that contemporary agonistic democracy is characterised by an exclusive emphasis on the constituent power in the modality of augmentation. This contrasts to the contemporary radical democrats, where there is a similarly exclusive emphasis on revolution. I explore the consequences of this difference in a moment, but Arendt's

---

[8] For a similar formulation see: Tully 2008b, 200–1.
[9] For a discussion see: Asman, 1992 and Pizer, 1995.

categories are more important still. As I argue in Chapter 2, this is because in her formulation of the revolutionary event Arendt shows, in explicit contrast to Sieyès and Schmitt, how the notion of absolute initiative is compatible with the agonistic circumstances of pluralism, tragedy, and the value of conflict. Indeed, it is a central claim of this book that there is nothing intrinsic in the agonistic perspective, which determines that we have to disavow the lost treasure of the revolutionary event.[10] In fact, a consistent theory of agonistic democracy requires that we (i) maintain the qualitative difference between revolution and augmentation, understood as distinct modalities of the constituent power, and (ii) recognise that they both represent authentic moments of republican freedom. In my own formulation of agonistic democracy in Chapter 7, I seek to combine these two moments in a theory of agonism and militant cosmopolitanism.[11]

One of the key diagnostic assertions of this study is that the moments of the constituent power characteristic of contemporary agonistic democracy are consonant with the Arendtean notion of augmentation. Indeed, in Part II we see that Connolly, Tully, Mouffe, and Honig all conceptualise the constituent power in terms of a non-dialectical augmentation of existing rules, practices, and institutions. This basic point is captured in different ways in Connolly's account of the politics of *enactment*, in Tully's Wittgensteinian conception of *autonomy* in terms of the indeterminacy inherent in the application of rules, in Mouffe's notion of the *articulation* of the principles of liberty and equality into more areas of social life, and Honig's account of the daily (re)foundation of democratic freedom in Derridean terms of *iterability* and *performativity*. These conceptions of the constituent power are explained in detail in the chapters that follow. As we have said, these formulations differentiate today's agonistic theorists from contemporary radical democrats. The term radical comes from

[10] Here, Benjamin is also an important figure. He was similarly a theorist and a scholar of the ancient *agon* (see: Benjamin, 1988; Asman, 1992; Adorno and Scholem, 1994, 231–5) and, like Arendt but unlike the contemporary agonistic democrats, Benjamin presented a model of the *agon* 'not only as a place of agony, struggle, debate, competition and sacrifice, but also as a place of revolution, rupture and escape where the judgement of the gods over humans is reversed' (Asman, 1992, 607). I return to Benjamin at a several points in this book, and it is precisely this association of the democratic *agon* with the revolutionary *Ursprung* that I seek to rework in my account of agonsim and militant cosmopolitanism.

[11] In his introduction to what is currently the best collection of essays on agonistic democracy, Schaap asks 'should we understand the *agon* as already internal to ... political unity or should it be defined precisely as that which threatens it? Or is it possible to think the *agon* as both external and internal to the political unity, and, if so, in what sense?' (Schaap, 2009, 2). This is a good question, to which Arendt's qualitative distinction between revolution and augmentation provides the best answer. Many of the essays included in Schaap's collection return to this question in one form or another, and I engage with some of them in the course of this study.

the Latin *radix*, meaning root or foundation, and neatly captures what is at stake for theorists like Badiou and Žižek who depict the constituent power instead as a decisive *event* – a moment of radical dislocation – that generates a fundamental transformation in the existing system. As Badiou puts it, the genuine political event 'is [always] a real break (both thought and practised) in the specific order within which the event took place' (Badiou, 2001, 42). The contemporary radical democrats do not draw explicitly on Arendt, and, as we will see in Chapter 2, there are significant differences between them. Nevertheless, in their depiction of the constituent power in terms of absolute initiative they are close to Arendt's account of the temporality of the modern revolutionary event elaborated in Chapter Five of her *On Revolution*.

Moreover, these alternative conceptualisations of the constituent power go hand in hand with different accounts of the emergence of democratic politics, with the agonistic democrats stressing the impact of new social movement politics, and the radical democrats taking moments of revolutionary upheaval, especially May 1968 in Paris, as paradigmatic of democratic freedom. Again, Arendt understood the distinctive qualities of both of these forms of politics, drawing attention to the importance of civil disobedience (exemplified perhaps in the American civil rights campaigns of the 1960s), as well as significant moments of revolutionary upheaval (not only the dramatic events of the late eighteenth century, but also the Russian revolutions of 1905 and 1917, the Hungarian uprising of 1956, and the other major revolutionary events of modern times) (Arendt, 1965, 28, 270). By way of contrast, we see in the two most important traditions of democratic theory to emerge from post-structuralism a regrettable tendency to present one or other of these alternatives as the only authentic form of political action.[12] This

---

[12] Some will object that the distinction between agonistic and radical democracy is over-drawn. For example, Laclau and Mouffe have published important work together, and Schaap is probably not alone in his feeling that Rancière belongs in the agonistic camp (Schaap, 2009, 2). Laclau and Rancière are certainty more nuanced than Badiou or Žižek, and I return to Schaap's depiction of Rancière as an agonist again below. I also explore Mouffe's co-authored work with Laclau in Chapter 5, but elsewhere I have examined the differences between them in some detail, and in the end I think they sit either side of this dividing line (Wenman, 2003c). For discussions (and examples) of the not insignificant differences between the radical democrats see: Žižek, 1999a, 2006b; Laclau, 2006; Marchart, 2007a; Stavrakakis, 2007. I offer a fuller account of radical democracy in Chapter 2, where the focus is again on the similarities between these thinkers. Indeed, together they provide an important point of contrast with the agonistic theorists examined in this book. Ultimately, all conceptual classifications involve the exercise of a degree of soft power around the edges, but the distinctions here are not arbitrarily imposed, and they capture some genuine fault lines within the main traditions of political thought associated (broadly) with post-structuralism.

represents a significant bifurcation in contemporary republican theory, and I argue that the agonistic democrats are ultimately unable to concep- tualise the exercise of the constituent power as revolution. The same is true of the radical democrats in respect of augmentation. Moreover, this division is regrettable and represents a regression *vis-à-vis* both Arendt and also Niccolò Machiavelli, who both recognised the importance of revolution and augmentation as two distinct and necessary moments of the constituent power. This does not mean that we can retrieve Arendt's theory without some important qualifications. Indeed, Arendt is herself often depicted a theorist of 'pure politics', rather than a nuanced theorist of alternate modalities of the constituent power, and this on account of her strict demarcation of the political (freedom and action) and the social (violence and necessity). I pick up on this aspect of Arendt's work in detail in chapters 1,2, 6, and 7, and my recovery of Arendt's categories of action, freedom, pluralism, augmentation, revolution, and reflective judgement is accompanied by a rigorous critique of aspects of her Hellenism and her false presentation of a basic topography of the social and the political. Thankfully, as we will observe in Chapter 6, Honig has already cleared much of the way for this retrieval, although we will also see that there are difficulties in her approach and especially in her repudiation of the Arendtean theory of revolution.[13]

The priority of the strategic question – or what is to be done?

The on-going importance of the qualitative distinction between aug- mentation and revolution, as well as the need to keep both these forms of politics in play, follows also from an additional feature of agonistic democracy, which is the inherently strategic nature of agonism. Here, the emphasis is on the range of possible moves available to situated sub- jects within any particular configuration of power relations. The strategic dimension of agonism is exemplified in Machiavelli and Foucault, and in contemporary theory this features most strongly in Tully's work. These ideas are examined in some detail in Chapter 1, but again we need a brief pointer here as a prelude to subsequent discussion.

---

[13] The secondary literature on Arendt is very extensive. For a flavour see: Canovan, 1983, 1995; Jay, 1986; Beiner, 1992; Villa, 1992a, 1992b; Honig, 1993; Keenan, 1994; Ben- habib, 2003; Markell, 2003; Zerilli, 2005; Kalyvas, 2008. Against those who read her as a proto-deliberative theorist, for example Benhabib and Kalyvas, Arendt is best under- stood as a sophisticated exponent of the *Existenz-philosophie*. For a discussion, see: Jay, 1986.

One of the most significant themes to remerge from contemporary agonistic and radical democracy is the idea of the difficult relationship between philosophy and politics, where philosophical enquiry has recurrently sought to subdue the constituent power, by subsuming the democratic tumult under a set of abstract principles or circumventing its creative energy through various notions of balance or good measure.[14] The importance of resisting these tendencies is at the heart of the agonistic critique of the excessive rationalism characteristic of much contemporary political theory, and I pick up on these themes in Chapter 2, where I consider in more detail the differences between agonism and the other contemporary models of democracy. Given the predatory nature of philosophy in respect of the democratic *agon*, it might be tempting to try to construct a political theory without reference to philosophical arguments at all, and perhaps to remain closer to the discipline of history, with its use of example, rather than abstract or foundational principles. However, this option turns out to be a chimera, because if we understand an ontological framework as something like a Kuhnian paradigm – such that ontology becomes a 'prerequisite to perception itself' (Kuhn, 1996, 113) – then it is clear that there is no way to bracket entirely or to get around ontological enquiry in the construction of political theory. Indeed, Connolly is correct when he says that every 'interpretation of political events, no matter how deeply it is sunk in a specific historical context or how high the data upon which it sits, contains an onto-political dimension' (Connolly, 1995a, 1). Consequently, as indicated above, the different agonistic theories come packaged in the form of an amalgam of different philosophical, sociological, historical, and ethical assumptions. There is no getting around this requirement, but, at the same time, my sense is that we need to develop an appropriate theoretical amalgam, one that retains both a sense of the irreducible centrality of political freedom and of the priority of the strategic question, i.e. of the range of actions or kinds of initiatives available to concretely situated subjects.

This attitude was exemplified in Machiavelli, who, as Louis Althusser said, managed to link together the movement of more general tendencies

---

[14] The standoff between politics and philosophy in fifth-century Athens was stressed by Arendt, and has been most carefully elaborated in contemporary political theory by Rancière (Arendt, 1958; Rancière, 1999). By Rancière's account, the age old attempt to eliminate the 'impropriety' of political freedom, by subsuming it under determinant forms originating in Plato, has taken three key turns: Platonic *Archi*politics (subsumption under the laws of the ideal state), Aristotelian *para*politics (a balanced constitution without tumult), and Marxist *meta*politics (politics conceived as super-structural to social and economic processes), see: Rancière, 1999, Chapter Four.

(for instance the incessant play between *virtù* and *Fortuna*), with a resolute focus on the strategic opportunities buried within the given conjuncture (Althusser, 1999, 16–17). With this example in mind, we could say that it is an important ethical objective to avoid closing down the strategic moves available to situated subjects, by invoking philosophical assumptions that present one form or other of politics as intrinsic. Indeed, democratic theorists who are concerned to analyse and expedite forms of political and social change ought not to constrain political actors by presenting them with a mono-typical account of democratic innovation. However, as we have said, it is precisely this tendency that is at work in the contemporary theories of agonistic and radical democracy. My central analytical concern in this study is, therefore, to identify the ways in which particular philosophical assumptions embedded in a given theoretical framework enable or constrain the emergence of the different modalities of the constituent power. The key question is what moments of the constituent power are conceivable from within the horizon of a particular theoretical framework?

At best, the agonistic theorists have a limited and inadequate account of revolutionary change, but I go further than this and argue that the strictly revolutionary moment is rendered inconceivable by the respective ontological frameworks presented by Connolly, Tully, Mouffe, and Honig. In short, if augmentation (*iterability* or one of its counterparts) strictly conditions all forms of politics, rather than being definitive of particular kinds of change, then the revolutionary moment is inconceivable. The radical democratic theorists do not fare any better. For them, moments of genuine politics are associated exclusively with the advent of radical innovation and monumental disruption, and all other moments of innovation are dismissed as bogus, as nothing but the ingenuous repetitions of the existing administrative or police order. By way of contrast to both these approaches, my claim is that *neither* augmentation *nor* revolution represents anything like the 'essence of the political'. Neither of these modalities of the constituent power has an ontological or ethical priority. Instead, they represent qualitatively distinct modalities of the constituent power, both of which always remain possible in some (often very conditioned) sense to situated subjects.

It is important also to point out that this strategic perspective does not presuppose a fully rational subject capable of calculating the options available. From the agonistic perspective, the subject of politics is effectively brought into being in the act of freedom. As Honig puts it, drawing on Arendt, strictly speaking action 'gives birth, as it were, to the actors in the moment' of its inception (Honig, 1995, 137). Action is therefore 'spontaneous, novel, creative, and, perhaps most disturbing, always self-surprising' (Honig, 1993, 80). Nevertheless, as various historical examples demonstrate, action comes in different forms, and, as we have said, a consistently agonistic approach needs to keep open the possibility of the emergence of the constituent power not only as augmentation but also as revolution. This brings us to the question of the relationship between agonistic democracy and liberal democracy, and to the difficult question of agonism and the possibility of historical transformation.

Agonism and liberal democracy, or the possibility of historical transformation

The question of the relationship between contemporary agonism and the broader framework of liberal democracy isn't straightforward, and, as we move through Part II of this study, we encounter a series of somewhat different responses to this question. However, despite their differences, the contemporary agonistic theorists are once again alike in their broad commitment to the traditions and practices of liberal democratic constitutionalism. This fidelity is both explicit and implicit in the work of each of the four main thinkers examined here. In an influential paper Jürgen Habermas has argued that, under conditions of modern constitutionalism, public and private autonomy are 'co-original', i.e. they are both necessary and interdependent elements of legitimate forms of government (Habermas, 2001). In Chapter 2 we will see that his position has been criticised from the agonistic perspective, and Honig in particular has stressed that Habermas' theory cannot really account for the co-originality of the constituent and constituted powers, because in his theory the former is ultimately subsumed under the latter in the form of a dialectical theory of progress (Honig, 2001a). These points are important, and I make the case that this difference reflects a more general distinction between agonism and the more mainstream conceptions of liberal democracy, which all tend to subordinate politics to constituted authority in one form or another. However, we will also see that the agonistic democrats nonetheless share the idea of the co-originality of democracy and constitutional liberalism. As Tully puts it, agonistic democracy is 'a more realistic reformulation of the "coarticulation" thesis under real-world conditions of hegemon-subaltern relations' (Tully, 2008b, 218). This suggests a certain proximity between agonistic democracy and the more mainstream perspectives, which is often overlooked by supporters and critics of agonistic democracy alike. Indeed, in Part II of this book we will see that each of the four thinkers examined here has sought to develop a conception of the constituent power that recognises genuine (i.e. non-teleological) innovation in modern politics (i.e. which asserts a relative priority of human freedom over juridical forms of constituted authority), but which nonetheless accepts the legitimacy of liberal democratic constitutionalism.

Moreover, in addition to this explicit endorsement of liberal democratic institutions and practices, the commitment to liberal democracy is also implicit in the agonistic insistence that augmentation is the necessary form of the constituent power. This is because the agonistic theorists associate the democratic contest with creative iterations of established institutions and practices – with, as Honig puts it, those *extra*ordinary moments of emergence within the (only apparently) ordinary circumstances of everyday politics – but not with the prospect of more radical innovation in social and political forms. So, democratic struggles appear destined to emerge repeatedly within the broader horizon of modern liberal democracy. This does not mean that those struggles remain confined within the perimeter of the nation-state, and, as we have said, with the exception of Mouffe, each of the agonists has stressed the value of those transnational or cosmopolitan social movements that increasingly challenge the authority of particular states. However, these political movements are not seen to enjoy the *potentia* to transgress the broader legitimacy of liberal democratic constitutionalism, with its basic grammar of democracy and individual rights, or popular sovereignty and the rule of law.

My sense, nevertheless, is that the leading theorists of agonism move too quickly to situate the *agon* within the horizon of liberal democracy, which after all contains a central commitment to the legal protection of forms of possessive individualism (Macpherson, 1962). Indeed, by taking liberal democratic constitutionalism as the basic horizon of agonistic politics, the contemporary theorists run the risk of unwittingly finding themselves co-opted into the idea that we have reached the 'end of history'. This notion was initially born of the self-confidence of liberal democratic regimes – and particularly the United States – after the collapse of the Soviet Union, which was understood to represent the total exhaustion of systematic alternatives to western liberalism (Fukuyama, 1992). Today, things look very different. This liberal idealism has given way to a growing cynicism and serious erosion in the legitimacy of western liberal democracies and their basic institutions, in the context of disciplinary neo-liberalism and the post–9/11 security state with its preemptive wars and its incapacity to address the global financial crises. Nevertheless, we also seem to find ourselves trapped in a situation where history (in the sense of prospects for radical change) really does appear to have been suspended, and the neo-liberal capitalist regime is able to 'present its order as permanent, eternal and necessary' despite all of its manifest pathologies (Hardt and Negri, 2001, 11). This is captured in the idea propagated by neo-liberal ideologues that 'there is no alternative' to the present system. In fact, we will see in Chapters 6 and 7, that one key to this predicament has been the transformation of the very notion of *crisis* or the *exception* from something that signalled historical movement to an internal element of governance within the present system (Hardt and Negri, 2001, 385; Agamben, 2005).

The contemporary agonists do seek to address these developments, and we will see that Tully and Honig in particular offer thoughtful and pertinent responses, respectively to the global consolidation of neo-liberal imperialism and to the new forms of sovereignty associated with the security state. However, their rejoinders ultimately fall short, and not least because of their basic assumption that democratic innovation unfolds within the horizon of liberal democratic constitutionalism. By way of contrast, I will argue that it is incumbent on agonistic theorists to hold on to the idea of radical innovation in response to the multiple and overlapping crises associated with neo-liberalism. In Chapter 7, I present a theory of agonism and militant cosmopolitanism which is predicated upon this ongoing possibility. Indeed, as the intensifying volume of protest movements around the world over the past few years has shown, there is presently a great yearning for systemic transformation, captured in the slogan that 'another world' and not just a reiteration of liberal democracy 'is possible'. Once again, Arendt's contribution is particularly important here, because, as we will see throughout this study, she combined an insistence on the pluralistic and open-ended conditions of political action with a keen sense of the miraculously creative power of the modern revolutionary *event*. Contemporary agonistic theory needs to rediscover this treasure, and to learn something from the generation who initiated our present forms of government, that, as Thomas Paine put it, political actors *always* retain the power to 'begin the world over again' (Paine, 1986, 120). This does not mean we need to recreate the whole of society from scratch, or gain control of the state and roll out a series of five-year plans, but it does mean we need to invent new social and political forms that introduce radical dislocation in the present forms of domination, that is, if we are to stand any chance of finding solutions to the financial, population, and climatic crises. These are, of course, contentious points, and I explore these ideas in more detail in Chapter 7, and in the concluding part of the book I also make some tentative suggestions about what this might mean for a conception of historical transformation, now that we have been liberated from the idea of the dialectic as the engine of World History.

Structure of the book

In Chapter 1 I provide a preliminary synopsis of the central components of the *agonistic* side of agonistic democracy. These are: (i) an emphasis on constitutive pluralism, (ii) a tragic vision of a world without hope of final redemption from conflict, suffering, and strife, and (iii) a belief that certain forms of contest can be a political good. These ideas are derived from Greek antiquity and they also feature prominently in Machiavelli. They are similarly important to Nietzsche, Arendt, and Foucault and are found – in different forms and with distinct inflection – in each of the four main thinkers examined in this book. In addition, I consider and reject the claim that a basic distinction can be drawn between those agonists who adequately address the problem of antagonism, i.e. Mouffe, and those who don't.

As I see it, the three components of the agonistic matrix represent constitutive dimensions of politics, and there is no reason why they should be associated exclusively with liberal democratic institutions or with any particular form of government. Moreover, there is nothing in these conditioning features of political life that precludes the possibility of moments of absolute initiative or radical innovation. Indeed, these basic circumstances of the democratic *agon* point towards the priority of the strategic question, and compel us to keep open the idea of the possibility of the emergence of alternative moments of the constituent power. As such, they frame my own elaboration of agonism and militant cosmopolitanism in Chapter 7.

Chapter 2 picks up the discussion about the priority of the constituent power. The chapter commences with a presentation of Schmitt's account of the constituent power as sovereign decision. We see that Schmitt's interpretation shares a great deal in common with Arendt, but, as Honig says, the Schmittean approach is predicated on a discourse about security and the simple maintenance of biological life, and so Schmitt lacked Arendt's insight into the creative and aspirational dimension of the constituent power. This discussion provides a prelude to a full account of Arendt's distinction between the antique Roman conception of augmentation and the modern revolutionary moment, exemplified in the French and, according to Arendt, especially in the American Revolution. These ideas are crucially important and structure the remainder of the book, but at this point we also glimpse the limitations of Arendt's approach, in her strict demarcation between the political and the social.

Through a comparison with Habermas' co-originality thesis, the chapter also examines in more detail how the contemporary agonistic theorists

place an exclusive emphasis on augmentation, and I explore again some of
the reasons why in the present context it is important instead to hold onto
the idea of the possibility of revolutionary innovation. In addition, the
chapter provides a brief survey of the mainstream approaches in contemporary democratic theory, and I show how they all tend to subordinate
the constituent power under constituted forms of authority in various
ways. I consider the principal assumptions of contemporary theories of
liberalism, as well as aggregative democracy, deliberative democracy, and
cosmopolitan democracy. We also return to the contribution of the radical democrats and see how their particular take on the priority of the
constituent power is combined with a stress on the intrinsically binary
nature of the political, and that they do not fully appreciate the conditioning circumstances of pluralism. These alternative approaches then
provide important points of comparison throughout the remainder of the
book.

The four chapters set out in Part II provide a comprehensive account of
agonistic democracy as it is represented in the four leading contemporary
proponents. Chapter 3 begins with an account of Connolly's evaluation
of two key ethical theorists: St. Augustine and Nietzsche. As Connolly
presents it, the 'Augustinian imperative' manifests in the pursuit of intrinsic moral order, and this gives rise to a politics of existential *ressentiment*,
where various 'heretics' effectively become responsible for human suffering. According to Connolly, this sentiment has had an enormous impact
on subsequent moral and religious doctrine, and is broadly felt today in
the present resurgence of forms of religious and secular fundamentalism.
By way of contrast, Nietzsche says 'yes' to life in all of its dimensions,
including the tragic dimension of suffering, and without *ressentiment*. On
Connolly's reading, the Nietzschean ethic is basically one of humility,
and this flows into the core components of his own ethical teaching, i.e.
the notions of 'agonistic respect' and 'critical responsiveness' which Connolly presents as the civic virtues appropriate to late modern pluralism,
and where democratic partisans are called upon to acknowledge the contestability of their convictions. I consider Connolly's various iterations of
the ends of agonistic politics – in terms of facilitating individuality, and
as a supplement to liberal conceptions of justice – and I stress that overall
his approach is best understood not as a radicalised form of liberalism,
but rather as part of a distinctly Madisonian tradition of republicanism
concerned with the ways in which agonism can prevent the tyranny of
intensive minorities. I also compare Connolly's position to Owen's reading of Nietzsche, and to his conception of agonistic democracy in terms
of a perfectionist struggle to establish a collective ranking of contending
values.

Connolly's account of critical responsiveness is linked to his conception of the creative power of agonistic politics in terms of 'pluralisation' or
democratic 'enactment', whereby new emergent movements periodically
displace established constellations of identity. This is Connolly's version
of the politics of augmentation, and represents a significant advance on
mainstream liberal theories. Connolly's theory of democratic enactment
captures much of what is going on in new social movement politics, but
it is also clear that his categories cannot envisage or facilitate moments
of radical innovation in democratic politics. In addition to this difficulty,
Connolly's theory is constrained by his basic tendency to translate the
necessary analysis of historically specific forms of domination into a discussion about the problems of existential *ressentiment*. This is apparent in
his reflections of globalisation, cosmopolitanism, and his recent account
of capitalism, and I discuss each of these points in some detail before
turning to Connolly's theory of 'immanent naturalism'.

Here Connolly has drawn on a variety of different sources including Deleuze, Baruch Spinoza, and William James, and this naturalist
approach has enabled Connolly to develop some remarkable insights into
the question of embodiment and of the temporality of social life. Nevertheless, Connolly's immanentist conception of politics carries several
problematic assumptions. Most significantly, like all forms of naturalism,
Connolly's thought is one of *process*, and although this is a dynamic conception taken from the latest developments in the natural sciences such
as complexity and chaos theory, Arendt has shown very cogently that the
uniquely human capacity for action must be understood as an interruption of natural and social processes. I argue that Connolly's astute probing
of complex processes has lots to offer, and this is because processes – of
globalisation, for example – *do* condition social life to a considerable
degree, but this insight only remains pertinent if we also recognise the
creative power of genuine human action as something essentially exogenous to process.

In Chapter 4 I commence with a discussion of Tully's understanding of the politics of recognition. Situating his reflections within wider
debates – with references to Charles Taylor, Will Kymlicka, Fraser,
Patchen Markell, and others – I show how Tully has developed a distinctively agonistic conception of the struggle for recognition, and how
this is intrinsically related to his particular stress on challenging domination, and with his understanding of agonistic democracy as a means to
republican independence. Having set out these important points I turn
to a detailed appraisal of Tully's application of Wittgenstein's later philosophy. Tully draws numerous insights from Wittgenstein, and in *Strange*

Multiplicity he employs Wittgenstein's comparative method to conduct a historical survey of the dominant strands of modern constitutionalism: liberalism, communitarianism, and nationalism. As Owen has said, Tully's approach here is close to the genealogical studies conducted by Nietzsche and Foucault, as well as Skinner's historical analyses of the concept of liberty. Tully also draws on Wittgenstein more generally in his depiction of agonistic dialogue, and, most importantly, Tully appropriates Wittgenstein's reflections on rule following, and develops Wittgenstein's insight that it is always possible to follow a rule in a variety of ways. This underpins Tully's version of the politics of augmentation, and I argue that he is right to dismiss conservative readings of Wittgenstein that see human agents as entirely rule-governed. Instead, Tully presents an agonistic conception of the political subject, who is always partially free to judge and amend a given rule in numerous ways, and in the course of its application.

However, it is also clear that Tully's approach, as well as that of others who rework Wittgenstein such as Aletta Norval, is unable to portray the specifically revolutionary moment of change. This is most apparent when we consider the temporality of the creative moment. In contrast to Arendt's theory, the Wittgensteinian subject is forever fated to *follow* a rule, albeit in many different and creative ways, and to transform rules on a case-by-case basis in the ordinary practices of daily life, she is also bound to keep some rules in place as necessary background conditions whilst others change, and she never finds herself in the miraculous locality of a moment of absolute initiative antecedent to the rule itself. Again, Tully presents a mono-typical theory of the constituent power, and, as various commentators have highlighted, in his approach this is also compounded by some fairly weighty normative assumptions that Tully attributes to agonistic dialogue and to the principle of *audi alteram partem*. These suppositions bring him close to deliberative theory, and I question whether Tully's normative conventions are really compatible with the tragic viewpoint of agonism, and show how his dialogic reasoning places limitations on the more strategic elements he appropriates from Foucault.

This limitation becomes all the more pressing when we turn to Tully's account of our current predicament in the second volume of his *Public Philosophy in a New Key*. Here, Tully presents an excellent account of the processes of globalisation as a continuation of Euro-American imperialism by other means. Tully focuses on the gross levels of inequality associated with neo-liberal globalisation, as well as the new forms of control associated with the network society. There can be no doubt that, on his reading, globalisation represents a form of imperial power and domination. However, Tully rightly stresses that the system of globalisation also provides conditions for the emergence of new forms of democratic agency, such as the World Social Forum. In fact, Tully identifies two basic forms of civic freedom to emerge in this changed context. He refers to those forms of direct citizen–citizen relationship, which, by Tully's account, are flourishing in the 'interstices' of global power regimes, and which he calls forms of glocal citizenship, and he also refers to new forms of agonistic conflict between hegemons and subalterns. I maintain that Tully's focus on direct citizen–citizen relations is problematic, and his analysis of the relationships between oppressed and oppressor is more important. However, in the end Tully has remarkably little to say about those struggles which seek to contest the dominant configuration of power, and I argue that his position is problematic from a republican viewpoint, because his glocal citizens effectively remain dependent on the arbitrary forms of power that tower over them.

Chapter 5 commences with an evaluation of Mouffe's post-Marxist theory developed in the 1980s with Laclau, and most notably in their co-authored *Hegemony and Socialist Strategy*. In some respects, this work stands on a fault line between agonistic and radical democracy. I emphasise the significance of post-structuralism, and especially Derrida's work, in their account of pluralism and the discursive construction of social subject positions. This perspective enabled Laclau and Mouffe to break with Marxist assumptions about the intrinsic priority of class relationships, and to explicate non-class political mobilisations associated with the new social movements around issues such as ethnicity, gender, and the environment. Drawing on Antonio Gramsci, Laclau and Mouffe theorised hegemony as a distinct mode of collective agency, built around a chain of equivalences between subordinate social struggles and aimed at a moment of emancipation from an oppressive force presumed to subjugate them all. These concepts provide important insights into the details of collective action under conditions of pluralism, and I offer an alternative reading of hegemony in my own account of agonism and militant cosmopolitanism. However, in marked contrast to Tully's glocal citizens, Laclau and Mouffe focus too intensely on the element of emancipation from the oppressor, and lose sight of the ultimate priority of the politics of innovation.

Despite these difficulties, at this stage in Mouffe's work the idea of a collective struggle for change was clearly at the forefront of her analysis. However, in her explicitly agonistic writings, from *The Return of the Political* onwards, this has given way to an altogether different emphasis. Instead, Mouffe has repeatedly stressed the challenge of 'the political' in the form of the friend/enemy antithesis and a corresponding threat of physical violence. She takes these ideas from Schmitt and, like Schmitt, sees the problem of antagonism as an 'ever present possibility' in human relations. This basic assumption provides Mouffe with the basis of both a negative critique of other contemporary forms of democratic theory and practice, and the building blocks of her own iteration of agonistic democracy. According to Mouffe, the problem with mainstream democratic theory and practice is that it closes down the *agon*, and fails to provide legitimate outlets for political contest. This is evident, for example, in the deliberative model, as well as in the prevailing political trends, which incline towards a consensus at the centre and a technocratic post-politics. As Mouffe sees it, these tendencies open the door to extremists, for example the rise of the far Right in Europe, who claim to offer a meaningful alternative to the mainstream consensus elites. In other words, the consensus at the centre leads to a 'return of the political' in the form of antagonism.

By way of contrast, the challenge of agonistic democracy is to transform relations of 'antagonism' into 'agonism' through the hegemonic construction of a shared symbolic space. Indeed, because of these assumptions, there is a strong emphasis in Mouffe's theory on the need for commonality as a prior condition of agonism. Mouffe also draws on Michael Oakeshott to develop a republican conception of the bonds of common loyalty between citizens, in their shared acknowledgement of the authority of the *respublica*. This is presented as a precondition of agonistic politics, understood in terms of a legitimate conflict between 'adversaries'. These ideas are linked in turn to Mouffe's account of liberal democracy as the basic horizon of agonistic politics, and her version of augmentation in terms of an on-going and open-ended extension of the paradoxical principles of liberty and equality into more areas of social life.

I argue that Mouffe is right to stress the incommensurability between the agonistic and deliberative models, and her critique of Third Way post-politics helps to explain significant tendencies in the present conjuncture. Nevertheless, Mouffe's overriding concern with the problem of antagonism means that she is in danger of losing sight of the positive goods of agonistic democracy. It seems that, for Mouffe, the primary, or perhaps even the exclusive, good of agonistic democracy has become the prudent circumvention of antagonism in order to ensure the maintenance of order and security. In this, she effectively invokes a Hobbsean view of politics in terms of a perennial need to sublimate a primordial tendency towards violence, and she comes perilously close to reproducing the neo-conservative position that underpins the post–9/11 security state. Mouffe is partly saved from this fate by her retrieval of the republican themes of *societas* and the *respublica*, and a discussion of this aspect of her work facilitates an understanding of the subtle differences between her and Tully.

Chapter 6 embarks on an evaluation of Honig's *Political Theory and the Displacement of Politics* in which she deconstructs the work of Kant, Rawls, and Michael Sandel, who are presented as exemplary theorists of political closure. Honig calls these more conventional approaches 'virtue' theories of politics, and they are contrasted primarily with the work of Nietzsche and Arendt but also with Machiavelli, whom Honig appropriates to develop an alternative politics of agonistic *virtù*. Honig's engagement with Nietzsche is covered briefly in Chapter 3 in relation to Connolly's work, and so in Chapter 6 I focus instead on her presentation of Arendt, who, by Honig's own account, 'forms the spiritual and conceptual centre' of the book. Honig's encounter with Arendt moves in two key directions, and I address each of these in turn. Firstly, Honig problematises Arendt's fixed topography of the political and the social, and she shows that Arendt's theory can be used to break down its own problematic binaries. This is because the qualities of innovation that Arendt associated with political action can cut into the realms of necessity that she attributed to the social, and Honig demonstrates this by drawing attention to the proximity of her reworked Arendtean categories and Judith Butler's notion of gender *performativity*. These are crucial insights, and Honig's reworking of the Arendtean topography demonstrates that Arendt's theory can be reclaimed for a critique of forms of social domination, and against those who insist that she is beyond recuperation in this way.

After this, I turn to Honig's reading of Arendt's *On Revolution*. Here, she wants to rescue Arendt from what she depicts as her poor formulation of the revolutionary event as moment of radical initiative. Honig develops her position through a critique of Arendt's reading of the American *Declaration of Independence*, and by appropriating an alterative reading based upon Derrida's understanding of the performative speech act. Whereas Arendt celebrates the *Declaration* as a 'purely performative speech act', and wants to rid the revolutionary event of any reference to a constative moment, and especially of any grounding in the transcendent power of the deity, Derrida understands instead that some allusion to a constative moment is part of the necessary aporetic structure of every constituent (speech) act. This analysis forms part of a more general appropriation of Derrida's position, and Honig presents *iterability* as a basic condition of all forms of politics. Her primary objective is to translate Arendt's idea of the revolutionary event into the more modest notion of a politics of perpetual (re)foundation in the day-to-day practices of the citizens. It is clear, then, that Honig trades in a framework that permits a distinction between alternate moments of the constituent act – augmentation and revolution – for a single framework of augmentation (or *iterability*) in the every day circumstances of the republic.

Moreover, this strategy of taking (only apparently) exceptional moments and translating them into the (only apparently) ordinary circumstances of everyday politics has become the defining feature of Honig's conception of agonistic democracy. This is clear in *Emergency Politics* where she brings this same approach to bear on Rousseau's depiction of the paradox of foundation, and to the tensions in his work between the 'general will' and the 'will of all', as well as in response to the Schmittean notion of the 'exception' that has recently been reworked so effectively by Agamben to explain the present circumstances of the security state. Honig's approach places the consistent power decisively in the hands of situated political actors, such as Louis Freeland Post, Assistant Secretary of Labour during the Wilson Administration, who was able to use his administrative discretion to resist and redirect executive decisions and priorities in the context of the first Red Scare. I argue that Honig provides an excellent account of the genuinely transformative power of agonistic augmentation, but with her exclusive emphasis on the politics of the *extra*-in-the-ordinary, she nonetheless runs the risk of complicity in the status quo, in the idea that there is no fundamental alternative to the security state and the neo-liberal capitalist regime.

Indeed, Honig's reticence about radical innovation and the possibility of genuine republican autonomy is more pronounced in *Democracy and the Foreigner*. This book works through a series of foreign founder myths from popular and high culture, and demonstrates that this figure is a 'fantasy construction', and one that enables the democratic polity to live with its own constitutive *aporia*. The central message of this book is the irreducibly alien quality to the law, and here again Honig is close to Derrida, and essentially to a Hebrew conception of the law as an unfathomable moment of divine command, which, by Honig's account of agonistic politics, can be perpetually resisted and redirected, but which precludes the possibility of the *demos* ever becoming the authors of the law. Again, it is clear just how far Honig has travelled from Arendt, whose great insight was to show how the modern revolutionary conception of authority as self-foundation, without reference to the divine or the transcendent, could be made consonant with the condition of human plurality.

Having surveyed the strengths but also the limitations of the four key theorists, in Chapter 7 I elaborate my own conception of agonism and militant cosmopolitanism. The chapter commences with a brief restatement of the principal challenges of the present conjuncture, in terms of the dominant characteristics of disciplinary neo-liberalism and the specific forms of control associated with the security state. Following this, I conceptualise the contemporary struggles against neo-liberalism in terms of a militant form of cosmopolitanism. The analysis moves through three separate discussions, which consider in turn (i) the vital role of reflective judgement in agonistic politics, and how the public sphere is forged in the dynamic tension between action and judgement, (ii) the importance of a politics of conviction, and how the actor strives to demonstrate her conviction by becoming a living example of her own values and principles, and (iii) the prospect of a new form of universalism, or militant cosmopolitanism, that emerges from the widespread recognition of the significance of a new beginning, so that it is picked up and carried forward in the multiple and open-ended judgements of diverse publics, and starts to have a real material impact on the lived experiences of citizens and on the priorities of governmental decision making.

In order to elaborate this theory, I work my way through a series of contributions, including: Arendt's use of Kant's theory of reflective judgement; Badiou's account of militant conviction in his book on St. Paul; Foucault's account of *parrhesia* which enables the actor to display her conviction by speaking freely in the public sphere; the original Hellenic conception of hegemony in terms of a literal reading of *leader*ship; and the Renaissance understanding of republican politics as built around an always provisional judgement of the *populus* on the *status* of the leader and the standing of his princely *virtù*. Each of these considerations is folded into my account of agonism and militant cosmopolitanism, where, crucially, the idea of cosmopolitanism refers to something more than simply transnationalism. Instead, the cosmopolitan moment is linked to the possibility of the emergence and subsequent augmentation of a radical new beginning, and in response to the present circumstances of multiple and overlapping crises.

This emphasis on absolute initiative brings us back to the difficult question of the historical conditions of agonism, and in the conclusion I link the democratic contest to the possibility of historical transformation. One of the great strengths of post-structuralism has been to liberate democratic actors from Hegelian and Marxist theories of history as teleological process, as well as from Kant's account of the Enlightenment and modernity as providential. The historical consciousness of the contemporary agonistic theories is represented in their genealogical studies of the contingent origins of particular contemporary practices and institutions. These are valuable contributions, but they cannot deliver a moment of more radical transformation, and the exclusive emphasis on genealogy reinforces the idea that augmentation represents the essential structure of the constituent power. By way of contrast, I link the *agon* to the revolutionary *Ursprung* as it was elaborated by Benjamin and Arendt. This is a radical leap into being, one that disrupts the historical continuum, and – when shorn of the messianic assumptions that are tied up with Benjamin's formulation – this could provide the key to the emergence of a new *princ*iple, or set of norms and values, which becomes rooted in the people through an on-going, open-ended, and expansive politics of contending judgements.

1 Agonism: pluralism, tragedy, and the value of conflict

In this chapter I set out a preliminary synopsis of the pivotal components of the *agonistic* side of agonistic democracy. As I have said, the term agonism comes from the Greek *agon* meaning contest or strife. More specifically, I make the case that there are three basic elements that comprise the *agonism* in agonistic democracy. These are (i) a conception of constitutive pluralism, (ii) a tragic vision of the world, and (iii) a belief that conflict can be a political good. These ideas are exhibited in each of the four thinkers examined in Part II, and represent a basic confluence of views that differentiate the agonists from other approaches. However, they also articulate these concepts in distinct ways, drawing on different sources, using contrasting terminology, and with divergent points of emphasis. Indeed, we will already start to see some important distinctions between the four thinkers in this opening chapter. Nevertheless, in my view, we should see these three core constituents of agonism as something like conditioning circumstances of politics. These ideas are derived from Greek antiquity, and we will see that they are similarly prefigured in Machiavelli, which reinforces the idea that contemporary agonistic democracy should be situated broadly within the republican tradition. They are also present in Nietzsche, Arendt, and Foucault. Furthermore, these core aspects of agonism both presuppose and reinforce the idea of the primacy of the constituent power and, as we have said, of the priority of the strategic question, i.e. of the sorts of moves available to situated subjects in any given conjuncture.

Constitutive pluralism

Over the past few decades the concept of pluralism has become a central point of reference across the spectrum of contemporary political theory, and this reflects the importance of the politics of diversity outlined in the Preface. According to John Rawls, our current predicament is defined by a basic need to establish constitutional principles of justice to regulate a society characterised by what he called the 'fact of pluralism'

(Rawls, 2005). However, whilst the terminology of pluralism is prevalent throughout contemporary political thought, this does not imply agreement about the meaning of this concept, and Rawls was wrong to present pluralism as a fact; instead, different conceptions of pluralism reflect different assumptions about how best to respond to the politics of diversity, and at least three features differentiate the agonistic conception of pluralism from the liberal conception elaborated by Rawls. Firstly, the agonists reject the idea that pluralism can be, or ought to be, mediated by a determinant set of rational principles; secondly, they insist that plurality does not only refer to differences between groups and individuals, but also to the circumstances that constitute and condition the identity of those groups and individuals; and, thirdly, the agonists have a keen sense of the ways in which plurality can be distorted and manipulated by dominant interests and values. I explore each of these points in turn.

To readers more familiar with the Anglo-American tradition, the agonistic view will resonate with the concept of value pluralism elaborated by Isaiah Berlin. For Berlin, value pluralism is understood as a diversity of 'ultimate ends' which differ 'not in all respects . . . but in some profound irreconcilable ways' and which are not 'combinable in any final synthesis', or as Gray puts it, drawing on Berlin, are not 'rankable' in any definitive 'scale of value' (Berlin, 1998, 8; Gray, 2007, 43). This understanding of value pluralism is shared by Berlin, Gray,[1] the agonistic democrats examined here, and various other contemporary theorists.[2] It is quite distinct from the Rawlsian version, where values can be ordered lexically and where 'justice is [always] the first virtue of social institutions, as truth is of systems of thought' (Rawls, 1972, 3). Although the agonistic democrats do not draw directly on Berlin, there is a shared lineage stretching back to Max Weber, who insisted that 'the various value spheres of the world stand in irreconcilable conflict with each other' as a consequence of the declining authority of Christianity in Europe under conditions of modernity (Weber, 1993b, 147–9), and Nietzsche, whose reflections on pluralism and nihilism are considered in detail in relation to Connolly's work in Chapter 3. Moreover, as Berlin has emphasised, there is a common root for all of these theorists in Machiavelli, who, on the earliest threshold of modernity, already recognised the fundamental incompatibility of Christian and pagan virtues (Berlin, 1997). Against conventional readings of Machiavelli, where he is thought to contrast Christian piety (the good) with the necessary evils of statecraft, Berlin insisted that the 'originality' of Machiavelli lay in his recognition of two

---

[1] Gray has described his approach as 'agonistic liberalism', see: Gray, 2007, 103.
[2] See, for example: Bellamy, 1999 and White, 2002.

competing conceptions of the good. On this reading, Machiavelli does not explicitly condemn Christian morality, he simply insists that, if 'one wishes to build a glorious community like those of Athens and Rome at their best, then one must abandon Christian education and substitute' an alternative Roman or classical conception 'better suited to the purpose' (Berlin, 1997, 47).

What is perhaps most significant about this constitutive or agonistic conception of value pluralism is that there is no transcendent *measure* by which to adjudicate between conflicting values. In Berlin's terms, competing values are often (but not always) 'incommensurable' and 'there might exist no single universal overarching standard that would enable a man to choose rationally between' them (Berlin, 1997, 69). The challenges associated with value pluralism are further complicated in politics, because, as Mark Philp says, the collective choices we make are typically 'multidimensional and . . . cut across a range of values' (Philp, 2010, 473). Decisions about whether or not to go to war, to regulate banker's pay, to cut expenditure on welfare, or to legislate on issues such as abortion or gay marriage inevitably invoke competing clusters of value commitments that include, for example, considerations of security, liberty, community, tolerance, and justice. Indeed, it is probably best to talk about elements of residual incommensurability between contending clusters of value because, in politics, we seldom if ever have to make straightforward choices between two opposed values, such as clemency or justice, or liberty or equality.[3]

This constitutive form of pluralism is not to be confused with relativism or the idea that 'anything goes', because, as Gray says, 'one may assert that the conceptions of the good expressed in the lives of Mother Teresa and Oscar Wilde are incommensurable, and yet confidently assert that the life of a crack addict is a poor one' (Gray, 2007, 43).[4] Nevertheless, to endorse this conception of pluralism as 'ineradicable', as Mouffe puts it, is to acknowledge that, in the absence of traditional forms of authority, there is no longer any justification for different values beyond individual and collective choice (Mouffe, 2000b, 102). Moreover, without leave to petition a set of foundational (or transcendent) principles this will 'not [be a] rational choice but [a] radical choice among incommensurables' (Gray, 2007, 100). On this view, political decision making cannot be rationally resolved with appeals to utilitarian calculation or a deontological use of public reason. Indeed, Mouffe and Honig both invoke Derrida's notion

---

[3] For an insightful discussion of value pluralism and the notion of incommensurability, see: Lukes, 1991.
[4] See also: Berlin, 1998, 9.

of the 'ordeal of the undecidable' to illustrate that every ethical and political decision is ultimately *groundless*, because no decision can appeal in a programmatic fashion to a given set of procedures to remove the burden of choice.[5] Tully on the other hand – drawing on Wittgenstein – defends an attenuated form of practical reasoning and a minimal set of dialogical conventions that guide the way in resolving disputes on a case-by-case basis. I evaluate this view in detail in Chapter 4 and consider whether this Wittgensteinian approach is in the end compatible with the groundlessness of constitutive pluralism.

A second distinctive feature of the concept of constitutive pluralism that underpins the agonistic approach is recognition that pluralism does not simply denote a system of differences between groups and individuals and their contending values, but is, in a way, more fundamental: in the sense that pluralism is a defining characteristic of the circumstances that condition the identity of groups and individuals. As Derek Edyvane puts it in his discussion of Stuart Hampshire, who also shares this view, it 'is not simply that inevitable differences in identities, lifestyles, and moralities might lead to conflict; it is rather that identities, lifestyles and moralities are in the first place formed by [pluralism and] conflict' (Edyvane, 2008, 329). In other words, on this reading, pluralism is a conditioning quality of political 'reality'. The agonists draw on various sources in continental philosophy to make this point. For example, Mouffe has repeatedly invoked the Derridean notion of constitutive *différance* – understood as a moving discord of difference and deferral – to articulate a conception of constitutive pluralism (Derrida, 1982, 9, 18; Mouffe, 1995a, 1534). This idea is elaborated in Chapter 5, and for now it will suffice to say that, for Derrida, *différance* forms part of a wider project to nominate the ultimately unnameable *excess* of relationality (syntactic, semantic, and temporal) which is constitutive of all signification and so, by his account, of all forms of identity (Derrida, 1982; Gasché, 1994). Connolly and Tully also acknowledge the value of the Derridean articulation of fundamental plurality, but they mostly make use of other sources to elaborate a conception of constitutive difference. These are, respectively, a Deleuzean conception of 'life' and 'multiplicity', and a conception of the constitutive nature of game-like 'dialogue' taken from Wittgenstein. As we will see in Chapter 6, Honig also draws extensively on Derrida and additionally invokes Arendt's distinctive conception of plurality: 'not

---

[5] Again, Weber makes the same point. He says: 'the ultimate possible attitudes towards life are irreconcilable, and hence their struggle can never be brought to a final conclusion. Thus it is necessary to make a decisive choice' (Weber, 1993b, 152). So too does Gray. He says deciding between incommensurables 'consists in making a decision or a commitment that is groundless' (Gray, 2007, 105).

only the *conditio sine qua non*, but the *conditio per quam* – of all political life' (Arendt, 1958, 7).

As we work our way through the chapters in Part II, we will see that there are important differences between these respective iterations of constitutive plurality. In Chapter 6 in particular I argue that we must resist the idea that *différance* represents a metaphysical principle that strictly conditions all forms of political action. However, for the moment we can refrain from exploring these differences and note instead that each of the thinkers examined in this book shares Mouffe's view that 'pluralism is not merely a fact... but rather an axiological principle' (Mouffe, 1995a, 1535), and so:

> The question of pluralism... cannot be envisaged only in terms of already existing subjects and restricted to their conceptions of the good. What must be addressed is the very process of constitution of the subjects of pluralism. This is indeed where the more crucial issues lie today. (Mouffe, 1993b, 149)

Moreover, at some level each of the agonistic thinkers associates pluralism with the qualities of contingency and unpredictability that necessarily condition political action and identify formation. Indeed, these ideas come together in a particularly compelling fashion in Arendt's conception of pluralism. For Arendt, human action is always action in concert, and so the actor consequently has little or no control over the significance of her action, which is inevitably taken up and judged by others and re/inscribed in multiple and unpredictable ways. She says:

> If [action] has any consequences at all, they consist in principle in an endless new chain of happenings whose eventual outcome the actor is utterly incapable of knowing or controlling beforehand. The most he may be able to do is to force things into a certain direction, and even of this he can never be sure. (Arendt, 1977c, 60)

This distinctly Arendtean take on constitutive pluralism forms a vital ingredient in my own account of agonism and militant cosmopolitanism elaborated in Chapter 7.

Because of their stress on the constitutive nature of pluralism, the agonists have also been acutely aware of the ways in which plurality is too often distorted by dominant sets of interests, ideas, values, practices, and institutions. Indeed, in contrast to the Rawlsean depiction of pluralism as an established fact, the agonistic emphasis on pluralism should not be taken as a defence of the status quo. On the contrary, from the agonistic viewpoint, *bona fide* plurality is always under threat from various demands for *uniformity* and *homogenisation*. This is evident, for example, in the politics of fundamentalism outlined in the Preface, and Connolly in particular has shown how the fundamentalist feels himself compelled to get rid of plurality in order to safeguard the purity and consistency of his own identity. However, this will-to-uniformity is also manifest in the politics of 'normalisation' explored by Connolly (drawing on Foucault), in the imperial practices (past and present) of Euro-American powers towards non-European and aboriginal peoples emphasised by Tully, and, more subtly perhaps, in the 'displacement of politics' that operates in numerous texts of contemporary political theory, challenged primarily by Honig and Mouffe. In addition, pluralism is also threatened by powerful forces of *disaggregation* or *fragmentation*, as we have seen especially, for example, in the ethnic conflicts in the Balkans, Rwanda, and elsewhere, and this danger of polarised division is particularly emphasised by Mouffe, drawing on Schmitt, in her account of the potential danger of 'antagonism'. Keeping both of these potential dangers in mind, we might think of constitutive plurality as being finely balanced between excessive claims to unity on one side, and the dangers of social or cultural fragmentation on the other. Indeed, we might view this construction as a contemporary rendition of the classical concern with the problems of tyranny (the illegitimate imposition of a single set of interests) and anarchy (the disintegration of the bonds of political community) respectively.[6] These two distinct ways of formulating the predominant threat to pluralism are not inconsequential, and again we return to these differences at various points in the book.

The rebirth of tragedy

The second component of the agonistic perspective affirmed by each of the thinkers considered here – although not, I shall argue, without equivocation in the work of Connolly and Tully – is a tragic view of the world. This follows necessarily from the notion of constitutive pluralism outlined above, and is captured in the idea of a world without hope of final redemption from suffering and strife. This tragic vision is ultimately derived from Greek antiquity, along with the concept of agonism itself that referred to the contest between adversaries in the athletic games and

[6] As Fossen has recognised, the affirmative 'valuation of pluralism' in agonistic democracy points to a corresponding commitment to 'emancipation', conceived in terms of 'a permanent attempt to lay bare and redress the harms, injustices or inequities caused by exclusions and restrictions of pluralism' (Fossen, 2008, 377). This confirms Khan's emphasis on the relationship between agonism and the republican conception of liberty as a struggle of freedom from domination (Khan, 2013).

rivalry among the characters in tragic drama.[7] In a recent commentary, Andreas Kalyvas has identified far-reaching discontinuities between 'the agonism of the ancients compared to that of the post moderns' (Kalyvas, 2009). As he sees it:

> The current revival of the agon in political theory does not suggest a nostalgic appeal to a pre-modern Greek past. It does not indicate yet another neo-classical revival. Quite the opposite... it represents a 'de-Hellenisation' of agonism, a considerable divestment of its ancient significations and a radical redefinition. (Kalyvas, 2009, 31)

Kalyvas is right to stress that contemporary agonism is in no way nostalgic for a return to small-scale face-to-face politics – in the same way that some modern participatory democrats have been – inspired by idealised renditions of the ancient *polis*. However, his main point of contention is that the post-modern agonists generally do not emphasise the relationship between agonism and the spirit of aristocracy, unlike in Greek antiquity where the *agon* was understood as 'a positive contest for greatness, glory and prominence' (Kalyvas, 2009, 24, 32). Kalyvas contrasts contemporary agonism with the aristocratic strains in the work of Nietzsche and Arendt, who – on his reading – were the two last 'ancient agonists' (Kalyvas, 2009, 16). I question this assessment of an apparent lack of aristocratic perfectionism in contemporary agonism below, in my discussion of the specific *value* of conflict. Nevertheless, it is important to stress that, irrespective of this point, Kalyvas misses a deeper affinity between the current accounts of agonism and Greek antiquity, which is manifest in the contemporary appreciation of the tragic wisdom of the ancients. Indeed, the ancient conception of the ineradicable strife of the world and of the human condition has filtered into contemporary political theory via the great modern tragedians – Nietzsche, Arendt, and also Sigmund Freud[8] – establishing a connection back once again

---

[7] For Jacob Burckhardt, the 'agonal age' stands in the interlude between the heroic epoch of Homer and the fifth century. This was a time of relative peace, when the competitive spirit could flourish, especially in the Pan-Hellenic festivals that are celebrated in the victory odes of Pindar (Burckhardt, 1998).

[8] Freud was immensely struck with the vision of Hellenic tragedy. This is evident not only in his repeated references to Greek mythology, and, of course, in the central importance of the Oedipal story in the psychoanalytical account of the psycho-social development of the child, but also in the basic Freudian depiction of the constant movement of unconscious desire, and its manifest displacements in slips of the tongue, dreams, obsessive thoughts, phobias, hysterical symptoms, and so on. The agonistic theorists examined in this book do not draw extensively on psychoanalysis, although, as we will see, there are some references to Freudian theory in Honig and Mouffe. Nevertheless, Samuel Weber has explicitly likened psychoanalysis to agonism, where the play of the unconscious and its 'resultant displacements mark the fitful rhythm of a game that can no longer be entirely

via Machiavelli to the original sources in the texts of fifth-century Attic drama, as well as to Thucydides' *History*,[9] and beyond that even to the epic poetry of the Mycenaean period.[10] Furthermore, this appreciation of Hellenic tragedy distinguishes contemporary agonistic democracy from the dominant rationalist accounts of liberalism and democracy, which, in one form or another, build upon the pre-eminent modern *anti*-tragic (or redemptive) philosophies of Kant and G. W. F. Hegel. It is important, therefore, to acknowledge the significance of the tragic vision before turning more specifically to the question of the value of conflict below.

Key to the tragic vision of both the ancients and the post-moderns is the idea that conflict, suffering, and strife are endemic in social and political life and not a temporary condition on a journey towards reconciliation or redemption.[11] For example, in Sophocles' *Theban Plays* as well as the epic poetry of Homer, this was dramatised in the rivalry between the key prot*agon*ists – Antigone and Creon in the *Antigone*, or Achilles and Hector in the *Iliad* – who should each be read as the embodiment of a distinct pathos, 'an ethical principle or 'spiritual power'' (Barker, 2009, 73). This is not to be misunderstood in terms of a modern Hollywood clash between good and evil, but rather as an impossible contest between two or more rivalrous but nonetheless legitimate powers, between incommensurate conceptions of the good, where neither has unqualified right or virtue on their side.[12] For example, *Antigone* is staged around a conflict between the divine law of ancestral burial rights and the private bonds of the *oikos*, invoked by Antigone, on the one side, and the equally imperative public bonds of the *polis* and the positive law of the state, represented

---

localised or determined, since it is constantly dislocating itself' (Weber, 1985, 109; see also: Gay, 1997).

[9] Various commentators have drawn attention to the essential element of tragedy in Thucydides' *History of the Peloponnesian War* (Lebow, 2003; Euben, 1990, Chapter 6). Indeed, Ned Lebow describes Thucydides as 'last of the great tragedians' (Lebow, 2003, 20). In the *History*, it is not only individuals but the *poli* themselves that embody different values, and the arrogance and loss of self-control (*sophrosyne*) that Athens displays, for example in the Melian Dialogue, leads to a basic *hamartia* in the Sicilian expedition, and *nemesis* in the form of the plague and subsequent defeat (Lebow, 2003).

[10] Although the form of fifth-century Attic poetry is distinct from earlier epic poetry, the tragic poets learnt much from Homer; particularly the central role of contest, and the idea that neither side has unqualified right on their side. See: Kaufmann, 1992, Chapter 5.

[11] For an overview of the deep impression made by Hellenic tragedy more generally on French post-structuralism, see: Leonard, 2005.

[12] The protagonists find themselves in circumstances of what Jean-Francois Lyotard called a *differend*, understood as a 'case of conflict, between (at least) two parties, that cannot be equitably resolved for lack of a rule of judgement applicable to both arguments. One side's legitimacy does not imply the other's lack of legitimacy' (Lyotard, 1988, xi).

by Creon, on the other.[13] The clash of wit and status between the central characters, the ambiguous moral standing of the tragic heroes, and the terrible fate that invariably awaits them, all point to the *ineradicable* strife at the heart of ethical and political life.

> Tragedy is inherently ambiguous and open to interpretation. Even when the events in the narratives are finished, they do not decisively resolve the questions they have raised. Rather than ethical closure, the plays demand open-ended discussion and deliberation. (Barker, 2009, 15)

Nietzsche is the modern thinker who has reflected most extensively on the lessons of Hellenic tragedy, and Connolly presents him as a 'modern Sophocles' who 'returns to haunt' contemporary dialecticians with the tragic spirit of Greek antiquity (Connolly, 1993c, 189). At the centre of several tragedies is the idea of the *hamartia* of the central heroic character, that is, a seemingly inescapable error of judgement that invites disaster, and here King Oedipus is the most well-known example.[14] In his earliest work *The Birth of Tragedy*, Nietzsche wondered what ethical teaching could possibly have been conveyed by the suffering and misfortune of the great tragic heroes whose fate was so utterly determined by divine forces beyond their control, so that 'no action of theirs can work any change in the eternal condition of things', and in whose contemplation, as Walter Kaufmann puts it, we 'feel seized and shaken by the whole misery of humanity' (Nietzsche, 1956, 51; Kaufmann, 1992, 45). He concluded that the only way to imagine Hellenic culture taking 'metaphysical solace' in tragedy was to see the message as one of courage or fortitude in response to the 'ghastly absurdity of existence' (Nietzsche, 1956, 51, 107). The 'heroic person praises his existence through tragedy', which installs in him a sense of 'bravery' in response to life – understood as a Dionysian flux of becoming with its perpetual cycles of destruction and renewal – so that he might find courage to face 'a powerful enemy, or noble hardship, or a problem that makes one shudder with horror'

---

[13] Antigone, in particular, has been a source of fascination for contemporary political and social theorists, and the specific values she is said to embody have been the subject of much discussion. See for example: Lacan, 1992; Butler, 2000; Žižek, 2001; Copjec, 2002; Honig, 2009a, 2010. However, the key point here is not any particular reading of the values that are exemplified in individual characters. Instead, the more basic message of Hellenic tragedy is that the *agon* is displayed in the clash between contending values. As Honig puts it, in the tragic plays 'each of the contending positions . . . is seen through the other's critical lens', the moral or ethical standpoint of each protagonist is 'amplified and criticized by surrounding characters', and the 'partiality and insufficiency of both contending forms . . . are on display' (Honig, 2009a, 25).

[14] For a discussion of the dramatic significance of the tragic misjudgement see: Aristotle, 1982, 57. The term *hamartia* initially meant missing the mark in archery, see: Lebow, 2003, 47.

(Nietzsche, 1998a, 56). Tragedy makes us 'realise that everything that is generated must be prepared to face its painful dissolution. It forces us to gaze into the horror of individual existence, yet without being turned to stone by the vision' (Nietzsche, 1956, 102). Moreover, the young Nietzsche thought that this 'tragic perception' also required the 'remedy of art' to make this experience of our radical insecurity and anguish bearable, and he saw the enormous achievements of classical art both as a product of this ancient tragic vision and as a form of solace for the tragic suffering of the world (Nietzsche, 1956, 95).

This emphasis on courage in the face of suffering remained a pertinent theme throughout Nietzsche's writings. Indeed, we will see in Chapter 3 that Connolly takes from Nietzsche the central ethical message that we should say 'yes to life, even in its strangest and hardest problems' and that this is the 'psychology of the tragic poet' (Nietzsche, 1998a, 81).[15] However, there is also awareness in Nietzsche's later work that the human condition is not so completely determined as this initial reading of the Greek plays suggested. Indeed, a more nuanced grasp of the tragic world of the Hellenes – of a cosmos understood as a complex of forces, where mortals find themselves in competition with a multiplicity of gods who are themselves set one against another – suggests perhaps that we are always partially free to engage and counter the forces that impact upon us. The tragic vision is not one of powerlessness in a cosmos of fate. As Connolly puts it, to accept our fate does not mean 'lapsing into passive resignation' (Connolly, 1993c, 163).[16] Indeed, we might even engage Nietzsche's texts in order to map out the tragic dimensions of life 'more robustly and [in order] to devise creative strategies through which to struggle against its violences' (Connolly, 1993c, 190). Honig also stresses that tragedy manifests 'in a call to action' (Honig, 2009a, 11). She insists that the vision of Hellenic tragedy points principally towards an agonistic *politics*, characterised by a limited human capacity to intervene in the world (as *natals*), and not exclusively, or primarily, to an ethical meditation on the universality of human suffering (as *mortals*) (Honig, 2010, 4).[17]

Nietzsche presented himself as the 'first tragic philosopher', and claimed to have 'looked in vain for signs' of this vision in previous

---

[15] See: Connolly, 2008, 136 and Deleuze, 1983, 19.

[16] See also: Connolly, 1993a, 118.

[17] Honig seeks to differentiate tragic wisdom from what she calls 'mortalist humanism', by which she means all those variegated approaches to ethics that see an underlying commonality in human 'vulnerability to suffering' (Honig, 2010, 1). By her account, we need to avoid elevating ethics – conceived as 'antipolitics' of grief – above 'the intractable divisions of politics' (Honig, 2010, 1, 6, 22–3).

'philosophers' with the exception of Heraclitus (Nietzsche, 1989, 273).[18] However, if we take the notion of 'philosopher' broadly then we can clearly see in Machiavelli's writings a modern love for this ancient wisdom three centuries before Nietzsche. This is evident in Machiavelli's account of the paradoxical interplay between chance and necessity throughout *The Prince* and *The Discourses*, and especially in Chapter XXV of *The Prince* entitled 'The Influence of Fortune on Human Affairs and How It May be Countered' (Machiavelli, 1947). Like Nietzsche, Machiavelli does not read the human condition as being completely determined by fate or *Fortuna*, rather we always find ourselves partially free to counter the tragic forces that shape our lives. The complex interplay of chance and necessity is summed up in Machiavelli's statement that 'without opportunity the... valour and wisdom [of great men] would... be... of no avail and without their talents the opportunity would... be... missed' (Machiavelli, 1947, 14).[19] As he puts it, 'if we are to keep' a sense of our capacity for action, then it must 'be true that fortune controls half our actions indeed but allows us the direction of the other half, or almost half' (Machiavelli, 1947, 73). This, of course, leads Machiavelli to his most notorious insight that good judgement in political affairs – both in princes and republics alike – lies in learning to play *Fortuna* at her own game, finding ways to adapt oneself to one's circumstances as much as is humanly possible, learning from experience, preparing against future obstacles, capitalising on the opportunities that life presents, and having the courage to face great challenges with wit and fortitude.[20] As he puts it, 'one must be a fox in avoiding traps and a lion in frightening wolves' and 'beyond doubt the greatness of princes lies in their ability to overcome obstacles and opposition, and therefore fortune' (Machiavelli, 1947, 50, 62).[21]

---

[18] The pre-Socratic philosophers turned away from allegory and myth and were the first to elaborate consistent forms of ontological argument, and yet they also participate in the ancient tragic vision. This is perhaps exemplified in Heraclitus, whose philosophy, says the early Nietzsche, represents a 'universal application' of the athletic *agon*, so that 'now the wheels of the cosmos turn on it' (Nietzsche, 1998b, 55).

[19] To the extent that the democratic *agon* can be legitimately figured as a game, then it is of the order of most card games, backgammon, and dominos, i.e. determined by a mixture of skill or prudence and blind luck, *virtù* and *Fortuna*. For a discussion along these lines, see: Caillois, 2001, 18.

[20] See especially: Machiavelli, 1947, 73, 75, and also Book Three Chapter 9 of *The Discourses* entitled: 'That it behoves one to adapt oneself to the times if one wants to enjoy continued good fortune' (Machiavelli, 1970, 430–2).

[21] Machiavelli thinks that a republic is better suited to adapt to fortune, because of the plurality of distinctive qualities that can be brought to bear in response to changing circumstances. He says 'for this reason a republic has a fuller life and enjoys good fortune for a longer time than a principality, since it is better able to adapt itself to

Again, we can see how the idea of tragedy (like the notion of constitutive pluralism) points towards the primacy of politics, to the centrality of the human capacity for action. In short, we could say that there is no pluralism without tragedy, and no tragedy without politics, understood in terms of the finite human capacity to contest fate and to bring new things into the world. Indeed, as I see it, agonism is ultimately a strategic doctrine concerned with the interplay between freedom and necessity, which is exemplified in Machiavelli. As Arendt says, human freedom is 'perhaps best illustrated by Machiavelli's concept of *virtù*, the excellence with which man answers the opportunities the world opens up for him in the guise of *Fortuna*' (Arendt, 1977b, 151). Foucault has forcefully reiterated this conception of agonism in twentieth-century theory in his essay 'The Subject and Power'.[22] Foucault is notorious for his idea of the omnipresence of power relationships. However, on his reading, this is not cause for despair because to say that there cannot be a society without power relations is not to say that the extant forms of constituted power and authority are necessary. Indeed:

Power is exercised only over free subjects, and only in so far as they are 'free'. By this we mean individual or collective subjects who are faced with a field of possibilities in which several kinds of conduct, several ways of reacting and modes of behaviour are available. (Foucault, 2002, 342)

Furthermore, Foucault associated agonism precisely with this human capacity for freedom. He said:

Rather than speaking of an essential antagonism, it would be better to speak of an 'agonism' – of a relationship which is at the same time mutual incitement and struggle; less of a face-to-face confrontation that paralyses both sides than a permanent provocation. (Foucault, 2002, 342)

On this Foucauldian reading, which I strongly endorse, agonism is a strategic and tactical doctrine concerned with the capacity of human agents to challenge the tragic forces that seek to govern their lives and determine their conduct.[23] In contemporary agonistic theory Tully comes

---

diverse circumstances, owing to the diversity found among its citizens, than a prince can do' (Machiavelli, 1970, 431).

[22] Foucault stressed that Machiavelli's advice to the Prince does not form part of the tradition of texts on the 'art of government' that emerged in the sixteenthth century, and which sought to introduce notions of efficiency and economy into the control of populations, and thereby gave rise to modern 'governmentality' (Foucault, 2009, 92). For a discussion of the Foucauldian notion of governmentality, see Chapter 4, below.

[23] Of course, some elements of political life can be subject to degrees of calculation, but – in contrast to rational choice and game theory approaches – the classical and

closest to this view. He says: 'any relation of power, no matter how strictly enforced, involves the possibility of freedom on the part of those over whom it is exercised' (Tully, 2008b, 81). There is 'always a certain "room for manoeuvre" (*Spielraum*) or field of possible comportments' in relation to the structures of power and domination that operate in social and political relations (Owen and Tully, 2007, 285).[24] As we will see in Chapter 3, Connolly also states a comparable view in his account of 'techniques of the self', which is again taken from Foucault.

We can see then that the tragic vision of contemporary agonistic democracy does not represent a thoroughly bleak or dismal assessment of the human condition.[25] Rather, it entails 'both a yearning to mediate and cope with conflict and an understanding that conflict is . . . ineliminable' (Barker, 2009, 5). This does mean, however, that the removal of conflict is not the *goal* of politics; rather, at best, political conflict can be perpetually displaced in ways that are mutually beneficial to contending parties. Nietzsche sums up this idea in his notion of the 'spiritualisation of enmity'. He says:

This consists in our profound understanding of the value of having enemies . . . Even in the field of politics enmity has nowadays become more spiritual – much cleverer, much more thoughtful, much *gentler*. Almost every party sees that its interest in self-preservation is best served if its opposite number does not lose its powers. (Nietzsche, 1998a, 22)

post-modern *strategos* appreciates the irreducible elements of chance, friction, and inertia that condition political life. Effective political agency, therefore, requires *both* knowledge and creative ability, but in the end is closer to an art than a science. In other words, the aspiration to fully calculate prudence, that underpins rational choice perspectives, demonstrates a basic lack of humility, which in turn draws into question the wisdom of these approaches.

[24] Classical realist theory also appreciates this irreducible element of strategy and tactics. The 'realist' appreciates that the realm of politics is not a fixed reality, characterised by hard facts or stable laws, nor is it ever fully governed by moral ideals or rational principles; the world of politics is rather a relentless mix of chance and necessity. The central *virtù* of the political actor is, therefore, the ability to read the moment, and this capacity can only ever be acquired through a mixture of learning, practical experience, intuition, and a fair measure of good luck (see Viroli, 2008, 22). Indeed, the basic conditions (or the 'reality') of politics place clear limitations on how much (fore) knowledge we can acquire about any concrete conjuncture, thereby limiting our predictive capacity, and suggesting instead that we turn to history as a storehouse of (only ever partially) enlightening examples. This wisdom of classical realist thought is for the most part lost on most modern political scientists and on moral philosophers alike, but is found not only in Machiavelli, but also in Sun Tzu, Thucydides, and Clausewitz, as well as some twentieth-century realists such as Hans Morgenthau. See: Handel, 2001; Howard, 2002; Lebow, 2003; Clausewitz, 2007; Sun Tzu, 2008; Strassler, 2008.

[25] Connolly distinguishes between tragic dramas – concentrated for example in a particular play by Sophocles or Shakespeare – and a 'tragic vision' that reflects a more general orientation to life (Connolly, 2008, 121).

This idea is shared in one form or another by each of the theorists examined in this book[26] and differentiates agonistic democracy from the mainstream perspectives in contemporary political theory, which are typically concerned to find ways to transcend conflict through appeals to determinant principles of justice or 'rationality'. Indeed, this distinction between the tragic wisdom of agonistic democracy and the 'rationalism' of contemporary neo-Kantians and dialecticians represents one of the front lines in current debates about how to address the politics of diversity and fundamentalism outlined in the Preface. This becomes more clear in the following chapter, which includes a brief survey of the mainstream perspectives in Anglo-American normative political theory and the variety of ways in which they seek to rise above tragic conflict and to subordinate the unruliness of the *polis* to the rule of law.[27] However, I say something briefly here about the most important precursors to the current rationalist philosophies in order to illustrate that the contest between rationalism and the tragic, or between philosophy and the democratic *agon*, has a long history.

In *The Birth of Tragedy* Nietzsche saw the original displacement of the tragic in the figure of Socrates 'the dialectical hero of the Platonic drama' and in his 'notion that knowledge alone makes men virtuous' (Nietzsche, 1956, 79, 88). Indeed, in the philosophy of Socrates and Plato the ancient wisdom of suffering is replaced by the pursuit of rational knowledge, and especially by the idea that truth is the necessary outcome of sound method or syllogistic reasoning. There is, says Nietzsche, an 'optimistic element in the nature of dialectics, which sees a triumph in every syllogism' (Nietzsche, 1956, 88). On Nietzsche's reading, the philosophers of late antiquity are not the highpoint of Hellenic culture, as they are generally understood to be, but rather its moment of decadence. These

---

[26] Bernard Williams also recognised this idea. He said: one 'very important reason' for thinking in terms of political as opposed to moral disagreement, is that the political decision – which temporarily brings disagreement to a close – 'does not in itself announce that the other party was morally wrong or, indeed, wrong at all. What it immediately announces is that they have lost' (Williams, 2005, 13). Treating our adversaries as political 'opponents', as opposed to moral or intellectual 'arguers', or 'fellow seekers after truth', can 'oddly enough, show them more respect' (Williams, 2005, 13). Honig sees this comparable vision in the work of Williams. However, Honig problematises William's tendency to present tragic situations as 'rare, exceptional, [or] extraordinary' events in moral life, and she stresses instead the 'radical undecidability' that 'touches all moral experience' (Honig, 1996, 262).

[27] As Honig puts it, most contemporary theorists 'read democratic theory according to the genre conventions of a popular or modern romance, as a happy ending love story' (Honig, 2001b, 109). By way of contrast, even when particular tragic plays do have happy endings, they do not offer solace through reconciliation, because along the way they have offered 'scenes of such intense and overwhelming suffering that the end did not outweigh them' (Kaufmann, 1992, 77).

'pseudo-Greek[s]' represent the 'counter movement against the ancient, noble taste, against the agonal spirit, against the *polis*' (Nietzsche, 1998a, 11, 78). Later, Nietzsche came to see an even more fateful opponent of the tragic vision in the Christian 'transcendental solution to the riddle of existence' and in the 'future anticipated bliss' of the Christian Gospels (Nietzsche, 1994b, 122). Machiavelli and Arendt also emphasised the impact of Christianity in 'the disappearance of the ancient city state' and its culture of tragedy (Arendt, 1958, 14; Machiavelli, 1970, 277). Indeed, Arendt emphasised the deep continuity between the 'Christian claim to be free from entanglement in worldly affairs' and 'the philosophic *apolitia* of late antiquity' (Arendt, 1958, 15). In the Platonic and Christian traditions alike 'Truth. . . can reveal itself only in complete human stillness', in a transcendence of the worldly experience of strife (Arendt, 1958, 14).

In Hegel's dialectic Greek philosophy and Christian doctrine are effectively brought together, so that the Good News of the Gospels works itself out teleologically in the movement of historical development, which is understood (retrospectively) as a necessary and rational process towards the realisation of 'the consciousness of Freedom' (Hegel, 1956). In this Hegelian view – which has had an enormous impact on modern thought – World History becomes the immanent movement of a 'cunning of reason' that forever negates conflicts so that together they constitute an all-encompassing spiritual Totality 'by dissolving themselves, and by making themselves into moments' of the Whole (Hegel, 1977, 20, 25). The 'end of history' is achieved when the conception of 'freedom. . . expressed in Christianity' (i.e. the doctrine of redemption through Christ) has 'cast off its otherworldliness' and 'become[s] the universal and actual principle of a new form of the world' (Hegel, 1991, 151, 380). This *telos* is finally knowable to human consciousness under conditions of modernity.

Hegel appreciated the value of Greek tragedy, which he saw as one of the highest achievements of Greek culture. Nonetheless, this was understood as a necessary 'moment' in the self-unfolding of the World Spirit, destined, along with the rest of Greek culture, to be *sublated*, that is, simultaneously overcome and preserved in higher or more rational forms of freedom. Indeed, Hegel reads the conflict between tragic characters as symptomatic of the basic contradiction of the ancient *polis*, which he presented as a simple 'immediate. . . Universality' (Hegel, 1956, 106). In the Greek World 'the individual will of the Subject adopts unreflectingly the conduct and habit prescribed by Justice and the Laws', and so there is no outlet for individual subjectivity, depicted, for example, in the figure of Antigone (Hegel, 1956, 107). By way of contrast, Hegel presents the modern state as a complex 'mediated whole' that accommodates subjective ethical freedom as an internal moment, expressed in the realm of civil society (Hegel, 1967, 133, 266). In other words, although (tragic) conflict is a central component in the movement of the dialectic, the Hegelian narrative is essentially one of redemption progressively realising itself in the world, and of reconciliation as immanent in the underlying structure of conflict itself.[28] As Deleuze puts it, the dialectic is 'not a tragic vision of the world but, on the contrary, the death of tragedy' (Deleuze, 1983, 18).[29] Although it is seldom presented today in the explicit terms of Hegelian philosophy, the dialectical conception of modernity and history (as a necessary movement whereby conflict is progressively overcome through progress towards freedom) remains an important underlying concept in many contemporary accounts of democracy. As we will see, for example in the following Chapter, this is evident in Habermas' conception of modernity as a self-correcting learning process. By way of contrast, the contemporary agonistic democrats – like Nietzsche and Arendt before them – recognise that a genuine conception of human freedom means we must resolutely reject dialectical and other notions of progress.

Kant was not as confident as Hegel would later be that history is a necessary dialectical process whose *telos* is the realisation of freedom and justice. Nevertheless, he was appalled at the tragic thought that history might be a haphazard set of events, where 'hopeless chance takes the place of reason's guiding thread' and he saw sufficient evidence in the European Enlightenment to allow himself at least hope that man's freedom can be brought into 'conformity with some definite plan of nature' (Kant, 1991a, 29, 30). However, Kant believed that the *concept* of right or justice could be formulated with 'mathematical precision' (Kant, 1991c, 135). Just like the 'purely formal concept of pure mathematics (e.g. geometry), reason has taken care that the understanding is likewise as fully equipped as possible with *a priori* intuitions for the construction of the concept of right' (Kant, 1991c, 135). 'Objectively', he insisted, 'there is utterly no conflict between morality and politics' and 'all politics must [ultimately] bend its knee before [the concept of] morality, and by so doing it can

---

[28] For an excellent account of the important – but nonetheless *Aufhebung* – role of tragedy in the Hegelian dialectic, see: Beistegui, 2000. He says: 'without wanting to "dramatize" Hegelian thought to the point of assimilating the true to the tragic, and at the cost of laughter or comedy, [and here we are reminded of Žižek's Hegel] one should recognise that the greatness of Spirit in history or of man in his action reveals itself primarily in sundering and in death, in sacrifice and in struggle, and that thought itself derives its depth only by taking the full measure of this tragic grandeur' (Beistegui, 2000, 27).

[29] The Hegelian reduction of tragic conflict to a dialectical negation and self-overcoming through *reconciliation*, is already prefigured in Aristotle's definition of tragedy, in terms of a *catharsis* – or purging – of the feelings of pity and fear (Aristotle, 1982, 50; and for a discussion, see: Beistegui, 2000, 11).

hope to reach, though but gradually, the stage where it will shine in light perpetual' (Kant, 1991b, 134, 135). On Kant's reading, history is understood as 'an unending process of *approximations*' to the rational concept of justice (Kant, 1991b, 139). Again, this Kantian formulation has had a significant impact on contemporary political theory, for example on liberal theories of justice and various forms of cosmopolitanism. In the following chapter it will become clear that in those contemporary theories that take their inspiration from either Kant or Hegel, tragic conflict – and as we will also see, political agency – is ultimately subsumed under the law, either the law *qua* the necessary unfolding of dialectical process in Hegel, or the law *qua* apodictic principles of right in Kant.

As I see it, the hallmark of an *authentically* tragic view of the world is the idea that no programme of action can be pursued without entailing loss. As Machiavelli put it 'all choices involve risks, for the order of things is such that one never escapes one danger without incurring another; prudence lies in weighing the disadvantages of each choice and taking the least bad as good' (Machiavelli, 1947, 67).[30] This tragic vision is irreconcilable with Christian notions of divine providence, and also with modern notions of progress through a human mastery of the world, but it does not rule out a constant striving for betterment in politics or a willingness to take a chance on this or that initiative. As Kaufmann puts it, 'Hell, purgatory, and heaven are not for us, except in so far as all three are here and now, on this earth', as, we might add, latent possibilities in the consequences of any action or decision (Kaufmann, 1992, xxi). This resolutely tragic vision is affirmed without equivocation in Mouffe and Honig, but we will see that there are elements at work in both Connolly's and Tully's theories designed to meliorate the tragic edginess of the human condition. Connolly claims to endorse a tragic view of the world, and his engagement with Nietzsche has done much to introduce the tragic into contemporary political theory. However, as I have argued elsewhere – and as others have also pointed out – there is a certain basic optimism in Connolly's account of agonistic democracy.[31] In Chapter 3 I identify the source of this optimism in Connolly's naturalist philosophy of 'life' and 'abundance' taken from various sources including Deleuze and Spinoza. In particular, this onto-softening of the tragic is manifest in the form of 'passive syntheses' that supposedly bring immanent forms of composition to political assemblages. Tully's desire to overcome the tragic is more explicit and he seeks to achieve this in a different way. In

---

[30] In Berlin's words we are 'doomed to choose, and every choice may entail an irreparable loss' (Berlin, 1998, 11). See also: Gray, 2007, 103.

[31] See: Wenman 2003b and Kalyvas, 2009, 33.

Chapter 4 I consider Tully's conception of practical dialogue developed from Wittgenstein, which – like all dialogic theories – seeks to translate tragic loss into a more manageable condition of 'reasonable' disagreement. We will see that Tully's seeks to bring otherwise incommensurable differences onto a 'common ground' that ought to mediate conflict with a set of regulative principles. In *Strange Multiplicity* this regulative element is embodied in the figure of Haemon – Antigone's lover and Creon's son – whom Tully presents as the 'exemplary citizen of the intercultural common ground' and who, on his reading, attempts to avert the tragic outcome of the play through his reasonable interventions (Tully, 1995, 23). Unlike mainstream deliberative theories, these regulative principles are presented as fully immanent to the negotiations and themselves subject to renegotiation in the course of the discussion. However, I make the case that these aspects of Tully's work are in tension with his otherwise clear appreciation of the strategic nature of agonism. As Hans Lindahl puts it, 'Tully cannot have it both ways: he must choose between an agonistic and a dialogical conception of politics' (Lindahl, 2008, 110–11).[32]

The value of conflict

From the mainstream perspectives in contemporary political theory, the tragic viewpoint of agonistic democracy is at best pessimistic and at worst dangerously nihilistic. Agonism is presented as being incapable of offering a conception of the political good, or, to the extent that the agonists allude to a normative position, they are said to be inconsistent, they fall into a performative contradiction. However, this is to misunderstand the fact that agonism is itself a political *value*, containing a conception of the good.[33] Indeed, one of the most prominent aspects of contemporary

---

[32] Honig has problematised Tully's reading of Haemon, and she also stresses how Tully appears 'dazzled by the deliberative ideal' (Honig, 2011). See also Tully's reply for a good discussion of the differences between these two iterations of agonism (Tully, 2011).

[33] Marc Stears describes the thinkers examined in this book as 'anti-liberal', and claims that the agonistic democrats are committed to the idea that politics is a thoroughly 'amoral' practice, which inevitably involves 'coercion' and 'domination' (Stears, 2007, 534, 541). A few pages later this stark assessment is toned down, and Stears acknowledges instead that these theorists typically 'present an account of what they take to be the ineliminable elements of politics and offer a view of how we should seek to change those aspects of our political world which are open to adaptation' (Stears, 2007, 545). Stears' initial evaluation of agonistic democracy is predicated on the untenable presumption that we face an either/or choice between liberalism and what he calls the politics of compulsion. This assessment can only be articulated from an idealised position of reasonable consensus presumably located somewhere beyond the struggles of political life. This viewpoint is incompatible with the realist idea that politics always comprises a mixture of consensus and conflict, which is a position that Stears himself later adopts, see Honig and Stears, 2011.

agonistic democracy has been an emphasis on the positive value of conflict. As Mouffe puts it, in 'a democratic polity, conflicts and confrontations, far from being a sign of imperfection, indicate that democracy is alive and inhabited by pluralism' (Mouffe, 2000b, 34). To affirm that there is no hope of final redemption from conflict is not to rule out the possibility of a typology of alternate *modes* of disagreement. Indeed, each of the thinkers examined in this book understands agonism to be a *constructive* mode of contest and rivalry.[34] This is contrasted both to forms of domination, where ascendant powers seek to shut down the *agon* through hierarchical modes of rule, and to antagonistic forms of hostility that lead to the mutual destruction of contending parties – as we have seen, for example, with the politics of fundamentalism outlined in the Preface.[35] This emphasis on the inevitable element of conflict in political life nevertheless suggests a kind of political realism, one that jars with the dominant normative, moralistic, and juridical tendencies in contemporary liberal and deliberative theories. However, from the agonistic viewpoint these theories presuppose a quasi-utopian view that conflict can be transcended or overcome through reasonable agreement, or at least this notion is presented as an ideal with which to evaluate existing forms of politics.[36]

The agonistic concern with the potential value of conflict was prefigured in Nietzsche's essay 'Homer's Contest' in which he presented agonism as a healthy and constructive aspect of Hellenic culture because it enabled men to express their 'envy, jealousy, and competitive ambition' in a manner that benefits the whole community (Nietzsche, 1994a, 190–4). Agonism leads men into the competition characteristic of the ancient Olympiad rather than into a 'hostile struggle-to-the-death' (Nietzsche, 1994a, 190–4). The Hellenic appreciation of the value of contest

---

[34] The agonistic emphasis on the value of conflict is also prominent in a number of thinkers who are not associated with the post-structuralist traditions of thought. See especially: Crick, 1964, and Hampshire, 1999; and see Edyvane, 2008 for a discussion of this aspect of Hampshire's thought.

[35] Bernard Crick similarly speaks in agonistic tone when he says to 'renounce or destroy politics is to destroy the very thing which gives order to the pluralism and variety of civilised society, the thing which enables us to enjoy variety without suffering either anarchy or the tyranny of single truths' (Crick, 1964, 26).

[36] In this regard, agonistic democracy forms part of what William Galston calls the 'ragtag band' of realist perspectives that circulate in contemporary political theory, who share a common antipathy to the 'high liberalism' of thinkers such as Rawls and Dworkin, and who commonly reject the idea that politics can be understood as a branch of applied ethics or morality (Galston, 2010, 385). In addition to the thinkers examined in this book, this broadly realist view is shared by Hampshire, Glen Newey, Williams, Gray, Raymond Geuss, Philp, and others. See: Hampshire, 1999; Newey, 2001; Williams, 2005; Gray, 2007; Geuss, 2008; Philp, 2010. For a discussion of the differences between some of these realist approaches, see: Stears, 2007, and Honig and Stears, 2011.

was encapsulated, according to Nietzsche, in the practice of ostracism, whereby overly powerful individuals would be banished from the city for a period of ten years in order to level out the playing field (Nietzsche, 1994a, 191). Indeed, we might think of agonism as a form of rivalry that ought to be characterised by a persistent disequilibrium of roughly approximate forces, or, as Foucault put it, as 'games of power [played] with as little domination as possible' (Foucault 1977, 298).[37]

This typology of distinct forms of conflict also points to what is apparently one of the most significant differences between the theorists examined in this book. I therefore explore this point further before turning more specifically to the reasons why agonism is understood as a political good. Mouffe, in particular, has been concerned to contrast agonism (constructive forms of rivalry) with antagonism (mutually destructive forms of hostility), and she has argued that the principal challenge today is to transform contemporary forms of antagonism – associated for example with the politics of fundamentalism or with the rise of the far Right in parts of Europe – into more constructive modes of conflict (Mouffe, 2000b, 100–3). As I said in the introduction, and this point is explored in detail in Chapter 5, Mouffe has drawn extensively on Schmitt to develop the notion of 'antagonism' understood as a hostile relationship of the 'friend vs. enemy type' (Schmitt, 1999, 208). For Mouffe, following Schmitt, the friend/enemy dichotomy is indicative of the *essence* of 'the political'. Even in its absence, this remains a latent potentiality in all human relationships, because social and cultural conflict can always intensify into relations of extreme conflict and antagonism. The 'political

---

[37] One advantage of the revival of the concept of agonism is that it renders problematic the predominant conception of the *polis* as a site of democratic unanimity and an idealised politics of the common good (for this point see: Kalyvas, 2009, 27). The communitarian image of Greek antiquity has been popular amongst modern advocates of participatory democracy. For example, Jane Mansbridge saw in the participatory politics of the New Left an echo of Aristotle's claim that the basis of life in the *polis* was 'friendship' (Mansbridge, 1983, viii). She called the tradition of small-scale face-to-face democracy 'unitary democracy', which was based upon common interests, equal respect, and where 'unanimity [homonoia] . . . is the principal aim of legislators' (Aristotle cited in Mansbridge, 1983, 3, 9, 14). On Mansbridge's reading, unitary democracies have recurred throughout history, for example in the New England town meetings of the early Republic, and the New Left communes of the 1970s, and she contrasts these experiences with the modern conception of democracy which she calls 'adversary democracy' (Mansbridge, 1983, viii-ix, 10). According to Mansbridge, it 'was not until the advent of the large-scale nation state and the market economy that the foundations were laid for a full-fledged system of adversary democracy' and since then 'westerners have increasingly accepted conflicting interests as an inalterable fact' (Mansbridge, 1983, 5, 15). On the contrary, as the agonistic theorists have shown, conflict is not an exclusive discovery of modern mercantile societies, and the European bourgeoisie did not invent adversarial democracy in the eighteenth century.

is the most intense and extreme antagonism, and every concrete antagonism becomes that much more political the closer it approaches the most
extreme point, that of the friend–enemy grouping' (Schmitt, 1996, 29).
In an earlier evaluation of agonistic democracy I identified this Mouffean concern with antagonism as the unique quality of her theory, and I
suggested this uncompromising realism gave her the edge over Connolly
and Tully (Wenman, 2003b).[38] Indeed, it is clear that Mouffe sees the
difference between her approach and the other agonistic theories in these
terms. She says:

> This antagonistic dimension, which can never be completely eliminated but only
> 'tamed' or 'sublimated' by being, so to speak, 'played out' in an agonistic way, is
> what, in my view, distinguishes my understanding of agonism from the one put
> forward by other 'agonistic theorists', those who are influenced by Nietzsche or
> Hannah Arendt, like William Connolly or Bonnie Honig. It seems to me that
> their conception leaves open the possibility that the political could under certain
> conditions be made absolutely congruent with the ethical, optimism which I do
> not share. (Mouffe, 2000b, 107)

However, I have come to see that this account of a clear distinction between Mouffean realism and a disproportionate optimism in the
other agonistic thinkers is only half right. Whilst it is perhaps true that
there is an excessive optimism in Connolly's writings, this is taken more
from Deleuze and Spinoza than from Nietzsche. Mouffe's assessment
of Arendt is not entirely correct either, and Honig certainly cannot be
read as an ethical thinker or as any less realist than Mouffe. In fact,
Nietzsche and Arendt both had a keen sense of the difference between
agonism and antagonism, in Arendt's terms between power and violence,
and recognition that violence can never be entirely eradicated from the
human condition. It is true that Arendt understood violence as a *prepolitical* phenomenon, and this idea is deeply problematic for reasons set out
below. However, we will also see that she was not entirely consistent in
her reflections on the relationship between politics and violence and, furthermore, that contemporary Arendteans such as Honig explicitly reject
her attempt to isolate the purity of politics from the realm of necessity and violence. Nevertheless, what *does* differentiate Mouffe from the
other agonists is her claim that defusing antagonism is the *primary*, and
at times it seems for her the *exclusive*, good of agonistic democracy. This
does set her apart from the other theorists who each develop agonism
in more aspirational terms. For Connolly, Tully, and Honig, as well as
for Nietzsche, Arendt, and Machiavelli before them, the *agon* produces a

---

[38]   Kalyvas also sees it in these terms, see: Kalyvas, 2009, 16.

number of different goods, and not only the sublimation of antagonism. I say something more about each of these points in turn.[39]

In 'Homer's Contest' it is clear that Nietzsche recognises the contrast between agonism and antagonism, and that antagonistic forms of conflict can only ever be tamed rather than entirely eliminated. He says 'if we take away [agonistic] competition from Greek life, we gaze immediately into that pre-Homeric abyss of a gruesome savagery of hatred and pleasure in destruction' (Nietzsche, 1994a, 193). Nietzsche cites Hesiod's *Works and Days* to illustrate this point, and it is worth quoting the passage at length. Hesiod says:

There are two Eris-goddesses [strife goddesses] on Earth... One should praise the one Eris as much as blame the other, if one has any sense; because the two goddesses have quite separate dispositions. One promotes wicked war and feuding, the cruel thing! [antagonism] No mortal likes her, but the yoke of necessity forces man to honour the heavy burden of this Eris according to the decrees of the Immortals. Black Night gave birth to this one as the older of the two; but Zeus, who reigned on high, placed the other on the roots of the earth and amongst men as a much better one. She drives the unskilled man to work; and if someone who lacks property sees someone else who is rich, he likewise hurries off to sow and plant and set his house in order; neighbour competes with neighbour for prosperity. This Eris is good for men [agonism]. Even potters harbour grudges against potters, carpenters against carpenters, beggars envy beggars and minstrels envy minstrels. (Hesiod cited in Nietzsche, 1994a, 189–90)

It is clear that Nietzsche recognised the need to pay homage to the first Eris and that she is never very far from human affairs. He says 'divine envy [antagonism] flares up when[ever] it sees a man without any competitor' (Nietzsche, 1994a, 194). Therefore, when Connolly gives the impression that we might thoroughly outwit the older Eris with his concepts of agonistic respect and critical responsiveness, which are explored in

---

[39] Political realism can lead quite readily to the conservative idea that the preservation of civil order against the (perceived) forces of anarchy is – as Galston claims – 'the *sine qua non* for every other political good' (Galston, 2010, 408). Indeed, according to Galston, this conclusion is one of the fundamental building blocks of realist political thought (Galston, 2010, 408). This conclusion certainly holds for thinkers such as Williams, Guess, and Philp, and in this study we will see that Mouffe comes very close to this same view. However, this conservative orientation does not capture the basic sentiments of the respective realisms espoused by Connolly, Tully, or Honig. Indeed, Honig has stressed that her approach ought not to be equated with a 'mere realism' but rather 'one that knows how things often are but also insists we can do better' (Honig and Stears, 2011, 190). Indeed, the realist might just as well be committed to the overarching significance of *freedom* (the struggle to bring new things into the world) rather than *order*. There is nothing in the basic order of things – the reality of politics *qua* pluralism, tragedy, and conflict – that leads inevitably to either one or other of these priorities; they reflect, instead, different commitments characteristic of individual thinkers.

Chapter 3, we should see a potential dereliction of Nietzsche's teachings rather than a confirmation of them.[40]

We have seen that Arendt identifies pluralism with the elements of creativity and contingency associated with action in concert. In *The Human Condition* these ideas are derived from an account of the Hellenic *agon* conceived in terms of the struggles between citizens in their reciprocal exchanges of words and deeds in the agora and the democratic assembly. On Arendt's account, the ancient *polis* is defined in terms of an on-going experience of equality (isonomy) entirely devoid of mastery and servitude, and where to be 'free meant to be free from the inequality of rulership and to move in a sphere where neither rule nor being ruled existed' (Arendt, 1958, 33). These aspects of Arendt's theory are well known, and Mouffe no doubt has these elements in mind when she derides the 'ethical optimism' which she sees in Arendtean versions of agonism. Indeed, for a number of commentators there is a clear distinction to be drawn between those contemporary agonists such as Mouffe who take their inspiration from Schmitt and those who take Arendt as their point of departure.[41] As Oliver Marchart puts it: 'what is stressed by all Arendteans is . . . [the] *associative* aspect (the aspect of *acting in concert* or *acting together*) versus the *dissociative* aspect of the political stressed within the Schmittian tradition' (Marchart, 2007a, 39, emphasis in the original). Certainly, this touches on an important variation. However, a number of significant points are overlooked on this demarcation. For one thing, this reading passes over the crucial point of commonality between Arendt and Schmitt in their shared emphasis on the absolute primacy of the constituent power. This is explored in detail in the following chapter, however; for the moment we stick to a comparison of these two key thinkers on the question of the position of violence in relation to agonistic politics.

For some commentators, Arendt's stress on equality and action in concert is reason to prefer what is perceived to be certain cheerfulness

---

[40] The passage from Hesiod should not be read from a modern perspective, which understands conflict in terms of economic competition. Nietzsche is clear that Hellenic agonism is distinct from the self-interested materialistic competition characteristic of the modern bourgeois economy. Agonism is not a means to the accumulation of wealth, but to public self-expression and was manifest in the great deeds of citizens in public oratory and in the games. 'For the ancients, the aim of agonistic education was the well-being of the whole, of state society . . . [The adversaries were not driven by] a boundless and indeterminate ambition like most modern ambition: the youth thought of the good of his native city when he ran a race or threw or sang; he wanted to increase its reputation through his own; it was to the city's gods that he dedicated the wreaths which the umpires placed on his head in honour' (Nietzsche, 1994a, 192).

[41] See, for example: Marchart, 2007a, 39, 42 and Schaap, 2007, 60, 66.

in Arendtean agonism, whereas for Mouffe this is evidence of her lack of realism and her tendency to reduce politics to ethics. However, what both these evaluations miss is that Arendt *did* recognise violence and constitutive exclusion as a prior condition of pluralism. In *The Human Condition* Arendt presented violence as a 'prepolitical act of liberating oneself from the necessity of life for the freedom of the world' in the *polis* (Arendt, 1958, 31). With this in mind, it should be clear that Arendt's theory is not more cheery than Schmitt's. In fact, her depiction of the ancient *agon*, comprising the reciprocal exchange of great words and deeds performed under conditions of isonomy in the assembly, is predicated on a scandalous refusal to pass judgement on the original exclusions that condition Hellenic pluralism. These exclusions are embodied not only in the walls of the city, the *nomos*, that separated citizens from other Greeks and barbarians, but also in the institutions of slavery (similarly walled up in the private realm of the *oikos*), which separate male citizens from the social drudgery of work and labour. As Honig puts it, Arendt's appropriation of Hellenic agonism without critical commentary on these practices, has the effect of condemning women and slaves to the 'tiresomely predictable, repetitious, and cyclical processes of nature and the despotism of the household, [where] they are determined [and] incapable of the freedom that Arendt identifies [exclusively] with action in the public realm' (Honig, 1995, 142). I return to these points at several turns in the book, and one thing is clear, which is that it is not possible to appropriate the Arendtean conceptions of pluralism, freedom, and action, without first addressing her misguided insistence on an untenable topographical distinction between the political (action and pluralism) and the social (prepolitical violence).

For some critics, this aspect of Arendt's thought renders her essentially beyond retrieval for any self-respecting conception of agonism committed to contesting contemporary forms of domination. According to Jean-Philippe Deranty and Emmanuel Renault, for example, it is simply not possible to apply Arendt's 'model of politics to the spheres in which she thought politics would be negated' (Deranty and Renault, 2009, 46). However, in Chapter 6 we will see that Honig manages to do just that. Indeed, one of the great contributions of Honig's work is to show that the Arendtean distinction between freedom and violence, politics and the social, can be reworked in such a way that does not lead to a naive celebration of pluralism, or a lack of consideration of the elements of violence and domination in political life. In fact, the resources exist in Arendt's work to deconstruct this untenable distinction. As Honig says, she can see no reason why 'if action is boundless and excessive', as it is in Arendt's account, 'it should . . . respect a public–private distinction that seeks, like a law of laws, to regulate and contain it without ever allowing itself to be engaged or contested by it' (Honig, 1993, 119). So the problem with Arendt's distinction between freedom and necessity, or freedom and violence, is not the analytical distinction as such, but the manner of their combination. This is problematic in *The Human Condition* – and likewise, as we will see in the following chapter, in *On Revolution* – because it is seen as one of mutual exclusion through a fixed topography. For Honig, Arendtean freedom becomes instead a moment of 'unstable fissure in an[y] otherwise highly ordered and settled practice or identity' (Honig, 1993, 123). I concur with this reading, and I similarly seek to combine the qualities that Arendt associated with action and pluralism with a critique of forms of domination in my own account of agonism and militant cosmopolitanism.

In this respect, it is important also to note that Arendt was herself less than consistent in her presentation of a clear distinction between freedom (politics) and violence (the social). Indeed, in her famous essay *On Violence*, she developed a more nuanced account, which appears to undermine her earlier topographical approach. She says 'no one engaged in thought about history and politics can remain unaware of the enormous role that violence has always played in human affairs' (Arendt, 1970, 8). Although she maintained an analytical distinction between constituent power (freedom) and violence, Arendt adds that 'these distinctions, though by no means arbitrary, hardly ever correspond to watertight compartments in the real world, from which nevertheless they are drawn' (Arendt, 1970, 46). In fact, 'nothing . . . is more common than the combination of violence and power, nothing less frequent than to find them in their pure and therefore extreme form' (Arendt, 1970, 47). In other words, the Mouffean distinction between agonism and antagonism has an established lineage in modern political thought, and is shared by Nietzsche and also (in a more convoluted fashion) by Arendt.

In fact these ideas have an even more established lineage, because they are once again prefigured in Machiavelli. Indeed, we can trace the first explicit formulation in western political thought of the agonistic idea of the positive value of conflict to Machiavelli's *The Discourses*, where he developed the idea that internal conflict can contribute to the vitality of the republic. Cutting against the grain of the entire tradition of western political thought stretching back to Plato and Aristotle – 'which had always condemned discord as both cause and effect of bad government and corruption' (Bock, 1990, 183) – Machiavelli identified internal 'tumults' as a feature of all the enduring constitutions of antiquity, and most notably of Rome whose longevity and vitality was a to a large extent a product of the 'friction between the plebs and the senate' (Machiavelli,

1970, 111, 115). We could say that Machiavelli writes a political tragedy in which the social classes embody distinct character traits, the nobility desire to dominate and the *populus* want only not to be dominated (McCormick, 2001, 298). According to Machiavelli:

> there are various *umori* or *sorte* or *qualita* of men – sometimes two (*nobili* and *popolo*), sometimes three (*nobili, popolo* and *plebe*) – and the enmities among them are natural, i.e. exist in every city, are inevitable and ineliminable, comprehensible and perhaps even legitimate. (Bock, 1990, 188)

Competition between *umori* provides an outlet for the ambitions of men from different classes and status groups and benefits the 'common good'. In 'competition one with the other, men look both to their own advantage and to that of the public; so that in both respects wonderful progress is made' (Machiavelli, 1970, 280). All 'legislation favourable to liberty is brought about by the clash between them' (Machiavelli, 1970, 113). In particular, popular hostility towards the nobles is one of the central causes of the maintenance of liberty.[42]

Furthermore, on closer examination, we can see that Machiavelli also appreciated the difference between agonism and antagonism. Indeed, as Gisela Bock has shown, Machiavelli was aware that 'some divisions harm republics', and, since 'the founder of a republic cannot make provisions against civil discord, at least he should take care that' they are the 'right kind' (Machiavelli cited in Bock, 1990, 197).[43] In contrast to the inevitable and productive conflict between *umori*, conflict between *sette* – that is between powerful rival families – should be avoided at all costs (Bock, 1990, 197).

> The *sette* are different from the *umori*... the latter are natural, unavoidable and may even lead, if checked and handled in a civilised way, to equality and the common good, the former are merely struggles for power, are avoidable and hence should be avoided. (Bock, 1990, 197)

Clearly then Mouffe's distinction between agonism and antagonism has a prehistory in the republican tradition, and does not distinguish her position from the alternative strands of agonism.

What does, however, distinguish Mouffe's position from other conceptions of agonism past and present is her insistence that this is the principal – and at times it seems for her the only – value of agonistic conflict, whereas for the other contemporary agonists (as well as for Machiavelli, Nietzsche, and Arendt) agonistic struggle gives rise to a

---

[42] For a discussion see: Viroli, 2008, 84, and McCormick, 2001.

[43] For a discussion of the positive value of contest, and the different modes of conflict in Machiavelli, see also: Miller, 2008.

number of goods. In fact, we can identify three specific goods which have been especially significant for contemporary agonists: these are (i) the idea that agonism facilitates the expression of individuality (which has been emphasised by both Connolly and Honig), (ii) that agonism is a condition of recognition and independence (which is the focal point in Tully's analysis) and (iii) that agonism can help to engender greater social equality (which is again a key point for Tully and was also Mouffe's principal concern before she became increasingly preoccupied with the Schmittian problem of antagonism).[44] The idea that agonism facilitates individuality can once again be traced to Nietzsche, who recognised that 'one is *fruitful* only at the price of being rich in opposites; one stays *young* only on condition that the soul does not . . . desire peace' (Nietzsche, 1998a, 22), and Machiavelli pre-empted Tully's emphasis on the relation between agonism and independence, because prolonged periods of peace can breed indolence and corruption and eventually lead to the ruin of the republic.[45]

One pertinent question, which has recently been raised by Thomas Fossen, is whether or not the positive goods of agonistic democracy should be understood in perfectionist or anti-perfectionist terms, where

[44] Honig and Stears refer to this 'agonistic realism' – which is attuned both to the conflictual and the aspirational elements of politics – as a distinctly *new* form of realism (Honig and Stears, 2011). However, there is nothing new about this wise combination of levelheadedness and a struggle for virtue or improvement. In fact this precise combination has been a defining feature of classical realist thought from Thucydides to Morgenthau, see: Lebow, 2003. As Marcus Raskin puts it, the classical realist 'is pledged to liberty and justice with crossed fingers' (Raskin, 1984, 89).

[45] Schaap describes Rancière as a *strategic* agonist, which he distinguishes from *pragmatic* and *expressivist* forms of agonism, represented respectively by Mouffe and Connolly (Schaap, 2009, 1). As I have said above, my own sense is that Rancière belongs instead with the radical democrats, and I reiterate this point below. However, Schaap's depiction of 'strategic agonism' is problematic for additional reasons, and this is because he associates the struggle against domination exclusively with Rancière's style of politics. He says that, unlike the pragmatic and expressivist forms of agonism, the strategic agonist 'understands struggle as orientated to overcoming social exclusion. The agon thus does not occur between co-citizens but between first- and second-class citizens, between those who are included and those excluded, and it seeks to abolish the social inequalities between them' (Schaap, 2009, 2). No doubt this is an accurate depiction of Rancière's objectives, but then, on a closer reading, the same basic orientation applies for Connolly, Tully, Honig, and Mouffe (at least in her early writings). Indeed, the idea that the existing political regime shelters sedimented forms of violence and oppression – and that agonistic democracy therefore involves a struggle against normalisation, excessive uniformity, imperialism, domination etc. – is explicit in each of the theories of agonistic democracy. As Fossen has said, this is inherent in their commitment to pluralism and, as Khan has stressed, this brings agonistic democracy within the orbit of the current republican revival. The different styles of agonism are therefore better established by concentrating on the alternate *ends* of the struggle with inequality and exclusion, rather than on the misguided idea that there are some forms of agonism that tackle inequality and exclusion and others that don't. This is not to say that they all tackle these questions equally well. Indeed they don't, for reasons I explore in the remainder of the book.

perfectionism 'signifies a commitment to the cultivation and continuous improvement of citizens' virtues and capacities' (Fossen, 2008, 377). As we saw above, the element of aristocratic perfectionism was, according to Kalyvas, a defining feature of ancient agonism. Ancient agonism represented an 'extraordinary encounter and blending of two opposed terms, democracy – isonomy and the rule of the demos, the many – and aristocracy – the competitive struggle for glory and individual distinction' (Kalyvas, 2009, 24). On Kalyvas's reading, these aristocratic elements in Hellenic agonism are absent from contemporary agonistic democracy, which is a form of 'post- or anti-heroic' agonism concerned exclusively with the facilitation of diversity and not with perfectionist struggles for individual and collective self-mastery (Kalyvas, 2009, 31). According to Kalyvas, this also sets the contemporary agonists apart from Nietzsche and Arendt, who retained the aristocratic goals of the Hellenic precursor (Kalyvas, 2009, 31). I briefly consider the aristocratic elements in Nietzsche and Arendt before turning to the question of perfectionism in contemporary agonism.

Clearly, agonistic perfectionism cannot take a conventional Aristotelian or Hegelian form, where the pursuit of the ideal represents the realisation of an inner *telos*, intrinsic to human nature or to the movement of history. Nevertheless, as we will see in more detail in Chapter 3, Nietzsche developed a non-teleological form of perfectionism, understood, as Fossen puts it, as 'a striving for perfection as continuous improvement, leaving open what counts as improvement, rather than [the] fulfilment of a preconceived ideal' (Fossen, 2008, 389). Indeed, the perfectionist elements were clearly at the forefront of both Nietzsche's and Arendt's elaboration of ancient agonism. For example, Nietzsche's emphasis, outlined above, on the institution of ostracism as a means to level out the playing field, should not be read as somehow out of step with the aristocratic thrust of Hellenic culture. On the contrary, this device was designed, according to Nietzsche, to remove any individual who monopolised excellence (and who thereby presented a permanent threat to competition), precisely in order to make way for a plurality of forms of greatness. Indeed, the Greeks assumed that 'there are always several geniuses to incite each other to action, just as they keep each other within certain limits, too' (Nietzsche, 1994a, 192). Arendt also emphasised that 'the *polis* was permeated by a fiercely agonal spirit, where everybody had constantly to distinguish himself from all others, to show through unique deeds or achievements that he was the best of all (*aien aristeuein*)' (Arendt, 1958, 41).[46] Moreover,

---

[46] Arendt's account of the aristocratic nature of the ancient *agon*, and the basic incompatibility of the ancient competitive spirit with economic activity, is surely also indebted to Burckhardt (Burckhardt, 1998, 182–5).

this struggle for glory in the *polis* was tied in an intrinsic way to Greek cosmology. In the absence of the later Christian notion of redemption – understood as an eternity of bliss that awaits the pious after death – the active life in the *polis* was stirred by an insatiable yearning for immortality (Arendt, 1958, 12). The Greeks saw 'their ability to leave non-perishable traces behind them' through great action as the only way to 'attain [a certain] immortality of their own and prove themselves to be of a divine nature' (Arendt, 1958, 19). 'Men entered the public realm because they wanted something of their own or something they had in common with others to be more permanent than their earthly lives' (Arendt, 1958, 55). Indeed, in the Greek world, only 'the best (*aristoi*), who constantly prove themselves to be the best... are really human' (Arendt, 1958, 19).

Although he does not spell it out, Kalyvas' essay suggests a certain longing for the heroic elements of ancient agonism and it is implicit in his essay that the perfectionist elements in Nietzsche and Arendt give them the edge over the contemporary agonistic democrats. Other commentators take a different view. For example, Hannah Pitkin has criticised the aristocratic elements in Arendt's agonism from a feminist perspective. She says that, although 'Arendt was female, there is a lot of *machismo* in her vision' of agonism and 'Arendt's citizens begin to resemble posturing little boys clamouring for attention ('Look at me! I'm the greatest!' 'No, look at *me*!')' (Pitkin, 2006, 223, emphasis in original). It is certainly true that perfectionism in any of its forms runs the risk of nurturing an elitist disdain for mediocrity, and this is often evident in Nietzsche's writings and in his contempt for the masses and their doctrines of democracy and socialism (Nietzsche, 1968, 458–9). Indeed, Nietzsche made no attempt to hide his scorn for mediocrity, going so far as to say that 'the great majority of men have no right to existence, but are a misfortune to higher men' (Nietzsche, 1968, 467). It is for this reason that many reject the idea that Nietzsche can be an important source for contemporary democratic theory, and I explore this point in detail in Chapter 3 in relation to Connolly's work.

Kalyvas might have identified Owen as one 'post-modern' democrat who *has* explicitly invoked the perfectionism of ancient agonism. Instead, this point has been made by Fossen who contrasts Owen's 'perfectionist agonism' with what he sees as the anti-perfectionist doctrines of Connolly, Mouffe, and Honig, for whom, he says, political contestation sets itself the more pragmatic objective of challenging violence and exclusion in the name of protecting pluralism (Fossen, 2008, 388). Owen's account of agonistic democracy draws extensively on Nietzsche, and he insists that late modern politics ought to be explicitly 'concerned with the character of nobility' (Owen, 1995, 160). For Owen, the renewal of democracy must be centred on 'an agonistic dialogue concerning what count as virtues and values [for the community] as well as how these virtues and values are ranked' (Owen, 1995, 160). I also consider Owen's perfectionist agonism in more detail in Chapter 3 in relation to Connolly's work, and I consider whether or not Connolly's agonism is really devoid of perfectionist elements, as Fossen claims. The anti-perfectionist view has been most obviously defended in recent times by liberals such as Rawls and Rorty, who in different ways insist on the strict relegation of projects of idealised self-making to the private sphere. They were pre-empted in this respect by Berlin, who insisted that we should entirely dispense with perfectionism in politics, which, on his reading, is invariably a 'recipe for bloodshed, no better even if it is demanded by the sincerest of idealists, the purest of heart' (Berlin, 1998, 15). Indeed, Berlin claimed that the doctrine of value pluralism inevitably pushes us in the direction of anti-perfectionism and towards a priority of negative liberty (Berlin, 1997, 78). Berlin's position is clearly in marked contrast to Owen. However, I think in this respect Berlin also moves in a different direction from all the contemporary agonists examined in this book, as they are each concerned in one way or another with rebuilding public life, and with the introduction of private ideals and values into the public sphere. It is true that, unlike Owen, Connolly does not explicitly endorse Nietzsche's perfectionism, but his account of agonistic democracy includes an emphasis on the importance of the cultivation of ideals in public life and is not an exclusively anti-perfectionist doctrine.

Conclusion

In this chapter we have seen that the matrix of agonism is comprised of pluralism, tragedy, and the value of conflict. These terms are synonymous respectively with an emphasis on the irreducible role of chance or *Fortuna*, with the agonising thought of a world without final redemption from conflict and strife, but where situated subjects nonetheless always retain a certain room for manoeuvre, or for agonistic *virtù*, and with the wisdom that teaches that there are alternate forms of conflict, some of which can produce political goods. Thus far, we have not seen anything here that suggests these elements of constitutive pluralism have an intrinsic relationship to liberal democratic constitutionalism. Instead, they are better understood as conditioning qualities of political life, and they point, above all, to the priority of the strategic question, to the need for an analysis of the range of possible moves available to situated subjects. Indeed, there is nothing here, it seems, that rules out the possibility of radical moments of innovation, at least not if we refrain from treating the

Part I

play of *différance* as a metaphysical principle, one that strictly conditions all forms of politics. Instead, what we need is an examination of alternate moments of political freedom, or of the constituent power, and it is to this analysis, and to the discussion of the difference between augmentation and revolution that we now return.

2 Democracy: the constituent power as augmentation and/or revolution

In the Introduction I invoked Wolin's insight that democracy is best understood as a constituting moment rather than a specific form or process of government. In this sense, democracy is intrinsically related to the emergence of the constituent power, to the irreducible element of/for creation associated with genuine moments of political action. This raises difficult questions about the relationship between the constituent power and constituted authorities, between a pre-judicial capacity for innovation (*potentia*) and the claims to legitimacy, lawfulness, and normativity embedded in extant social and political forms (*potestas*). We saw that it is possible to envisage both an absolute and a relative priority of the constituent power, where the former is associated with radical moments of innovation and the latter with the power of emergence and expansion within the horizon of a given constitutional form. These differences are best captured by Arendt's distinction between revolution and augmentation, and I suggested that the leading contemporary theorists of agonistic democracy focus exclusively on the latter, whereas a consistently strategic form of agonism will keep both these qualitatively distinct options in play. In this chapter, I return to these discussions and offer a fuller account of the Arendtean categories. At an analytical level, this facilitates a better understanding of how contemporary agonistic democracy is positioned in relation to liberalism as well as to other contemporary models of democracy. However, we will also reconsider some of the strategic reasons why, in the present conjuncture, it is important not to associate agonism exclusively with augmentation.

The chapter commences with a discussion of Schmitt's reflections on the absolute priority of the constituent power, figured as a moment of 'sovereign decision'. We see that Schmitt's formulation is close to Arendt's notion of revolution in many respects, but that there are also crucial differences between them, and the Schmittean notion of absolute 'sovereignty' is incompatible with agonistic pluralism. This point is then picked up and explored further in Chapters 6 and 7 in response to Agamben's analysis of the contemporary security state as a resurgent mode of sovereignty. Having identified some of the differences between Schmitt and Arendt, I then offer a detailed account of the latter's distinction between ancient Roman augmentation and modern revolution. I also consider her preference for the American over the French Revolution, and what this tells us about the strengths and the limitations of her rendition of the revolutionary event. Following this, I offer an initial account of the forms of augmentation presented by the contemporary agonistic democrats, by considering more closely their proximity and their distance from Habermas' co-originality thesis. The unique versions of augmentation presented by each of the four main contemporary theorists of agonism are then explored in detail in Part II of the book. The latter sections of this chapter offer a brief synopsis of the main alterative models of liberalism and democracy: liberal constitutionalism, aggregative, deliberative, and cosmopolitan democracy. We see how they all seek to subsume the constituent power under constituted forms of authority in various ways, and this is in contrast also to the radical democrats who present an exclusive emphasis on revolution. The agonistic democrats are right to criticise the radical democrats for their singular emphasis on the moment of radical transformation, but it does not follow that the idea of revolution is entirely incongruent with the agonistic circumstances of pluralism, tragedy, and the value of conflict, and a consistently agonistic viewpoint will retain both of these two qualitatively distinct moments of the constituent power.

Carl Schmitt: the absolute priority of the constituent power figured as sovereign decision

In the previous chapter we explored whether or not a basic distinction can be drawn between Schmittean and Arendtean forms of agonism. We considered and rejected Mouffe's claim that her version of agonistic democracy has a monopoly on clear thinking and self-honesty about the irreducible role of violence in politics. We noted that Nietzschean and Arendtean forms of agonism should not be dismissed (or celebrated) as cheerful ethical forms of agonism, in contrast to Mouffean realism. However, we also noted that, unlike the other theories, Mouffe's does place an *exclusive* emphasis on the need to sublimate violence and antagonism. In Chapter 5 I look at Mouffe's theory in more detail and we see that she repeatedly invokes Schmitt's *On the Concept of the Political* (1927), with its core thesis of the friend/enemy relationship, to elaborate a notion of elementary antagonism. However, we will also see that Mouffe does not draw on a wider range of potential resources in Schmitt's thought,

and, in particular, she has little to say about his specific formulation of
the constituent power in his magnum opus *Constitutional Theory* (1927)
and in the brilliantly insightful *Political Theology* (1922). These texts were
published on the verge of the crisis of the Weimar Republic that would
soon see Adolf Hitler delivered to power and the Weimar constitution
overturned. The relationship between the clarity of Schmitt's thought
and his proximity to these events is probably not a coincidence. As I
said in the Introduction, the contingency of constituted authorities *vis-
à-vis* the absolute priority of the constituent power is most apparent in
times of crisis. Indeed, we need a more detailed examination of Schmitt's
account of the constituent power at this point, partly because he offers
a prescient rendition of the ultimate priority of the constituent power,
but also because there are key points of similarity and difference between
Schmitt and Arendt on the manifestation of the constituent power, and
so this discussion provides an essential prelude to the consideration of
Arendtean revolution and augmentation in the following section. It is
also important to engage Schmitt here, because his position provides the
basic framework for Agamben's analysis of sovereignty, which we discuss
in Chapters 6 and 7.

In *Constitutional Theory* Schmitt argued that every constitution in the
limited sense, i.e. as a system of basic laws, whether codified in a particular document or not, presupposes a constitution in a broad sense, understood as the 'political . . . and social order of a particular state' (Schmitt,
2008, 59). Moreover, the existence of the social order is not derived from
the constitution in a narrow sense, but ultimately from the constituent
power, which, in Schmitt's terms, is manifest as 'a pre-established, unified will' (Schmitt, 2008, 64–5). The constitution in the narrow sense
endures only 'by virtue of the existing political will of that which establishes it. Every type of legal norm, every constitutional law, presupposes
that such a will already exists' (Schmitt, 2008, 76). This emphasis on
the absolute priority of the constituent power as 'unified will', *vis-à-vis*
specific constitutional forms leads Schmitt to a fundamental critique of
liberalism, which is a false and apolitical doctrine that seeks to reverse
this priority.[1]

The aspiration of the bourgeois *Rechtsstaat* . . . is to repress the political, to limit
all expressions of state life through a series of normative frameworks, and to
transform all state activity into competencies, which are jurisdictions that are
precisely defined and, in principle, limited. Thus, it is evident that the bourgeois

---

[1] For discussions of Schmitt's critique of liberal constitutionalism see: Scheuerman, 1996;
Lindahl, 2007; Kalyvas, 2008; and the essays collected in Dyzenhaus, 1998.

Rechtsstaat component [i.e. a written constitution, the bill of rights, etc.] can constitute only a part of the entire state constitution [in the broad sense], while another part contains the positive decision over the form of political existence. (Schmitt, 2008, 93)

Moreover, unlike particular constitutional laws which can always be amended, by Schmitt's account the constitution in the broad sense is 'inviolable', unless and until it is 'annihilated' by the act of another constituent power, another 'sovereign will' (Schmitt, 2008, 80, 147).

Although there are clear differences, as we will see in a moment, it is nonetheless important to first acknowledge the key point of coincidence between Schmitt and Arendt, their common insistence on the absolute priority of the constituent power.[2] As we saw in the introduction, for Arendt the constituent power manifests in decisive action, understood always as an interruption of a given process or state of affairs, and in these formulations she was undoubtedly influenced by Schmitt's *Political Theology*, where he described the constituent power as an exceptional moment that 'breaks through the crust of a mechanism that has become torpid by repetition' (Schmitt, 2005, 15). Both thinkers were concerned to reassert the primacy of political action not just against liberalism, but also in contrast to Marxist and other progressive or evolutionary conceptions of history. Like Arendt, Schmitt differentiated genuine political action from any mechanical or organicist conceptions of state and society: the constituent power is a decisive intervention that disrupts social and historical processes otherwise understood as a 'continual series of development' or 'organic evolution' (Schmitt, 1988, 56). Similarly, Schmitt invoked the idea of a miracle to depict this non-dialectical, a-teleological, and unpredictable capacity of/for origination (Schmitt, 2005, 36).

Given these important points of connection we can see that the claims we examined in the previous chapter, i.e. that there is a basic difference between Schmittean and Arendtean theory, move too quickly over this aspect of their respective contributions. Nevertheless, this does not mean that the differences are unimportant; indeed they are also crucial, and we turn now to these differences because they start to provide an insight into how Arendt, unlike Schmitt, developed a conception of absolute innovation that is well suited to pluralism. In the introduction we said it is not possible to depict the miraculous human capacity of/for innovation without making some conceptual and probably also some ethical priorities, which inevitably become worked into the nomination. This is all

---

[2] Negri recognises this profound point of connection between Schmitt and Arendt, in their common emphasis on the 'ontological intensity' of the 'constitutive act' (Negri, 1999, 19).

too clear in Schmitt's account of the constituent power as absolute and 'unified will'. In fact, on this point he strictly follows Sieyès in associating the constituent power with the unified will of 'the Nation'. As Sieyès puts it, the 'nation exists prior to everything: it is the origin of everything. Its will is always legal. It is the law itself' (Sieyès, 2003a, 136). In Schmitt's terms, when, under conditions of modernity, the National Will displaces 'princely absolutism' as the source of authority in the state, the 'nation puts itself in the prince's place just as absolutely' (Schmitt, 2008, 102). So, for example, in the context of the founding of the Weimar Constitution in 1918, he says:

> The unity of the German Reich does not rest on the . . . 181 articles and their validity; but rather on the political existence of the German people . . . The Weimar Constitution is valid because the German people 'gave itself this constitution'. (Schmitt, 2008, 65)

Moreover, Schmitt did not appeal to an organic conception of the *Volk*, and so here we start to see how his conception of the constituent power *is* linked in an intrinsic way to his concept of the political as antagonism. This is because, in Schmitt's account, the identity of the National Will, i.e. the constituent power, is effectively 'awakened' into being in reaction to the external threat of the existential enemy (Scheuerman, 1996, 305–6). Indeed, the constituent power, as National Will, becomes most alert in times of crisis such as a civil war or violent insurrection, when the 'normal situation' gives way to the moment of 'exception' (Schmitt, 1996, 33, 43; 1999, 199, 203). The 'principle of unity' becomes absolutely 'definitive in critical cases of conflicts', and at this point the constituent power as National Will, which is forged through a relation of enmity and exclusion, becomes embodied in the form of 'sovereign decision', or, as Schmitt famously put it, sovereign is 'he who decides on the exception' (Schmitt, 2005, 5; 2008, 59). This need for unity and self-preservation in the moment of crisis is also expressed in the constitution, in the limited sense, i.e. in Article 48 of the Weimar Constitution that granted emergency powers of commissarial dictatorship to the *Reichspräsident*. Schmitt's theory consequently becomes a defence of a plebiscitary democracy focused on the executive, in which the *Reichspräsident* becomes the personal embodiment of the 'national will' or of the constituent power.

When we consider the sequence of this argument it becomes clear that the Schmittean formulation of the absolute priority of the constituent power is incompatible with the circumstances of agonistic pluralism that we examined in the previous chapter. We will have to wait till Chapter 7 for a detailed account of how the moment of absolute initiative can be made consonant with pluralism. However, we have already seen that the meaning and significance of political action is always picked up upon and judged by a plurality of human agents, action is always action in concert, and so the actor is never fully in control of the reception, consequences, or outcome of her or his action. This Arendtean understanding of constitutive pluralism effectively precludes the possibility of the emergence of the constituent power in the form of 'sovereignty' and 'unified will'. The presentation of the constituent power as sovereign 'will' projects the hubris of omnipotence, and we are left with a depiction of politics as a zero sum game whereby the sovereign exists in perpetuity, unless and until it is annihilated by another equally unified sovereign will. This delusion of omnipotence can only possibly be sustained through a violation of human plurality and so as Arendt put it:

Under human conditions, which are determined by the fact that not man but men live on the earth, freedom and sovereignty are so little identical that they cannot even exist simultaneously...If men wish to be free, it is precisely sovereignty they must renounce. (Arendt, 1977b, 163)[3]

This passage strikes an ominous tone when we consider the trends towards extra-judicial executive power in the current conjuncture. We return to a fuller discussion of the machinations of sovereignty and to Agamben's reworking of Schmitt, in the notion of a 'permanent state of exception' in Chapters 6 and 7.[4] However, at this point we turn to Arendt's alternative depiction of the distinct moments of the constituent power, but, first, we should also note an additional observation that Honig has stressed about the difference between these two thinkers, because this also remains pertinent in the present conjuncture. Ultimately, at the core of these different delineations of the constituent power is a set of assumptions about what we might expect from politics. Honig summarises the difference neatly. In the Schmittean problematic of friends and enemies, of emergency, and of the sovereign decision, politics, she says, is essentially 'biological', concerned simply with the

---

[3] For a detailed discussion of Arendt's critique of sovereignty, see: Kalyvas, 2008, 210–22.

[4] For Negri, the 'juridical' notion of the constituent power is inappropriately hemmed in; all the while it remains in a strained relationship (i.e. as both constitutive of and disruptive of) constituted authority (Negri, 1999, 13). Like Schmitt, he also figures the constituent power in terms of 'omnipotence'. However, in contrast to the category of 'sovereignty', by Negri's account the 'constitutive strength never ends up as power, nor does the multitude tend to become a totality but, rather, a set of singularities, an open multiplicity' (Negri, 1999, 14). In Negri's thinking, this conception of the constituent power as 'absolute process' is also tied to the Marxist idea that the constituent strength 'finds its own capacity for innovation' in the 'spontaneity of living labour' (Negri, 1999, 13, 32). I pick up on the problems associated with these formulations at various points in the chapters that follow.

maintenance and protection of life, whereas Arendt's theory is 'aspirational', concerned instead with a yearning for 'more life' (Honig, 2009b, 103) – concerned, that is, with the open chanciness and possibilities associated with the politics of innovation. It is to Arendt's presentation of the two key moments of the politics of innovation that we now turn.

The constituent power as augmentation and revolution

One of the central themes of Arendt's *On Revolution* (1963), as well as of the essay 'What is Authority?' is a detailed account of the exercise of freedom in the mode of augmentation. The notion of *augmentation* derives from the specific experience of the constituent power characteristic of Roman antiquity, 'from the beginning of the republic until virtually the end of the imperial era' (Arendt, 1977a, 120). At the core of the Roman practice of augmentation was a certain reverence for the foundations of the city, so that 'all innovations and changes remain tied back to the foundation which, at the same time, they augment and increase' (Arendt, 1965, 203). Indeed:

Roman freedom was a legacy bequeathed by the founders of Rome to the Roman people; their freedom was tied to the beginning their forefathers had established by founding the city, whose affairs the descendants had to manage, whose consequences they had to bear, and whose foundations they had to 'augment'. (Arendt, 1977b, 165)

This meant that action in the form of absolute initiative, without reference to established authority or tradition, was literally inconceivable in the Roman republic (Arendt, 1977a, 124). Indeed, the 'word *auctoritas* derives from the verb *augere*, 'augment' and what authority or those in authority constantly augment is the foundation' (Arendt, 1977a, 121).

This is why the Romans [unlike the Greeks] were unable to repeat the founding of their first polis in the settlement of colonies but were capable of adding to the original foundation until the whole of Italy and, eventually, the whole of the western world were united and administered by Rome, as though the whole world were nothing but Roman hinterland. (Arendt, 1977a, 120)[5]

---

[5] This passage demonstrates the link between Roman augmentation and the experience of imperialism. This point has been stressed by Mikael Hornqvist and others as a critique of contemporary theorists of republicanism such as Skinner and Viroli, who largely sidestep this problem in their re-appropriation of the tradition (Hornqvist, 2004). However, as we will see in more detail below, the contemporary agonists have a solution to this difficulty and they refigure the element of augmentation so that it does not result in imperial 'acquisition' but rather in a conception of augmentation as (re)politicisation and as 'continual world-building' (Honig, 1993, 112).

In the Roman experience authority was embodied in the Senate or the *patres*, and Arendt attributes the great longevity of Rome to the specific combination of authority, tradition, and religion, and, of course, the Catholic Church also effectively reworked this admixture after the fall of the empire. Arendt didn't think it was possible or desirable to reproduce the details of the Roman experience under conditions of modernity. However, she did think it was feasible to rework the practice of augmentation in a way that is suited to modern conditions, as we will see below.

However, Arendt also proceeds to contrast this inherently Roman conception of freedom with the qualitatively distinct modern experience of revolution. According to Arendt, the correspondence between freedom and the 'experience of a new beginning' is once again decisive for understanding the revolutions of the modern age (Arendt, 1965, 21). However, the vital difference here is that the practice of freedom or initiative is manifest in a way that does not simultaneously call up or supplement an original foundation. This change is evidenced in the subtle but highly significant shift in the meaning of the term 'revolution' from the seventeenth to the eighteenth centuries. Reflecting on the upheavals of the seventeenth century – for example the 'Glorious Revolution' of 1689 – Arendt shows that the modern concept of revolution originally meant 'restoration', the removal of tyranny or a corrupt form of government and the 'restoration of monarchical power to its former righteousness and glory', or the return of 'freedom by God's blessing restored' (Arendt, 1965, 36). This was not unlike the antique Roman conception of augmentation, where the exercise of freedom was conceptualised as the return of a corrupted state of being to an original state of liberty. Indeed, the seventeenth-century agents of change 'pleaded in all sincerity that they wanted to revolve back to the old times when things had been as they ought to be' (Arendt, 1965, 37). However, in the course of the eighteenth-century, the term revolution took on an altogether different connotation.

Once again actors on both sides of the Atlantic initially envisaged themselves as (re)constituting the Roman foundation, and this was evident in their enthusiasm for dressing themselves and their actions up in antique Roman costume, pseudonyms, and other accoutrements.[6] Nevertheless:

---

[6] Numerous commenters on the eighteenth-century revolutions have remarked on this tendency of the revolutionaries to refer back to the Roman experience, and perhaps most notably Karl Marx and Derrida (Marx, 1983c, 287–8; Derrida, 1994). Derrida sees this as indicative of the 'law of an invincible anachrony' that constitutes the conditions of (im)possibility of the revolutionary *event* (Derrida, 1994, 140). He says, 'the more the new erupts in the revolutionary crisis, the more the period is in crisis, the more it is "out of joint" the more one has to convoke the old, [or] "borrow" from it' (Derrida, 1994, 136). This predicament is ultimately a consequence of the quasi-transcendental conditions of

when the Americans decided to vary Virgil's line from *magnus ordo saeclorum* to *novus ordo saeclorum*, they had admitted that it was no longer a matter of founding 'Rome anew' but of founding a 'new Rome', that the thread of continuity which bound Occidental politics back to the foundation of the eternal city and which tied this foundation once more back to the prehistorical memories of Greece and Troy was broken and could not be renewed. (Arendt, 1965, 213)

On Arendt's reading, this was a development of unprecedented importance, introducing an altogether different experience of political freedom, or of the constituent power. Unlike augmentation, the modern revolutionary pathos is specifically manifest in the emergence of the 'absolutely new, of a beginning which would justify starting to count time in the year of the revolutionary event' (Arendt, 1965, 30). In other words, this distinctively modern concept of revolution is bound up with a specific temporality, revealed in the idea that 'the course of history suddenly begins anew, that an entirely new story . . . is about to unfold' (Arendt, 1965, 17).

It is as though . . . [the revolution] . . . came out of nowhere in time or space. For a moment, the moment of beginning, it is as though the beginner had abolished the sequence of temporality itself, or as though the actors were thrown out of the temporal order and its continuity. (Arendt, 1965, 207)

Again, there is a clear connection between Arendt's formulation of revolutionary innovation and Benjamin's rendition of the *Ursprung*. Indeed, Arendt was influenced by Benjamin's depiction of the revolutionary 'now time' in his *Theses on the Philosophy of History*, understood as a 'present which is not a transition, but in which time stands still and has come to a stop', but nonetheless where the revolutionary actor 'remains in control of his powers, man enough to blast open the continuum of history' (Benjamin, 1999, 254).

Some have suggested that *On Revolution* should be read as a critique of absolute beginnings,[7] and it is not uncommon in this regard for commentators to note the elements of continuity that Arendt described as

différance that ensure that 'no time is contemporary with itself', including the 'time of the Revolution' (Derrida, 1994, 136). Derrida's reading stands in marked contrast to Arendt and effectively serves to ensure augmentation (transformation plus continuity, or (re)*iter*ation) as the only game in town. I return to this difference between Arendt and Derrida in my discussion of Honig's evaluation of *On Revolution* in Chapter 6. For an example of what post-revolutionary militant politics might look like from this Derridean viewpoint, see: Arditi, 2008.

[7] For example, Kalyvas acknowledges that Arendt identified an important distinction between absolute and relative new beginnings, but he mistakenly claims that 'she rejected the idea of total breaks and absolute foundings' (Kalyvas, 2008, 192, 223–31). This conclusion can't be sustained from a reading of *On Revolution*, or the essay 'On Freedom', or Arendt's subsequent reiteration of these ideas in *The Life of the Mind*.

preparing the way for the American Revolution: the link back to the Mayflower compact, the experience of relative self-governance in New England during the colonial period, made possible by the physical distance from the British Crown, etc. However, the decisive point comes at the end of Chapter 5, where Arendt stresses unequivocally the moment of radical innovation in spite of these preliminary elements of continuity (Arendt, 1965, 213). Moreover, when she summarised her arguments about the uniqueness of modern revolutions vis-à-vis the Roman experience years later, in *The Life of the Mind*, Arendt reiterated what she called the 'abyss of freedom' or the 'abyss of nothingness that opens up before any deed that cannot be accounted for by a reliable chain of cause and effect' (Arendt, 1978, 207).

Moreover, although this distinctly modern consciousness of time and of radical innovation only became manifest in the eighteenth-century experience, Arendt nonetheless also pointed to the first stirrings of this idea in Machiavelli. In the previous chapter, we saw that Machiavelli provided the first explicit account of the value of internal conflict within the republic, and how this was linked to augmentation. However, as Arendt noted, Machiavelli was also the first to hint at what hangs in the balance in the modern conception of revolution (Arendt, 1977a, 136). Indeed, 'like Robespierre and Lenin and all the great revolutionaries whose ancestor he was, [Machiavelli] wished nothing more passionately than to initiate a new order of things' (Arendt, 1977a, 140). His admiration for founders – for Moses, Cyrus, Theseus, and Romulus – is evident in both *The Prince* and *The Discourses* and, although Machiavelli understood that 'there is nothing more difficult to plan, more doubtful of success, nor more dangerous to manage than the creation of a new system', he reiterated that there was also nothing more likely to 'bring a prince into greater respect' than the successful foundation of a new state (Machiavelli, 1947, 15, 65; 1970, 133). Similarly, in his short book on Machiavelli, Althusser stressed that the Machiavelli was the original theorist of the absolute beginning and, moreover, that he understood the importance of revolution *and* augmentation as two distinct moments of innovation, with the first being the principal focus of *The Prince* and the latter brought to the fore in *The Discourses*, and, as we will see below in Arendt's discussion of the great advantages of the American revolution, with the two qualitatively distinct moments of the constituent power forming a necessary union in the best examples of republican politics (Althusser, 1999, 64–5).[8]

[8] On Arendt's account, Machiavelli has an ambiguous relationship to the Roman past. Like the Romans he understood the importance of founding, but he envisaged the new beginning as a violent act of making, rather than a moment of innovation or origination, and this paves the way for Robespierre, Marx, and Lenin (Arendt, 1977a, 139).

I come back to the importance of this formulation in my own account of agonism and militant cosmopolitanism in Chapter 7, and shortly we will return to the way in which the contemporary agonistic theories are characterised by an exclusive emphasis on augmentation. First, however we need to probe Arendt's notorious preference for the American over the French Revolution as this tells us something more about the limitations of her approach, but also provides some important insights about how the absolute beginning might be made consonant with pluralism.

Arendt's preference for the American Revolution follows from five key points, one of which is utterly indefensible, though the other four are highly pertinent. On Arendt's account, the French and American Revolutions were emphatically alike in their common understanding of the absolute priority of the constituent power, in their emphasis on the precedence of the 'constituting act' as resolutely 'antecedent' to the consolidation of political institutions (Arendt, 1965, 205). This stress on the originary event was not the source of the violence of the French revolution. Instead, Arendt's preference partly reflected her untenable views about the need to draw a fixed distinction between the political and the social and her renunciation of the prospect of any political transformation of social relations. Things went wrong in France because 'it appeared to revolutionary men more important to change the fabric of society . . . than to change the structure of the political realm' (Arendt, 1965, 17). Indeed, she attributed what she judged to be the failure of the French Revolution to the moment 'when the poor, driven by the needs of their bodies, burst onto the scene' and 'unleashed the terror and sent the Revolution to its doom' (Arendt, 1965, 54, 55). From Arendt's perspective 'nothing . . . could be more obsolete than to attempt to liberate mankind from poverty by political means; nothing could be more futile and more dangerous' (Arendt, 1965, 110). This reading is deeply problematic for reasons we have touched on already, and which we will discuss in detail in Chapters 6 and 7. Indeed, we might say instead that nothing is more obsolete today than the Arendtean attempt to establish a fixed topography of the political and the social, and to deny any possibility of the political transformation of social relations.

However, in her evaluation of the French Revolution, Arendt raised three additional points of criticism, which are only indirectly related to her misguided analysis of the 'social question', and each of which remains highly pertinent. Firstly, she stressed that from the outset the French protagonists tended to figure the Revolution in metaphors taken from nature, as a wild force or energy, and consequently lost sight of the fact that the Revolution was a uniquely human creation (Arendt, 1965, 43). From this, the second *hamartia* swiftly followed, which was to see the Revolution no longer 'as the work of men' but rather as a product of history, understood as 'irresistible process' (Arendt, 1965, 43). Whereas in America the revolutionaries never really lost sight of the fact that they themselves were the authors of this innovation, in France this sentiment was readily transformed into a 'feeling of awe and wonder at the power of history itself', and, by Arendt's account, this idea would go on to to have an enormous impact on the Hegelian and Marxist traditions (Arendt, 1965, 45). Finally, the French revolutionaries depicted the constituent power in terms taken from the philosophy of the subject, as a unified or sovereign 'will' of the nation, and this misconception, which, as we have seen, was reiterated in Schmitt, effectively delivered the dictatorship in the figure of Napoleon, who, to the 'applause of a whole nation', could so easily declare 'I am the *pouvoir constituant*' (Arendt, 1965, 162). Each of these observations is crucially important. Indeed, we will see that Arendt's stress on the uniquely human quality of the constituent power, and her depiction of the act of human freedom as something essentially exogenous to natural processes, provides an important critique of Connolly's attempt to figure agonistic politics on the basis of a naturalist philosophy. Her stress, with Benjamin, on the revolutionary event as disruptive of any notion of historical process, or progress, provides an important component in my own account of militant cosmopolitanism,[9]

---

[9] Arendt's critique of the Marxist conception of history is important; she anticipates more recent discussions amongst post-structuralists, and neither of her conceptions of action (i.e. as revolution or augmentation) is compatible with any kind of dialectics. Republican freedom is always a creative interruption of a given *process*, and so to present revolution instead as an internal moment within the dialectic of history is to deny the actors the dignity of their specific innovations. However, she was only half right when she said that the conception of political revolution as an *outcome* of historical development was 'what the men of the Russian Revolution . . . learned from the French Revolution' (Arendt, 1965, 51). The conception of history as determinate process was most explicit in the evolutionary framework of Second International Marxism, and the debates in Russia turned on the question of whether or not a socialist revolution could occur in a largely 'backward' agrarian society and therefore in spite of the framework of the historical schema. Indeed, the priority of the strategic question was most acutely felt in February 1917, when Lenin perceived how the 'unique historical situation' of the imperialist war had produced a golden opportunity for revolution in Tsarist Russia. In fact, in his 'Letters from Afar', written in March, he also drew attention to the importance of the 1905 Revolution in preparing the Russian people for action, in much the same way that Arendt discusses the foregrounding of the American Revolution in the New England town meetings, and he similarly refers to this fortuitous combination of circumstances as a 'miracle' (Lenin, 2002). Žižek has recently stressed this aspect of Lenin's 1917 writings (Žižek, 2002). Nevertheless, at no point in the context of the Russian Revolution did the major protagonists fully dissociate the strategic question from a determinant theory of history. This latter idea was central to Trotsky's notion of 'permanent revolution', which was his answer to the question of whether or not, under the direction of the revolutionary proletariat, a backward country could skip different historical stages and move directly from a bourgeois democratic revolution to the socialist revolution (Trotsky, 2007). And,

and, as I have already said, her critique of sovereignty and the constituent power figured as 'unified will' provides insights into how we might respond to the present day security state. We return to each of these points in due course.

However, in addition to these negative criticisms of the French experience, Arendt's final reason for preferring the American event was because of the great wisdom of the founders. Unlike the French and the Russian revolutionaries, the American protagonists understood the need to institutionalise the experience of the revolutionary event, to be 'enacted further, to be augmented and spun out by their posterity' (Arendt, 1965, 40). In other words, they grasped the importance of combining the moment of radical initiative with a subsequent augmentation. This insight was evident, for example, in Thomas Jefferson's sentiment that 'a little rebellion now and then is a good thing', because it 'prevents the degeneracy of government, and nourishes a general attention to the public affairs' (Jefferson, 1999b, 108). In a sense, this Jeffersonian instinct has found a place in modern democracies in the organisation of periodic elections for executive and legislative power. And in this regard we might think of Lefort's insight that, under conditions of modern democracy, following the withdrawal of the theological foundations of political legitimacy, 'division' has become 'in a general way, constitutive of the very unity of society', because in modern democracies no 'group can be consubstantial with' sovereignty, and the 'locus of power becomes an empty space' (Lefort, 1988, 16–18). More specifically, however, in Arendt's account, the wisdom of the American founders and their profound appreciation of the value of reworking the Roman notion of augmentation, is evident in the doctrine of the separation of powers, elaborated by John Adams and especially by James Madison in *The Federalist* Number 10 (Hamilton *et al.*, 1987, 123, 125, 319). Indeed, when the Founders insisted that 'power must be opposed to power, force to force, strength to strength, interest to interest, as well as reason to reason, eloquence to eloquence, and passion to passion' this was not – according to Arendt – to put 'impotence in the place of power' but 'rather [an] instrument to generate

---

of course, this idea also underpinned Lenin's conception of the vanguard party as the guardian of historical consciousness, which he formulated in 1902, and his insistence, in August 1917, that the liberation of the oppressed class was impossible without a violent appropriation of state power, and the instigation of a revolutionary 'dictatorship of the proletariat' that would guide the great mass of the population in the organisation of a socialist society (Lenin, 1978, 1943). These Marxist assumptions about revolution all reflect the dialectical theory of history, and, thankfully, each of these debates becomes redundant in an agonistic theory of revolution, where democratic struggles rediscover their specificity and their dignity, and they are not explained or justified with reference to any wider historical process.

more power, more strength, more reason' (Arendt, 1965, 151). Indeed, the 'principle underlying the whole structure of separated powers' was 'deliberately designed to keep the power potential of the republic intact and prevent any of the multiple power sources from drying up in the event of further expansion' (Arendt, 1965, 149, 153, 155). Moreover, in this insight they were directly drawing on Montesquieu's intuition that ultimately 'only power (of the people, i.e., constituent power), and not laws, can check power (of the state, i.e. constituted power)' (Vatter, 2005, 131).[10]

Furthermore, it is precisely in amongst these particular insights that we need to situate the contribution of the contemporary theories of agonistic democracy. In Part II, I show how Connolly, Tully, Mouffe, and Honig all offer distinct iterations of agonistic politics in terms of augmentation through contending powers. Of course, this does not commit them to any narrow definition of American constitutional arrangements, and we will need to look closely at where the agonistic theorists locate the sources of augmentation and how their positions differ from deliberative theories, as well as from liberal interpretations of the constitution; but it does commit the agonistic theorists to the more general spirit of republican expansion and revitalisation though democratic contestation. In this, Connolly, Tully, Mouffe, and Honig all share something like the antique Roman view that freedom is constantly (re)generated through the introduction of novel forms of action that simultaneously produce innovation *and* supplement or increase the foundations; except now the foundations are no longer those of the 'eternal city' instituted by Aeneas, but rather the revolutionary events of the eighteenth century themselves which have become *our* foundation, have become the basis of modern constitutional democracy with its foundational principle of the co-originality of public and private autonomy. As I have said, the *exclusive* emphasis on augmentation is problematic, and not least because this effectively positions the democratic *agon* forever within the broad horizon of modern liberal democratic constitutionalism. I come back to this point at the end of this chapter and then, in Part III, I offer an alterative account of agonism, one that seeks to retain the qualitative distinction between revolution and augmentation and to think through the manner of their combination. However, firstly, in Part II, the more immediate objective is to provide a detailed analysis of the different versions of contemporary agonistic augmentation, and, as a prelude to this enquiry, I briefly consider here the points of similarity and difference between the contemporary agonistic approach

---

[10] For Montesquieu's discussion of power, liberty, and the role of competing powers in ensuring liberty, see: Montesquieu, 1989, Part 2, Book 11.

and Habermas' take on 'co-originality'. Indeed, we will see that one key point of emphasis in the agonistic conception of augmentation, contra Habermas, is the crucial importance of its non-dialectical qualities.

Against the dialectical reading of modern constitutionalism

In his influential paper entitled 'Constitutional Democracy: A Paradoxical Union of Contradictory Principles?' Habermas effectively picks up where Arendt leaves off (Habermas, 2001). Habermas takes the eighteenth-century foundation of modern constitutionalism as given, and so the (potentially) contradictory principles of public and private autonomy are presented as 'co-original'. Indeed, modern constitutionalism is defined by an acknowledgement that expressions of democratic 'sovereignty' and the constitutional guarantees that protect individual rights, are both necessary and interdependent components of legitimate forms of government (Habermas, 2001, 767; 1997, 49). This particular combination represents the horizon of possibility for contemporary democratic struggles. Under conditions of political modernity 'the laws of the republic . . . set limits on the people's sovereign self-determination' and 'the rule of law requires that democratic will-formation not violate human rights that have been positively enacted as basic right' (Habermas, 2001, 766). In other words, modern constitutionalism implies a necessary degree of containment of the constituent power by the rule of law (Habermas, 2001, 766). However, in contrast to some liberal conceptions of the absolute priority of the law, which we explore briefly in a moment, Habermas claims that on his model freedom and right are in a relationship of mutual dependence.

> The two concepts . . . are related to each other by material implication. Citizens can make an appropriate use of their public autonomy, as guaranteed by political rights, only if they are sufficiently independent in virtue of an equally protected private autonomy in their life conduct. But members of society actually enjoy their equal private autonomy to an equal extent . . . only if as citizens they make an appropriate use of their political autonomy. (Habermas, 2001, 767)

Moreover, in order to further establish the credibility of this account of modern constitutionalism, Habermas appeals to a dialectical conception of modernity understood as a 'self-correcting learning process' in which the *populus* becomes increasingly competent in the exercise of its democratic freedom in 'the course of applying, interpreting, and supplementing [existing] constitutional norms' (Habermas, 2001, 771, 774–5). From this perspective:

the allegedly paradoxical relationship between democracy and the rule of law [between the constituent power and constituted authority] resolves itself in the dimension of historical time, provided one conceives the constitution as a project that makes the founding act into a on-going process of constitution making that continues across generations. (Habermas, 2001, 768)

On this confident model of political modernity, the 'still-untapped normative substance of the system of rights laid down in the original document[s] of the [eighteenth-century] constitution[s]' are progressively realised as each new generation 'tap[s] the system of rights ever more fully' (Habermas, 2001, 774–6).

This distinctive account of modern constitutionalism has enjoyed widespread recognition, and clearly bears some resemblance to the Arendtean delineation of the Roman experience of augmentation. We have also said in the introduction that contemporary agonistic theories accept the basic premise of the legitimacy of modern liberal democratic constitutionalism, and they seek to offer an alternative iteration of the co-originality thesis. Nevertheless, Habermas' position has been criticised, especially by Honig and Mouffe, and the differences here are instructive (Honig, 2001a; Mouffe, 2005a). Honig sees in 'Habermas' effort to establish co-originality . . . an admirable attempt to stem the translation tide of liberal constitutionalism and give participation its due' (Honig, 2001a, 801). However, whilst his thesis overturns strictly foundationalist conceptions of law, Habermas ultimately subordinates democratic agency to another form of law: the dialectical law of progressive development towards the reconciliation of public and private autonomy. Although Habermas acknowledges that political modernisation is not 'immune to contingent interruptions and historical regressions', his conception of progress nonetheless represents an up-to-date version of the theories of providence and teleological development elaborated by Kant and Hegel, which we considered in the previous chapter (Habermas, 2001, 774). Honig says, when 'Habermas characterises his hoped-for future in progressive terms, he turns that future into a ground. Its character as a future is undone by progress' guarantee' (Honig, 2001a, 797). This narrative of progress misunderstands the tragic dimension of politics, and effectively constrains the constituent power of present and future generations by encasing them in a unilinear temporality destined to perfect the ideals of modern constitutionalism that were laid down in the eighteenth century. As Honig puts it, 'in what sense can the people [really] be said to have free authorship . . . if they understand themselves to be bound to a progressive temporality in and out of which constitutional democracy in its full, unconflicted expression is required to unfold' (Honig, 2001a, 795)?

Indeed, this dialectical framework 'launches us into a subsumptive logic' in which genuine moments of democratic innovation 'are assessed not in terms of the new worlds they may bring into being but rather in terms of their appositeness to . . . models already in place: incomplete, but definitive in their contours' (Honig, 2006, 110). In other words, Habermas' theory, along with those inspired by him, does not fully grasp the politics of invention, because like all forms of dialectical and teleological thought, he 'restrict[s] the autonomy of action by placing it in the context of a larger . . . necessity' (Villa, 2006, 123). In fact, Habermas confirms this assessment when he says:

Because the practice of civic self-determination is conceived as a long-run process of realising and progressively elaborating the system of fundamental rights, the principle of popular sovereignty comes into its own as part and parcel of the idea of government by law. (Habermas, 2001, 778)

Indeed, Habermas' subsumptive logic (subtly) privileges the *logos* (dialectical development) over the constituent power (genuine innovation), and this marks a basic dissonance between Habermas and the contemporary theorists of agonistic democracy.

These criticisms of Habermas are significant, and, by way of contrast, the contemporary agonists do manage to combine, paradoxically perhaps, the possibility of genuine innovation in democratic politics with a stress on the basic legitimacy of liberal democratic constitutionalism. Although the current theorists of agonism reject the possibility of the absolute priority of the constituent power, and so the democratic agon *is* hemmed in within a certain horizon, the horizon of liberal democratic constitutionalism and its basic set of values founded in the last great revolutions, contemporary agonistic democracy is nevertheless built around the idea of a genuinely open-ended, a-teleological, and adventurous experience of democratic augmentation.[11] Honig puts it in precisely these terms. She says agonistic freedom represents a form of 'augmentation that is committed not to [the] entrenchment or [eventual] settlement [of pre-established constitutional norms] but to a utopian possibility of [democratic freedom understood as] a perpetual . . . self-overcoming' (Honig, 1993, 157). Agonism presents citizens with 'opportunities for political activity other than revolution by committing [modern liberal democracies] institutionally to continual world building' (Honig, 1993,

---

[11] As Mouffe and Honig have both stressed, in order to grasp the tensions within modern constitutional government in a genuinely open way it is necessary to acknowledge the inherently paradoxical, rather than dialectical, relationship between democratic freedom and liberal constitutionalism (Mouffe, 2000b; Honig 2007). I come back to these formulations again Chapters 6 and 7.

112). The emergence of the constituent power repeatedly opens up 'new spaces of politics and individuation for others to explore, augment, and amend in their turn' (Honig, 1995, 155).

This experience of democratic politics is exemplified in the politics of the new social movements from the late 1960s. As Connolly has said, retrospectively people treat these movements as having 'either exposed hypocrisy in the profession of universal rights by the dominant group or prompted a cultural dialectic that fills out the [progressive] logic [supposedly] already implicit' in modern societies (Connolly, 1999b, 52). However, these mistaken ways of thinking force new social movements into 'disabling identifications' as we inevitably judge them through existing criteria of justice, and so underestimate their transformative power as they introduce genuine novelty into existing democracies (Connolly, 1995a, xv, xvi). From the agonistic perspective, it is precisely this conception of democratic augmentation – what Connolly calls 'the politics of enactment' – which should be the focal point of democratic theory and practice, and in Part II I examine a variety of different ways of formulating this conception of the constituent power. First, however, we need to take a brief detour and outline the other contemporary models of liberalism and democracy, which also provide important points of contrast with the agonistic viewpoint. Apart from the theory of radical democracy, we see that there is a marked tendency in contemporary democratic theory to try to subsume the innovative capacity of the constituent power under constituted forms of authority in a variety of distinct but comparable ways.

Contemporary theories of liberal democracy

In the introduction we spoke about the age-old quarrel between politics and philosophy, where philosophy has recurrently sought to bring the generative power of political action under some version or other of the rational principle. Once again, the tension between the constituent power and constituted authority, between *potentia* and *potestas*, helps to explain this difficult relationship. This is because we not only encounter claims to constituted right (*potestas*) embedded in extant social and political forms, and their associated norms and practices, in modes of constitutionalism in the narrow sense, etc., we also come across claims to authority in the law like *principles* – of right, justice, and progress, etc. – elaborated by political philosophers. Indeed, contemporary political philosophy, especially in the Anglo-American academy, has to a large extent been concerned with elaborating rational conditions of validity for the rightful expression of the constituent power, and to subsume the creative power of the *demos* under some set of determinant principles. In this respect, much contemporary liberal democratic theory follows, very broadly, in the rationalist traditions of Kant and Hegel, explored in the previous chapter, for whom it was imperative to transcend the tragic circumstances of politics with principles of right or to incorporate the *agon* into the overall movement of a dialectical cunning of reason. We have just seen how Habermas presents another iteration of these same broad ambitions in his presentation of modern constitutionalism as a dialectical learning process, and we also find comparable versions of these basic objectives in most contemporary democratic theory. In short, these theories typically provide examples of what Rancière calls parapolitics. From the agonistic perspective these attempts to subsume the constituent power under norms of balance and good measure are ultimately futile, since, as Kalyvas says, the constituent power 'always escapes subsumption under any rule or norm because, in fact, it constitutes their ultimate origin' (Kalyvas, 2005, 228). Nevertheless, the various attempts to achieve this impossible end are instructive and provide important points of contrast with the agonistic perspective. This tendency is certainly prevalent in the predominant liberal perspectives, but it is also pretty much central in a range of alternate models of democracy, and I turn now to a (necessarily brief) synopsis of the most important examples.

Liberal constitutionalism

The foundationalism of liberal constitutionalism is expressed most clearly in the social contract tradition, and in early modern doctrines of the natural rights of Man. From this perspective, the purpose of government is essentially to protect a determinant set of basic rights, the existence and validity of which is understood to be prior to all forms of political constitution. This aspiration was more or less approximated in the early Rawls, and especially in the work of Ronald Dworkin, for whom legally sanctioned basis rights necessarily trump the particular decisions of democratically elected legislatures (Rawls, 1972; Dworkin, 2005). Indeed, from the viewpoint of liberal foundationalism, the cut and thrust of democratic politics presents a potential threat to individual liberty, and so the 'liberal ... needs a scheme of civil-rights, whose effect will be to determine those political decisions that are antecedently likely to reflect strong external preferences, and to remove those decisions from majoritarian political institutions altogether' (Dworkin 1978, 134). However, more recent liberal thought has moved in much the same direction as Habermas, and is characterised instead by an acknowledgement of the need to reconcile constitutionalism with the importance of democratic sovereignty. This adjustment is seen, for example, in the passage from the early to the later Rawls, from the foundational status of a hypothetical 'original position' that ensures impartiality, to an emphasis on a *de facto* use of 'public reason', and this revised version of liberal constitutionalism is exemplified in the work of Bruce Ackerman (Rawls, 1972, 2005; Ackerman, 1991). On this modified theory, there is an appreciation of the role of the constituent power in moments of significant constitutional change, but this influence is delimited within a two-track model of the process of law making, which established a fixed distinction between 'normal' majoritarian politics expressed through Congress, and 'higher law-making' where the Supreme Court is the authoritative institution (Ackerman, 1991, 6).[12] Moreover, on this model the Supreme Court is the pivotal institution in moments of constitutional augmentation, understood as the branch of government that embodies principles of justice and reciprocity, and which 'serves as the exemplar of public reason' (Rawls, 2005, 231). Overall, these revised models of liberal constitutionalism are still orientated towards an insistence on the authority of a set of transcendent principles of right over and above the innovations of the democratic constituent power. As Frank Michelman says, for example: 'whoever is engaged in higher law making for a country . . . is, in that engagement, answering to some still higher law [of reason] that is already there' (Michelman, 1995, 230).

Indeed, at the core of contemporary liberal theory is the idea that the locus of constituted authority resides in an independent judiciary whose function is to prevent any excessive exercise of power by upholding and amending the constitution and guaranteeing the negative freedom of citizens understood as a sphere of individual private right. From the agonistic viewpoint, the ongoing predominance of liberal constitutionalism in Anglo-American political theory is indicative of a dangerous trend towards a juridification of politics. As Gray says, the basic objective of the current theories of liberal constitutionalism is to 'supplant' politics by law, and, as Mouffe puts it, the 'increasing moralisation and juridification of politics, far from being a progressive step in the development of democracy, should be seen as a threat to its future existence' (Gray, 2007, 9; Mouffe, 2005b, 123). This degeneration has been evident in some dramatic events – such the Supreme Court's decisive role

---

[12] Indeed, in the context of the wave of revolutions in 1989/90 that brought an end to Soviet rule in Eastern Europe, Ackerman even stressed the importance of a liberal theory of revolution, where the revolutionary constituent power is seen as an opportunity for the judiciary to consolidate a new constitutional document and a framework of basic law (Ackerman, 1992).

in settling the outcome of the 2000 US Presidential Election – and, less remarkably, in the ever increasing hold of administrative procedures on the day-to-day activities of citizens, as political questions are understood in juridical terms and decided upon by lawyers and experts as opposed to the people and their elected representatives.

Most importantly, agonistic theory rejects the liberal presentation of the Supreme Court Justices as the pivotal element in 'higher law making'. For example, Arendt stressed instead the decisive role of civil disobedience in the on-going augmentation of the republic (Arendt, 1972). As she put it, the law can 'stabilise and legalise change once it has occurred, but the change itself is always the result of extra-legal action' (Arendt, 1972, 80). For example, the Supreme Court's eventual enforcement of the Fourteenth Amendment in the Southern States, only followed the 'drastic change in attitudes of both black and white citizens' brought about by the civil rights campaigns (Arendt, 1972, 81). Moreover, the occurrence of civil disobedience cannot itself be explained with reference to acts of individual moral conscience or appeals to a higher law, but should be understood simply in terms of the unpredictable emergence of minorities of citizens associated together in the common conviction of some particular opinion (Arendt, 1972, 56). Similarly, for the contemporary agonistic democrats, augmentation is engendered not through supermajorities and juridical review, nor (primarily) through simple majorities and the 'normal' legislative process, but most importantly through direct action, civil disobedience, and the identity-transforming emergences of the politics of the new social movements. It is precisely this periodic (re)emergence of the constituent power – and not the rulings of constitutional lawyers – which provides the generative movement of democratic politics.

Aggregative democracy

The term 'aggregative democracy' refers to models that present the democratic system as a mechanism for the aggregation of economic interests. This outlook can be traced to the work of Joseph Schumpeter in the late 1940s, and the focus in this tradition is on the negotiation of interests in the day-to-day workings of democracy, in various forums of majoritarian decision making (Schumpeter, 1970). This includes rational choice models, exemplified in the writings of Anthony Downs, Mancur Olson, and William Riker, which have become predominant in political science since the late 1960s, as well as the tradition of interest group pluralism

developed by writers such as David Truman, Robert Dahl, Charles Lindblom, and Nelson Polsby, which was similarly prominent in the 1950s
and 1960s.[13] Many important debates surround these contributions,
and I can only touch on a few key issues here. I focus on the pluralist
approach, because, unlike the rational choice model, it shares a certain
proximity to agonism.[14] Indeed, the conventional pluralists understood
interest group politics to be typified by many cross-cutting cleavages and
multiple lines of contestation, and Dahl and others stressed the idea of
the positive value of conflict. Like the contemporary agonists, and in contrast to deliberative theories, the pluralist writers understood democratic
politics to be sewn together by its own inner contests. Nevertheless, in the
late 1960s and early 1970s the pluralist approach was subject to extensive
criticism, and was widely derided as a conservative doctrine, concerned
above all with the stability of the American system of government in the
context of the Cold War.[15] The most significant criticisms included the
following claims, that the conventional pluralists: failed to account for
the constitutive exclusions from the decision-making arenas of poorly
articulated interests, and so worked with a limited and superficial view of
political power; understood the contests of democratic decision making
to move inherently towards a condition of stable equilibrium; assumed
that a background consensus, or the democratic 'rules of the game',
could be taken as given; were cynical about the high levels of apathy in
modern democracies, and saw this as contributing to the overall stability
of the system; were unable to account for the politics of innovation; and
propagated a narrow instrumentalist vision of democracy that could not
give rise to any wider public goods.[16] Out of these debates emerged
various theories of 'participatory democracy' in the 1970s and early
1980s, which insisted instead on the vital importance of meaningful
participation for any credible theory and practice of democracy, and
in some respects these interventions prepared the ground for the

[13] For the rational choice approaches, see: Downs, 1985; Olson, 1977; and Riker, 1984;
and for some of the key texts of American pluralism in its heyday see: Dahl, 1956, 1961;
Truman, 1962; Dahl and Linblom, 1976.
[14] For an account of the differences between pluralism and social choice theory, see:
Miller, 1983. These theories diverge in their respective assessments of the consequences
of repeated suboptimal decision making for the well being of democratic institutions
over time. The pluralist emphasis on the overall value of conflict, as a consequence of
recurrent sub-optimality in the aggregation of preferences, resonates with the agonistic
model.
[15] See, for example: Walker, 1966, 289; Eisenberg, 1995, 158, 165.
[16] For critical commentaries on post-war pluralism, see: Bachrach and Baratz, 1962; Duncan and Lukes, 1963; Walker, 1966; Bachrach, 1969; Connolly, 1969, 1995a; Pateman,
1970; Skinner, 1973; Lukes, 1974; Macpherson, 1979; Mansbridge, 1983; Barber,
1984.

more recent models of deliberative democracy.[17] I come back to this point below.

One reason why these discussions are significant here is that Connolly was an important contributor to these debates, and a prominent critic of conventional pluralism in the late 1960s (Connolly, 1969). However, in the mid 1990s he presented his particular iteration of agonistic democracy as an alternative model of pluralism, and partly as a reconstruction of the American pluralist tradition (Connolly, 1995a). Nevertheless, Connolly also remained critical of the conventional pluralists – and precisely for what he saw as their lack of appreciation of the politics of innovation and change. In the recent interpretive literature on Connolly's work a consensus has emerged that he offers a distinctly new form of pluralism, one that breaks categorically with the conservatism of the post-war writers.[18] However, I have argued elsewhere that the various criticisms of conventional pluralism identified above don't stand up to scrutiny, and, in fact; the post-war writers anticipated Connolly's conception of augmentation as 'pluralisation' in many important respects.[19] Indeed, Dahl and Lindblom in particular should not be read as conservative figures, but rather as important forerunners of contemporary agonistic democracy, and especially close to the Connollian iteration. I pick up on this point briefly in the following chapter, but for now we should note how all three writers follow in the Madisonian tradition, where on-going pluralistic democratic contests are seen to contribute to an open-ended expansion of the republic, and can help prevent domination in the form of a tyranny of the majority (Madison) or of intense minorities (Dahl and Connolly). As Dahl put it, pluralism can help 'minimise government coercion' of social life, 'curb hierarchy', 'prevent domination', and facilitate 'mutual control' (Dahl, 1982, 1, 32).

Despite these important points of connection, there is at least one area where the aggregative and agonistic models of democracy do diverge in important respects, and this follows from the exclusive emphasis on the politics of 'interest' in the aggregative model. This contrasts with the agonistic model, where, as we will see in the following chapters, there is a much wider focus on democratic politics as a means of constituting identities, as well as values, interests, and preferences. Furthermore, there is a tendency in the aggregative model – or at least in the rational choice

---

[17] For the generation of participatory theories see: Walker, 1966; Bachrach, 1969; Pateman, 1970; Macpherson, 1979; Mansbridge, 1983; Barber, 1984.

[18] See for example: Carver and Chambers, 2008, 1, 4; Campbell and Schoolman, 2008, 9.

[19] I appreciate this is a controversial claim. There is not the scope to argue the case here. For a full account, see: Wenman, forthcoming.

variants – to present these 'interests' as always already constituted, in the form of fixed preferences, at the point they enter the democratic arena, and so the constituent power of democratic politics is delimited to a negotiation and rearrangement of those pre-established preferences, preferably in ways which are efficient and fair. In this regard, there is no scope for a conception of democratic politics as a constitutive force that shapes the identities (interests and preferences) of social actors.[20] As Owen puts it, by way of contrast, from the agonistic perspective:

> The interests that one understands oneself and/or one's fellow citizens as having or sharing are always already conditional on the way in which one understands the form and substance of our relationship to one another as citizens – and this requires acknowledging the priority of a view of constitutional democracy as the *medium* through which we work out our civic identities rather than as the *vehicle* through which we negotiate conflicts of interest. (Owen, 2009, 72)

Moreover, the stress on fixed preferences (at least) in the (rational choice variants of the) aggregative model also contrasts with deliberative democracy, which shares with the agonistic view an understanding of democratic politics as a constituent power that transforms social identities, interests, and preferences. Nevertheless, whilst the agonistic and the deliberative models share this emphasis *vis-à-vis* the aggregative model, we will now see that the deliberative democrats add an additional clause, which is that these transformations ought to be in the direction of generalisable interests or something like the 'common good'. Moreover, in their formulation of this additional requirement, the deliberative democrats typically aim to bring the constituent power under clear principles of the 'public use of reason'.

Deliberative democracy

The model of deliberative democracy has established a strong hold in the discipline over the past two decades.[21] Unlike the juridical

---

[20] For a discussion of this aspect of the aggregative model see: Warren, 1992, 8–9. In an earlier paper, I explored this tendency in the conventional pluralist model, see: Wenman, 2003a. However, on closer inspection it becomes clear that the pluralists had a more nuanced grasp of the political formation of 'interest'. As Dean Mathiowetz has shown, Arthur Bentley for one understood 'interests' as forged in the active contestation of political life (Mathiowetz, 2008, 632–3; Bentley, 1908). Again, for a discussion of the close proximity between Connolly and Bentley, see: Wenman, forthcoming.

[21] The literature on deliberative democracy is now very extensive and this highlights the increasingly hegemonic position of deliberative approaches within contemporary democratic theory. For a selection, see: Fishkin, 1991; Benhabib, 1996; Gutmann and Thompson, 1996; Cohen, 1997; Elster, 1997; Habermas, 1997; Bohman, 1998; Dryzek, 2002; Fraser, 2008.

foundationalism of liberal constitutionalism, the deliberative model acknowledges the relative priority of the constituent power, and deliberative theorists are not primarily concerned with the constitutional protection of basic rights, but with the need instead to reform institutions in western democracies in order to improve the quality of democratic debate and public deliberation. For example, Amy Gutmann and Dennis Thompson have applied the deliberative model to areas of deep moral disagreement such as abortion, capital punishment, and affirmative action (Gutmann and Thompson, 1996). Whereas, in the hands of John Dryzek, Seyla Benhabib, Fraser and others, deliberative democracy becomes a more far-reaching critique of existing societies, concerned with widespread reform of liberal democratic institutions. From this more radical perspective, a whole series of developments – such as the increasing alienation of ordinary people from the political process, the enormous influence of large media corporations, and the increasing bureaucratisation of political decision making – are explained in terms of the debasement of rational forms of communication by a politics of narrow self-interest. This corrupted state of affairs is contrasted to an idealised conception of democratic deliberation – overseen by principles of inclusion, transparency, and reciprocity – which serves as a normative criterion by which to evaluate the actual workings of contemporary institutions.

In contrast to the aggregative model, the emphasis here is on the constituent power of deliberative processes to transform partisan and short-sighted interests, preferences, values, and opinions *specifically* in the direction of the public good.[22] Deliberation is presented as a reflective process of political judgement and decision making, whereby participants gradually become more informed about a range of issues as they listen to the opinions of others in the course of the discussion (Benhabib, 1996). Through this process, interlocutors progressively come to see themselves as partners working out shared solutions to shared problems, and this enables a certain detachment from their narrow self-interest (Cohen, 1991, 221). On this model the general interest – or common good – emerges from rational public debate, as 'everyone is required to take [on board] the perspective of everyone else' and to develop an

---

[22] Many of the earlier theories of participation shared the same basic objective as contemporary theories of deliberation. Participation was 'designed to develop responsible, individual and social political action', where citizens 'learn that the public and the private interest are linked' (Pateman, 1970, 24). See also: Barber, 1984, 136. The deliberative model was also prefigured in the early twentieth century in the work of John Dewey (See: Dewey, 1977, 211–15).

'extended 'we' perspective' (Habermas, 1988, 58). The idea is that processes of transparent deliberation generate distinctly rational moments of the constituent power, or of 'communicative action', based exclusively on the 'force of the better argument', which can be brought to bear in a 'steering capacity' upon legislative debates, electoral campaigns, legal institutions, and the formation of public policy. For the more radical elements within deliberative theory, as well as for Habermas in his earlier work, this rational communicative power needs to be extended to 'alternative venues' that might include autonomous public spheres or 'civil-society in confrontation with the state . . . or workplace democracy' (Dryzek, 2002, 27).

From the agonistic perceptive, the deliberative emphasis on 'appropriate' or 'rational' forms of democratic will formation, ultimately tries to subordinate the constituent power to determinant principles of rationality. In the deliberative model, the constituent power is either governed normatively from the start by transcendent principles of inclusion and reciprocity, and/or locked into a dialectical movement, where interlocutors progressively learn these virtues as they move towards the ideal of 'unconstrained rational consensus'. These ideas can ultimately be traced to Kant and/or Hegel and, as we saw in the previous chapter, these rationalist viewpoints are incommensurate with a tragic view of the world, where reciprocity is necessarily limited and conditional and where conflict is understood as an ineliminable feature of human relations and not a temporary condition on a journey towards any kind of reconciliation. In response to these kinds of criticism, some deliberative theorists have sought to qualify the idea of 'rational consensus' and to insist that unanimous agreement is not necessarily the goal of democratic politics. For example, Gutmann and Thompson have said that, although the consensus reached through democratic deliberation under conditions of fairness and inclusion is 'binding in the present on all citizens', it nonetheless remains 'open to challenge in the future' (Gutmann and Thompson, 2004, 7). Indeed, with respect to issues of deep moral disagreement – such as abortion and gay marriage – consensus may not be the goal of democratic debate, but we might expect deliberative processes to enable the interlocutors to 'find greater common ground than they had before' thus making the issues 'more tractable' (Gutmann and Thompson, 2004, 54; Dryzek, 2002, 17). By practising an 'economy of moral disagreement' participants still promote 'the value of mutual respect (which is at the core of deliberative democracy)' (Gutmann and Thompson, 2004, 7). This qualification is accompanied by an increasing emphasis on feasibility, and an acknowledgement that – because of the constraints of time and imperfect information – voting and bargaining also have a part to play in democratic processes (Elster, 1997, 9).[23] As James Bohman puts it, 'few deliberative democrats now think of deliberation independently from voting or bargaining. The question is only how to make them more consistent with deliberation rather than undermining it' (Bohman, 1998, 415).[24] However, as Mouffe has said, even where the achievement of rational – that is fair and transparent – deliberation is 'conceived as an 'infinite task' or only a 'regulative idea', this still presents a rationalist constraint on the democratic constituent power (Mouffe, 1996a, 11; 1996b, 138). As Andrew Schaap says, the deliberative principles of fairness and reciprocity predetermine what counts as legitimate political action (Schaap, 2006, 257).

The question of the relationship between the agonistic and deliberative approaches has generated significant debate. Some commentators have suggested that Habermas' theory is more attentive to forms of conflict than his agonistic critics suppose (Brady, 2004, 331; Markell, 1997, 391). Fraser thinks that the distinction between agonism and deliberation is overdrawn, and that they both have a part to play in democratic politics (Fraser, 2008, 74). As we will see in Chapter 4, Tully also places agonistic and deliberative democracy on a continuum and presents his particular take on agonistic democracy as part of a more general deliberative turn in contemporary political theory. However, these readings fail to grasp the basic incommensurability between a model of democracy where contest and fallibility are understood as contingent limitations on otherwise potentially rational forms of democratic will formation, and the wholeheartedly tragic vision of agonistic democracy where conflict is understood as intrinsic to political life. As we saw in the previous chapter, this does not mean that agonistic democracy is an immoral doctrine devoid of any normative claims. But it does mean that we should examine prospects for alterative forms of contest, and think of agonism in terms of the artful innovations of games of power played with a minimum of domination, rather than judging the relations between protagonists from any 'reasonable' or 'impartial' viewpoint deemed to be somehow beyond the democratic *mêlée*. Indeed, as we will see in Chapter 5, one of the strengths of Mouffe's contribution has been her resolute critique of the deliberative viewpoint. Fuat Gursozlu is correct when he insists that the two approaches are fundamentally distinct, and Schaap is right when he says that it is not possible to combine these approaches 'without according

---

[23] Bohman describes these developments in terms of deliberative democracy 'coming of age', whereas Stephen Elstub distinguishes between different 'generations' of deliberative democracy (Bohman, 1998; Elstub, 2010).

[24] For comparable claims see: Habermas, 1997, 47; Elster, 1997, 14; Elstub, 2010, 296.

priority to the claims of one over the other, which would not be a matter of combination but cooption' (Gursozlu, 2009, 356; Schaap, 2006, 257). The cooption of the agonistic to the deliberative viewpoint is perspicuous in Fraser's attempt to combine the two viewpoints (Fraser, 2008), and, as we will see in Chapter 4, Tully comes very close to repeating this miscalculation.

Cosmopolitan democracy

In addition to the models of democracy examined thus far, a sizable literature has emerged over the past few decades promoting notions of cosmopolitan democracy and global justice. This development needs to be seen as a response to the changing circumstances of democratic politics under conditions of globalisation. Again, this literature is very extensive, but some of the major contributions include those of David Held and Daniele Archibugi who focus on the institutional reforms required to ensure effective forms of transnational governance; Richard Falk and Mary Kaldor who emphasise instead the importance of transnational social movements and 'global civil society'; Simon Caney and Kok-Chor Tan who have sought to extend Rawlsian principles of distributive justice across state borders (Caney, 2005; Tan, 2004); and a range of thinkers – including Gutmann and Thompson (2004, 39), Dryzek (2006, vii), Benhabib, and Andrew Linklater (1998b) – who have conceptualised cosmopolitan forms of deliberative democracy. These theories differ in their respective accounts of the agents and institutions of cosmopolitan democracy, and in their precise formulations of the principles of right and justice that are said to ground cosmopolitanism. Nonetheless, they all share the basic Kantian view that there are reciprocal forms of moral duty which bind humans to one another, and which transcend the particularistic loyalties and forms of identification that tie citizens to the nation-state (see for example: Beetham, 1998, 60; Linklater, 1998a, 113, 127).

From the perspective of Archibugi and Held, global, social, and economic problems require global solutions and these can only be brought about through social democratic reform of the United Nations, and the use of transnational institutions to strengthen global governance and to ensure the effective implementation of international human rights law (Held, 1993, 1995). These theorists do not envisage that we will dispense entirely with democracy at the national level, but national forms of democracy need to be supplemented by an elaborate architecture of transnational institutions. In the long run, this variety of institutions will be brought together to 'create a [single] multi-ethnic, transnational social democracy which protects the legal, political, social, and cultural rights of all members' (Linklater, 1998a, 118). The idea is to 'integrate and limit the functions of existing states with new institutions based on world citizenship. These institutions should be entitled to manage issues of global concern as well as to interfere within states whenever serious violations of human rights are committed' (Archibugi, 1998, 216). Before the present crisis, the European Union was often presented as a model for the effective pooling of sovereignty, which is inherent in this model of transnational democratic governance (Archibugi, 1998, 200, 209, 220). These approaches exhibit a clear institutionalist and technocratic bias. However, Falk and Kaldor emphasise instead the importance of transnational social movements and NGOs understood as the carriers of cosmopolitan values, and of global civil society presented as a site of active participation, collective solidarity, and the renewal of democratic self-determination that rises above the parochial concerns of national politics (Kaldor, 1998, 109; 2003; Falk, 1999). Environmental groups, community organisations, and NGOs can bring pressure to bear both on nation-states and the transnational institutions of the UN and other organisations such as the WTO and the IMF, and these theorists emphasise the constituent power of a globalisation from below (Falk, 1995, 171).

From the agonistic viewpoint, this second depiction of cosmopolitanism is much more promising and, as we will see in Part II, Connolly and Tully in particular have also drawn attention to the opportunities presented by globalisation for novel forms of social movement politics that transcend the boundaries of the nation-state. I also share the view that this is where innovative forms of cosmopolitan consciousness might emerge, and this basic supposition underpins my account of agonism and militant cosmopolitanism elaborated in Chapter 7. However, in their representations of global civil society, the Kantian theorists make a number of pivotal assumptions that are deeply problematic from the agonistic viewpoint. Once again, the difficulty is that these theories try to subsume the constituent power of a globalisation from below under predetermined principles of right. The transnational movements are depicted as the standard bearers of a 'law of humanity' that is supposedly already prefigured in the framework of international law and human rights, which has been partially established since the end of the Second World War (Falk, 1995, 163, 164, 170). In turn, these developments represent the Kantian ideal of moral agents as 'co-legislators within a universal kingdom of ends' (Linklater, 1998b, 44). The contemporary Kantian theorists don't assume that globalisation will inevitably deliver a fully-fledged cosmopolitan democracy, and they are mindful of the powerful forces pulling in the opposite direction; such as the resurgence of ethnic conflict, the emergence of novel forms of warfare, and the threat of international terrorism. Nevertheless, despite the many challenges associated with globalisation, these theorists share Kant's idea that the European Enlightenment has provided us with a vision of progress in which we can be reasonably confident that man will eventually be brought to 'establish a way of thinking that . . . transform[s] the crude natural capacity . . . into a moral whole' (Kant, 1991a, 32, 39). Through the federation of democratic and peaceable forms of government, the human race can gradually be brought ever closer to a 'universal cosmopolitan state' (Kant, 1991a, 38; 1991b, 118). As Linklater puts it, the realisation of the cosmopolitan ideal is 'already immanent within contemporary patters of social, economic, cultural and political change' (Linklater, 1998a, 120).

Tully and Mouffe in particular have stressed the element of imperialism inherent in these approaches, as they presume the cultural superiority and universal status of European principles of justice and right (Mouffe, 2005b, 91). As Tully puts it, the 'Kantian idea of free states and federation is not culturally neutral but is the bearer of processes of a homogenising or assimilating European cultural identity' (Tully, 2008b, 23). In their quick and easy association of cosmopolitanism with these culturally specific and predetermined principles of right, the Kantian theorists effectively impose an arbitrary model of cosmopolitanism on the democratic movements of the globalisation from below. This reflects and reinforces the role of the major western NGOs in the current global human rights regime. As Tully says, these organisations have been responsible for 'reproducing and expanding some of the [most] undemocratic features' associated with globalisation (Tully, 2008b, 192). As the soft power agents of Euro-American imperialism, these organisations often discount the 'traditional forms of communication and cooperation' of 'excluded peoples' when they bring them 'into the major government and corporate development networks', and they effectively 'assimilate them to the . . . form of . . . subjectivity they bring with them, rather than nurturing non-assimilative forms of inclusion' (Tully, 2008b, 192).

In Part II, we see that each of the agonistic theorists has been critical of these Kantian models of cosmopolitan democracy and, as I said in the Introduction, with the exception of Mouffe, they all present alternative models of cosmopolitanism. One underlying sentiment in these agonistic modes of cosmopolitanism is that the new forms of transnational solidarity associated, for example, with the World Social Forum, should be grasped in terms of their capacity for innovation, and not represented as the embodiment of any predetermined principles of right. In Tully's contribution, in particular, the stress is on the linking together of culturally specific forms of a globalisation from below. These are important insights, but the agonistic theorists generally evade the question of link between cosmopolitanism and universality. By way of contrast, in my own formulation of agonism and militant cosmopolitanism, I make the claim that cosmopolitanism is something more than simply transnationalism, and that it is possible to reconfigure the universal as something other than simply a rational (European) imposition on the globalisations from below. Instead, in Chapter 7 I draw on Arendt's reworking of Kant's theory of reflective judgement, as well as a theory of leadership, to figure the universal as a moment of absolute initiative; one that is increasingly recognised to be of broader or more cosmopolitan significance, so that it is taken up by diverse publics at the local, national, and transnational levels and begins to provide an alternative set of priorities in response to pressing issues such as climate change and global poverty. Ironically perhaps, we will see that this alternative reading of cosmopolitanism is also derived from Kant (via Arendt), but this is from the hidden, subversive, (post-modern) Kant of the third critique, and is entirely out of step with Kant's own reflections on morality and politics.

Radical democracy

I have surveyed a range of alternate models of liberalism and democracy, and we have seen that the predominant trend in contemporary democratic theory is to try to contain the creative power associated with moments of democratic innovation and to subsume the constituent power under constituted authority in various ways – specifically: under inviolable principles of constitutional right and justice (constitutionalism liberalism), in respect of the constituted inertia of fixed preferences (some forms of aggregative democracy), beneath the rational principles of inclusion and reciprocity (deliberative democracy), below the universal status of international human rights law (Kantian theories of cosmopolitanism). By way of contrast, the contemporary agonistic theorists emphasise the relative priority of the constituent power, in the form of a non-dialectical expansion that sees genuine innovation periodically introduced into liberal democratic constitutionalism. In a moment we will return to the strategic question, and whether or not it is wise to place an exclusive emphasis on augmentation in the context of the present conjuncture. However, as a prelude to this discussion I first return briefly to the radical democrats, who, as I have said, place an equally exclusive emphasis on the absolute priority of the constituent power in the form of revolution.

In the Introduction I briefly invoked the tradition of radical democracy, represented by Badiou, Laclau, Rancière, and Žižek, as the other major strand of democratic theory to emerge from post-structuralism. These thinkers don't draw on Arendt, and they are critical of her contribution, and especially her inadequate reflections on the 'the social question'. Nevertheless, I suggested that these theorists present conceptions of the constituent power which are strictly analogous to Arendt's depiction of the temporality of the modern revolutionary event. I now look more closely at this point of association, and reconsider the limitations of contemporary radical democracy because, unlike Arendt and Machiavelli, these theorists place an equally exclusive emphasis on revolution, understood as something like the essence of the political, and fail to grasp the crucial significance of augmentation. The limitations of radical democracy are perhaps especially pronounced in Badiou and Žižek, and these thinkers in particular lack the wisdom of the agonistic democrats and their grasp of the conditioning qualities of pluralism, tragedy, and the value of conflict.

One of the central features of contemporary radical democracy is the idea that genuine moments of the constituent power, *always* take the form of a radical break. In this respect, their approach is indelibly marked by the events of May 68. I cited Badiou on this point in the Introduction, but the other thinkers make the same claim. As Žižek puts it, the revolutionary event situates the actor 'in the *ex nihilo* of the interstices of reality, momentarily suspending the very rules that define what counts as (social) reality' (Žižek, 2001, 176). In Laclau's terminology, 'the genuine ethical act, is always subversive; it is never simply the result of an 'improvement' or a 'reform'' (Laclau, 2005, 228).

The passage from one hegemonic formation, or popular configuration, to another will always involve a radical break, a certain creation *ex nihilo*. It is not that all of the elements of an emerging configuration have to be entirely new, but rather the articulating point, the partial object around which the hegemonic formation is reconstituted as a new totality, does not derive its central role from any logic already operating within the preceding situation. (Laclau, 2005, 228)

Whether or not they are aware of it, these formulations are exactly congruous with Arendt's depiction of modern revolution.[25] As we have seen above, what singles out the modern revolutionary moment from the Roman experience of augmentation, is that revolution radically interrupts the continuity of the temporal sequence and marks the origin of an absolutely new beginning. Again, as I have said, the common root of this conception of revolutionary change is Benjamin's understanding of the *Ursprung*.

---

[25] This important point of connection between Arendt and Žižek and Badiou is stressed by Marchart, see: Marchart, 2007b, 105.

This formulation of the absolute priority of the constituent power has been criticised from the contemporary agonistic viewpoint. Indeed, the radical democrats are inattentive to moments of genuine innovation found in less dramatic forms of politics, and their exclusive emphasis on the originary event harbours authoritarian tendencies. As Norval puts it, the radical democrats:

> work with too sharp a distinction between the moment of the political, which is usually understood in terms of the institution of regimes, and the ordinary on-going business of politics, in which they denigrate the latter in favour of the former. (Norval, 2007, 11)

Indeed, the exclusive emphasis on revolution results in 'a dualistic narrative according to which the great and rare emancipatory event is opposed to the always repressive machinations of the state' (Marchart, 2007a, 132). For example, in Rancière's theory 'politics exists when the natural order of domination is interrupted by the institution of a part of those that have no part. This [revolutionary] institution is the whole of politics as a specific form of connection... Beyond this set up there is no politics', there is only the regulatory administrative power of what he calls the police order (Rancière, 1999, 12). This tendency to depreciate any moment of innovation that falls short of the monumental event is compounded in Badiou and especially Žižek, because of their criticisms of the politics of cultural diversity, and an insistence on the essentially violent nature of the revolutionary transformation.[26]

Agonistic democracy as augmentation and/or revolution

I concur with a great deal of what the agonistic theorists have to say about the limitations of radical democracy.[27] There are many moments

---

[26] See: Žižek, 1999a, 236, 238; 2001, 6; 2006a, 250; 2008, 119; Badiou, 2003, 10, 13; and for criticisms of these tendencies see: Coles, 2005; Marchart, 2007a; Norval, 2006, 237, 246; Stavrakakis, 2005, 195.

[27] Two additional features of radical democracy differentiate these theorists from the contemporary agonistic democrats, as well as from Arendt; their stress on the intrinsically binary nature of authentic political contests, and their formulation of political universalism in terms of a part that comes to stand in for the whole. On the first point see: Laclau, 2005, 77 and Rancière, 2007, 34. On the second see: Laclau, 2000, 35, 55; 2001, 5; Žižek, 2006a, 198. There is not scope here to examine these features of radical democracy in any detail, but I do pick up on the question of the binary nature of political struggles and how this relates to pluralism in Chapters 4 and 5, and one of my objectives in Chapter 7 is to make use of Kant's notion of reflective judgement to present an alternative account of the emergence of the universal, one that is compatible with pluralism and which is never consolidated, even temporarily, in the form of a Whole. In contrast to Schaap's locating of Rancière in the agonistic camp, we should also reiterate that all three elements I have identified here with radical democracy – i.e. the exclusive

of genuine innovation in modern democratic politics that do not take the form of an absolute initiative or of the grand revolutionary event. The repeated emergence of social movement politics is indicative of a relative priority of the constituent power over extant norms and practices, and we should not dismiss these emergences as mere repetitions that do not have any transformative effect; we should not simply sit around and wait for the absolute priority of the constituent power to become manifest again in a moment of profound transformation. However, as I said in the Introduction, the exclusive emphasis on augmentation characteristic of contemporary agonistic democracy is equally problematic. The idea of augmentation denotes moments of innovation that bring about genuine (i.e. open-ended and non-dialectical) change in existing norms and practices, but also, and at the same time, refer back to and expand a prior moment of authority or foundation. In Part II, we will see that, despite their differences, Connolly, Tully, Mouffe, and Honig, all present formulations of agonistic politics where this is the essential structure of the constituent power. Indeed, the idea of radical origin is inconceivable from within the paradigm of any one of their respective approaches. In addition to these theoretical delimitations of the constituent power to a particular type of politics, the agonistic theorists also explicitly endorse the traditions and practices of modern liberal democracies, and their basic grammar of the co-originality of public and private autonomy. The combined effect of these assumptions is to limit agonistic politics to a non-dialectical expansion of the basic social and political forms that were founded in the eighteenth-century revolutions. These conclusions are problematic because the forms of domination that shape the current conjuncture call for more radical moments of innovation, and in order to tackle problems such as climate change. Indeed, Arendt herself also remarked on the eventual 'failure' of the American Revolution to 'provide...a lasting institution' of its freedom (Arendt, 1965, 234). This corruption was evident in the steady displacement of 'public freedom, public happiness, [and the] public spirit' by the insistence on the priority of civil liberties and the pursuit of private property (Arendt, 1965, 131, 223). In other words, whereas the French Revolution quickly collapsed into a cycle of violent destruction, the American Revolution suffered a more prolonged disappearance brought about by the slow stranglehold

emphasis on extra-ordinary moments of rupture, on the intrinsically binary nature of these events, and on the linking of the part with the whole – are all intrinsic to his account of political disagreement, understood as a 'fundamental dispute' that 'actually happens very little or rarely', and that reveals the *demos* – or part that has no part – as 'identical to the whole: the many as one, the part as whole, the all in all' (Rancière, 1999, 10, 13, 17, 42).

of bourgeois 'negative liberties'. The central principle that effectively became foundational for the eighteenth-century events was the idea of the legal protection of forms of possessive individualism, and today the corruption of this principle has become systemic and entrenched, and we find ourselves in the stranglehold of disciplinary neo-liberalism.[28]

Thankfully, we do not have to choose either revolution or augmentation as the only authentic form of republican politics. In fact, we saw in the previous chapter that the principally strategic nature of agonism compels us to keep open the range of possible moves available to situated subjects. In the contemporary agonistic literature Tully comes closest to this view. In response to the extant forms of power that condition their subjectivity, he says:

> individual or collective agents . . . are [always] faced with a limited field of possible ways of thinking, speaking, acting, organising and conducting themselves *within* the (rules of the) relationship . . . [of power] . . . And, furthermore, if they refuse to be governed in this way and to work within the relationship, there is also a range of possible ways of directly confronting and negotiating the limits of the relationship itself, from the acceptable procedures of grievance and negotiation, strike and direct action to strategies of disobedience, revolt and revolution. (Tully, 2008b, 276)

These are crucial observations, and in this passage the inspiration of Foucault, who is one of the major influences on Tully's iteration of agonism, shines through. However, in Chapter 4 we will see that the significance of these insights is undermined in Tully's contribution, because at an ontological level he presents a mono-typical account of the constituent power in the form of augmentation, and on the basis of a series of theoretical assumptions taken from Wittgenstein. By way of contrast, if we really are to grasp the priority of the strategic question then we also need to maintain the qualitative distinction between revolution and

---

[28] In her account of the distinction between reform and revolution, Rosa Luxemburg grasped the qualitative difference between augmentation (as *reform*) and revolution (as decisive moment of transformation). In contrast to Edward Bernstein, for whom reform is a means to revolution as the end, she said 'during every historic period, work for reforms is carried on only in the direction given to it by the impetus of the last revolution, and continues as long as the impulsion of the last revolution continues to make itself felt . . . work for reforms is carried on only in the framework of the social form created by the last revolution' (Luxemburg, 2008, 90). These are important observations that help us to see some of the consequences of the contemporary agonistic theories and their *exclusive* emphasis on augmentation. Although this expansion is figured in non-dialectical terms, and is dissociated from any notion of progress, it nonetheless remains bound within the horizon of the basic forms of life that originated in the last great revolutions. Of course, Luxemburg's insights remained limited because of her Marxist theory of history, where revolution is seen ultimately as a product of underlying social processes.

augmentation that is elaborated in Arendt's *On Revolution*. However, this qualitative distinction between augmentation and revolution is inconceivable from the perspective that Tully develops from Wittgenstein. In fact, Tully, Norval, and Owen, who all draw on Wittgenstein, have arrived at exactly the opposite conclusion, i.e. that there is no qualitative distinction to be drawn between the kind of politics that found a new regime or a new framework of law, and the agonic freedom of citizens to challenge the constituted forms of authority from within the horizon of a given constitutional arrangement (Norval, 2007, 185; Tully, 2008b; Owen, 2009, 78–9). As Owen puts it, this distinction is a matter of degree and not kind: 'because (i) the activity of politics extends across both (a) contests within the current constitutional rules and (b) contests over those rules, and (ii) because there is no sharp line between (a) and (b)' (Owen, 2009, 79).

We will have to wait until Chapter 4 to really appreciate the limitations of these claims, but suffice it to say at the moment that these formulations are made from within a theoretical framework where augmentation represents the essential modality of the constituent power. Consequently, from this Wittgensteinian viewpoint, revolution becomes at best a particularly acute or intense form of augmentation. In Chapter 6 we will see the same basic sentiment at work in Honig's desire to translate the truly extraordinary event into an agonistic politics of the little bit *extra-in-the-ordinary*. There are several problems with these approaches, and not least that, from this perspective, we lose any capacity to differentiate genuinely extraordinary moments. Of course, there are sometimes truly astonishing qualities to what passes for everyday politics, and the agonists are right to draw attention to these moments of *virtù* that emerge from the many democratic struggles within the horizon of liberal democratic constitutionalism. However, these democratic emergences should not be confused with those genuinely exceptional moments that institute and announce the *novus ordo saeclorum*. So one of the central claims in this study is that we need to keep open Arendt's qualitative distinction between revolution and augmentation and envisage forms of agonistic democracy where these unique moments of the constituent power each have a part to play. Tied to this claim is the additional assertion that the experience of radical origin is not incongruent with the agonistic circumstances of pluralism, tragedy, and the value of conflict. This is evident in Arendt and Benjamin, but not in Schmitt or the contemporary radical democrats. Again, we will have to wait to Chapter 7 for a fuller account of this contention, but we have already glimpsed in Arendt's account of pluralism, in her critique of the Schmittean depiction of the constituent power in the form of a 'unified will', and in her discussion of the differences between the French and American Revolutions, some indications of how this might be possible. Indeed, the idea of absolute initiative is not equivalent to omnipotence, and in this regard Laclau is right to stress in the quote above that the idea of radical origin does not mean that everything has to change, but only that a new principle emerges that is entirely unaccounted for in the present conjuncture.

In fact, we will see in Chapter 7 that the originator of new forms needs the conditioning circumstances of pluralism and of on-going, multiple, and open-ended judgements, if her initiative is to have any prospect of continuing and expanding. Indeed, Arendt's most significant insight, which she shared with Machiavelli and the American founders, is that the radical leap of the origin requires subsequent augmentation, that is, if it is to root itself in the people. These two qualitatively distinct moments of the constituent power have become separated into different models of democracy in the current debates between radical and agonistic democrats. However, one principal challenge today is to rediscover this important combination of the constituent powers, in order to generate profoundly new forms of communal and ecologically sustainable ways of being, forms that might endure and expand and become the basis of a new militant cosmopolitanism. We will pick up this discussion in Part III, but first we turn to a detailed examination of the forms of augmentation presented by the four leading contemporary theorists of agonistic democracy. This is the focus of Part II, where we map the terrain of contemporary agonistic augmentation.

Part II

3   An ethos of agonistic respect: William E. Connolly

William Connolly has made important contributions to political theory for more than four decades. His career began by critically engaging the pluralism of American political science and the claims to value neutrality characteristic of behaviouralism, and this initial phase culminated in the prize-winning *The Terms of Political Discourse* (1974) (Connolly, 2006, 1969, 1993d). Since the early 1990s Connolly has developed his own distinctive conception of 'deep' or 'rhizomatic' pluralism, which is presented as the ontological, or what Connolly calls the 'onto-political' conditions of his account of agonistic democracy. Connolly has published many books during this period, including: *Identity/Difference* (1991), *The Augustinian Imperative* (1993), *Political Theory and Modernity* (1993), *The Ethos of Pluralisation* (1995), *Why I am not a Secularist* (1999), *Neuropolitics* (2002), *Pluralism* (2005), *Capitalism and Christianity American Style* (2008), and *A World of Becoming* (2011). This long list is testimony to the breadth of Connolly's interests, and in these volumes he explores a wide range of subjects including: the politics of faith and the conceits of secularism, the politics of crime and punishment, the impact of globalisation, the latest advances in neuroscience, and the nature of contemporary capitalism. Throughout the pages of these books Connolly has also developed a distinctive theory of agonistic democracy, which coalesces around a core set of themes, most importantly the onto-political themes of temporality, embodiment, and pluralisation, and the ethico-political values of agonistic respect and critical responsiveness. In this chapter I present a comprehensive overview of Connolly's theory, which reconstructs and evaluates these core themes and concepts, drawing broadly from each of these publications.

Connolly's focus on ethical questions follows from his particular reading of two aspects of the tragic circumstances of agonism that were outlined in Chapter 1. The core assumption, which really underpins the sum of Connolly's project, is the idea that certain dimensions of human suffering and conflict are 'rooted in the human condition itself' (Connolly, 1991, 191). In contrast to some forms of social criticism, which locate suffering exclusively in forms of social domination, for example in the injustices associated with the capitalist system, Connolly argues instead that we should 'refuse to reduce suffering [exclusively] to defects in the structure of society' and acknowledge the importance of responding to residual forms of existential suffering which would exist even in the good society. We need to acknowledge this in order to prevent resentment hardening into an attitude of 'bad faith' or *ressentiment* (Connolly, 1991, 191).[1] Tied up with this observation is Connolly's agonistic appreciation of politics as the medium through which identities are constituted, rather than, for example, as a distinct realm which can be isolated from the rest of society and conducted by professionals. Instead, forms of agonistic contest are found throughout society, because 'each identity is fated to contend – to various degrees and in multifarious ways – with others it depends upon to enunciate itself' (Connolly, 1991, 92; 1993a, 28). Given these two assumptions, the ethical question – of how an identity 'defines itself with respect to different identities' – becomes centrally important (Connolly, 1991, 9).

Keeping these suppositions in mind, the first section of this chapter focuses on Connolly's evaluation of two key ethical thinkers: St. Augustine and Nietzsche. We see that Connolly identifies in Augustine's thought a paradigm case of the problem of *ressentiment*, which has had a lasting impact and helps to explain contemporary developments such as the politics of normalisation and the rise of secular and religious forms of fundamentalism. By way of alternative, Nietzsche offers an affirmative ethos, one that has the courage to defy the lure of *ressentiment*, and in the second section we see how Connolly draws on Nietzsche, as well as Foucault, to develop his own ethical values of agonistic respect and critical responsiveness, along with the associated ideas of genealogy and the importance of ethical work on the self. I consider Connolly's various formulations of the ends of agonistic politics – in terms of facilitating individualism, providing a supplement to liberal theories of justice, and presenting a potential antidote to the prospective tyranny of intensive minorities – and I argue that it is really the latter point which provides the core ethico-political goal of Connolly's version of agonistic democracy. Indeed, in contrast to the widely held view that Connolly really presents a more radical form of liberalism, I argue instead that he belongs specifically within the Madisonian strand of republican theory. Moreover, he

[1] Connolly uses the term *ressentiment* to indicate something more than simply resentment, frustration, or indignation at this or that particular set of circumstances or perceived injustices. *Ressentiment* refers specifically to existential resentment, to a deep resentment at the finitude and suffering constitutive of the human condition.

shares this tradition with Dahl and Lindblom, and this despite his earlier criticisms of their contribution.

Connolly's position is then brought into sharper focus through contrast with Owen's alternative iteration of agonism. Owen also draws on Nietzsche, but he figures the democratic contest instead as staged around a collective ranking of values. We will see that there are important differences between these two approaches, but Connolly's theory is not a strictly anti-perfectionist doctrine, and I claim that a consistent theory of agonism will incorporate the underlying impulses in each of these contributions.

Indeed, Connolly's presentation of agonism is valuable in many respects, especially his account of the politics of pluralist enactment set out in the *Ethos of Pluralisation*, which he formulates with theoretical categories that are exactly congruent with the Arendtean depiction of augmentation. However, we will also see that Connolly places an exclusive stress on augmentation, and this is problematic for the reasons I set out in the previous chapter. Moreover, this difficulty is compounded in Connolly's particular contribution by a second problem that is unique to his approach, and this stems from the first of his two core assumptions identified above. Whilst Connolly is no doubt correct to say that some forms of suffering are rooted in the human condition, and that suffering cannot be fully explained with reference to specific forms of social injustice, discrimination, etc., it does not follow that this observation should become the focal point of a theory of democratic agonism. However, in Connolly's work we see that this priority leads to a marked tendency to focus on discussions about existential *ressentiment*, which effectively come to displace a proper analysis of historically specific forms of domination. In fact, more problematically still, Connolly tends to explain the manifestations of socio-economic injustice as largely a consequence of existential anxiety, and so he looks for solutions in personal ethics rather than in the possibility of a transformation in the basic structures or processes of society. These critical observations underpin my analysis of Connolly's account of globalisation, capitalism, and cosmopolitanism in section three, where we see how these limitations repeatedly undermine his otherwise important contributions.

In the final section, I turn to Connolly's theory of immanent naturalism, and here again we find some very important observations mixed with significant limitations. This aspect of Connolly's work should be situated more generally within the 'new materialist' tendency that has emerged in contemporary theory, and in Connolly's iteration a wide range of thinkers – including Spinoza, Nietzsche, Deleuze, William James, Henri Bergson, as well as the latest developments in the natural sciences, represented, for example, in chaos and complexity theory – are worked together in some remarkable analyses of the circumstances of time and embodiment. We will set out the detail below, but one central theme is the idea that the latest understandings of natural processes – with their focus on the self-organising properties of nature, as well as on complex forms of emergent causality – can be generalised to explain social and political processes, as well as the composite imbrications of various kinds of processes. These insights are potentially very fruitful, because processes *do* condition social life to a considerable degree. However, there are also some real dangers lurking in these analyses and, most importantly, we need to retain Arendt's insight that genuine political innovation is always something exogenous to process and disruptive of process. Connolly's critique of secularism is not examined here, but in Chapter 7 I integrate his observation that we cannot draw a clear distinction between faith and modern reason into my account of agonism and militant cosmopolitanism.

Ethical sensibility: Augustine vs. Nietzsche

Throughout his work since the early 1990s, Connolly has engaged with the ethical and moral teachings of a variety thinkers, including the Buddha, Jesus, Kant, Spinoza, Deleuze, James, and the Dalai Lama. However, two figures stand out as particularly significant; these are St. Augustine of Hippo and Nietzsche. Augustine was one of the Church Fathers and he wrote in the fourth century, in the traumatic context of the collapse of the Roman Empire in the west. In this conjuncture, Catholic doctrine was slowly being consolidated, and was not yet secure in respect of paganism as well as other beliefs closely associated with Christianity, such as Aryanism, Gnosticism, and also Manichaeism from which Augustine had converted in 386AD. Connolly sees in the Augustinian vindication of Christianity a paradigmatic example of how the quest for moral unity and certainty is often invoked in an impossible attempt to displace the inevitable circumstances of human mortality and suffering. He engages with Augustine most extensively in *The Augustinian Imperative* (1993), but also at several other points in his work, and his encounter with Augustine sets down the central concern of his theory of agonistic democracy, which is the problem of existential *ressentiment*.

The Augustinian imperative is manifested in 'the insistence that there is an intrinsic moral order' – the doctrine of the one true God – which is 'susceptible to authoritative representation' (Connolly, 1993a, xvii). This doctrine has difficulty explaining the presence of suffering, unlike, for example, the dualism of Manichaeism, which postulated good and evil as two distinct cosmic forces. For Augustine, the problem of evil is explained in terms of original sin, which is passed down from Adam and Eve to each of us through the conjugal act, and which manifests as 'a division within the will itself', and as Connolly says this gives rise to a morality of *ressentiment* 'built around the priorities of will, blame, guilt, and responsibility' (Connolly, 1993a, 53, 73; Augustine, 1998). Indeed, the Augustinian imperative 'is linked to an obligatory pursuit: the quest to move closer to one's truest self by exploring its inner geography' and rooting out those inner 'monstrosities that appear to break' with the moral design (Connolly, 1993a, xvii, 40). Moreover, on the Augustinian model, sources of corruption are not only located in the self, but also in the 'heresies' of those who do not share the moral Truth. In a time of great uncertainly says Connolly, Augustine sought to secure the identity of the Christian Church and doctrine by defining the propagators of other truths as carriers of 'evil' (Augustine, 1983, 156–7; Connolly, 1993a, 78).

On Connolly's reading, this moral imperative has subsequently become deeply engrained in western civilisation. All too often other identities cease to be figured as simply different. Instead, the other is figured as 'delinquent' or as 'deviant' from my own (or our own) true identity (Connolly, 1991, 3). The problem of *ressentiment* denotes a 'paradoxical element circulating through relations of identity/difference' (Connolly, 1999b, 144). Every 'identity needs a set of differences through which to define itself, while its imagination of wholeness can also translate that affirmative condition of possibility into a primordial threat' (Connolly, 1999b, 144). Indeed, human beings can best tolerate the tragic circumstances of life if 'they can find some agent who is responsible for [their] suffering, an agent who can become the repository of *ressentiment*' (Connolly, 1993c, 153).

Clearly there is a resonance between Augustine's doctrine and the kind of mutual intolerance associated with the politics of fundamentalism, which I outlined in the Preface. Indeed, Connolly has identified the proximity between Augustine and contemporary religious fundamentalism. He says 'Augustine's doctrine of divinity, will, grace, universal authority, and evil is too close for comfort to the doctrine of Sayyid Qutub, the radical cleric whose version of Islam is said to [have] inspire[d] Osama bin Laden' (Connolly, 2005, 17). For Connolly, fundamentalism is characterised by the 'tendency to define your faith as absolutely authoritative for others, and to treat it as under severe assault or even persecution until it is confessed by every one with whom you interact' (Connolly, 2005, 18). This undoubtedly helps to explain the psychology of religious fundamentalism, as it has been manifest for example in the mobilisation of the Christian Right in the US around issues such as abortion and against the teaching of Darwinism in schools, as well as the fanaticism of radical Islamists in their more general critique of western secular values. Connolly also draws attention to the same tendency in modern secular ideologies, such as the experience of McCarthyism, and more controversially he says also in the dominant trends in contemporary liberalism, which tend to 'project fundamentalism solely onto the other and fail to recognise its strains in themselves' (Connolly, 1995a, 123, 125; 2005, 6).

Furthermore, Connolly detects existential *ressentiment* not only in the politics of fundamentalism, but also in the more subtle practices of normalisation that underpin modern societies. Following Foucault, Connolly shows how a normalising society bestows 'institutional privilege' on a 'restrictive set of identities' defined as normal in relation to various 'standards of abnormality such as irrationality, irresponsibility, immorality, delinquency, and perversity' (Foucault, 1991b, 181–4; Connolly, 1991, 81; 1995a, 88). Adopting Foucault's genealogies of key modern institutions such as the clinic and the prison, Connolly argues that in contemporary societies the state can become the site of a 'politics of generalised *ressentiment*' (Foucault, 1989; 1991a; Connolly, 1991, 207). The dominant groups employ the key institutions of the state in order to ensure their own identities, 'by making "foreign" a variety of "external" and "internal" identities' that threaten to disrupt the conventional norms and values of the society (Connolly, 1991, 207). The politics of *ressentiment* finds expression 'in a variety of institutions, including those of work, investment, church assemblies, educational practices, modes of consumption, voting habits, electoral campaigns [and] . . . economic theory' (Connolly, 1995a, xxv, 48; 2008, 3, 5). This is especially evident in the criminal justice system, which becomes the vehicle of 'accumulated desires for social revenge', directed for example at ethnic minority groups in inner-city neighbourhoods (Connolly, 1995a, xxvi). Indeed, these tendencies reveal the clear limitations of the predominant liberal theories with their focus on the so-called 'fact of pluralism'. As Connolly says, there is 'plenty of variety in a normalising society', but this is a distorted or manipulated form of pluralism which privileges a dominant set of norms, and in which 'numerous groups and individuals who deviate are shuffled into multifarious categories of . . . irresponsibility' and 'personal defect' (Connolly, 1995a, 90). The result is a 'disciplinary society' and a normalised individual who keeps up self-surveillance in order 'to avoid treatment for delinquency, mental illness, or sexual perversity' (Connolly, 1984, 231; 1991, 85). We will come back to these observations in the following chapter, where we see how these 'disciplinary' and 'normalising' mechanisms have been steadily overlaced and complicated by new modalities of power associated with the society of 'control'.

If these normalising elements of contemporary politics can ultimately be traced to the 'Augustinian imperative', then Connolly looks to Nietzsche for a solution. Where Augustine sought to consolidate Christian doctrine in late antiquity, Nietzsche was a self-proclaimed 'anti-Christ', and the most vocal of a number of nineteenth-century commentators to announce the scandal of the 'death of God'. We moderns have killed him, and with his passing we have undermined all that he held in place in the order of tradition, authority, and unexamined truth. Nietzsche saw numerous trends in the West (going back to Plato's devaluation of the world of appearances), which culminate in modern nihilism, but it is the epistemological scepticism that defines post-Cartesian Enlightenment science and philosophy that really spells the end of the authoritative status of scripture and revealed truth (Nietzsche, 1990, 80). When the method of hyperbolic doubt becomes a precondition for any positive knowledge, we have started on the road to a (post-)modern condition where gnawing anxiety and doubt accompany every truth claim, (eventually) including (also) those of the modern sciences, and everybody, whether or not they have the courage to admit it to themselves, subconsciously knows it. Indeed, this is the definitive characteristic of modern man, his basic propensity towards generalised 'unbelief' (or nihilism). Modern man essentially 'knows not which way to turn', and this is because the world has been stripped of its highest values, and 'there is no longer a word left of what was formally called "truth"' (Nietzsche, 2003, 162).

When the ancient idea of the universe as a meaningful whole in which the individual can immerse himself is no longer believed, and when the idea of a transcendent world of bliss beyond this world has similarly become untenable, then we are in the terrain of modern nihilism. (Nietzsche, 1968, 13)

Nietzsche's work is often misapprehended as a *passive* nihilism, as if he was simply endorsing the agony of the 'terrible thought' of 'existence as it is, without meaning or aim, yet recurring inevitably without any finale of nothingness' (Nietzsche, 1968, 35). However, this is to miss the fact that Nietzsche saw the trauma of modern nihilism as an ambiguous development, which can be read both passively and actively, and which prepares the way for the advent of a truly vigorous and active spirit (Nietzsche, 1968, 17; 2003, 184). Indeed, a positive report on the (post-)modern condition recognises in the shock of nihilism 'a sign of [an] increased power of the spirit' a sign that 'the spirit may have grown so strong that previous goals ("convictions", articles of faith) have become incommensurate', coupled with the courage to 'posit for oneself, productively, [and groundlessly] a goal, a why, a faith' (Nietzsche, 1968,

17, 18). This leads Nietzsche to his portrayal of the greatest potential of modernity in the possibility of the *Übermensch* (Overman), who struggles incessantly to 'embody his own justification' (Thiele, 1990, 910). This is an 'autonomous individual who is not bound by moral rules as customary constraints, but as the freely endorsed commitments through which he gives expression to his own character' (Owen, 2009, 73).

This predicament, and opportunity, of nihilism is on Nietzsche's reading the central significance of the European Enlightenment and modernity. Indeed, for Nietzsche, the trauma of nihilism is not only devastating for the traditional status of revealed truth, but also for the foundational claims characteristic of modern reason. I come back to this point in more detail in Chapter 7, but here we should note how Nietzsche's appraisal of nihilism corresponds with the account of tragic pluralism we elaborated in Chapter 1. Indeed, Nietzsche pre-empts the delineations of modernity presented by Weber and Berlin in terms of a plurality of values, which are incommensurable in certain respects, and which cannot be ordered rationally or grounded in anything beyond individual and collective choice. Moreover, this dual emphasis – on value plurality combined with groundlessness – leads to another caricature of Nietzsche's thought, as opening the door to immorality, to a situation where 'anything goes'. However, as Connolly, Honig, and Owen have all emphasised, this is to overlook the fact that Nietzsche was a theorist of ethical responsibility (Connolly, 1993c; Honig, 1993, 47; Owen, 1995, 119). As Owen puts it, 'far from being ethically abhorrent', Nietzsche's teaching shows that in order to confront nihilism the individual must 'become the authority for himself which is also to say to become responsible for himself' (Owen, 1994, 75; 1995, 119). In fact, we might say that Nietzsche's thought teaches a hyper-responsibility, where the autonomous individual – denied recourse to customary or rational foundations – confronts every moment as a potential ethical dilemma. This is illustrated, for example, in Nietzsche's notion of the 'eternal return', which, on one reading at least, can be understood as a thought experiment designed to provoke the individual to reflect on his or her action, and to decide whether or not she can will herself to affirm this or that deed for eternity (Owen, 1994, 73). In other words, the Nietzschean Overman exhibits a 'will to self-responsibility that is manifest in the perpetual striving to increase, to expand, one's powers of self-government' (Owen, 2002, 119).

Indeed, Nietzsche's emphasis on autonomy is related to the importance of the affirmative more generally in his ethical teaching that we also spoke about briefly in Chapter 1. The central message of Nietzsche's ethics is that we should find the courage to affirm 'life, even in its strangest and hardest problems' (Nietzsche, 1998a, 81). Nietzsche offers a philosophy of action as an antidote to the Christian doctrine of guilt and remorse. Here the emphasis is literally on a solution to (re)*sentiment*, because, as Honig says, the Christian doctrine 'locks us into [backward-looking] cycles of guilt, vengeance, violence, and self-loathing' rather than pointing beyond them (Honig, 1993, 53). Indeed, it is 'only through new, creative, and powerful activities, not through remorse, or guilt' that we can get beyond the 'vengeful rage' that otherwise fastens the will to the past and makes affirmative action in the present impossible (Honig, 1993, 57). This emphasis on the 'nobility of action and its superiority to reaction' is manifest in Nietzsche's preference, like Machiavelli, for the values of Greek and Roman antiquity (Deleuze, 1983, 18). His *On the Genealogy of Morality* sought to rediscover these ancient aristocratic values, and to show how they were historically displaced by the Judeo-Christian 'slave's revolt in morality' (Nietzsche, 1994b, 21). On Nietzsche's reading, the ancient values were predicated on a clear order of rank, or on what he calls a 'pathos of distance', which associated the 'good' with 'strong, free, happy action', and where the 'bad' simply referred, 'with no derogatory implication', to the 'common man' and 'in contrast to the nobility' (Nietzsche, 1994b, 13–14, 18). This aristocratic, life-affirming order of rank was subject to an 'awe-inspiring reversal', first by the Jewish people and then later consolidated in Christianity, where 'only the poor, the powerless, and the lowly are good', and the noble and powerful are seen to be 'eternally wicked, cruel, lustful . . . godless' (Nietzsche, 1994b, 19). On Nietzsche's reading, Christianity is a life-denying doctrine, and, as we have seen, Connolly sees this exemplified in Augustine and his emphasis on original sin and its manifestations in desire and in heresy. Indeed, Connolly shares Nietzsche's preference for pagan antiquity, he says the 'Greek gods, heroically, assumed responsibility for human suffering. They absorbed guilt into themselves, reducing the store of poison to be absorbed by humans' (Connolly, 1993c, 158).

However, Nietzsche was not melancholic for the lost object of pagan antiquity. He says 'one recognises the superiority of the Greek man and the Renaissance man – but one would like to have them without the causes and conditions that made them possible' (Nietzsche, 1968, 471). As Owen says, Nietzsche recognised that ancient noble autonomy was 'grounded on an unreflective internalisation of the social order of rank' tied up with the authority of tradition and impossible under conditions of modern nihilism (Owen, 1994, 60). Indeed, the general effort to reverse the Judeo-Christian order of values is not meant to enable a return to Greek antiquity, but rather to help make possible the emergence of a new aristocracy who find the courage to affirm life and truth under the groundless conditions of modern nihilism. This possibility of the

Overman stands in contrast to the 'last man' who is the 'manifestation of the dystopian (anti-)ideal of comfortable freedom', who seeks to escape ethical responsibility in the superficial satisfaction of a materialistic and secular society (Owen, 1995, 122).

Clearly then, there is an undeniable aristocratic strain in Nietzsche's thought, and he explicitly condemns all those elements of 'plebeianism' in modern mass politics, including movements for democracy and socialism, which he associates with the last man (Nietzsche, 1968, 25, 459; 1994b, 15). Understandably, this leads many to dismiss the idea that Nietzsche has anything to contribute to a democratic theory of modern politics. However, Connolly rejects this conclusion, claiming instead that Nietzsche 'makes a compelling contribution to the spirituality and ethos most appropriate to democratic life in late modern times' and despite his own intentions (Connolly, 1993c, 197). Connolly recognises that certain 'alterations' are needed in Nietzsche's thought in order to extract 'an agonistic ideal of democratic politics' (Connolly, 1991, 186). However, he makes no apology for simply adopting those aspects that he finds compelling and rejecting the rest. He says, Nietzsche's emphasis on the importance of 'greater diversity and generosity in life' and his 'ethic of letting be' can be divorced from his 'aristocratic solution in which the few – defined not economically but by criteria of relative strength in affirming the contingency of existence – separate themselves from the herd' (Connolly, 1993c, 159, 161; 1995b, 131). Indeed, on Connolly's account, the Overman ceases to be a 'set of distinctive dispositions concentrated in a particular caste or type' of people, and becomes instead 'a set of dispositions that may compete for presence in any self'; the Overman becomes effectively 'a voice in the self contending with other voices, including those of *ressentiment*' (Connolly, 1991, 187).

We should note, at this point, that this reading is probably not something Nietzsche himself would have accepted. Indeed, according to Nietzsche, there is an *intrinsic* link between his doctrine of self-affirmation and the spirit of aristocracy. He says, 'if you do away with firm opposition and differences in rank, you will also abolish all strong love, lofty attitudes, and the feeling of individuality' (Nietzsche, 1968, 494). In a moment we will see that Connolly's position contrasts with Owen's theory of agonistic democracy. Owen is close to Connolly in many respects, but nonetheless he retains the aristocratic sentiments underpinning Nietzsche's thought whilst seeking to divorce them from any connotations of social or political hierarchy (Owen, 2008, 220). However, before we arrive at this discussion, we need to first look in more detail at the different element and purposes of Connolly's 'politicised left-Nietzscheanism' (Connolly, 1991, 190).

A post-Nietzschean ethical sensibility of agonistic respect

Connolly's account of the ethical sensibility appropriate to agonistic democracy is comprised of four basic components. These are: (i) the strategic importance of genealogy as a way of disrupting established claims to normality; (ii) the significance of an attitude of agonistic respect as the key to constructive forms of agonistic contest; (iii) the need to cultivate this attitude through techniques-of-the-self, and (iv) the associated idea of critical responsiveness, as a way of practising agonism specifically in respect to new emergences. Connolly describes genealogy as a conceptual tool for tracing the 'discrete' and arbitrary foundations of ideas, values, and institutions, i.e. the constituted powers and authorities that we now 'take for granted . . . as if they were natural, or given, or established by reason' (Connolly, 1993c, 151). This is exemplified in Nietzsche's *Genealogy* (1994b) as well as Foucault's genealogy of the modern prison system and its concomitant mechanisms of punishment (Foucault, 1991a). As we have seen, Connolly's book on Augustine shares the same basic objective, i.e. of unearthing the forgotten origins of contemporary modes of normalisation and fundamentalism (Connolly, 1993b, 366–7). Indeed, in Chapter 1 we saw that one central objective in agonistic democracy is to contest the methods of tyranny that seek to subdue or control genuine plurality, and here this objective is clearly at work in Connolly's understanding of genealogy. This is an indispensable tool in a world were the *agon* is always under threat from 'the pursuit of unity, coherence, and harmony' (Connolly, 1995a, 87). However, Connolly also acknowledges that these strategies have the potential to cause anxiety, because they are designed to reveal the contingency of the dominant norms and values that we often take for granted, and so Connolly worries that genealogy may end up fuelling the very *ressentiment* that its 'advocates are tying to curtail' (Connolly, 1991, 185; 1993b, 370).

Connolly moves from this observation to the claim that it is crucial to combine genealogy with a positive 'ethos of engagement' or agonistic respect (Connolly, 1991, 58; 1993b, 368, 381; 1999b, 36). Agonistic respect is the centrepiece of Connolly's ethico-political schema and is presented as an ethos or sensibility, which can be practised by the carriers of any faith, identity, or doctrine, if they can only come to terms with the 'comparative contestability' of their beliefs (Connolly, 1993b, 382; 1999b, 143–156; 2000a, 611). More specifically, Connolly urges the protagonists to 'strive for reciprocal modesty' and greater 'responsiveness to difference' which become 'presumptive virtues in pluralist politics' (Connolly, 1995a, 69; 1999b, 9; 2002, 16; 2005, 123). As Connolly puts it – citing Nietzsche – '"rival" you shall say, but not heretic', and, on his reading, the widespread dissemination of agonistic respect 'offers the best opportunity for diverse faiths to coexist without violence', the best antidote to the politics of normalisation and fundamentalism, and this ethos needs to become embedded in the institutions and public values of modern democracies (Connolly, 1993a, 88; 2005, 65). The reader will, of course, recognise clear resonances with the liberal notion of tolerance. Indeed, Connolly sometimes describes his theory as a (post-modern) strand of liberalism, and there is a fairly widespread view in the secondary literature that this is how best to make sense of his contribution.[2] In a moment I will scrutinise Connolly's formulations of the ends of agonistic politics more carefully, and offer an alterative account of where to situate his theory. However, for now we should simply note that these formulations of agonistic respect don't commit Connolly to an insistence on the priority of negative liberty in the manner of Berlin, or to a clear constitutional demarcation of the public and private spheres, which is the central objective of most contemporary liberal theories. Instead, Connolly refers to agonistic respect as a civic virtue, and the basic ambition is to fold 'forbearance into the inevitable element of [public] conflict between alternative identities' (Connolly, 1991, 166; 1993c, 190; 1999b, 3, 6; 2005, 5). As we have said, the democratic *agon* can emerge in all areas of society, and this is because the circumstances of tragedy and constitutive pluralism render 'inescapable the intensive entanglement of everyone with everyone else' (Connolly, 1991, 188). Connolly's hope is that the dissemination of agonistic respect will facilitate a more constructive form of contest, where the protagonists increasingly engage in 'respectful competition and selective collaboration' (Connolly, 1993c, 135).

In line with this presentation of agonistic respect as a basic attitude or civic virtue, Connolly also draws attention to the importance of ethical work on the self. In the absence of any rational grounding for principles of moral duty in the manner of the Kantian tradition, Connolly shares an emphasis with Foucault on the need for individuals to work 'patiently on specific contingencies' in themselves, in order to *cultivate* an ethical sensibility they can affirm without *ressentiment* (Connolly, 1993c, 157; 1995a, 69). Again, this should not be confused with a kind of apolitical individualism. Like Foucault, Connolly points instead to the link between the care of the self and the value of civic responsibility (Connolly, 1991,

---

[2] See: Moon, 1998, 63–71; White, 1998, 73–81; 2000, 143–4; Vazquez-Arroyo, 2004; Brown, 2008, 254; Owen, 2008, 215.

76).[3] Moreover, in the form of 'micropolitics', the techniques-of-the-self become explicitly collectivised in the form of 'action by the . . . small scale assemblage upon itself', such as the family, the school, and the neighbourhood (Connolly, 1995a, xxi, xxv; 1999a, 27; 1999b, 149). This aspect of Connolly's contribution reiterates the essentially strategic nature of agonism I stressed in Chapter 1, which is exemplified in Machiavelli and Foucault. Indeed, the emphasis on the techniques-of-the-self and micro-politics reflects the interplay of necessity, chance, and freedom inherent in the agonistic conception of politics. The idea here is that 'through much obstinate, faithful, repetition of the same labours' individuals and groups acquire a finite capacity to engage and redirect the forces that impact on their lives (Connolly, 1993c, 163). This is unlike Aristotelian conceptions of self-making, where the idea is to realise the true self, and it does not imply a fully sovereign individual who completely masters his mode of being in the world.[4] As Connolly says, echoing Machiavelli and Foucault, 'we are not sovereign agents who will the codes of desire that circulates through us, even though we do possess variable abilities to move or modify particular patterns of desire by tactical means' (Connolly, 1995a, 65). We will come back to this point below in the discussion of immanent naturalism, where we will see that this strategic conception of agency would be rendered impossible in a fully immanentist conception of politics.

The final part of Connolly's ethico-political composition is the idea of critical responsiveness, but before we explicate this particular ethos we need to take an initial dip into the central theme of his onto-political analysis, which is the experience of pluralisation or of the politics of 'pluralist

---

[3] Foucault traced the emergence of the idea of the care of the self to the Hellenistic period and the Roman world, and he emphasised how this development is often misinterpreted as a substitute for civic activity following the demise of the classical *polis* (Foucault, 1988, 86). However, in contradistinction, he says 'it is not in opposition to the active life that the cultivation of the self places its own values and practices' (Foucault, 1988, 86). Indeed, the idea of the care of the self was originally formulated as a means to enable the citizen to conduct his civic duty in the increasingly complex structures of the Roman Empire (Foucault, 1988, 95).

[4] Although the content of Connolly's ethical sensibility resembles liberal tolerance, the form of his argument is closer to communitarian ethics (Connolly, 1993b, 370). The difference is that Connolly distances his approach from those who link the practice of ethical work on the self to an 'intrinsic purpose susceptible to attunement or recognition' (Connolly, 1999a, 21). He says that 'a post-Nietzschean ethic is "Aristotelian" in its drive to cultivate a sensibility inscribed in practice rather than to authorise a full moral theory; [but] it is "Nietzschean" in its drive to appreciate ways in which the pool of life exceeds every settled moral economy rather than to cultivate attunement to a design in god or an intrinsic purpose in nature' (Connolly, 1993c, 193). Rather than a theory of the morally encumbered self, we might say that Connolly's presents a theory of the temporally and existentially encumbered self.

enactment'. This idea was first elaborated in *The Ethos of Pluralisation*, where Connolly focused on the constituent power of social movements to bring 'new possibilities of being into the existing matrix of pluralism' (Connolly, 1995a, xix; 1995b, 134). Drawing on examples of struggles from the late 1960s around issues such as gay rights, women's rights, and the anti-war movement, Connolly describes agonistic democracy in terms of moments of innovation whereby 'established definitions of normality and rationality' are 'challenged periodically by new movements' and 'contested . . . in multifarious ways' (Connolly, 1991, 85; 1995a, xiv; 1995b, 134; 1999b, 5). Indeed, Connolly's initial formulation of the politics of enactment is closely akin to Arendt's rendition of the constituent power in terms of moments of creation. Similarly, on Connolly's reading these democratic inventions possess the capacity (*potentia*) to interrupt the constituted powers and authorities, or what Connolly calls the 'contemporary self-satisfied unities', and they likewise bring about an overall expansion, because when an emergent movement 'succeeds in placing a new identity on the cultural field' it 'changes the shape and contour of already entrenched identities' (Connolly, 1991, 85; 1999b, 57, 70).

Critical responsiveness is a further elaboration of the idea of agonistic respect, in the hope that it might also become an 'indispensable lubricant' for these constitutive circumstances of an open-ended and non-dialectical politics of becoming (Connolly, 1995a, xvii; 1999b, 51; 2000b, 195). Again, the basic objective is to avoid the attractions of *ressentiment*, and Connolly understands those who are on the receiving end of the new emergences to be most exposed to this temptation. This is because anxiety will often be provoked in the 'self-confidence of established identities', as the democratic movements introduce novel possibilities that disrupt conventional norms and values (Connolly, 1995a, xv). Connolly therefore petitions those who find themselves unsettled in the politics of enactment to try to 'respond reflexively to the next set of surprises' (Connolly, 1995a, xv; 1999a, 36; 2002, 166). Most importantly, the lesson is to avoid translating the new initiatives into categories of 'immorality and abnormality' (Connolly, 1995a, xv, xviii, xix).

> The ethos of critical responsiveness . . . does not reduce the other to what some 'we' already is. It opens up cultural space through which the other might consolidate itself into something that is unafflicted by negative cultural markings. (Connolly, 1995a, xvii)

This passage epitomises Connolly's desire to articulate the genuine inventiveness of the politics of enactment, and his portrayal of agonistic augmentation neatly discloses the limitations of the predominant liberal perspectives, which seek to subsume the new emergences under existing codes of justice, as well as of dialectical theories that read the new beginnings as evidence of a necessary 'logic [of progress] already implicit' in liberal democratic society (Connolly, 1999b, 52). We come back to the relationship between Connollian critical responsiveness and liberalism in a moment, and we explored the difficulties with dialectical theories in the previous chapter, and in respect of Habermas' account of modern constitutionalism as a learning process.

This aspect of Connolly's theory is very compelling, and, as I said in the previous chapter, the agonistic stress on the power of creative invention associated with the new social movements is important for several reasons – not least because it reveals the limitations of the radical democratic theories with their exclusive emphasis on the grand revolutionary event. However, it is also clear that Connolly's theory of enactment focuses equally exclusively on the *relative* priority of the constituent power. Connolly understands the disruptive power of enactment as a capacity for innovation that emerges *within* liberal democratic societies, and he says the politics of innovation presupposes 'pre-existing pluralism as one of its supporting conditions' (Connolly, 1995a, xiv; 1999b, 58, 68). The new movements simultaneously produce novelty and refer back to existing codes of normality and justice. Consequently, as White says, Connolly's 'radicality does not lie in proposals for a wholesale transformation of the basic structures of liberal democracy, but rather in a form of "micropolitics" that might animate those structures differently' (White, 2000, 117). Indeed, Connolly explicitly rejects the idea of revolution, which he thinks has become an outmoded and hazardous form of politics under conditions of late modernity (Connolly, 2008, 113). In the previous chapter I argued to the contrary, and this is because the grave circumstances we face today require that we hold onto the possibility of the radical invention of new social and political forms. I come back to this in Chapter 7.

However, it is important to appreciate that Connolly's exclusive emphasis on augmentation does not follow only from his particular political commitments and his explicit rejection of the idea of revolution. More significantly, it is also inherent in his theoretical categories, and this is because the originary break is literally inconceivable in his formulation of the politics of becoming. Indeed, Connolly presents augmentation as the essential structure of the constituent power. In agonistic politics a 'productive tension is [always] maintained between political governance through electoral accountability and political disturbance of closures in conventions and identities that have become fixed or naturalised'; a 'tense balance must be maintained' between 'claims of regularity, predictability, and commonality and those of experimentation, artistry, and becoming' (Connolly, 1993c, 179; 2002, 162). In fact, these formulations reflect something like a metaphysical reading of the eternal return, where the politics of becoming is understood as a perpetual movement of pluralism/pluralisation identity/difference, governance/disturbance, being/becoming etc. I come back to this in my discussion of immanent naturalism below. However, as we said in the previous chapter, this single explanatory framework represents a regression vis-à-vis Arendt's stress on the qualitative distinction between the two primary moments of the constituent power.

Agonism and the ends of democratic politics

We have said that the overriding goal in Connolly's theory is to provide a corrective to those assertions of moral unity and certainty that often flow from existential *ressentiment*, and this reflects his commitment to pluralism. However, within this overarching objective Connolly also elaborates the ends of agonistic democracy more specifically. The values of agonistic respect and critical responsiveness are said to (i) contain the potential to facilitate individualism, (ii) provide an important supplement to liberal theories of justice, and (iii) help address the threat of intensive minorities. I briefly consider each of these aims and I argue that it is the third aspiration that really represents the core of Connollian agonism, and this places him within a distinctly Madisonian mode of thinking about democratic politics.

Connolly stressed the importance of individualism in *Identity/Difference* and also in *The Ethos of Pluralisation*, and his emphasis was on the power of individuality, or on alternate 'styles of living', to help subvert the pressures of normalisation and to stretch the 'boundaries of identity' available to the self (Connolly, 1991, 75, 85, 91; 1995a, 106). In much the same way as John Stuart Mill, Connolly celebrates non-identity with the dominant conception of the self as a 'sign of individuality' (Connolly, 1991, 75).[5] In *The Ethos of Pluralisation* these sentiments are combined with a critique of the predominant trends in contemporary liberalism for their restricted focus on the priority of justice. Mainstream liberal theory celebrates 'diversity within settled contexts of conflict and collective action',

---

[5] Mill's critique of the 'increased regularity of conduct' characteristic of modern democracy, and the 'small number of moulds which society provides in order to save its members the trouble of forming their own character' is close to Nietzsche and pre-empts Foucault's and Connolly's critiques of normalisation (Mill, 1978, 62, 65). As Mill put it: 'Protection . . . against the tyranny of the magistrate is not enough; there needs [to be] protection also against the tyranny of the prevailing opinion and feeling, against the tendency of society to impose, by other means than civil penalties, its own ideas and practices as rules of conduct on those who dissent from them' (Mill, 1978, 4).

the so-called fact of pluralism, but fails to appreciate the crucial impact of the politics of enactment, as new movements seek to place novel demands onto the 'register of justice' (Connolly, 1991, 81; 1993c, 178; 1995a, xiii, x, 111; 1999b, 63) Consequently, the predominant liberal theories are blind towards the modes of suffering and subordination 'subsisting below the public register of justice', and they do not appreciate the constituent power of new movements to genuinely transform the standards of judgement and recognition built into the existing codes of justice (Connolly, 1995a, xvi; 1999b, 10). However, despite these criticisms, Connolly nonetheless presents critical responsiveness as a supplement to liberal theories of justice and not as a substitution. As White says, Connolly's formulations reveal the 'exposed flank of liberalism' rather than seeking to go entirely beyond the liberal tradition (White, 2000, 149).[6] In this regard, Connolly's iteration of agonism clearly exhibits certain proximity to liberalism, and, as we have said, he shares this basic fidelity to liberal values and institutions with each of the thinkers examined in this book. However, we also need to consider Connolly's location within the liberal democratic tradition more carefully, and it is important to resist the conclusion that his version of agonistic democracy represents simply, or primarily, a complement to liberalism.

Instead, Connolly reworks a distinctly Madisonian view of politics, where the focus is not primarily on justice or on the constitutional protections of the bill of rights, but rather on the capacity of the on-going and open-ended democratic contest to provide a potential counterpoint to domination. This is especially evident in Connolly's reflections on the dangers of intensive minorities, where he effectively reworks the vision of democratic politics elaborated by Dahl and Lindblom in the 1950s and early 1960s. In the previous chapter, I suggested that these (so-called) 'conventional' pluralists actually anticipated contemporary agonistic democracy in important respects. This reading contrasts with the predominant view that Connolly's contribution represents a radical break with the 'old' pluralism of the post-war political scientists (Campbell and Schoolman, 2008; Carver and Chambers, 2008). However, these readings move too quickly to accept the well-known criticisms of Dahl and Lindblom, that they were conservative thinkers concerned above all with the value of stability, whereas, in fact, they were also advocates of the augmentation of the republic through the medium of democratic contest, and they offered sophisticated interpretations of the politics of change that anticipate Connolly's account of the politics of

---

[6] For a detailed evaluation of Connolly's work in relation to liberalism see: White, 2000, 145–50.

becoming.[7] Indeed, we need to look a little more closely at Connolly's proximity to Dahl and Lindblom, because this reveals that his theory of the democratic *agon* is, like theirs, importantly different from liberalism.

In the *Federalist* No. 10 Madison outlined the values of the new constitution in terms of its ability to manage the effects of faction and to prevent the concentration of power in the hands of 'the superior force of an interested and overbearing majority' (Hamilton *et al.*, 1987, 123, 125, 319). In *A Preface to Democratic Theory* 1956 Dahl described this as the 'central ethical goal of the Madisonian system' (Dahl, 1956, 10). Unlike Dahl, Lindblom, or Connolly, Madison's focus was primarily on the role of political institutions – the principle of federalism and a constitutional separation of powers – understood as a series of 'intergovernmental checks' on the influence of officials, and essentially designed to ensure that power was not concentrated in the legislature. However, Dahl also stressed that Madison understood the importance of the 'social checks and balances existing in [a modern] pluralistic society' (Dahl, 1956, 22). Against conventional wisdom at the time, the Federalists argued that throughout society 'ambition must be made to counteract ambition' and that 'a greater variety of parties and interests' are to be welcomed, because when an electorate is extended in size and 'diverse in interests', as Dahl put it, 'a majority faction is less likely to exist, and if it does exist, it is less likely to act as a unity' (Hamilton *et al.*, 1987, 128, 319; Dahl, 1956, 17). In his account of 'polyarchal democracy', Dahl further developed the idea of the positive value of societal contests, arguing that 'no constitutional arrangements can produce a non-tyrannical republic' in the absence of a set of social checks and balances (Dahl, 1956, 83). Similarly, in *The Intelligence of Democracy* (1965) Lindblom reworked the classical discussion about the importance of the struggle between factions and developed a theory of democracy in terms of what he called 'partisan mutual adjustment' (Lindblom, 1965, 9). Lindblom identified the benefits of the democratic contest above all with the possibility of 'large scale coordination . . . through mutual adjustment of persons not ordered by rule, central management, or dominant common purpose' (Lindblom, 1965, 4). In other words, the on-going contests associated with the democratic *agon* might enable people to 'coordinate with each other without anyone's coordinating them' (Lindblom, 1965, 3). This is a positive way of formulating the idea of a non-tyrannical republic:

[7] In fact, Connolly's theory is best understood as the resumption and enhancement of a distinct canon of pluralism in American political thought, which is shared not only by the post-war writers, but also by Bentley, and has a common root in the pragmatist tradition and the work of James. See: Wenman, forthcoming.

the open-ended clashes characteristic of modern democracy have the potential to help maintain liberty or self-government.

Dahl also claimed that Madison's argument has been a victim of its own success. Indeed, latter-day pluralists need to be less concerned with majority tyranny because – as Madison rightly predicted – 'majorities are likely to be unstable and transitory in a large and pluralistic society' (Dahl, 1956, 30). On Dahl's reading, the challenge of pluralist democracy is, therefore, to understand the ways in which different minorities seek to use the instruments of government to 'frustrate the ambitions of one another', against the backdrop of 'the passive acquiescence or indifference of a majority of... voters' (Dahl, 1956, 133). In other words, the real danger in twentieth-century democracy is the prospect of the tyranny of a well-organised and motivated minority, and a successful system of polyarchy is one in which it is less likely that 'any given minority will have its most valued freedoms curtailed [by another minority] through governmental action' (Dahl, 1956, 83, 135).

In some of his more recent work Connolly has similarly argued that present-day capitalist systems proliferate 'minorities of many types' (Connolly, 2008, 27). Indeed, we now live in a 'world of interlocked minorities' – a world of immigrants, alternative lifestyle movements, religious groups, feminist movements, and ethnic minorities – and the national majority has become 'a symbolic centre consisting of fewer people than the sum of the minorities' (Connolly, 2008, 27). Under these conditions, says Connolly, the key to democratic politics is to prevent the tyranny of those 'intransigent unitarians' who would seek to impose their interests and values on everybody else (Connolly, 2005, 125). For example, Connolly diagnoses this threat in what he calls the 'evangelical capitalist resonance machine' (Connolly, 2008). This depicts the alliances between Christian evangelists, advocates of neo-liberalism, large media corporations, and elements within the Republican Party that has come to be a major force in American politics, and, in Connolly's iteration of the agonistic ideal, any attempt by this (or any other) minority – or assemblage of minorities – 'to claim that it embodies in itself the essential virtues of the nation is stymied by multiple constituencies banding together to resist the outrageous presumptiveness of that claim' (Connolly, 2000b, 192; 2008, 2, 39).[8]

---

[8] In Schoolman's terms, Connolly is concerned with the 'problem of violence towards difference', and his emphasis on contestability is designed to deny 'sovereignty to every idea and practice' (Schoolman, 2008, 18, 58). This is said to represent a qualitatively new set of pluralist values (Campbell and Schoolman, 2008, 9). However, this is really an elaboration of what Dahl and Lindblom call the 'the first problem of politics', that is 'the antique and yet ever recurring problem of how citizens can keep their rulers [which in a democracy, emerge from amongst themselves] from becoming tyrants' (Dahl and Lindblom, 1976, 273).

Connolly says that this model of agonistic democracy 'makes the checks and balances of Madisonian . . . pluralism . . . look like child's play' (Connolly, 2002, 127). His version is more sophisticated in many important respects, and most significantly in his emphasis on the civic virtues appropriate to the democratic *agon*, which we elaborated above. Nevertheless, Connolly's presentation of agonistic democracy as a system of partisan mutual adjustment retains the normative core of earlier iterations of pluralism. The purpose of agonistic democracy is (with Dahl) to prevent domination or, conversely (with Lindblom), to facilitate self-government in the form of the immanent self-direction of the societal processes. In this respect, Connolly's contribution is closer to the normative foundations of the American Republic than contemporary liberal theory, as it has been developed for example by Rawls, Dworkin, or Ackerman (Rawls, 1972; Dworkin, 2005; Ackerman, 1991). In contrast to liberal ideals of juridical impartiality, of the constitution as an overlapping consensus on basic principles of justice, of rights as trumps, or of higher law-making as somehow above the fray of democratic decision making, Dahl and Connolly have both emphasised the way in which the Supreme Court Justices, and the legal institutions more generally, are necessarily implicated in the on-going and open-ended contests of democratic politics.[9] Similarly, the ideal of Connolly's agonistic theory is closer to Madison than it is to the Rousseauian standards of deliberative democracy, where democratic politics is seen instead to be (or potentially to be) oriented towards something like the common good through rational public debate. As Connolly says, the agonistic conception of partisan mutual adjustment 'is at odds with the Rousseauian ideal of identity between subject and sovereign . . . even while it is committed to the primacy of democratic politics' (Connolly, 1993c, 184).

These important points of connection between Connolly and the earlier pluralists reaffirms Khan's observation that agonistic democracy should be understood as part of a more general republican renewal (Khan, 2013). Indeed, at this point, it will also be instructive to briefly compare Connolly and Owen's respective iterations of agonistic democracy, because Owen similarly draws on Nietzsche and he likewise stresses the link between agonism and republicanism, but his theory also appears to differ from Connolly in significant respects. Owen presents democracy as the 'domain within which substantive comprehensive doctrines contest with each other' and, in contrast to Connolly, he is more conformable with the idea of recovering the aristocratic elements in the 'public culture of Greek society . . . in which citizens strove to surpass each other and

---

[9] See: Dahl, 1956; Connolly, 2005, 145.

to set new standards of nobility' (Owen, 1995, 164; 2002, 125). As he sees it, the *agon* ought to take the form of the 'on-going construction, destruction and reconstruction' of communities of judgement, whereby citizens make collective decisions about contending values and how they ought to be ranked, and without recourse to foundational principles or to any public use of reason (Owen, 1994, 77; 1995, 133, 160). This reading of agonistic democracy has a greater fidelity to Nietzsche's critique of mediocrity and of the tendency for modern societies to produce 'petty, bland, and unheroic types', to produce the last man (Owen, 1995, 167). In contrast to Connolly – who, as we have said, translates the Overman into a voice within the self – Owen endorses an explicitly perfectionist iteration of agonistic democracy where everybody is 'called on, and aided, to develop their capacities for self-government' and where servility is understood as a 'fundamental democratic vice' (Owen, 2002, 120, 129). However, this does not commit Owen to a formally aristocratic society, only to a mode of democratic politics that is staged explicitly around an on-going and open-ended struggle to (re)determine collective standards of virtue. On his account, we 'can easily imagine a community in which formal respect for other persons . . . is twinned with substantive disdain for them (because we hold that the ordered set of values they recommend is lacking by our lights)' (Owen, 1995, 162; 2002, 125; 2008, 220).

In some respects, this avowedly perfectionist brand of agonism pulls in a very different direction to Connolly's ethos of agonistic respect. Indeed, there is no account in Connolly's version of agonistic democracy of any requirement to establish a collective ranking of values. As we have seen, the primary emphasis is instead on the disruptive capacity of agonism to disturb established configurations of normalisation, and to mitigate the forces of *ressentiment* that flow from human existential anxiety and suffering. This might appear to leave Connolly without a more constructive theory of the purposes of democratic decision making. As Dryzek sees it, for example, in Connolly there is 'no suggestion that there are collective decisions to be made, social problems to be solved' (Dryzek, 2002, 78). However, in Chapter 1, I resisted Fossen's claim that Connolly offers a strictly anti-perfectionist doctrine (Fossen, 2008). Unlike Berlin or Rawls, Connolly does see an important role for the democratic negotiation of contending values and ideals. However, in his theory of democracy the point is not to focus on any given particular ranking of those values, but rather on how the repeated contests characteristic of democratic decision making might, in the long run, prevent any combination of those ideals from monopolising public space. In this respect he is once again close to Dahl and Lindblom. Of course,

Owen also stresses the importance of on-going public contest. The point in his theory is not to deliver any conclusive ranking of the priority of the goods. So perhaps, in the end, these two iterations of agonistic democracy are not too far apart; they just highlight different components of the democratic *agon*, i.e. the need for collective decision-making about the relative priority of alternate goods, and the need for an open-ended augmentation of those decisions through the politics of agonistic enactment.

Globalisation, cosmopolitanism, and capitalism

Having set out the core components of Connolly's ethico-political schema, and looked at his formulations of the ends of agonistic democracy, we turn now to his reflections on the current conjuncture. Here we see that Connolly has offered some valuable insights into globalisation, and the possibility of novel forms of transnational democratic agency. However, we also explore more carefully his overriding concern with the problem of existential *ressentiment*, and we see how this tends to obfuscate Connolly's social critique, as it prevents him from developing an adequate account of the structures of domination associated with globalisation. This difficulty has been particularly pronounced in his reflections on capitalism.

Since the early 1990s Connolly has examined the impact of globalisation, and his analysis points beyond the usual focus on increasing interconnectedness. He has been especially interested in the massive quickening of speed in the reproduction of social processes associated with globalisation (Connolly, 2000b, 186; 2000a). This is evident, for example, in 'the acceleration of population flows accompanying the globalisation of economic life . . . the acceleration of speed in military delivery systems, cultural communications, civilian transportation, disease transmission, ecological change, and political mobilisation' (Connolly, 1995a, xi). Drawing on Virilio, Connolly shows how these developments have engendered a profound transformation in the social experience of time (Virilio, 2006). Virilio highlights the negative impact of 'real time' communications on democracy. These processes deny the *populus* the necessary time to reflect on political decisions, and so the citizens tend to become passive 'tele-spectators . . . transfixed' on the images packaged by large media corporations (Virilio, 1991, 1–16). We will explore these developments in more detail in the following chapter, but Connolly is right to stress that this is not the entire story, and that the impact of 'real time' communications is an ambiguous development, one that also helps to facilitate forms of democratic activism above the level of the nation-state (Connolly, 2000a, 597). Indeed, this is one of the principal strengths of Connolly's analysis of globalisation: his recognition that the 'globalisation of capital, labour, and contingency must be shadowed by a corollary globalisation of politics' (Connolly, 1991, 215). He rightly identifies the opportunities that globalisation presents for new forms of transnational social movements, which extend the politics of enactment beyond the frontiers of the nation-state (Connolly, 1995a, 13; 2000a, 604). Connolly also refrains from an idealised view of these developments. He recognises that the nation-state remains an important institution in world and domestic politics, that new movements can apply pressure on the priorities of particular states, for example, the world-wide movement against Apartheid in South Africa in the 1980s, but he does not think that these developments will ever congeal into constituted forms of authority at the global level, and he suitably stresses that the future direction of these transnational forms of democratic politics is still very uncertain.[10] I agree with each of these observations, which I incorporate into my own account of agonism and militant cosmopolitanism in Chapter 7.

However, in Connolly's consideration of globalisation we already start to perceive the difficulties with his exclusive emphasis on the problem of *ressentiment*. Connolly stresses the way in which the new temporality associated with globalisation leads to an intensification of the experience of contingency, which in turn taps into the temptations of *ressentiment*. Indeed, for Connolly, this is the principal cause of the rise of religious fundamentalism in the context of globalisation (Connolly, 1995a, xi; 2000b, 186). This is because 'those who resent the fragility of their own fundamentals are apt to blame some other group or doctrine for this obdurate condition' (Connolly, 1995a, 22; 1999b, 8). In some respects, this observation is also in line with Castells, who similarly sees the rise of religious fundamentalism as a 'defensive reaction against the impositions of global disorder and uncomfortable, fast paced change' (Castells, 1997, 64–5).

These analyses are pertinent, and this stress on the increase in temporal dislocation captures some of the most pronounced experiences associated with globalisation. However, for Connolly, unlike Castells, this experience is said to ratchet up the deeper problem of existential *ressentiment*, and this emphasis has two particular consequences. Firstly, it means that Connolly once again looks to personal and collectivised ethics for a solution. Indeed, he envisages transnational movements carrying

---

[10] See: Connolly, 1991, 218–19; 1993a, 152, 156; 1993b, 380; 1993c, 179; 1995a, 132; 1999b, 181; 2000a, 603; 2005, 7.

the democratic sentiments of agonistic respect and critical responsiveness beyond the boundaries of the state (Connolly, 1993b, 380). This is 'designed to limit the evils that states do to each other', and also to alleviate the effects of fundamentalism (Connolly, 2005, 34). Because:

> Even fundamentalists . . . can participate in such relations of complementary dissonance, to the extent, first, they acknowledge how their own faith appears contestable and offensive in some respects from other points of view, and to the degree, second, they affirm restrictions in the ways they press their demands in light of this first awareness. (Connolly, 1993a, 29)

However, these formulations of the purposes of the new transnational democratic movements do not match up to the scale of the challenges we face today. This follows from the second consequence of Connolly's focus on existential *ressentiment*, which is that it draws attention away from a much-needed structural analysis of the historically specific forms of domination associated with globalisation. Indeed, the present upsurge in religious fundamentalism and corresponding developments such as Islamic terrorism are better understood as a response to the specific inequities and privations associated with neo-liberalism, such as widespread poverty and the effects of western imperialism, rather than as any kind of traumatic encounter with existential anxiety.

Connolly also describes his rendition of the new global politics as a form of cosmopolitanism. He is rightly critical of the predominant Kantian modes of cosmopolitanism for their imperious view that the new transnational forms of politics can be grounded in a unique set of rational principles of right or morality, or in deliberative notions of reciprocity supposedly immanent in the fact of communication (Connolly, 2000a, 602). By way of contrast, Connolly says that the purpose of his agonistic cosmopolitanism is simply to 'inspire participants in each religious and metaphysical perspective to come to terms with its comparative contestability and to explore creative lines of connection to other orientations' (Connolly, 2000a, 611). However, in the previous chapter I argued that the idea of cosmopolitanism is inherently linked with the notion of universality, and, importantly, that it is possible to envisage forms of universality that are engendered from within the globalisation from below, that are congruent with the agonistic circumstances of pluralism, tragedy, and the value of conflict, grounded in nothing beyond the power of reflective judgement, and which always remain ungoverned by any (liberal or deliberative) principles or standards. We will return to these ideas in Chapter 7, where we will also see that the emergence of this militant universalism is crucially important in the context of the current global crises. However, for now we should note that Connolly seeks to disassociate agonistic cosmopolitanism from any kind of universality (Connolly, 1995a, xx).

For a long time, Connolly has stressed how the 'ethos of diversification and the reduction of inequality set conditions of possibility for each other' (Connolly, 1999b, 49). This is an admirable sentiment. However, in Connolly's recent work, where he has focused more directly on the dynamics of contemporary capitalism, it is clear that he is unable to deliver an effective analysis of the present conjuncture (Connolly, 2008, 2011). Indeed, Connolly's evaluation of capitalism is less than satisfactory in several key respects, and the underlying problem is, once again, that he repeatedly neglects the need for a structural analysis of the dynamics of the present system, and he focuses instead on what he sees as the underlying problem of existential anxiety and suffering. In fact, Connolly typically treats the problem of existential *ressentiment* as the primary cause of specific forms of domination, as we have seen, for example, in his analysis of normalisation; the implication being that we might find solutions to our present predicament in the civic virtues of agonistic respect and critical responsiveness, rather than in, say, a radical transformation of the present system of global inequality and domination. This deficiency in Connolly's analysis is evident, for example, in his explanations of the consolidation of the neo-conservative agenda in the US, post 9/11, with its 'expansion of the aggressive, punitive arm of the state' (Connolly, 2008, 29). Connolly rightly draws attention to the important connections 'between evangelical Christianity, cowboy capitalism, the electronic news media, and the Republican party' (Connolly, 2008, 2, 39). However, his explanation for this development is that the discrete elements of this assemblage come together around comparable 'affinities of spirituality'; they all seek 'revenge against other people or [against] existence as such' (Connolly, 2008, 3, 5, 40). However, the idea that we can explain the consolidation of neo-conservatism primarily in terms of each one of these constituencies trying to circumvent their own anxious inner ordeal over the circumstances of human mortality seems more than problematic. Missing from this picture is a structural analysis of the specific modalities of power associated with the present socio-economic conjuncture in their own terms.[11] By way of contrast, we

---

[11] Jonathan Simons thinks that 'Connolly is more sophisticated than Foucault' because Connolly 'distinguishes between necessary or existential injustice inherent in the human condition and systemic or social injustice which could be removed if the existing order were transformed' (Simons, 1995, 120). Connolly does make this distinction. However, there is a clear tendency running throughout his work to move too quickly from an analysis of specific forms of domination to discussions about existential anxiety. In fact, the problem is deeper, because Connolly typically reads extant modalities of

will see in the following chapter that Tully provides an excellent account of globalisation in his *Public Philosophy in a New Key* (2008), in terms of the intensification of a system of 'informal imperialism [which] has been in operation, with varying degrees of success, since the end of the nineteenth century' (Tully, 2008c, 75). This needs also to be combined with Agamben's explanation of the neo-conservative security state in terms of a new modality of power, built around the idea of a 'permanent exception'. Each of these developments needs to be understood in their own terms, and neither of them can be adequately explained by referring them back to deeper causes in existential *ressentiment*.

Moreover, when Connolly does turn to more specific socio-economic questions, his analyses tend to be underdeveloped. For example, in *Capitalism and Christianity American Style* (also 2008), Connolly deliberately restricted his enquiry to the US context. This is explained on the basis that the United States 'remains the dominant state in global capitalism; [and] its conjunctions and priorities set conditions to which others are compelled to adjust or resist' (Connolly, 2008, 28). There is some truth in this observation, although in this regard we should also note how quickly things seem to be moving post-2008, and especially the rise of China. But even if we grant Connolly this point, it is an outmoded strategy to focus on developments in one national economy, at a time when all the important analysis has focused instead on the global dynamics of capitalism. Similarly, in this book, when Connolly turns to consider possible solutions to the neo-liberal program, he offers an analysis focused on a conventional social democratic agenda, and the need for 'state support for modes of consumption that are inclusive rather than exclusionary in form' (Connolly, 2008, 108).[12] Again, it is not that these aren't laudable intentions, but there is now widespread recognition that national governments are to a large extent incapable of directing economic processes: for example, they are largely unable to raise taxes to fund the social welfare programs that Connolly proposes, because in the era of globalisation this leads to capital flight and to a relocation of production to the developing

---

power – for example normalisation and the will-to-punish – as externalisations of existential *ressentiment*, and at the expense of a more systemic or structural analysis of the causes of inequity and suffering. As Antonio Vazquez-Arroyo sees it, Connolly fails to 'consider structural and institutional aspects of power in contemporary capitalist democracies' (Vazquez-Arroyo, 2004, 10). This is too strong. Connolly does consider the structural dimensions of power; the point is rather that his analysis is inadequate because he refers them back to manifestations of existential *ressentiment*. Foucault, on the other hand, kept his focus squarely on complex institutional modalities of power, and the need to contest them, and he did not trace these back to deeper existential causes.

[12] For an earlier discussion along the same lines, see: Connolly, 1995a, 81–2.

world where costs are low and workers' rights are not adequately protected.

Thankfully, Connolly has moved beyond these limitations in his most recent writings. He now describes neo-liberalism as a 'global antagonist machine' that has been progressively consolidated since the end of the Cold War, and he stresses the need for militant action in response to these developments.[13] This change of tack is timely and apposite. However, the trouble is that Connolly's theory lacks the resources to adequately diagnose the current forms of domination, which he continues to describe in terms of an amplification of 'already existing resentments about human mortality' (Connolly, 2011, 140–7). By way of contrast we need to acknowledge that the challenges we face today, such as climate change, the massive levels of inequality both within and between regions, especially between the global north and the global south, and the changing security context with its shift toward pre-emptive war, are all better understood as historically specific forms of domination, which can be subject to democratic transformation and redirection.

In short, Connolly needs to let go of the repeated stress on existential *ressentiment*, and supplement his valuable account of globalisation in terms of the changed experience of time, with an analysis of globalisation as a system of social and economic domination.[14] However, there is an additional problem with Connolly's analyses, which is his reticence to acknowledge that the different modalities of power do come together in a single system of domination. Indeed, he says capitalism is 'neither [a] mechanism, nor organism, nor a system of tight contradictions. It is too messy and volatile to fit those images' (Connolly, 2008, 25). Messy it may well be – and in the following section we look closely at the benefits and also the dangers lurking in Connolly's use of complexity theory to explain the morphology of social and other processes – but, despite the increasing complexity of social processes, it is also crucial to see that the different forms of domination reinforce one another in a single system of global control. In the following chapter we will see that Tully makes a compelling case that globalisation is a novel form of imperialism, and in Chapter 7 I show how globalisation sutures together several distinct

---

[13] See: Connolly, 2011, especially Chapter 5.

[14] Whilst we would not want to endorse the problematic of true and false needs taken from the young Marx, we might nonetheless note how Connolly's approach represents the complete obverse of someone like Herbert Marcuse, for whom the key point of social critique was not to think through the ethical consequences that follow from the irreducible elements of repression associated with the human existential condition, but rather to analyse the avoidable 'surplus-repression' involved in the maintenance of historically specific forms of social domination (Marcuse, 1966, 155).

forms of domination, without being reduced to the dynamics of any one of them.

Immanent naturalism

From the late 1990s Connolly has expanded his conception of the politics of becoming into a more developed account of 'immanent naturalism' (Connolly, 1999a, 21; 1999b, 13).[15] This is a materialist ontology that depicts the world as a layered immanent field of 'infrasensible forces' (Connolly, 1999a, 21). In his elaboration of this theory Connolly has drawn on several sources including Spinoza, Nietzsche, James, Deleuze, and the latest developments in the natural sciences, represented for example in the work of the neuroscientist Antonio Damasio and the Nobel Prize winning chemist Ilya Prigogine. This aspect of Connolly's work also needs to be situated in relation to other contemporary theorists who have sought to apply Deleuze's work to democratic politics, as well as more generally to the vitalist and new materialist approaches which have recently emerged in political theory.[16] We will see that Connolly's conception of immanent naturalism has enabled him to develop some very significant insights into processes of temporality, open systems, and the circumstances of embodiment. Each of these interventions helps us to better understand the complex processes associated with globalisation, as long as we don't lose sight of the fact that these processes overlap and reinforce one another in a single system of domination. However, there are two crucial difficulties with the immanentist approach, which are (i) the assumption that forms of political organisation can be modelled on the self-organising qualities of nature, stressed, for example, in complexity theory, and (ii) the idea that the politics of innovation itself becomes something endogenous to process. Both of these ideas are deeply problematic, in fact, more than that, they are dangerous because they effectively collapse the distinction between natural process and the uniquely human capacity for action. Indeed, in a consistent naturalist approach, human agency and innovation (*potentia*) become just part of a wider story of *natura naturans*, and in this respect there can no longer be any site for individual or collective techniques-of-the-self. Indeed, we will

---

[15] This was first articulated in a journal article entitled 'Brain Waves, Transcendental Fields, and Techniques of Thought' published in *Radical Philosophy* in 1999, it re-emerges in *Why I am not a Secularist*, and it is an explicit theme throughout *Neuropolitics*, *Pluralism*, and *A World of Becoming*.

[16] For other prominent Deleuzean contributions see: Buchanan and Thoburn, 2008 and Patton, 2000; and for the new materialism see: Bennett, 2010a; 2010b and the essays collected in Coole and Frost 2010.

see that this aspect of Connolly's work is potentially in profound tension with his earlier stress on the inherently tactical and strategic nature of agonism. Interestingly, however, Connolly pulls back from these conclusions, which are nonetheless asserted more resolutely by other immanent naturalists.

One of the principal influences on Connolly's immanent naturalism, and more generally on the new materialist approaches is the metaphysical monism of Spinoza (Spinoza, 1955). Spinoza rejected Cartesian dualism, with its ontological distinction between mind and matter, and advocated instead a monistic ontology where 'God or Nature is the immanent cause of all things' (Hampshire, 2005, xxi). For Spinoza, God is *natura naturans* and *natura naturata,* [understood as] two aspects of a single substance' (Hampshire, 2005, xix). Deleuze's philosophy represents a rigorous reworking of Spinozan immanentism, where 'what is involved is no longer the affirmation of a single substance, but rather the laying out of a common plane of immanence [understood as a conceptual-affective continuum] on which all bodies, all minds and all individuals are situated' (Deleuze, 1988, 122). For Deleuze, it is not 'one thing that returns but rather returning itself is the one thing which is affirmed of diversity or multiplicity' (Deleuze, 1983, 48). Deleuze presents an inorganic vitalism where 'life' is figured as an emergent or virtual multiplicity that incessantly 'enters assemblages and leaves them' without inherent purpose or design (Connolly, 1993a, 161). For Deleuze, it 'is primary affirmation (becoming) which is being', understood as the 'continual, renewed creation' of the world from chaos (Deleuze, 1983, 186). Indeed, another influence here, on both Connolly and Deleuze, is the more metaphysical strand in Nietzsche's thought, because Nietzsche also depicted 'life' as an elementary flux in which 'all events, all motion, all becoming' are 'determination[s] of degrees and relations of force' (Nietzsche, 1956, 102; 1968, 299). Likewise, Connolly defends a 'joyous materialism' that 'mixes nature and culture' in an immanent process, that 'function[s] without the aid of a divine or supernatural force', but is nonetheless also the 'encompassing whole in which we are set' (Connolly, 2001, 548; 2002, 45, 53, 57, 61, 66, 85).

Connolly has stressed how this immanentist ontology of an emergent virtual multiplicity is also reinforced by the latest developments in the natural sciences. In contemporary cosmology, evolutionary biology, and neuroscience, for example, we find models of evolution where open systems possess powers of self-organisation and seemingly minor variations can initiate distinct new trajectories, so that change cannot be fully predicted (Prigogine and Stengers, 1984; Connolly, 2010, 223). In each of these fields, the 'emergence of new formations, is irreducible to patterns of efficient causality, purposive time, simple probability, or long cycles of recurrence' (Connolly, 2010, 225). Moreover, in *Pluralism* (2005) Connolly similarly finds an important source of these ideas in James' metaphysical pluralism. Early in the last century James developed an ontology that he called 'radical pluralism' or 'radical empiricism'. In contrast to the Hegelian conception of Totality with 'no loose ends hanging out', James postulated instead a genuinely 'pluralistic and incompletely integrated universe' (James, 1909, 45, 35, 103, 106). For James, radical pluralism is a 'coherent world, and not an incarnate incoherence' (James, 1909, 325). However, its coherence is constitutively unstable, and from every claim to identity 'something like a pluralism breaks out' (James, 1909, 37–8). As Connolly puts it, in James' view 'the overlapping forces propelling the world are themselves messy. Pluralism is the philosophy of a messy universe' (Connolly, 2005, 70).

Together this collection of ontological resources has enabled Connolly to probe the processes of temporality, open systems, and embodiment. James' 'pluralistic universe' was partly inspired by Bergson,[17] and in *Pluralism* Connolly draws on Bergson and James to disrupt 'the chronological idea of time, the idea that time consists of one punctual moment after another' (Connolly, 2005, 74). These thinkers have enabled Connolly to develop a conception of time as 'duration' in which temporal trajectories resemble a 'flux in which elements from the past fold into the present and both of those into future anticipation' (Connolly, 2010, 232). The experience of time as duration is 'marked by feedbacks and alterations that deform continuity without eliminating it' (Connolly, 2005, 75). The temporal flux is characterised by an open trajectory that is occasionally disrupted by unexpected 'forks' or 'swerves' in time (Connolly, 2005, 97–130). This leads to a stress on open systems that are susceptible to periods of acute disequilibrium. Unlike 'systems in equilibrium', unstable systems (for example in biochemistry) are 'marked by an element of internal unpredictability, by capacities of self-development, by periods of significant openness to outside forces, and by a trajectory of irreversible change' (Connolly, 2002, 55).

In Connolly's view, analysts of politics need to be informed by these developments in natural science, in order to adequately explain the morphology of social and political systems. This does not mean that the world of politics is unrecognisable as a system. Instead, from Connolly's perspective there 'are periods... of relative stability or equilibrium' in social and political systems just as there are in nature (Connolly, 2010, 225). The point is rather to address 'constitutive variations in rates of

---

[17] James, 1909, 228–30, 252–3, 262; Bergson, 1960.

acceleration and deceleration, being and becoming, flux and stabilisation, relative equilibrium and radical disequilibrium' (Connolly, 2008, 87). Moreover, today the 'world [is] composed of multiple systems' – social, economic, cultural, ideological, as well as natural – 'periodically colliding, colluding, and comingling', and so we need a theory 'that draws attention to the complex interactions between systems in various degrees of disequilibrium' (Connolly, 2008, 69, 87).

Connolly is right to insist that we address this complexity if we are to keep up with the challenges we face today 'such as the sources and effects of climate change, the volatile potentialities of capitalism, the activation of intense religious movements, and the exchanges between all three zones' (Connolly, 2008, 87). Indeed, processes of various kinds do condition social and political relations, and so these nuanced analyses of their morphology, extending notions of complexity from the natural sciences, offer real insights into some of the forces at work in the present conjuncture. Connolly's position is also more sophisticated than Negri's naive account of the emergent as a limitless multiplicity, as a fully unbounded or 'absolute process', which in turn underpins his equally limited conception of Empire as a single system of domination predicated on the exploitation of free living labour (Negri, 1999, 13). Nevertheless, we should note that Connolly's account of the world of becoming in terms of several unique and yet related processes, characterised by relative rates of acceleration, does not preclude a reading of globalisation as an overall process that configures these various processes into a single system. Connolly is reluctant to present it in this way. However, we will return to something like this in the following chapter in respect of Tully's account of imperialism as a complex system that sutures together several distinct modes of domination, and I present a similar view in Chapter 7.

The originary break, as Arendt and Benjamin conceive it, i.e. the *ex nihilo* event, has no place in this immanentist theory. Importantly, however, these naturalist approaches probably can furnish a model of absolute initiative, i.e. when systems are 'far from equilibrium' and so they reach a 'tipping point' in the emergence, say, of a new species in Darwinian theory, or when t=0 in the moment of the Big Bang. However, this is not Connolly's concern, and instead he stresses that the 'introduction of radical disequilibrium into too many zones at once would defeat the very possibility of human life' (Connolly, 2002, 56; 2008, 87). However, at this point in the analysis, the question of whether or not we can sustain the qualitative distinction between absolute and relative moments of initiative, actually gives way to a more basic question, which is whether or not it is possible to maintain a conception of the constituent power at all on the basis of Connolly's naturalism, or for that matter on the basis of

Negri's contribution or any other Deleuzean approach. This is because, from the naturalist viewpoint, we are on the verge of losing sight of the constituent power understood as a uniquely human capacity for action, as something essentially disruptive of natural and social processes, rather than as an internal mode within the overall movement and creative power of nature. I come back to this all-important question in a moment.

Connolly's naturalism has also enabled him to develop some remarkable insights into the circumstances of embodiment, or what he calls the 'visceral register of subjectivity' (Connolly, 1995a, 57, 204; 1999b, 163). By Connolly's account, human consciousness is constituted at the juncture of a 'dense interweaving of genetic endowment, image, movement, sound, rhythm, smell, touch... trauma' and 'affect-imbued' memory traces (Connolly, 1995a, 38; 2002, 13). He also draws attention to the way in which, in the media-saturated context of the present conjuncture, the democratic *agon* is increasing staged at this visceral level of the 'body/brain/culture networks' (Connolly, 1995a, 71; 2002, 13). Indeed, the Republican Right in the United States has been particularly adept at 'working actively' at this level, through the 'organisation of TV evangelical programs, talk shows, authoritative patterns of gossip, authoritative patters of narrative, and so forth' (Connolly, 1999b, 176). Again, these are very pertinent observations, and we return to a similar analysis of the new infra-sensible mechanisms of control in the following chapter. However, we should also note how these formulations suggest that political actors *do* retain a degree of strategic capacity to partially direct these complex bio-political processes. This appears to problematise the notion of 'pure immanence', and might just restore the dignity of an always finite, and (only ever partially) exogenous, capacity for action that we associated with the tragic vision of agonism in Chapter 1.

As I said above, there are two principal difficulties with Connolly's naturalist approach. The first is the idea that the self-organising qualities of nature can be extended to explain political forms of organisation. Although, as we have seen, the emphasis in the new sciences is on the often unpredictable emergences associated with open systems, it is nonetheless important to appreciate that these theories also stress the complex self-organising qualities of life and matter. Moreover, this same principle is also at work in Deleuzean theory, where, as Nathan Widder has said, life is animated by a 'disjunctive synthesis' that always 'remains unrepresentable while structuring representation and meaning' (Widder, 2002, 42, 147–8). This disjunctive synthesis is distinct from the dialectic, because the Deleuzean matter in movement, or 'heterogeneous folding', is not driven by any moment of negation, and its 'actualization is [always] a genuine creation' that escapes the finality of a teleological Whole

(Widder, 2002, 148, 153). These are important differences, but the proximity between Deleuze and the dialectic is also significant, because in both approaches the idea of an immanent self-organising synthesis is doing quite a lot of work.[18] Similarly, Connolly imagines the movement of 'passive syntheses' that 'weave their repetitions' in public life generating 'proximate regularities' that nonetheless remain 'underdetermined by any logical, narrative, or explanatory line of progression' (Connolly, 2002, 69, 94).[19] This conception of the immanent emergence of modes of association is designed to lessen the agony of the tragic view of politics, and lies at the heart of what we referred to in Chapter 1 as an excessive optimism in Connolly's theory. Indeed, this undercuts White's claim that Connolly's 'ontological figuration of abundance is too radically undetermined to prefigure by itself all the qualities Connolly wants to include in the ethical attitude of critical responsiveness' (White, 2000, 129).[20] In fact, Connolly's theory is ontologically too weighty in the sense that this presumption, i.e. of the self-organising qualities of society, makes possible the untenable claim that the virtues of agonistic respect and critical responsiveness might be all we need to enable 'multifarious styles of life to coexist' (Connolly, 1993b, 381).[21]

Nowhere is this ontological presumption more obvious than in Connolly's delineation of the immanent emergence of 'assemblages'. Connolly has sought to elaborate the mode of collective action we need today in order to take on the evangelical capitalist resonance machine, and he makes several important observations when he says the nascent assemblage will:

not take the form of a general consensus, in which each constituency supports the programs in question for the same reasons as the others. Nor would it reflect the will of a nation, organised around a unified language, ethnicity, race or religion. Nor would it amount to a simple coalition of interests. (Connolly, 1995a, 95)

However, in his attempt to address the crucial question of how to build an association that doesn't violate pluralism, Connolly ends up abrogating the need for strategic action in concert, and so the emerging assemblage becomes instead just part of the immanent movement of social

---

[18] On this important point of connection between Deleuze and Hegel, see: Badiou, 2000, 64.

[19] For comparable formulations, see also: Connolly, 1995a, 100; 1999a, 95.

[20] See also: White, 1998.

[21] Kalyvas also recognises the relationship between Connolly's existential optimism and his ontology of 'life'. He says, if 'one probes deeper, one discovers that this normative ideal [of agonistic respect] is derived from the fundamental value ascribed to the principle of the greatest inclusion of differences, which itself presupposes a particular ontology of life' (Kalyvas, 2009, 33).

processes. The elements of the assemblage 'must loop into each other, with each loop amplifying those that precede it, generating a positive resonance machine more powerful than the elements from which it was formed' (Connolly, 2008, 117). The 'loosely associated elements fold, bend, blend, emulsify, and resolve incompletely into each other, forging a qualitative assemblage resistant to classical modes of explanation' (Connolly, 2008, 40). The trouble is that all this resonating, flowing, looping, amplifying, folding, and bending does not a politics make. These formulations draw attention away from important questions about action, alliance building, and modes of reciprocal judgement that are always involved in the hard work of constructing assemblages, or action in concert. Connolly does not focus on these questions, and this is because he tends to see the emergence of assemblages as immanent to the morphology of social processes. By way of contrast, to borrow a comparable sentiment from a different conjuncture, we might say that 'processes don't march on the streets'.

Indeed, it is at this point that we arrive at the crux of the problem, which is that, taken literally, the naturalist approach collapses the distinction between human agency and natural process. This underlying monism is inherent in the Spinozan legacy. In his response to the overblown dualism of Descartes – where the *res cogitans* entirely transcends the realm of nature and its movements of cause and effect – Spinoza rejected the idea that human beings are at all 'exceptional in nature' and argued instead that all of the qualities that apparently distinguish human beings from the rest of nature, are actually products of natural processes (Hampshire, 2005, xxi, Descartes, 1986; Spinoza, 1955). From Arendt's perspective, this is a most perilous proposition. Indeed, as she says, nothing could be 'theoretically more dangerous than the [introduction of the] tradition of organic thought in political matters' (Arendt, 1970, 75). We touched on this briefly in the previous chapter, in respect of Arendt's reflections on the French Revolution, which tended to be seen by the protagonists as a wild force of nature. The problem with these assumptions is that they deny the uniqueness and dignity of human freedom, and so political actors find themselves 'doomed to swing forever in the ever recurring cycle of becoming' (Arendt, 1958, 245).

What makes man a political being is his faculty of action; it enables him to get together with his peers, to act in concert, and to reach out for goals and enterprises that would never enter his mind, let alone the desires of his heart, had he not been given this gift – to embark on something new . . . none of the properties of creativity is adequately expressed in metaphors drawn from the life process. To beget and give birth are no more creative than to die is annihilating;

they are but different phases of the same, ever-recurring cycle in which all living things are held as though they were spellbound. (Arendt, 1970, 82)

Moreover, in her critique of the use of the bio metaphor for explaining political action, Arendt not only targeted conventional forms of organicism in political theory, she also had in mind Nietzsche and Bergson who, by her account, cannot properly conceptualise political action, because 'their ultimate point of reference is not action; it is life and life's fertility' (Arendt, 1958, 313 f76).

Connolly rejects Arendt's formulation of the distinction between action and natural process. He says:

the Arendtean duality between active thinking and corporeal automatism obscures the extent to which numerous dimensions of corporeality are always already *objects* of extensive political action as well as protean *sources* from which new possibilities of thinking and being might be cast into the world of public appearance. (Connolly, 1999b, 182, emphasis in the original)

Connolly is right to discard Arendt's tendency to present this distinction – between action (politics) and process (the social, which is concerned with the reproduction of life) – in the form of a fixed topography. As I said in Chapter 1, this is untenable. However, in Chapter 6 we will see, with Honig, that this distinction can be *reworked*, and in such a way that we envisage action instead as an always-delimited capacity to act into the social, but where crucially this alteration does not (must not) result in a dissolution of the distinction itself. Because to lose the distinction between action and process is to lose any sense of what is unique about the human capacity for innovation.

Indeed, the hazards associated with just such a venture are brought to the fore in the recent work of Jane Bennett, who is the most consistent, and therefore also the most perilous, of the new materialists. In her *Vibrant Matter* (2010), Bennett rejects any qualitative distinction between human and non-human forms of agency, and she folds the former entirely into a story about the creative movement of matter itself, understood as an 'impersonal vitality' that runs through all things; one that 'coordinates parts on behalf of a whole, without following a rigid plan', that 'answers events innovatively and perspicuously, deciding on the spot and in real time which of the many possible courses of development will in fact happen', and that 'animates, arranges, and directs the bodies of the living' (Bennett, 2010b, 55). Bennett likens this overall animating force to the movement of Machiavelli's *Fortuna* (Bennett, 2010b, 55). But without the concrete person of the prince who struggles with this blind force of nature, we are left with a (a)theology of generalised vitality rather than a theory of politics.[22] Indeed, despite the important differences between vitalist and dialectical approaches, the same critique that Arendt levelled at the Hegelian and Marxist theories of history (as process) are relevant here. In other words, in a consistent theory of 'pure immanence' the dignity and uniqueness of specific moments of human action are translated into parts (or folds) within the great (virtual) chain of vitalist becoming.

Thankfully, we do not have to choose between Cartesian dualism, where the uniquely human qualities (presented in terms of thinking rather than acting) are said to fully transcend natural processes (a presumption that runs from Descartes through Kant to Habermas), and the idea of 'pure immanence' (shared by Spinoza, Deleuze, and Bennett), where, as Deleuze says, the 'immanent... [carries] with it the events or singularities that are merely actualised in subjects and objects' (Deleuze, 2001, 29). This is because there is a third alternative, which is the properly agonistic viewpoint, exemplified in Machiavelli and Foucault. Here, the crucial distinction between action (freedom) and process (determinism) is refigured in terms of those moments of partial transcendence that always open up in a given conjuncture, in the form of a range of possible moves available to concrete, situated, human subjects. In fact, Arendt was also pretty close to this position, despite her overdrawn distinction between the political and the social, and this is evident in her presentation of pluralism as a condition of action, and in her insistence that the actor is never sovereign, because she never possesses control over the outcome, consequences, or significance of her action, which is inevitably taken up by multiple others and reworked and expanded upon in unpredictable ways. We have seen that this properly strategic view of human freedom was crucially important in Connolly's earlier reflections on the techniques-of-the-self and micro-politics, and, in fact, he has repeated this view in his more recent writings on immanent naturalism, where he continues to depict the human subject in an 'active relationship' with the 'immanent field of forces' that operate below consciousness, and where the field of protean forces is susceptible to some extent to practices of self-discipline, self-regulation, and technique (Connolly, 1999a, 21, 25;

[22] This is not to reassert the gendered priority of the manly *vir* over the feminine playfulness of the new vitalism. Indeed, as Honig has said, following Pitkin, the Machiavellian gendered binary is disrupted by its own deeper message, i.e. that the 'highest overall excellence of Machiavelli's man of *virtù* is his ability to be like *Fortuna*, to be as capricious, unpredictable, and wily as she is' (Honig, 1993, 16; Pitkin, 1999). However, the key point here is that, from the agonistic view, this capacity for agency must be embodied in the talent of particular human actors rather than located in a disembodied vital or natural force.

2002, 13). Indeed, this same strategic view is repeated in the passage above, where Connolly does not so much collapse the Arendtean distinction between action and the corporeal 'object', but rather he moves it to a more nuanced level of mutual imbrications. Indeed, Connolly shares with Arendt the conclusion that human 'agency is never consummate', and we only ever 'participate in creation, more than being masterful agents of it' (Connolly, 2011, 27–8). Unlike other immanent naturalists, Connolly appears not to lose sight of the distinctive qualities of human agency and, in this respect, he is faithful to his agonism, but this is not strictly a theory of 'pure immanence'.

Conclusion

We have seen that Connolly develops a sophisticated theory of agonistic democracy that comes together around the ontological themes of temporality and becoming and the ethico-political virtues of agonistic respect and critical responsiveness. The core objective is to find a potential answer to, or at least an alleviation of, the underlying problem of existential *ressentiment*. *Ressentiment* manifests in various forms, from the practices of normalisation that underpin modern societies, to the rise of fundamentalism in the current conjuncture, and the perils of the 'evangelical capitalist resonance machine'. In response, Connolly petitions groups and individuals to cultivate a sense of the contestability of their most cherished values, and he hopes this will generate more constructive modes of democratic contest. These contests unfold throughout all areas of society, and transnational movements are also said to potentially carry these virtues as they apply pressure on the established priorities of particular states.

Connolly's position resonates with liberal notions of tolerance and individuality, but overall is better understood as part of a distinctly Madisonian tradition, which he shares with Dahl and Lindblom, where the emphasis is on the capacity of the democratic *mêlée*, over the long term, to prevent any tyrannical occupation of public space. These are valuable insights, and they are also combined with an emphasis on augmentation, whereby the politics of enactment repeatedly propels new norms and values into the existing configurations of identity within modern liberal democracies. Nevertheless, Connolly does not have an adequate grasp of the challenges we face today. This is evident, for example, in his analysis of capitalism, which remains conventional in many respects, and his tendency to repeatedly come back to discussions about personal ethics at the expense of a critical theory and analysis of historically specific forms of domination. This inclination follows inevitably from his overriding concern with the problem of existential *ressentiment*, i.e. with the Augustinian tendency to displace inner anxiety about mortality into a politics of blame, guilt, and the causes of 'evil'.

Connolly is surely correct when he says that some sources of suffering are rooted in our existential condition, but one is left wondering how and why this observation ends up becoming the central focus of his political theory, rather than a significant but secondary concern. For instance, Connolly's account of the politics of fundamentalism no doubt captures aspects of the psychology that underpins the present manifestations of religious fanaticism. However, the current rise of radical Islamism, for example, does not stem primarily from any underlying encounter with existential anxiety, but is better explained in social and political terms, i.e. as a manifestation of specific resentments (not *ressentiment*) against perceived injustices in Gaza and Iraq, and ultimately as a reaction against economic globalisation understood as a historically specific extension of Euro-American imperialism. In the following chapter, we turn to Tully's contribution, which, we will see, includes an analysis of the present conjuncture in exactly these terms. Tully takes his Foucault without Deleuze, and this is the source of his more effective and more pronounced emphasis on the priority of the strategic question. However, we will see that Tully's iteration of agonistic democracy also contains some significant limitations, and this time because he is drawn in the direction of deliberative theory and a professed need to construct a normative theory of agonistic dialogue.

4   Agonistic struggles for independence: James Tully

James Tully has set out his rendition of agonistic democracy in *Strange Multiplicity* (1995) and the two volumes of *Public Philosophy in a New Key* (2008).[1] In this chapter I present a thematic account of Tully's approach, moving back and forth between these works as well as other important papers. We see that the conceptual core of Tully's theory runs consistently throughout these writings, but I also identify some not insignificant differences between the earlier and later books. Tully has been especially concerned with the struggles of aboriginal or indigenous peoples for independence and in response to European imperialism and colonialism. In *Strange Multiplicity* he says that their struggles can be seen as exemplary of the broad spectrum of demands for cultural recognition characteristic of the new politics of diversity (Tully, 1995, 4). This is because their 'unique perspective' brings both historical forms of oppression and current modes of domination sharply into view (Tully, 1995, 4). In the opening section, I consider Tully's reflections on the politics of recognition and how he has reworked this idea in terms of multifarious struggles for 'acknowledgement'. We see that Tully develops a characteristically agonistic conception of the struggles for recognition, which take him beyond communitarianism and also past those contemporary theorists who focus primarily on the need to establish a legal recognition of group rights. By way of contrast, in Tully's theory the struggle for recognition is intrinsically open-ended, and this is linked to the republican conception of liberty as independence from arbitrary forms of power.

Tully's reframing of the politics of recognition includes many significant insights, and his focus on the link between agonism and the struggle of/for independence is more clearly formulated and explicit than that of the other thinkers examined in this book. However, to gain a fuller understanding of Tully's theory we also need to consider his use of Wittgenstein's later philosophy, and this is the focus of the second section. Indeed, Tully's project can be seen as a detailed application of

---

[1] Henceforth: *Public Philosophy*.

Wittgenstein's method to political theory and practice. We see that Tully takes many important ideas from Wittgenstein's *Philosophical Investigations* (1953), and, most significantly, in *Strange Multiplicity* he applies Wittgenstein's comparative method to develop a critical survey of the predominant forms of constitutionalism in modern political theory. More generally, he develops a conception of agonistic dialogue predicated on Wittgenstein's insights into the essential freedom and indeterminacy inherent in the application of the rules of linguistic exchange. Again, there is much that is valuable in these analyses, and Tully presents a mode of agonistic augmentation built around the capacity of situated subjects to judge and amend a given rule in multifarious ways.

Tully draws attention to the proximity between Wittgenstein, Arendt, and Foucault, and he claims that they all broadly contribute to an agonic conception of the freedom of citizens (Tully, 1999a). I probe the connections between these thinkers in the course of this chapter, and we see that despite their shared emphasis on the priority of the constituent power, there are also crucial differences between them. Indeed, it is clear that Tully's Wittgensteinian approach cannot adequately portray the revolutionary moment of change. Again, this is most apparent when we consider the temporality of moments of political innovation, where we see that the absolute priority of the constituent power is inconceivable from within the Wittgensteinian framework. In contrast to Arendt's theory, the Wittgensteinian subject is forever fated to *follow* a rule, albeit in many different and creative ways, and to transform rules on a case-by-case basis; she is also bound to keep some rules in place as necessary background conditions whilst others change, and this theory simply cannot envisage an occasion of absolute initiative antecedent to the rule itself. In other words, Tully presents a mono-typical delineation of the relative priority of the constituent power, and, as I said in Chapter 2, this represents a regression in respect of Arendt's theoretical framework elaborated in *On Revolution*.

More generally, as several commentators have pointed out, there is a strong normative component running through Tully's concept of agonistic dialogue. Tully associates agonism with the values of reciprocity and mutual respect, and in his account the relations between the protagonists are said to be mediated by various normative principles, and most notably the principle of *audi alteram partem*. We look closely at the status of these principles, which Tully says cannot be given any transcendental position or grounding, and we see that he also insists they are themselves always up for negotiation in the course of the struggles. Nevertheless, despite these qualifications, this aspect of Tully's approach closely resembles deliberative theory. This is a dangerous digression from the properly tragic viewpoint of agonism, and this tendency is in tension with the more strategic orientation that is otherwise well pronounced in Tully's theory, and which he acquires from Foucault.

The struggles of aboriginal peoples for independence has remained a focal point in Tully's writings, and in the second volume of *Public Philosophy* this has culminated in an excellent account of globalisation as the continuation of Euro-American imperialism by other means. Tully stresses the gross levels of inequality rooted in the neo-liberal policies propagated by the World Bank and the IMF, and he also delineates the new forms of power and control associated with the revolution in information technology. I consider his account of the new imperialism in the penultimate section of this chapter, and his analyses also serve as the starting point for my own theory of agonism and militant cosmopolitanism in Chapter 7. However, in the final part of this chapter I also demonstrate the limitations of Tully's reflections on how best to respond to these challenges, his version of the globalisation from below which he calls 'glocal citizenship'. Although Tully's version of cosmopolitanism contains many valuable insights and, most importantly, a strategic assessment of the opportunities available to situated subjects in the present conjuncture, his analyses fall short of adequately addressing the challenges we face today. Tully categorises two forms of civic freedom that emerge in this changed context. He identifies direct citizen–citizen relationships, which, he says, are flourishing in the 'interstices' of the global power regimes, as well as forms of agonistic conflict between hegemons and subalterns. However, Tully's focus is almost exclusively on the former of these two categories, and he actually has very little to say about the need to confront the mechanisms of top-down power and domination that he otherwise identifies and explains so effectively. This position is, in the end, incompatible with his republican viewpoint, because, without a more radical transformation of the existing power structures, Tully's 'glocal citizens' remain in *potestate domini*.

Agonism and the politics of recognition

Strange Multiplicity opens with a discussion of the politics of diversity in terms of contending struggles for cultural 'recognition'. Tully identifies the many different demands for recognition that have emerged in the present conjuncture, including: nationalist movements for political autonomy within multinational states such as Canada and the UK, the demands of linguistic and ethnic minorities, of feminist movements, and the struggles of indigenous peoples for recognition of their 'diverse cultures, governments, and environmental practices' (Tully, 1995, 2–3).

Tully's focus on cultural diversity and his emphasis on the politics of recognition place his contribution within wider debates about recognition that have been prominent in Anglo-American political theory over the past two decades. Indeed, Tully shares a broad set of concerns with authors such as Iris Young, Kymlicka, Bikhu Parekh, and Taylor who all identify the need for greater recognition for minority and disadvantaged groups as indispensable for ensuring equality and justice in contemporary western democracies.[2] These theorists reject liberal claims that state intuitions are, or can be made, impartial in respect of the cultural diversity of the citizens. Instead, the supposedly neutral set of 'difference-blind principles' of liberal theory, are really a 'reflection of one hegemonic culture' (Taylor, 1992a, 43). State institutions, constitutional norms, and forms of citizenship tend to privilege the 'dominant linguistic, cultural, ethnic, national and religious groups', whilst the voices of diverse others are 'silenced, ignored, deemed unreasonable, or marginalised' (Tully, 1999a, 172; 2002a, 541). In response, the theorists of recognition have argued that we need to 'treat members of different groups differently for the sake of promoting equality or freedom' (Young 2007, 62). Despite their differences, each of these authors points to the importance of institutional mechanisms for ensuring the legal recognition of the rights of minority groups. These institutional devices might include the devolution of power to sub-national units, exemptions for minority religious groups from certain laws (such as Jews and Muslims being exempt from legislation regarding humane slaughter for animals), quotas for under-privileged groups in areas such as higher education and the professions, and the recognition of minority religious festivals in the public calendar.[3]

In *Strange Multiplicity* and elsewhere Tully advocates a comparable list of proposals,[4] but his particular concern with the struggles of aboriginal peoples leads to a more militant stance, because the claims of indigenous and aboriginal peoples cannot be equitably accommodated in terms of 'distinctive minority... group rights within the exclusive sovereign authority of former colonial powers such as Canada or the United States' (Tully, 2000b, 50). What is required instead is recognition of their prior, continuing, and coexisting forms of autonomy and shared jurisdictions (Tully, 2000b, 52–4). Indeed, the overall objective of *Strange Multiplicity*

---

[2] See: Young, 1990; Taylor, 1992a; Kymlicka, 1995; Tully, 1995; Parekh, 2006.

[3] Despite a basic convergence on the need for a range of institutional designs to protect the rights of minority groups, Kymlicka is primarily concerned with questions of cultural identity, whilst Young was more focused on the problem of inequality, and with the emancipation of structurally disadvantaged groups (Kymlicka, 2002, 329; Young, 1990, 184, 187; 1995, 67, 75).

[4] See: Tully, 1995, 2; 2000a, 470; 2008b, 34.

is to figure a more radical mode of the politics of recognition, which moves away from a narrow focus on formal institutional methods of recognition and the importance of group 'rights'. Tully describes his alternative as a form of 'diverse federalism', and in which aboriginals, women, and migrants are able to express themselves in public life 'in their diverse cultural forms' and where each constituency 'listens to the voices of the others in their own terms' (Tully, 1995, 57, 24–5). In order to appreciate the detail of Tully's distinctive take on the politics of recognition we need to look at what is at issue in the concept or philosophy of recognition, and this means passing through several significant debates, and also looking at how Tully's claims have developed subsequent to *Strange Multiplicity*. A good place to start this discussion is Taylor's communitarian rendition of the politics of recognition in his *Multiculturalism* (1992). Taylor's discussion of recognition helps to explain the basic orientation of *Strange Multiplicity*, but we will also see how Tully later breaks decisively with the communitarian elements of Taylor's conception of recognition.

In *Multiculturalism* Taylor contrasts the experience of pre-modern societies – where 'what we would now call identity was largely fixed by one's social position' – with the dynamics of modernity where 'we define our identity [instead] always in dialogue with, sometimes in struggle against . . . our significant others' (Taylor, 1992a, 28, 33). Under conditions of modernity, cultural identity therefore 'crucially depends upon . . . relations with others', and so withholding recognition amounts to a form of oppression (Taylor, 1992a, 32, 36). When majority groups subject minority groups to misrecognition or non-recognition, those groups end up internalising a picture of their own inferiority, and so they effectively become 'imprisoned in a false, distorted, and reduced mode of being' (Taylor, 1992a, 25). As Kymlicka put it, the lack of appropriate recognition for minority groups in the dominant institutions and narratives of the state can result in 'serious damage to people's self-respect and sense of agency' (Kymlicka, 2007, 43). However, Taylor's justification of the politics of group rights is underpinned by some weighty claims he wants to make about the importance of *culture*, understood as the context where individuals develop their 'goals of self-fulfilment and self-realisation' (Taylor, 1992a, 28, 31, 66). This leads to the controversial claim that equitable political institutions must afford 'respect to [all] actually evolved cultures', and through 'variations in the kinds of law we deem permissible from one cultural context to another' (Taylor, 1992a, 37, 42, 61). This is predicated on the communitarian idea 'that all human cultures that have animated whole societies over some considerable stretch of time' are intrinsically worthy (Taylor, 1992a, 64). These claims have been especially unpalatable to liberals. As Brian Barry and

Susan Moller Okin have said, claims to cultural group rights are often advanced by traditional groups who seek to oppress their own internal minorities and especially women, and so from the liberal viewpoint the value of different cultural practices is not intrinsic, but ought to be measured by context transcending principles of justice or individual rights (Barry, 2001, 132; Moller Okin, 1999, 5).

Furthermore, as Markell has shown, Taylor's argument is inconsistent. The communitarian element in Taylor's conception of recognition is ultimately in tension with his dialogic account of the construction of identity. Taylor tries to combine two irreconcilable conceptions of identity: firstly, the idea of identity as a construction, and therefore of recognition as the 'intersubjective activity through which identities are formed and transformed', and secondly, a 'view of identities as antecedently given facts about us' (Markell, 2003, 41, 58). Indeed, the second view is intrinsic to the communitarian conception of injustice, understood as a 'failure to accurately perceive and/or appropriately respect people as who they already really are' (Markell, 2003, 59). This tension, between the dialogic and the communitarian conceptions of identity, is also evident in *Strange Multiplicity*. In many respects, the dialogic conception of identity formation is the central theme of Tully's book. He explicitly repudiates the conception of cultural group identity as internally homogenous, and – in keeping with the agonistic idea of a constitutive pluralism that I outlined in Chapter 1 – Tully emphasises that plurality is not a fact, but refers instead to the circumstances that constitute and condition the identities of groups and individuals. Indeed, from Tully's dialogic standpoint, the identity of each cultural constituency 'consist[s] in the innumerable ways it relates to and interacts with . . . others', and to the point where the experience of otherness becomes 'internal to one's own identity' (Tully, 1995, 10, 13, 14, 204).

Even an ascriptive identity, such as ethnicity or language, is not given, but the construction of dialogue and negotiation. What the ascriptive identity is, who possesses it and who does not, and how it is recognised, interpreted, and implemented are questions that are answered in the course of . . . on-going discussions among the members of the group. (Tully, 2000a, 474)

However, in *Strange Multiplicity* this view is in tension with an insistence on the intrinsic value of 'cultural continuity'. Tully says the 'loss or assimilation of any of the other cultures is experienced as an impoverishment of one's own identity' (Tully, 1995, 205). This suggests a communitarian reading of identity, and in this respect, Tully feels compelled to address liberal concerns about the need to safeguard 'minorities within the group', and to prevent the problem of 'illiberal and undemocratic enclaves' (Tully, 1995, 191; 2000a, 474). In so doing, he invokes more general principles of consent and reciprocity, which come into play in the politics of recognition, and which ought to 'protect the provinces and nations of a multinational confederation [and] also apply to the citizens within them' (Tully, 1995, 191). In the end, the principles of consent and reciprocity are given priority over the principle of continuity, in the sense that those cultural practices that do not reflect these more general principles, racist or patriarchal practices for example, ought presumably to be discontinued.[5] The consequences of this priority are not spelt out in *Strange Multiplicity*, however, where the three principles of consent, reciprocity, and continuity are treated as equally fundamental.

In a moment we will examine the sources and the status of these principles, and how, according to Tully, they differ from the foundationalism and transcendentalism of liberal and deliberative approaches, and explore whether or not his position is commensurate with the tragic viewpoint of agonism. However, for the moment I bracket this discussion and explore further the subsequent development of Tully's conception of the politics of recognition. This is because following *Strange Multiplicity* Tully has weeded out the remnants of the communitarian notion of authentic identity, dropped any references to the idea of the intrinsic value of cultural 'continuity', and reworked the recognition in terms of an agonistic politics of 'acknowledgement' (Tully, 2000a, 479). Indeed, at this point he fully embraces and extends the view that dialogic relations are constitutive of the politics of recognition, and that consequently cultural identities do not 'pre-exist their articulation and negotiation in some unmediated or ascriptive pre-dialogue realm' (Owen and Tully, 2007, 282). In his development of these themes, Tully makes several pertinent observations about agonistic democracy, and we need to isolate these advances from his problematic assumption that these agonistic modes of politics are mediated by principles of reciprocity. Tully's most significant insights into the agonistic politics of recognition are: (i) his stress on the priory of independence over and above the need for a legal recognition of group rights, (ii) his advocacy of an extended conception of recognition, understood as an intrinsic component of all forms of democratic struggle, rather than a distinctive quality of certain kinds of struggle, (iii) his emphasis on the pluralistic quality of the struggles, over and above

---

[5] In this respect, Tully's position in *Strange Multiplicity* is not too dissimilar from Kymlicka's attempt to 'combine group-specific multiculturalism policies with difference-blind common rights'; this position leads Kymlicka to the claim that minority rights are only 'consistent with liberal culturalism if (i) they protect the freedom of individuals within the group; and (ii) they promote relations of equality (non-dominance) between groups' (Kymlicka, 2002, 342; 2007, 46).

binary forms of division, and (iv) his elaboration of the non-teleological and open-ended nature of the struggles for recognition. These points are all valid and important, and I consider each of them in turn.

Whether they take the form of exemptions from generalised norms (in the case of cultural minorities), or the use of quotas to ensure social justice (for disadvantaged groups), the theorists of group recognition tend to focus on legal and institutional mechanisms to protect the rights of minorities. This inclination is evident for example in Kymlicka's work, where he sets out in fine detail, and in the manner of a law maker, a framework of different rights and entitlements tailor made for different kinds of minority groups, including: 'self-government rights, polyethnic rights, and special representation rights', etc. (Kymlicka, 1996, 155). By way of contrast, Tully's formulation is marked by a strong emphasis on the importance of autonomy. The struggle for recognition is ultimately a demand for liberty, in the republican understanding of that term, i.e. as self-government or independence (Tully, 1995, 6). Formal legal recognition in the narrow sense remains important; however, the institutional and juridical focus of the conventional theories has generated its own set of problems.

The most powerful and vocal minorities gain public recognition at the expense of the least powerful and most oppressed; the set of rights tend to freeze the minority in a specific configuration of recognition; they fail to protect minorities within the groups who gained recognition; and they do little to develop a sense of attachment to the larger cooperative association among the members of minorities, occasionally increasing fragmentation and secession. (Tully, 2008a, 300–1)

Consequently, from Tully's perspective, the moment of formal legal recognition needs to be understood as only ever a 'codification of the state of processes of identity negotiation at a particular time, a reification of a moment of the more primary activities', the struggles of the citizens themselves (Tully, 1999a, 171; 2000a, 477).

Indeed, the element of legal recognition needs also to be grasped as just one aspect in a more general ontological understanding of the concept of 'recognition', presented as an intrinsic component of every form of political struggle (Tully, 2008a, 294). This feature of Tully's theory is close to Axel Honneth's elaboration of recognition (Honneth, 1995). From Honneth's viewpoint, society is primarily constructed on the basis of struggles for symbolic meaning and significance,[6] and

---

[6] Honneth develops his theory from a reading of Hegel's early Jena writings (before he became preoccupied with the dialectic of self-consciousness elaborated in the *Phenomenology of Spirit*), where Honneth discovers a distinctive model of *Sittlichkeit*, one

consequently – from the viewpoint of this more general understanding of 'recognition politics' – all kinds of political demands, including those for economic redistribution, can only be rendered intelligible as part of a wider struggle for the value and significance of various social identity claims (Owen and Tully, 2007, 268). In other words, this extended conception of recognition sets Tully apart from those theorists, such as Fraser, who draw a qualitative distinction between the politics of *recognition* and struggles for economic *redistribution*. For Fraser, recognition politics is concerned exclusively with questions of *public status*, and is typically advanced by groups in society who have been portrayed in an inferior position in the politics of normalisation, even though they might not be economically disadvantaged (Fraser, 2008, 60). By her account, progressive political movements should only endorse those forms of recognition claims that complement the struggle for economic equality. This might well include gay rights, for example, but would exclude the struggles of traditional patriarchal cultures for recognition of practices such as forced marriage or the exclusion of women from education. Whilst it is important to be able to distinguish between legitimate and illegitimate forms of recognition claims, from Tully's perspective Fraser's conceptual schema is overly simplistic, because a 'complex interaction between distribution and recognition appears to be characteristic of political struggles today' (Tully, 2008a, 299). Indeed, he says, each 'successful struggle for recognition redistributes the opportunity of citizens to gain economic and political power', and so we need a framework that comprehends recognition and redistribution as different dimensions of each struggle 'rather than distinct types of struggle', and, most importantly, from his agonistic viewpoint the struggles themselves are the 'primary thing' understood as the manifestation of freedom (Tully, 2000a, 469).

Tully also rejects the long established idea that struggles for recognition are essentially binary in nature. This can be traced to Hegel's dialectical account of the politics of recognition, in terms of the struggle between lord and bondsman, in the *Phenomenology of Spirit* (Hegel, 1977, 111–19; Tully, 2008a, 205). By way of contrast, Tully says we need to think instead of a 'multilateral web of relations' of mis/recognition and their 'effects among actors of different types' (Tully, 2000a, 474). This stress on plurality is important, but also needs some qualification.

that emphasises how 'a struggle among subjects for the mutual recognition of their identity' can generate 'inner-society pressure towards the practical, political establishment of institutions that would guarantee freedom' (Honneth, 1995, 5). On Honneth's view, this conception of social conflict in the early Hegel contrasts with the atomistic model of society understood in terms of a struggle for self-preservation and associated, for example, with Hobbes (Honneth, 1995, 7–10).

Most significantly, Tully reaffirms the agonistic idea of the constitutive nature of pluralism that we examined in Chapter 1. In contrast to the radical democrats, who typically present binary conflict as the intrinsic form of 'the political', Tully is right to stress that the multiple contests of/for recognition always emerge from, and are conditioned by, the circumstances of plurality (as well as tragedy and conflict). However, the question of the relationship between agonism and the binary form of political struggle is a debated point. Indeed, in the following chapter we will see that Mouffe understands the effective negotiation of binary division, in the form of the friend/enemy relationship, as something like a prior condition of agonistic democracy, understood in terms of pluralistic struggles between adversaries. In my discussion of Mouffe's contribution I also show that it is possible to figure the binary division in either aspirational or reactionary terms: respectively in the form of struggles between oppressed and oppressor (where the objective is to overcome domination), or between friends and enemies (where the focus is instead on the need to ensure order and security). Unfortunately, we see a clear journey in Mouffe's work from a focus on the former kind of division to the latter. Nevertheless, my sense is that we should not move too quickly to dissociate agonistic democracy entirely from the first of these two modes of the politics of division. Indeed, the many varied struggles characteristic of the democratic *agon* will also nonetheless be minimally binary, in the sense that they emerge partly through an opposition to contemporary forms of domination, and so, as John Holloway puts it, they represent an affirmation of all that is currently denied (Holloway, 2005, 167, 212). In other words, the agonistic struggles *of* freedom will always also contain a demand *for* liberation from the oppressor, as Tully has himself argued in one particularly important essay (Tully, 2000b). Without this important qualification, the pluralistic *agon* of the politics of innovation and the struggles for recognition risks becoming incapable of disrupting the present forms of the constituted powers and authorities; and, in fact, we will see below that Tully himself falls into this error in *Public Philosophy* in his formulation of 'glocal citizenship' and of horizontal citizen–citizen relations.

In addition to the three important points we have examined thus far, Tully also says that the politics of recognition does not gravitate towards a comprehensive 'end state', understood as the 'form of mutual recognition [that] all those concerned demand' (Tully, 1999a, 175). As we have seen, this disavowal of teleology is definitive of the agonistic viewpoint, and Tully reaffirms the idea that politics is interminable and not orientated towards some higher form of reconciliation. Full recognition is constitutively impossible, and not least because the *agonic* struggles of citizens always shape cultural 'identities in unpredictable ways' (Tully, 2000a, 476–7). Moreover, if full recognition is not the end point of democratic politics, then this widens the assortment of possible goods that might emerge from the on-going struggles for acknowledgement. For example, Tully says that the 'game of reciprocal disclosure . . . is a way of dispelling *ressentiment*' which might 'otherwise be discharged in more violent and anti-democratic forms of protest' (Tully, 2000a, 479). However, his proclamation of the goods of agonistic democracy is richer than Connolly's account, with its overriding concern with the problem of *ressentiment*. On Tully's account, the principal advantage of the democratic *agon* is not to provide an antidote to existential *ressentiment*, but rather to facilitate autonomy or independence, and because agonism helps us to envisage the ways in which 'the prevailing forms of recognition' can be challenged, and how 'mis-recognised and non-recognised minorities' can gain 'access to and exercise of political power' (Tully, 1999a, 172; 2000a, 470). This clear and unequivocal stress on the importance of autonomy is one of the key strengths of Tully's approach, and he also shows how this overall objective contains within it a range of related goods. The contests 'generate levels of self-respect and self-esteem' among marginalised groups even if they fall short of achieving their demands in terms of formal legal recognition; counterintuitively, they might generate a sense of common belonging between contestants as they come to 'recognise each other *as* members' of a mutual dialogue; and in turn this might generate a process of 'citizenisation', whereby an interlocutor 'comes to acquire an identity *as* a citizen through participation' in 'bonds of solidarity across real differences' (Owen and Tully, 2007, 290; Tully, 1999a, 170; 2000a, 479, 481; 2005, 209; 2008a, 211, 293, 311).

In a moment we turn to Wittgenstein's philosophy to get a fuller sense of Tully's conception of agonistic 'dialogue'. We will see that Tully introduces some strong normative claims, and he develops a conception of agonistic freedom presented exclusively in the mode of augmentation. These aspects of Tully's theory are problematic, but they have only a contingent relationship to the points I have outlined thus far. Indeed, with the necessary qualifications about the binary division in place, we can conclude that each of these four substantive components of Tully's reworked version of the politics of recognition is significant. However, before we examine Tully's appropriation of Wittgenstein, it is important first to briefly also consider Markell's critique of Tully, because this illustrates significant differences between alternate strands of agonistic theory.

In his *Bound by Recognition* (2003), Markell credits Tully for having introduced important qualifications into the conventional theory of recognition, but he says Tully's reflections:

do not go far enough, for they leave the notion of successful recognition in place as a regulative idea, a constantly receding horizon toward which our politics nevertheless ought to strive, interminably. They treat recognition as necessarily provisional, but . . . they do not force us to consider the more challenging possibility that the pursuit of recognition . . . might be an incoherent and therefore potentially costly enterprise. (Markell, 2003, 16)

Rather than engaging in a struggle for recognition, Markell counsels political actors to turn their attention instead to the underlying 'motives, investments, and experiences that sustain misrecognition' in the first place (Markell, 2003, 21). In much the same manner as Connolly's diagnosis of normalisation, Markell explains the structures of misrecognition built into contemporary Euro-American societies as a displacement of an existential confrontation with the 'ineliminable fact of finitude' (Markell, 2003, 22). Unlike Connolly, Markell does not locate the source of finitude in the fact of mortality, but rather in the circumstances of openness and unpredictability that, following Arendt, he associates with human plurality (Markell, 2003, 5). Nevertheless, the sequence of his argument is very much the same as Connolly's, in the sense that Markell thinks the experience of finitude is traumatic for the subject who is said to possess a 'desire for [full] sovereign agency', and the impact of this trauma, i.e. in the contradiction that unfolds between the subject's desire for fullness and his encounter with finitude, gives rise to the various structures of super- and subordination in society (Markell, 2003, 5). In short, these are designed to sustain the prestige of the dominant group, thereby shoring up their otherwise fragile sense of sovereignty and 'enabling them to live' with this contradiction 'at other peoples' expense' (Markell, 2003, 22).

The political consequences that follow from this analysis are also in line with Connolly. Essentially, contemporary protagonists are advised to give up claims to the recognition of (the fullness of) their identity, and to appreciate instead that the 'pursuit of recognition involves a 'misrecognition' of a different and deeper kind: not the misrecognition of an identity, either one's own or somebody else's, but the misrecognition of one's own fundamental situation or circumstances' (Markell, 2003, 5). The key point then is that acknowledgement is in the 'first instance self- rather than other directed', and so political actors need to set about working on the self in order to overcome the initial desire for fullness (Markell, 2003, 38). This is key to a form of agonistic politics where we could celebrate the 'uncertain risks and pleasure of activity' over the 'satisfactions' of recognition and identity (Markell, 2003, 33).

Markell's book has been very influential, and his arguments have gone a long way towards exposing the inconsistencies in Taylor's communitarian conception of recognition that we discussed above. But I think there are several difficulties in Markell's formulations, both analytically and politically. Most importantly, Markell assumes an *intrinsic* relationship between the struggle for recognition and the desire for fullness or 'sovereignty'. This perhaps follows from his careful analysis of the communitarian idea, represented in his account not only by Taylor but also by Johann Gottfried Herder, where the demand for recognition does take the form of an appeal for an acknowledgement of a pre-established (full) identity. Markell's characterisation of the subject as driven by an impossible desire for fullness also neatly describes the Lacanian view, and he rightly identifies Laclau as someone who explicitly conceives of the subject in these terms (Markell, 2003, 184). But it is not clear why it should follow that this claim to sovereign fullness is necessarily carried over, in the form of a 'regulative idea', into Tully's reworked theory of 'acknowledgment'. Certainly, Tully doesn't put it in those terms himself, but Markell's point is rather that these assumptions are inherent in the very notion of 'recognition'.

Nevertheless, Markell also accepts that politics will always include a recognition dimension, because 'recognition helps give our lives depth and continuity, and a world completely lacking signposts of identity would be unnavigable' (Markell, 2003, 1). Indeed it would, and my sense is that this is really what is at stake in Tully's reworked conception of the politics of acknowledgement. In other words, Tully envisages an agonistic contest where different groups and individuals strive to recalibrate the existing configurations of meaning and signification in society, or the relationships of identity/difference, in order to disrupt the relations of super- and subordination built into the dominant norms and practices, by exposing the mechanisms of domination that sustain the privileged status of particular groups and drawing attention to the need for greater acknowledgement of under-represented or subordinate groups. But this game is not necessarily the same thing as a struggle built around a perpetual striving for fullness. In short, political concepts such as 'recognition' are not determined by some inner notion, and it does not follow that the communitarian understanding of recognition (of fullness) is necessarily carried over into Tully's theory, understood as an impossible but regulative ideal.

Moreover, it is not only these analytical categories that are at issue. Perhaps the more important difference between Tully and Markell resides in their respective political strategies. As we have said, Markell joins Connolly in the recommendation that political actors turn their attention inwards, and focus above all on the need to acknowledge their own finitude. However, in a context of structured inequality, these proposals represent a politically disabling strategy for those on the receiving end of misrecognition. As Antonio Vazquez-Arroyo puts it, in response to Connolly's notion of agonistic respect (which, remember, is built around an inner acknowledgement of the contestability of your own political claims), he says, these practices do not seem appropriate:

for those who do not share in power, for the dispossessed, the inhabitants of urban ghettos, poor inner city neighbourhoods, or forgotten countryside areas. Rather, the strong emphasis placed on forbearance seems [better] directed to those already sharing power, privilege and status. (Vazquez-Arroyo, 2004, 15)

The problem with Markell's analysis is that we once again end up with a discussion about personal ethics, where we really need a militant form of politics and a critique of historically specific forms of socio-economic and cultural domination, i.e. in their own terms as distinct mechanisms of power, rather than referring them back to supposedly deeper causes in the existential encounter with human finitude. Markell appreciates that the established relationships of recognition structure forms of entrenched domination, but he does not present a systematic account of the actual workings of these structures, and this reflects his concern instead to problematise the motivations of the actor and his supposed demand for sovereignty. In this sense, he is a long way from Tully, who, as we will see later in this chapter, offers a series of very insightful reflections on the actual operations of power, domination, and imperialism that define the present conjuncture, and this reflects his central concern, i.e. not with personal ethics, but rather with the public struggle for acknowledgement, and how this is linked to the goods of autonomy and independence.

Wittgenstein and agonistic 'dialogue'

To get a fuller sense of Tully's theory of agonistic dialogue, we need to turn now to his use of Wittgenstein. Indeed, in many respects, Tully's work represents a rigorous application of Wittgenstein's late philosophy to an analysis of political thought and practice. In the *Philosophical Investigations* Wittgenstein developed a critique of the predominant understanding of language in western philosophy, where language is conceived as a nomenclature. In this conventional picture of human language – which goes back at least as far as Augustine – individual 'words in language name objects, [and] sentences are [simply] combinations of such names' (Wittgenstein, 1967, No. 1). This view informed Wittgenstein's earlier work in the *Tractatus*, where, as part of the more general philosophical movement of logical positivism, Wittgenstein sought to provide a meta-theory of language in terms of the relationship between elementary propositions and objective states of affairs (Wittgenstein, 1974). By way of contrast, Wittgenstein's later philosophy represents a survey of the ordinary use of language, and this was designed explicitly to help liberate us from the dominant impression of the relationship between language and the world (Wittgenstein, 1967, No. 122, No. 115). The purpose of Wittgenstein's *Philosophical Investigations* was not to find a rational solution to the question of the essence of language, but rather to survey the grammar of the everyday use of words, in order to bring them back from their association with the metaphysical picture of language to the rich detail of actual linguistic practices. By Wittgenstein's account, the meaning of any given term is defined not by its correspondence with an object in the world, but rather by its use in the game-like practices of everyday language (Wittgenstein, 1967, No. 7, No. 43).

One of the immediate consequences of this approach is that we can never fully abstract ourselves from the everyday use of language and the 'actions into which it is woven' which together make up our world, and Wittgenstein's thought is in many ways a profound critique of the entrenched tendency towards abstraction and foundationalism in western philosophical enquiry (Owen, 2003, 88). Wittgenstein, therefore, provides a 'radically different "worldview" to the one that pervades much contemporary political theory' (Tully, 1995, 111). For example, Habermas' work represents a paradigmatic case of this tendency to abstraction. As Tully has shown, Habermas shares with Wittgenstein an appreciation of the way in which language is 'woven so deeply into human action that the whole – language and the ways of acting – itself provides the grounds in the light of which criticism and change take place' (Tully, 1998, 8). However, in Habermas' theory political practices ought to be regulated by universal principles (of inclusion, transparency, and reciprocity), determined by 'reason . . . turn[ing] back on itself', making explicit what is implicit in our daily communication, and presented in the form of a 'transcendental . . . court of appeal' (Tully, 1989, 174–8). In the Habermasian view, 'our customary agreements are rational only if the participants could give reasons that justify them; that is, that they could redeem [them], through argument aimed at validation' (Tully, 1989, 177). Tully explicitly rejects this view. As he puts it, there is no 'metacontextual political theory', there is no Archimedean point outside of political practices from which to adjudicate rationally and impartially between, for example, competing demands for recognition (Tully, 2002a, 544).

However, Tully does not only seek to displace the drive towards abstraction characteristic of Habermas' thought. He has also challenged more generally the view that 'political life is free and rational only if it is founded on some form or other of critical reflection' (Tully, 1989, 172). Tully calls for a reorientation of political philosophy, so that 'no type of critical reflection can play the mythical role of founding patriarch of our political life', and he has drawn extensively on Wittgenstein to give expression to this more modest form of political theorising (Tully, 1989, 199; 2002a, 554). In particular, Wittgenstein's philosophy is central to Tully's method of historical survey and his normative account of agonistic dialogue, and I consider each of these in turn.

One of Tully's central objectives in *Strange Multiplicity* is to reveal the contingent circumstances of historical ascendancy that underpin the currently predominant schools of constitutional theory. He focuses on liberalism, communitarianism, and nationalism, and shows how they have 'elbowed aside entire areas of the broader language of constitutionalism... such as the common law, earlier varieties of whiggism and civic humanism' (Tully, 1995, 37). Tully aims to engender an awareness of the wider range of possibilities for the politics of recognition by revealing the arbitrary foundations that condition the presently hegemonic ways of thinking about constitutionalism (see, for example: Tully, 2002a, 548). As Owen has pointed out, in this sense Tully's application of Wittgenstein not only resembles Foucault's critical genealogies of modern institutions, but also Skinner's explorations into the history of the concept of liberty (Owen, 2003, 87). These methods also correspond with Connolly's genealogy of the politics of *ressentiment*, which we explored in the previous chapter. All of these approaches 'are characterised by a historical comparative sensibility' designed to free us from our captivation by the currently predominant pictures (of sovereignty, liberty, constitutionalism, or morality), by bringing back to the surface historical alternatives that have been suppressed or concealed (Owen, 2003, 86, 96). As Tully puts it, his is a:

historical application of Wittgenstein's method of dissolving philosophical problems, not by presenting yet another solution, but by a survey that brings to critical light the unexamined conventions that govern the language games in which both the problem and the range of solutions arise. (Tully, 1995, 35)

Moreover, when it is applied in this way, political theory becomes a 'discursive technique in a practice of resistance' (Tully, 2000b, 43). Indeed, in *Strange Multiplicity* Tully seeks to expose the 'male, imperial and Eurocentric bias' that underpins the predominant forms of modern constitutional theory (Tully, 1995, 31, 44). His survey reveals that – despite basic differences between them – liberal, communitarian, and nationalist narratives of constitutionalism, each represent homogenous understandings of political life that are detrimental to the 'endless diversity and strife' of human relations (Tully, 1995, 9, 104). More specifically, in *Strange Multiplicity* Tully identifies seven conventions of modern constitutionalism that serve to exclude or assimilate cultural diversity (Tully, 1995, 104, 41). I briefly summarise these points here, which give a foretaste of Tully's on-going concern with imperialism, which is examined in more detail below.

Firstly, the different language games of modern constitutionalism converge around the idea that the sovereign people are culturally homogenous; whether that unity is grounded in a shared national identity, a common set of values, or the enjoyment of a uniform set of rights; secondly, the modern constitution is tied to a stages view of history, in which the advanced status of modern liberal democracy is contrasted not only with 'pre-modern European constitutions' but also with 'the customs of non-European societies at "earlier" and "lower" stages of historical development'; thirdly, modern constitutionalism (in its various manifestations and justifications) presupposes legal uniformity, and this is typically contrasted to the irregularity of non-European constitutions, and to 'the assemblages of laws, customs, and institutions of Europe prior to the peace of Westphalia'; fourthly, modern constitutionalism is bound to the theories of modernisation and sociological progress, exemplified in the nineteenth century, but which first emerged in the eighteenth-century idea that the development of modern civil(ised) society would gradually undermine the 'ancient constitution of customs and ranks' and eventually produce a 'society of one "estate" or "state" of equal and legally undifferentiated individuals with similar "manners"'; the fifth element of modern constitutionalism identifies legitimacy exclusively with European political institutions; the sixth convention is the idea that the constitutional state possesses a necessary identity as a 'nation'; and finally this is supported by the view that the modern constitution originated in a single discontinuous moment, which is 'reinforced by the popular images of the American and French revolutions as great founding acts performed by founding fathers at the threshold of modernity' (Tully, 1995, 59, 64–9).

I suspect that point four is really inextricable from point two, and in Chapter 2 I questioned the idea that the modern understanding of revolution is incompatible with pluralism, and I come back to this again in Chapter 7. However, for the moment, we remain with Tully's account and note the way in which these seven characteristics, which are said to be shared by the three predominant language games of modern constitutionalism, have both engendered and masked the 'abhorrent history of attempts to bring the overlapping cultural diversity' of the peoples of the world 'in line with the norm of one nation, one state' (Tully, 1995, 10). This is the history of attempts to 'exclude, dominate, assimilate or exterminate' cultural diversity that runs from the 'American holocaust' against indigenous peoples, to the more recent wars of extermination and genocide, for example, in Bosnia and Rwanda (Tully, 1995, 10, 97). From the perspective of any one of these three language games, the story of European imperialism – of the 'invasion of America' and the 'imposition of European economic and political systems' on Aboriginal peoples – is 'replaced with the captivating picture of the inevitable and benign progress of modern constitutionalism' (Tully, 1995, 78). In some respects, the contrast with Connolly here is striking. Tully's focus is clearly on the historical specificity and detail of these different modes of domination, and they are not referred back to any deeper underlying causes supposedly rooted in existential *ressentiment*. This is an important difference between the two thinkers, and, as we see below, Tully's focus on the specific mechanisms of forms of domination leads in turn to his excellent analyses of globalisation as a new form of imperialism. Nevertheless, we should also note a significant correspondence between the two agonists, which is that Tully shares Connolly's broad concern that the fragility of *bona fide* pluralism is threatened by excessive claims to unity and homogenisation. In Tully's case, the pluralism of pre-Westphalian Europe and aboriginal forms of constitutionalism is imperilled by the tyranny of modern European 'constitutionalism' in its three predominant forms: liberalism, communitarianism, and nationalism.

In addition to this critical survey of the dominant language games of constitutional theory, Tully also applies Wittgenstein's philosophy to develop his normative theory of 'agonistic dialogue'. The starting point here is an emphasis on the familiar or taken-for-granted in the everyday use of words (Wittgenstein, 1967, No. 116–20). Tully says that social and political practices are conditioned by forms of speech activity, in which actors 'are already in tacit agreement and understand one another in [their] thoughtful, confident, rational yet unreflective uses of words' (Tully, 1989, 182).[7] Indeed, Wittgenstein emphasises the important role of custom and training in the acquiring of linguistic competence, and he suggests that all differences of opinion take place within the context of a particular 'form of life' (Wittgenstein, 1967, 201, 226). He says, 'if language is to be a means of communication there must be agreement not only in definitions but also (queer as this may sound) in judgements' (Wittgenstein, 1967, 242). This means that, on Wittgenstein's model, interpretation is subordinate to pre-reflexive 'understanding', indeed interpretation is a practice we engage in 'only when our customary

---

[7] For a comparable view, see: Williams, 2005, 24–5.

understanding and use of signs is in some way problematic or in doubt'
(Tully, 1989, 182–3, 196).

This aspect of Wittgenstein's theory has generated a number of conservative readings. According to János Kristóf Nyíri, for example, the
purpose of Wittgenstein's philosophy is 'to show that the given form
of life is the ultimate givenness, that the given form of life cannot be
consciously transcended' (Nyíri, 1982, 59). From this perspective, linguistic 'rule following is, in the last analysis, blind: it cannot be explained
or justified . . . it cannot actually be criticised . . . [because] [a]ll criticism
presupposes a form of life, a language, that is, a tradition of agreements'
(Nyíri, 1982, 59). Furthermore, by Wittgenstein's account, language is
inextricably bound up with wider social and cultural practices, and so
for some commentators these implications follow more generally for the
status of social norms. Peter Winch most notoriously advanced this view
in *The Idea of a Social Science* (Winch, 1973). Indeed, Winch focused on
this aspect of Wittgenstein's theory to argue that 'all behaviour which is
meaningful (therefore all specifically human behaviour) is *ipso facto* rule
governed' (Winch, 1973, 52). This is true for the 'free thinking anarchist'
as much as it is for the disciplined routines of a monk or a soldier (Winch,
1973, 52). Although the rules that govern the anarchist's way of life are
not as explicit or tightly drawn, the 'anarchist's way of life is [still] a *way
of life*. It is to be distinguished, for instance, from the pointless behaviour
of a berserk lunatic' (Winch, 1973, 52–3, emphasis in the original).

As David Cerbone has observed, common to these conservative readings is 'a conception of our concepts and judgements as located within,
and so circumscribed by, something else: a tradition, a culture, a society,
a form of life' (Cerbone, 2003, 49). However, this picture is actually a
'target' of Wittgenstein's criticism, rather than the 'cornerstone' of his
theory, because these accounts fail to take on board a second and crucial
aspect of Wittgenstein's understanding of language games, which is his
emphasis on the inherent freedom and indeterminacy involved in the
reiteration of the rules of linguistic exchange (Cerbone, 2003, 51). As
Tully says, the emphasis on an agreement in the form of life is only the
first line of argument in Wittgenstein's theory (Tully, 1995, 107). Of
particular interest to Tully is Wittgenstein's additional insight that language games are never bound by hard and fast rules (Wittgenstein, 1967,
Nos. 19, 83). This is because language users inevitably find themselves
in the position where they are able to alter the rules of the game as they
go along (Wittgenstein, 1967, No. 83; Tully, 1995, 108). According to
Tully, no matter how elaborate a general rule for the meaning of a given
term might be, it 'is always possible to interpret and apply it in various

ways' (Tully, 1995, 106).[8] No language 'game is [ever] completely circumscribed by rules', and the 'condition of being "rule-bound"' is 'constantly subverted in practice' (Tully, 1999a, 164, 168).[9]

Like Arendt, this Wittgensteinian approach draws attention to the important distinction between the human condition and the casual determinism that defines natural processes and systems. Unlike natural laws, social rules and norms are human conventions that can always ultimately be re-inscribed and subverted in multifarious ways. As Taylor puts it, this suggests a 'reciprocal relation between rule and action, the fact that the latter does not simply flow from the former but actually transforms it' (Taylor, 1992b, 181–2). In Wittgenstein's formulation:

A rule stands there like a signpost. – Does the signpost leave no doubt open about the way I have to go? Does it shew which direction I am to take when I have passed it; whether along the road or the footpath or cross-country? But where is it said which way I am to follow it; whether in the direction of its finger or (e.g.) in the opposite one? – And if there were, not a single signpost, but a chain of adjacent ones or of chalk marks on the ground – is there only one way of interpreting them? – So I can say, the signpost does after all leave no room for doubt. Or rather: it sometimes leaves room for doubt and sometimes not. And now this is no longer a philosophical proposition, but an empirical one. (Wittgenstein, 1967, No. 85)

In other words, on this view, 'rule following is [an] interactive [practice] rather than passive obedience to a prescribed norm' (Tully, 2008a, 296). Citing Wittgenstein, Tully says it is 'our acting, which lies at the bottom of the language game' (Tully, 1989, 184). Indeed, this is the cardinal point in Tully's conception of agonistic democracy.[10] In agonistic politics individuals and groups struggle incessantly to 'free themselves from and [to] modify the conventions' that govern their 'thought and action in the present' (Tully, 1999a, 166; 2000a, 479). This is the source of the constituent power, which has the capacity to introduce novelty into extant practices. For example, the relationships and 'self-understandings of men and women, of Muslims and Christians, French and English and indigenous peoples and non-indigenous peoples has changed

---

[8] In *The Post-Modern Condition* Lyotard also drew on Wittgenstein's conception of language games to develop a theory of 'general agonistics' (Lyotard, 1986, 10, 15). Lyotard similarly stressed the creative element of agonism, in its perpetual disruption of established patterns of connotation (Lyotard, 1986, 10).

[9] For a comparable discussion and a similar set of conclusions, see: Williams, 2005, 34–7.

[10] See also: Tully, 2000a, 472; 2008a, 199. Importantly, from this perspective, rule following/amending is a uniquely human practice. So Tully does not get tied up in the difficulties we explored in the previous chapter in relation to Connolly's naturalism.

enormously over the last decades' through on-going 'conflict, negotiation and discussion' (Tully, 2008a, 303).

By Tully's account, this power 'to call something [new] into being... can irrupt in almost any organised form of human activity', and 'differentially situated players' always retain varying degrees of freedom 'no matter how explicit the rules' that seek to govern their conduct (Tully, 1999a, 164; 2008b, 286). In fact, Tully's Wittgensteinian perspective requires a third and final conceptual paradigm shift; not just an emphasis on the inherently situated context of (linguistic and social) rules, or the inescapable element of freedom in the application of those rules, but finally – as one commentator put it – an acknowledgement of a 'sceptical dimension in the rule itself' (Laugier, 2006, 37). Indeed, on this revised view, we turn full circle so that the rule of law itself comes to be seen not as a mode of command, but rather as a 'system of norms over which there is always [on-going] reasonable disagreement' (Tully, 2008a, 306).[11]

This presentation clearly reiterates the ultimate priority of the constituent power over forms of constituted authority, and Tully depicts this paradigmatic shift in general terms as a movement from a civil to a *civic* theory of law and politics. The civil:

tradition makes a fundamental distinction between the institutional rule of law and the citizen activities that take place within the boundaries of these institutional settings. The institutionalised rule of law exhibits a systemic or functional quality of formality and independence from the agents who are subject to it and act within its boundaries. This picture is encapsulated in the mantra, 'rule of law not of men'. (Tully, 2008b, 285)

By way of contrast, the civic understanding situates the rule of law within 'a network of relationships of negotiated practices' where dissent is seen as inevitable and constructive (Tully, 2008b, 286). This also requires a reorientation in political and legal theory, so that the goal of political theory is not understood in terms of:

reaching final agreements on universal principles or procedures, but to ensuring that constitutional democracies are always open to the democratic freedom of calling into question and presenting reasons for the negotiation of the prevailing rules of law, principles of justice, and practices of deliberation. (Tully, 2005, 208)

---

[11] Tully is one of a number of political theorists who converge on a broadly agonistic conception of rule following derived from Wittgenstein. See, for example, Taylor, 1992b; Zerilli, 2001; Pohlhaus and Wright, 2002; Williams, 2005; Laugier, 2006; Norval, 2007. This perspective is also equivalent to Butler's claim that the norms of social regulation do not ultimately have any fixity apart from their daily (re)iteration. This point is explored in relation to Honig's work in Chapter 6.

Tully describes this as 'democracy in the extensive sense: the exercise of the abilities of the governed to negotiate the way their conduct is guided' (Tully, 2008b, 57). This is 'not to deny the importance of institutionalised procedures' or principles of right, but the constituted powers are always subject to the uncertainty, the suspense, and the 'possibility of irreversible change', which 'surrounds all significant action, however "rule guided"' (Tully, 2008a, 307).

In other words, from Tully's Wittgensteinian perspective, the key to political freedom is, as in Arendt, the exercise of freedom itself, understood as a 'form of activity with others in public' (Arendt, 1958, 202; Tully, 1999a, 162). However, at this point we need to turn to an additional presumption in Tully's approach, which clearly demarcates him from Arendt. Following Wittgenstein, Tully insists that at any given moment in the struggles of agonistic politics 'some constituents are held firm and provide the ground for questioning others' (Tully, 1999a, 170). Indeed, any rule is 'in principle open to dissent, discussion, consideration and, if necessary, alteration' but only 'in accord with the totality of rules that are not in question in any particular case' (Tully, 2008a, 199). These elements that remain stable – whilst other criteria are 'questioned, reinterpreted, and tested' – are presented as conditions of possibility of agonistic politics (Tully, 2002a, 543, 547). They play the 'hinge role' in agonistic democracy; they are the riverbed of agonistic politics, not the river (Tully, 2000b, 58).[12] Indeed, the agonism of intercultural dialogue 'takes place against, and is justified with reference to, the broad and relatively stable background of customary agreements in judgement that are not questioned in any given critical discussion' (Tully, 1995, 40).

These formulations strongly reiterate the antique Roman conception of augmentation, where the moment of freedom or initiative generates innovation, but, at the same time, remains inscribed within and expands the terrain of established norms and authorities.[13] Moreover, because,

---

[12] Zerilli makes the same point (see: Zerilli, 2003, 140). For Wittgenstein's metaphor of the river and the riverbed see Wittgenstein, 1975, 97 and 99.

[13] Norval makes a similar point in her discussion of aspect change, taken from the second part of the *Investigations*, where Wittgenstein discusses a change in the visual perception of an object, one with which we are already familiar. Wittgenstein emphasises that the change in visual perception is never total or absolute, but rather partial (Wittgenstein, 1967, 196). As Norval puts it, when we experience an aspect change 'things simply are no longer the same; our way of looking at things has changed. But . . . this is not a break that denies all that has gone before. To the contrary, it is dependent upon what has gone before, but that before is also rearranged – resignified – in important respects' (Norval, 2006, 238). Moreover, 'it is precisely this emphasis on rearrangement that allows one to think through a conception of political change that steers a path between radical rupture and continuity', if 'we lack the new, we are forever trapped in tradition; if tradition is entirely absent, the new will be unintelligible' (Norval, 2006, 238, 243). Again, these formulations restate the Roman experience of augmentation.

on Tully's Wittgensteinian view, these claims are presented as necessary conditions of political action rather than, as I have suggested following Arendt, as characteristic of particular examples of freedom, this approach also represents a mono-typical account of the emergence of the constituent power. Indeed, the idea of absolute initiative, in the form of the radical *Ursprung*, is inconceivable from the Wittgensteinian perspective. We will explore this difference between Wittgenstein and Arendt in more detail in a moment, but we first need to pursue Tully's approach a little further, and this is because he does not only make the claim that some undefined elements must necessarily remain firm, whilst others are challenged and subject to resignification. In fact, he goes much further than this and identifies the content of those norms which he says play the 'hinge role' in agonistic politics.

As I have said, in *Strange Multiplicity* Tully identifies the content of this anchorage point with the principles of mutual recognition, consent, and cultural continuity (Tully, 1995, 30). These 'conventions' are said to be immanent to the dialogues between citizens and cannot be demonstrated in the manner of Habermas' ideal of dialogue as fair deliberation: they 'cannot be represented in universal principles or . . . in universal institutions' (Tully, 1995, 131). Nevertheless, they gradually gain their authority and are given the 'appearance of a transcendental standard' by acts in conformity with them on all sides (Tully, 1989, 188; 1995, 116, 138). Indeed, Tully clearly wants the conventions to do some of the heavy normative lifting that Habermas attributes to the 'presuppositions of argumentation' that supposedly underpin the exchange of public reasons. The three conventions are 'immune from direct criticism', and, Tully says, to contravene these conventions is to fall into a performative contradiction (Tully, 1995, 177; 2000a, 474; 2000b, 58). At other times the normative status of the conventions is presented more as an aspiration. Tully hopes that the practice of intercultural dialogue will help cultivate 'the principle of reciprocity or mutual recognition', and foster a change in civic attitude, so that citizens start to 'affirm diversity itself as a constitutive good' (Tully, 1995, 177; 2000a, 474).[14] As we have said, after *Strange Multiplicity* Tully jettisons the communitarian principle of cultural continuity and, in his later works, the rules of democratic

---

[14] At times in *Strange Multiplicity* Tully slips into a more explicit ideal of harmony and reconciliation. Referring to the sculpture *The Spirit of Haida Gwaii* by Bill Reid – which is appealed to as a metaphor for 'post-imperial' pluralism – Tully says that 'for all the celebration of diversity and the vying for recognition . . . the ship of state glides harmoniously into the dawn of the twenty-first century' (Tully, 1995, 28). Indeed, in some respects, the ideal of *Strange Multiplicity* appears to be more in line with deliberative approaches. The objective is not to face tragedy with courage and fortitude (in the lineage of Nietzsche and Machiavelli) but rather to find reasonable ways to 'avoid . . . tragic fate' (Tully, 1995, 211).

negotiation are boiled down to the first 'principle of democratic deliberation [which] is *audi alteram partem*, "always listen to the other side",
for there is always something to be learned from the other side' (Tully,
2005, 208).[15] This move away from communitarianism is not insignificant, and, for the reasons set out above, this enables Tully to adopt a
more thoroughly constructivist understanding of identity formation and
the politics of recognition. Nevertheless, whether it is one or three conventions that are said to mediate agonistic politics, the key issue is really
the status of these immanent rules that are said to condition the legitimate exercise of democratic freedom. We need to examine whether or not
Tully's various formulations of their immanent and negotiable status are
really compatible with the properly tragic viewpoint of agonism. Again,
we come back to this shortly.

Another crucial question is how the convention(s) relate to modern liberal democratic constitutionalism? As we have said, in *Strange Multiplicity*
the institutions and practices of modern constitutionalism are presented
as just one constitutional language game amongst many. They form part
of a wider historical survey that rediscovers the validity of pre-modern
forms of constitutionalism, the common law, and aboriginal treaty constitutionalism (Tully, 1995, 124, 61, 116). However, Tully also claims
that this reassessment will enhance rather than diminish the 'primary
goods of individual liberty and equality, which are correctly associated
with modern constitutionalism' (Tully, 1995, 31).[16] As his position has
developed in his subsequent writings, it is clear that Tully thinks of his
rendition of agonistic dialogue as a better understanding of the values
inherent in modern constitutionalism, and, as was said in the Introduction, this is most evident in Tully's explicit endorsement of Habermas'
notion of the co-originality of public and private autonomy. As he puts
it, a given constitutional democracy is 'legitimate only if both principles
inform the basic institutions in an equally fundamental way' (Tully, 2005,
191, 194–5).[17]

This means that the constituent power is always to some extent 'rule
governed (to be constitutionally legitimate), but [at the same time] the
rules must also be open to democratic amendment (to be democratically legitimate)' (Tully, 2005, 193). In other words, in a manner that
is characteristic of the theorists examined in this book, Tully thinks of
agonistic democracy in terms of a constitutive augmentation of existing

---

[15] See also: Tully, 1995, 110, 174; 2000a, 475. This resonates with Hampshire, for whom
justice must be thought of a 'fair weighting and balancing of contrary arguments' under
the 'single prescription *audi alteram partem*' (Hampshire, 1999, 21).

[16] See also: Tully, 2008a, 252.   [17] See also: Tully, 2008a, 196.

liberal democratic institutions. Most importantly, from Tully's perspective, the constituted powers and authorities are legitimate if they enable the 'politics of recognition to be played freely from generation to generation, with as little domination as possible' (Tully, 2008a, 189). Even though the present rules of recognition may 'harbour elements of injustice and non-consensus' the system is legitimate if the prevailing rules of law can be subject to on-going 'disagreement, negotiation, amendment, implementation, and review' (Tully, 2005, 196).[18] The primary objective of Tully's conception of agonistic democracy is therefore 'to ensure that those subject to and affected by any system of governance are always free to call its prevailing norms of recognition and action coordination into question' (Owen and Tully, 2007, 287). This iteration of the democratic *agon* offers key insights into the politics of innovation, and how situated subjects can introduce genuine augmentation into existing liberal democracies. However, given his formulation of the democratic contest in terms of these fine balances between the constituent and constituted powers, it is not surprising that Tully has found himself in the position of being criticised on one side by liberals for not providing adequately secure foundations for constitutional authority and, on the other side, by radical democrats for being insufficiently critical of the juridical paradigm of liberal constitutionalism.[19]

Tully and his critics

From the viewpoint of liberal constitutionalism, Tully's position appears inconsistent. To acknowledge the norm of reciprocity is to 'introduce the relevance of abstract and prescriptive reason. This norm, after all, is neither universally accepted, nor self-interpreting' (Blake, 2005, 241). Tully makes a 'prescriptive statement capable of philosophical defence and elucidation', and so, when he denies the possibility of a grounded or transcendent justification of normative principles, he finds himself

---

[18] See also: Tully, 2000a, 477; 2005, 195; 2008a, 215–16; Owen and Tully, 2007, 286.

[19] Connolly finds himself caught in the same predicament. He is criticised on one side by liberals for undermining the foundational status of justice (Moon, 1998), and on the other side by radical democrats for his 'relentless commitment to liberalism' (Vazquez-Arroyo, 2004). These polarised responses – to Connolly and Tully alike – corroborate the idea that the contemporary agonistic viewpoint is demarcated by a typical desire to walk a tightrope (of augmentation), poised between an emphasis on the ultimate groundlessness of political action and simultaneously an acknowledgement of the basic legitimacy of liberal constitutionalism. These acrobatics will inevitably appear inconsistent to those who are lead more decisively in the direction of one or other of these alternatives.

in a performative contradiction (Blake, 2005, 231).[20] As we saw in Chapter 2, constitutional liberalism is predicated on a core anxiety about the vulnerability of basic rights to the whims of majoritarian decision making, and in response to this dilemma the liberal typically regards 'certain norms and principles as being legitimately outside the reach of collective deliberation and control' (Blake, 2005, 231). Consequently, when Tully suggests that basic constitutional norms are themselves up for debate in the on-going negotiations of democratic politics, his position is not only contradictory but also dangerous, and Tully's liberal critics have reasserted instead the foundationalist view that there are in fact 'many rules . . . that should never be open to democratic challenge and amendment' in this way (Leif, 2005, 245–6). These exchanges reaffirm the essential differences between liberalism and agonistic democracy, and these frightened responses to Tully's provocations confirm that liberal foundationalism is not a theory of politics, but a juridical statement of the absolute priority of constituted right (*potestas*), most often in the form of determinant principles of justice, and which aspire to contain the constituent power through the rule of law.

However, Tully's position also appears inconsistent from the more militant viewpoint of radical democracy. Tully wants to 'control political agonism by subordinating struggle to the normative principle of reciprocity', and so, as Lindahl says, one 'cannot help noting that, whatever their differences, Habermas, on the one hand, and . . . Tully, on the other, agree on the essential' (Lindahl, 2009, 57; 2008, 110). The bone of contention between Tully and theorists of deliberative democracy is 'whether the criteria of what counts as . . . "reasonable" struggle [are] transcendent or immanent' (Lindahl, 2009, 65). But, like the deliberative theories, Tully's 'interpretation of political agonism takes for granted: that there are reasonable and unreasonable forms of struggle' and 'that the principle of reciprocity determines what counts as reasonable' (Lindahl, 2009, 65).[21] Tully 'overlooks the decisive point that political reciprocity is always a limited reciprocity' and 'to lose sight of this is to deprive politics of its specificity, and to transform political philosophy into a theory of applied morality' (Lindahl, 2008, 113). In the terms of this study, what Lindahl is driving at here is the basic difference between the aspiration to regulate or transcend conflict that underpins all forms of rationalism in politics, and the properly tragic vision of agonistic democracy, where

---

[20] Rainer Forst presents a similar response to Tully but from a critical theory perspective, he says the 'critique of contingent social practices of domination does not, pace Tully, rest on contingent resources but on a strong and solid foundation' (Forst, 2011, 120).

[21] Honig and Stears also pinpoint this tendency towards 'normativising' in Tully's approach (Honig and Stears, 2011, 199).

conflict is more fundamental, and where the best we can achieve is an artful redirection of conflict, but where we also relinquish any hope of doing so without moments of genuine loss. On this front, Tully's contribution appears to fall within the orbit of the deliberative or 'reasonable' approaches. As we have said, Tully sees his contribution as part of a more general deliberative turn in political theory, and he sometimes refers to his position as an explicit radicalisation of deliberative democracy (Tully, 2008a, 302). However, we have also said that there is no middle ground between agonistic and deliberative theory, and so Lindahl is right when he says that, in the end, Tully will have to choose between the two.

However, Lindahl also presses Tully on another question, and this takes us back to the discussion about the difference between the relative and the absolute priority of the constituent power. Lindahl provides an excellent restatement of this distinction in his account of alternate forms of disorder in respect of legal norms, where he draws a contrast between what he calls moments of 'illegality' as opposed to '*a*legality'. The first form of disorder 'concerns the distinction between legal and illegal acts' and comes into being when the exercise of human freedom 'breaches a [given] legal norm. The second, primordial form of legal disorder involves acts that challenge the very distinction between legality and illegality, as drawn by a [particular] political community' (Lindahl, 2009, 57). Moreover, Lindahl associates these '*a*legal' moments, of the absolute priority of the constituent power, with events of political foundation. He says:

The founding acts of legal order are themselves *neither legal nor illegal* because both terms of this binary opposition already presuppose a legal order as the condition for their intelligibility. Instead foundational acts [of the constituent power] are *a*legal: they institute the distinction itself between legality and illegality. (Lindahl, 2009, 59, emphasis in original)

In the terms of this study, Lindahl's distinction between alegality and illegality is analogous to the Arendtean distinction between revolution and augmentation. The moment of alegality refers – with Arendt, Benjamin, and Schmitt – to a moment of radical origin, one which is entirely unaccounted for in a pre-existing framework of normativity; whereas the moment of illegality refers instead to a moment of augmentation, one that ruptures a given framework of norms, but nonetheless emerges from and remains explicable within its broader horizon of meaning and legitimacy. Like Arendt, Lindahl insists that these represent qualitatively distinct moments of the constituent power, and he rightly stresses that it is important to keep open this distinction. However, we have seen that the moment of radical origin is inconceivable from within the Wittgensteinian theoretical framework. On this model, democratic freedom manifests as a simultaneous alteration and repetition of an existing rule or norm, and the emphasis is empathetically on the indisscociable mix of change and continuity. Consequently, in Lindahl's terms, Tully 'level[s] down alegality to (il)legality' (Lindahl, 2009, 67). Or, in my narrative, Tully presents a mono-typical account of the emergence of the constituent power that is equivalent to the Arendtean conception of augmentation.

In Chapter 2, we saw that Tully and other contemporary Wittgensteinians such as Owen and Norval have argued to the contrary that there is no qualitative distinction between moments of foundation and the agonic freedom of citizens to amend norms and practices within the context of a constitutional set of norms (Norval, 2007, 185; Tully, 2008b; Owen, 2009, 78–9). Instead, these different modalities of the constituent power exist on a continuum, with moments of foundation being just acute forms of the more general capacity of situated subjects to redirect rules and norms in many varied and creative ways. As Owen sees it, Lindhal's categories presuppose an overblown 'regulist picture of norms', where the rules (of law) exist in a relation of externality to the subjects who contest or actualise them, and Lindahl cannot grasp Wittgenstein's insight that freedom is instead always already immanent to the very reiteration of any given norm (Owen, 2009, 77, 79, 81). Owen is right to stress that we should not conceive of constituted authority as something that regulates freedom from a point of externality. Such a picture of authority is perhaps inherent in Schmitt's depiction of the source of legality in a moment of sovereign decision, one which is then held in awe, or at least up until it is annihilated by another sovereign power. However, Arendt's categories are more nuanced. Her retrieval of the Roman conception of augmentation is intended precisely to reveal those moments of freedom that always remain immanent within any claims to authority or of the rule of law. However, she did not lose sight of how this experience is qualitatively distinct from the moment of radical origin.

Indeed, the qualitative distinction between the absolute and the relative priority of the constituent power, between *a* and *il*legality, ultimately comes down to the temporality of the constituent act, and this can again be neatly illustrated by contrasting Arendt and Wittgenstein on the temporality of freedom. Whereas the Wittgensteinian subject of agonistic democracy always *follows* a rule (the 'rule stood there like a signpost' etc.), albeit in many free and creative ways, the Arendtean subject of revolution miraculously finds herself in a moment of absolute initiative, in the revolutionary *Ursprung* that is somehow antecedent to the rule itself. This means that what distinguishes the moment of radical innovation in respect of the rule or norm, is that it gives rise to its own principle, as opposed to augmenting or reiterating an existing rule or norm. Indeed:

What saves the act of beginning from its own arbitrariness is that it carries its own principle within itself, or, to be more precise, that beginning and principle, *principium* and principle, are not only related to each other, but are coeval. The absolute from which the beginning is to derive its own validity and which must save it, as it were, from its inherent arbitrariness is the principle which, together with it, makes its appearance in the world. (Arendt, 1965, 214)

Moreover, Arendt further illustrated this crucial distinction between the two alternate temporalities of the constituent power with reference to the fact that there are two verbs for 'to act' in both Greek and Latin:

The two Greek words are *archein*: to begin, [or] to lead . . . and *prattein*: to carry something through. The corresponding Latin verbs are *agere*: to set something in motion; *gerere*, which is hard to translate and somehow means the enduring and supporting continuation of past acts whose results are *res gestae*, the deeds and events we call historical. (Arendt, 1977b, 164)[22]

In Chapter 7 we see just how important it is to keep both of these distinct moments of freedom in play. Indeed, there I present a conception of the democratic *agon* as situated to a large extent in the precarious interface between the moment of radical origin and the subsequent 'carrying through'. Moreover, it is precisely in the successful arrangement of these two distinct moments that we might find the greatest chance for the emergence of a militant form of cosmopolitanism. By way of contrast, from the viewpoint of contemporary Wittgensteinian agonism, political subjects are denied this capacity for radical innovation and they are fated instead to perpetually rework the existing system of rules in diverse, unique, and unpredictable ways. In other words, they never get the opportunity to set something original in motion, it is rather all about the innovative ways of 'carrying through'.

Globalisation as the new imperialism

Tully's concern with European colonial rule over indigenous peoples was at the core of *Strange Multiplicity*, and in second volume of *Public Philosophy* this is further elaborated into an extensive account of globalisation as the continuation of Euro-American imperialism by other means. Tully's critique of globalisation focuses on the gross levels of inequality deriving from neo-liberalism, as well as the new networked forms of control associated with the impact of information technology. His analysis is more

[22] See also: Arendt, 1958, 189; 2005, 126.

advanced than the other theorists examined in this book, both in terms of the depth and detail of his scholarship and of his basic insight into the new forms of domination and exploitation associated with globalisation. I pretty much concur with the details of Tully's analysis of globalisation. I set out the main points here, and in Chapter 7 I take his account as the starting point for my own formulation of a theory of agonism and militant cosmopolitanism.

Drawing on Foucault, Tully distinguishes between the formal institutions of *government* (which, since the Treaty of Westphalia, have been associated primarily with the nation-state), and the wider strategies and techniques of *governance* (understood in terms of the 'multiple, complex, and overlapping ways of governing individuals and groups') (Foucault, 1991b, 92; Tully, 2002a, 538). Mainstream political theory is often blind to the complex operations of governance that operate below the 'uniform edifice of sovereignty', because of an exclusive concern with the role of government in the narrow sense, and a typical preoccupation with a juridical conception of power (Foucault, 1980a, 96; 1980b, 104–6). As we will see, in many respects, the specific forms of governance associated with modern disciplinary societies, located primarily in institutions such as prisons, schools, and factories, etc., and which were mapped so effectively by Foucault, have been steadily displaced in the context of globalisation with new forms of discipline, centred instead in the market and the large corporations and also associated with the new digital technologies. This has generally been described in terms of the transformation of a disciplinary society into a society of control. Nevertheless, Foucault's basic insight that we need to focus on complex modalities of governance, rather than on government in the narrow sense, also becomes especially pertinent in the current conjuncture, where it is increasingly acknowledged that state sovereignty has been progressively compromised by overlapping and multi-layered networks of governance associated with the reproduction of international law, and manifest in the role and function of supra-state bodies such as the UN, the WTO, the major NGOs and the transnational corporations.[23]

Reiterating what is now a widely accepted thesis, Tully shows how economic globalisation has undermined democratic institutions at the level of the nation-state (Tully, 2008b, 51). Most of the dispersed practices of supra-state governance are not democratic. They are typically 'authoritarian or systemic' and coordinate the interaction of social actors 'behind their backs', without their say, through market mechanisms and bureaucracy (Tully, 2008b, 50). Increasingly, these novel forms of constituted

---

[23] See: Tully, 2002a, 538; 2002b, 210; 2005, 197; 2008b, 199.

power have the 'capacity to override domestic and national constitutions, forcing them to . . . free the economy from the democratic control of existing nation-states' (Tully, 2005, 199). In particular, the globalisation of capital becomes insulated from democratic discussion and control, and this is particularly evident in the increased power of transnational corporations *vis-a-vis* national governments, as well as the instability caused by capital mobility (Tully, 2008b, 51, 213). The impact of these processes has been most acute in the 'developing' countries, often through the direct intervention of the IMF and the World Bank, whereas in the 'developed' world they have generally taken the more subtle form of a race to the bottom, an erosion of welfare programs, and a consolidation of the idea that there is no alternative to market liberalisation. Overall, economic globalisation reproduces a basic structure of inequality between advanced economies (the G8) and the developing world, and also manifests in terms of what Marxists call uneven and combined development, both within the system as a whole, and within different regions, nations, and cities.[24] As Tully puts it, the 'processes of globalisation in the various domains affect different regions, sectors and peoples differently' and in 'the poorest and weakest states even the basic democratic rights of assembly, association, and free speech are curtailed and sweatshop work conditions imposed' (Tully, 2005, 201; 2008b, 61). We should also note that these same strategies have been felt more acutely in countries on the periphery of Europe since the publication of *Public Philosophy*, and in response to the European sovereign debt crisis, with the imposition of severe austerity measures and an unelected technocracy in Italy and Greece.[25]

Indeed, the processes of globalisation hold 'enormous structures of social and economic inequality in place' and reproduce systemic relations of 'dependency and exploitation' (Tully, 2008b, 67, 267). In line with other prominent theorists such as Negri, Edward Said, and David Harvey, Tully presents globalisation as a continuation of European imperialism by other means.[26] On this view, a new form of informal or 'free

---

[24] See for example: Harvey, 2006.
[25] Tully's analysis of imperialism is more sophisticated than conventional Marxist approaches. He recognises that the enforcement of capitalist wage-labour relations forms part of a more complex structure of domination, and is not in itself the motor force of European colonial expansion. Nevertheless, the imposition of the Europeans' uniform economic institutions of 'private property and commodity production' on non-European indigenous peoples has been a key component of modern empire (Tully, 1995, 77). I return to the question of the relationship between economic exploitation and other aspects of domination in the following chapter and again in Chapter 7.
[26] See: Said, 1994; Hardt and Negri, 2001; Harvey, 2003; and for a fuller discussion of points of similarity and differences between Tully and Negri see: Ivison, 2011, 132–3.

trade' imperialism has been emerging in one form or another since the end of the nineteenth century, and has become the dominant form of imperialism since the processes of decolonisation after World War Two (Tully, 2008b, 195, 196, 212; 2008c, 75). Under informal imperialism the great powers 'recognise the imperialised or subalternised peoples as [formally] self-governing constitutional states' (Tully, 2008b, 196). They nonetheless continue to exert domination over them 'by means of military threats and military intervention' and a 'host of other informal techniques of indirect legal, political, educational and cultural rule' (Tully, 2008c, 73). In the era of globalisation, the old European duty to civilise is reconfigured in 'the form of the trade agreements of the WTO and imposition of neo-liberal structural adjustment and privatisation programmes by the World Bank and the IMF' (Tully, 2008b, 215). As we said in Chapter 2, the major NGOs are also implicated in the new imperialism as the soft power agents of assimilation, and, all in all, globalisation therefore represents the latest stage in 'five hundred years of relentless "tyranny" against local citizenship and self-reliance' (Tully, 2008b, 192, 267).

To some readers, this narrative might appear overly pessimistic. Perhaps this account does not adequately acknowledge the progress which has been made in tackling absolute poverty in many parts of the world, and examples of apparently successful development can be identified in different regions – for example, in the so called BRIC countries. However, as Tully says, the figures speak for themselves. The levels of global inequality are 'worse now than at the height of the ruthless phase of western imperialism at the turn of the nineteenth century' (Tully, 2008b, 265). Today:

Approximately 840 million people are malnourished. There are 6 million children under the age of five who die each year as a consequence of malnutrition. Roughly 1.2 billion people live on less than $1 a day and half the world's population lives on less than $2 a day. Ninety-one out of every thousand children in the developing world die before they reach the age of five. Twelve million die annually from lack of water, and 1.1 billion people have no access to clean water. About 2.4 billion people live without proper sanitation, while 40 million live with AIDS, and 133 million children have no basic education. One in five does not survive past forty years of age. (Tully, 2008b, 266)

Moreover, this picture of systemic inequality and oppression has been intensified as a consequence of the global financial crisis, which has brought the prospect of chronic indebtedness to the 'developed' world, and produced greater austerity, rising unemployment, rising inflation and the prospect of a global economic slump.

However, in addition to this account of systemic global inequality and top-down forms of power, Tully emphasises two novel developments, associated with the consolidation of neo-liberalism. Firstly, he draws attention to the protracted decline in public life. As Tully says, neoliberalism is an ideology or worldview that is predicated on the priority of negative forms of liberty, foremost of which is the 'liberty to participate in the private economic sphere... the right to own property and enter into contracts' (Tully, 2008b, 251). This is the centrepiece of a disciplinary regime, which has been consolidated since the end of the Cold War and in which individuals are increasingly assimilated into 'the dominant identity of a [passive] consumer of lifestyles' and 'many hard won social and economic rights nationally and internationally [are dismantled] in the name of spreading market forces' (Tully, 2005, 216; 2008b, 254). In addition to the privatisation of citizenship, publically limited corporations have acquired rights to private acquisition and so they too operate as private persons (Tully, 2008b, 251). The doctrines and institutions of neo-liberalism eat away at our capacity for democratic agency, and so increasingly individual citizens do not acquire the 'experience of, nor subjective interest in, democratic participation' (Tully, 2005, 216). Moreover, because of these tendencies, individuals 'tend in the extreme to cohere instead around the protection of their capitalist patterns of consumption at one end and the protection of their excluded religious and cultural identities at the other' (Tully, 2005, 217). These observations suggest an altogether different explanation for the current rise of fundamentalism than Connolly's depiction of religious fanaticism as a displacement of existential anxiety. The causes of the present surge in religious fundamentalism are contingent rather than existential, and they follow from the consolidation of economic globalisation understood as a historically specific mode of disciplinary control.

The other major component in Tully's assessment of the new forms of domination associated with globalisation is his account of the novel forms of control made possible by the revolution in information technology. Indeed, an understanding of this development is crucially important, because the digital technologies provide the material basis of globalisation (Tully, 2008b, 171; see also Castells, 2000, 1). These technologies have transformed not only 'the way humans communicate', but also 'the way they carry out their communicatively mediated activities: production, distribution, finance, consumption, governance, war, resistance, culture, intimacy and much else... They tend to modify the practices so that they too are organised along the lines of a network' (Tully, 2008b, 172; see also Castells, 2000, 70). Like Connolly, Tully stresses that these developments are ambiguous, and how they have presented opportunities for innovative, networked forms of transnational democratic agency. I come back to this in a moment. However, we first need to consider how and why these developments have generated new forms of control. The impact of the new technologies has had a number of immediate consequences for the conventional institutions and practices of democracy centred in nation-states. Again like Connolly, Tully stresses how the instantaneous speed of communication means that social and economic processes, such as the circulation of capital, now effectively outrun 'the time frame of traditional democratic decision[-making] procedures', as well as operating on a scale that transgresses 'the jurisdictional boundaries of traditional nation states' (Tully, 2008b, 171). As a consequence, many social processes now effectively disregard 'the representative and legal institutions of modern citizenship that are supposed to bring them under representative authority' (Tully, 2008b, 301). Moreover, in contrast to those who see in the diffuse nature of the network a model of democratic and egalitarian organisation, Tully shows how the communication networks are not straightforwardly democratic or egalitarian spaces, but, taken as a whole, tend rather to 'reproduce the unequal nodes of communication, commerce and military rule laid down over five hundred years of European-American imperialism' (Tully, 2008b, 176).

In addition, the new technologies have made possible a new form of bio-power that shapes our conduct 'infrastructurally' by working directly on our desires and aspirations (Tully, 2008b, 51, 65). Again like Connolly, Tully shows how the new-networked relationships establish forms of control that tend to operate at the level of pre-reflective modes of conduct. Because of the instantaneous speed of electronic communications, we are increasingly 'governed by immanent norms of efficient interaction' rather than formal laws (Tully, 2008b, 66–7). What 'moves along the information highways is not so much ideas' – which can potentially be subject to democratic debate and deliberation – but 'images that structure the... consciousness of the recipient' immediately, or apparently without recourse to conscious reflection (Tully, 2008b, 174). Taking all of these points into consideration, Tully's analysis of globalisation leads inexorably to the conclusion that the 'twentieth century has experienced a shift from direct, territorial forms of control characteristic of the long age of European and American imperialism to new forms of non-territorial imperialism based on control of peoples and markets by indirect, infrastructural control' (Tully, 2008b, 57–9).

Indeed, Tully has been very adept at mapping the new networked forms of control, and his depiction of globalisation as a continuation of Euro-American imperialism by other means is very compelling. However, he also offers a series of reflections on how we might resist and transform these developments. Indeed, he says 'contemporary political globalisation is not composed of processes in which humans are powerless', and the fact that a variety of new forms of democratic agency have emerged in the context of globalisation demonstrates that 'we are not completely determined by the systems [of constituted power] in which we are [currently] engaged' (Tully, 2008b, 52, 84). In fact, opportunities for resistance and transformation are built into the ambiguous nature of the technologies themselves. This is because, unlike earlier communications technology – such as radio and television – networkers also interact directly with the new technology, often generating new forms of social relations in the process (Castells, 2000, Chapter 5). Consequently, the modes of control associated with the new technologies are distinct from the disciplinary procedures characteristic of the high point of modernity, where individuals were constituted through systems of surveillance and a 'tightly-knit grid of material coercions' within specific institutions (Foucault, 1977, 212, 222; 1980b, 104; 1980c, 155). By way of contrast, in the present conjuncture, subjects are always:

encouraged to see network communication from two perspectives. From one side, it is absolutely necessary to submit to commands, functions and routines as an assembling condition of becoming a networker and learning the rules of the game. On the other hand, it is a flexible and open-ended game in which networkers are treated as free players, as interactive and creative communicators, modifying the rules of the game as they play. (Tully, 2008b, 185)

This means that the current forms of domination can sometimes appear understated and indirect, with the predominant powers trying to nudge subjects in particular directions by structuring the 'field of possible actions of the subaltern actors in the network through strategically controlling the flexible and hierarchical infrastructural relations of communication, technology, research, finance, security, [and] norm creation' (Tully, 2008b, 179).

As we saw in Chapter 1, Foucault associated agonism with an ingrained capacity for manoeuvre that is retained by situated subjects, by his account, even in a highly determined context such as a psychiatric hospital. The new infrastructural forms of domination have amplified this strategic dimension of the democratic *agon*, because the digital technologies make possible many new and varied kinds of movements and operations, which 'can be mobilised instantaneously and across the multi-jurisdictional global space of network effects' (Tully, 2008b, 189). Indeed, situated subjects assemble the new technologies to coordinate various forms of transnational struggle, and this has been evident in the huge upsurge in forms of global protest over the past few years, from the uprising in Iran in 2009 to the Occupy movement and the Arab Spring. In each of these cases, the protagonists have made widespread use of various forms of 'real time' communication. Indeed, one of the most valuable components of Tully's later writings has been his stress, with Foucault, on the strategic nature of the democratic contest (Tully, 2002a, 540; 2008a, 295, 311). As we saw at the end of Chapter 2, Tully emphasises the many different forms of action available to situated subjects in the context of globalisation, up to and including the possibility of the 'general strike, direct action, [and] revolution' (Tully, 2008b, 202). Nevertheless, he also says that, in his view, the 'classic picture of a . . . people overthrowing their unjust regime and setting up a new government as they see fit within bounded states' has 'quite limited application' today (Tully, 2008b, 299). Indeed, Tully draws attention to the experience of the revolutionary decolonisation struggles of the mid twentieth century, and how they have not effectively emancipated oppressed peoples from European imperialism, because the former colonial governments have been replaced by the new informal modes of imperial governance (Tully, 2008b, 299). This has led many activists to reject the idea of revolution, and to turn instead to 'organising nonimperially and modifying the imperial dimensions of constitutional democracy from within' (Tully, 2008b, 204).

There is, undoubtedly, a great deal of truth in the observation that the idea of revolution in terms of overthrowing or seizing state power has become obsolete. There are many reasons for this, including the long-term demise of the nation-state vis-à-vis the global forces of capital and other social processes. However, Tully's depiction here of the 'classical picture' of revolution does not get to grips with what is at stake in the Arendtean depiction of revolution. We will have to wait till Chapter 7 to consider more carefully how we might rework the idea of revolution in the present conjuncture, but we can confidently say that it does not entail a violent overthrow of the state. Alternatively, as Wolin says, what is at issue in the revolutionary moment is the human capacity to create new forms (Wolin, 1992, 249). More specifically, the idea of revolution testifies to a human capacity for *radical* initiation, to generate new modes of being in the world, which cannot be accounted for in the present conjuncture.[27]

---

[27] Tully derives this depiction of revolution from his early work on John Locke. Locke shared the republican 'hypothesis that political institutions and traditions rest upon the political freedom and popular sovereignty of the people', and so, in the extreme case the people always retain the power to overthrow 'an unjust government and set . . . up a new one' (Tully, 1990, 521; 1993, 41; 2005, 198). Locke is an important figure who understood the revolutionary moment of republican freedom and the absolute priority of the constituent power. However, the details of Locke's account are quite distinct from Arendt, and the fact that the 'classic picture' of republican revolution – with its focus on the substitution of one government (in the narrow sense), or set of state institutions, for another – is largely outmoded, does not mean that the idea of radical innovation and the

As I have said, this moment of radical origin is literally inconceivable from Tully's Wittgensteinian viewpoint, that is, from a perceptive which insists that every form of constituent innovation is always also a continuity; that some norms and practices must remain uncontested, thereby providing background conditions, whilst others are brought into critical judgement; that the subject of freedom always necessarily *follows* a rule; and, on Tully's iteration, that these innovations are also always mediated by immanent rules of reciprocity. It is important to appreciate that, when Tully and other contemporary Wittgensteinians insist that there is no qualitative distinction to be drawn between alternate moments of the constituent power, the effect is to secure this particular rendition (of the constituent power as augmentation) as the only game in town; in effect, revolution becomes just an intense form of augmentation. In other words, Tully's admirable (Foucauldean) emphasis on the range of moves available to situated subjects in the theatre of strategic action is hemmed in by certain intrinsic assumptions derived from a (Wittgensteinian) theoretical framework that does not appreciate (with Arendt) the qualitative distinction between those alternate moments of freedom. These limitations should be borne in mind, when we turn now to his more detailed account of how we might respond to the forces of global imperialism.

Glocal citizenship

In addition to Tully's mapping of the new modes of imperialism, the second volume of *Public Philosophy* also includes a detailed account of the novel transnational forms of democratic agency that he calls 'glocal citizenship'. Tully presents these movements as a new, rigorously bottom-up form of cosmopolitanism, which he distinguishes from the Kantian model. Indeed, Tully delivers a thorough critique of the predominant models of cosmopolitan democracy, which, he says, present 'successive idealisations of modern Euro-American citizenship as the uniquely universal model for all human societies' (Tully, 2008b, 247). These theories reproduce the seven components of the 'empire of uniformity' that Tully exposed in his survey in *Strange Multiplicity* of the prevailing forms of modern constitutionalism, and which we discussed above.[28] If we

possibility of the emergence of a new principle is similarly fated. Indeed, in Chapter 7 we explore the ways in which these Arendtean themes remain highly pertinent in the context of globalisation.

[28] For Tully's critique of Kantian cosmopolitanism see: Tully, 2008b, 25, 63, 257–9.

'take respect for cultural diversity and democratic freedom seriously', we therefore need to 'go beyond the imperial Eurocentric uniformity of the Kantian framework' (Tully, 2008b, 15). Instead, 'glocalisation' refers to the 'global networking of local practices of civic citizenship' and this 'takes countless forms in different locals' (Tully, 2008b, 246–7). More specifically, Tully distinguishes between two basic forms of glocal citizenship. Glocalisation manifests in both (i) the vertical struggles between subalterns and hegemons and (ii) in the horizontal relations between glocal citizens themselves. This categorisation is problematic – for several reasons that we will now explore.[29]

As Tully says, masters and subalterns find themselves positioned in vertical relations in the 'vastly unequal field of institutions' characteristic of globalisation, and the forms of 'power codified in the prevailing system of misrecognition' systematically reproduce these relationships (Tully, 2008a, 214; 2008c, 99). Indeed, subaltern peoples – particularly in the 'developing' world – are dominated in all manner of ways in the present conjuncture:

They are repressed by their own dependent elites, democratic rights are further reduced or eliminated, and the governments become more authoritarian. Or, if the people manage to gain power, the repertoire of covert and overt informal means available to the great powers is employed to destabilise and undermine the government, bring about regime change and institute neo-liberal structural adjustment policies that promote tier one [that is negative, private] liberties of individuals and corporations. (Tully, 2008b, 264)

However, Tully rightly stresses that the imperial relationships of inequality, dependency, and exploitation are not automatic processes. These structures are 'the target of confrontation strategies', and so masters and subalterns are 'mutually constituted to a considerable degree by their strategic-tactical interaction over time' (Tully, 2008b, 266; 2008c, 98). Tully acknowledges that more work 'needs to be done' to understand 'the type of modifications that are possible in this complex field' of vertical relationships (Tully, 2008c, 100). However, in the end he says very little about the agonistic struggles between oppressor and oppressed, and this is somewhat curious, given the lengths he goes to in *Public Philosophy* to deliver a detailed map of the manifestations of imperial power.

---

[29] Tully's use of the term 'hegemon' is also problematic, because he equates this with domination, whereas in fact the term means leadership and is commensurate with agonistic freedom. I come back to this in Chapter 7. However, Tully would be better off using the term *dominus* or master (as opposed to hegemon) as the antonym of the subaltern.

One thing is clear, however, which is that the struggles between masters and subalterns cannot be effectively accounted for in terms of the relatively symmetrical game-like exchanges that Tully associates with agonistic 'dialogue'. If political legitimacy follows from the idea that a given framework of rules is open to a meaningful degree to on-going negotiation and amendment, then the current structures of neoliberal governance and the networked forms of control, analysed so effectively in *Public Philosophy*, cannot be described as legitimate. On Tully's own account, these are broadly entrenched systems of hierarchy and domination, where citizens are denied a democratic voice and increasingly subject to subtle forms of administration through infrastructural mechanisms of control. Here, Tully's theory resembles (other) deliberative approaches in drawing a distinction between a model of domination (e.g. Habermas' systematically distorted communication) and an ideal of reciprocal dialogue, and the division starts to look unbridgeable, because it is not clear how the ideal can be brought to bear on the harsh realities of the present modalities of power. In fact, Tully doesn't adequately address this difficulty. Instead, he looks elsewhere for evidence of the lived practices of agonistic dialogue, which he finds instead in the terrain of the horizontal relations between glocal citizens.

Tully sees these citizen–citizen relations flourishing in the 'interstitial locations' within globalisation; they emerge from the 'nooks and crannies in and around the dominant institutions' (Tully, 2005, 193). Examples of these 'diversity-savvy' forms of solidarity include 'not-for-profit organisations', 'urban communes', the World Social Forum and the Zapatistas (Tully, 2008b, 233, 291, 306). Here, glocal citizens experiment with cooperatives, fair trade, local democracy, deep ecology, and mutual aid (Tully, 2008b, 220). They establish non-violent civic partnerships in and between the north and global south (Tully, 2008b, 306). These 'cooperative federations' do not contest the state or the capitalist mode of production, nor do they 'confront and negotiate with governors to change this or that regulation', they simply 'avoid assimilation and sustain alternative worlds' by participating directly in unconventional practices of citizenship (Tully, 2008b, 269, 293). Reiterating one of his conclusions in *Strange Multiplicity*, Tully says that the current proliferation of these horizontal citizen–citizen relations is indicative of the 'rich sources' of pluralism that always persist in the 'day-to-day practices of millions of people' and 'beneath the dead machinery of [imperial] uniformity' (Tully, 2008a, 219, 256).[30]

---

[30] For the earlier articulation of this view in *Strange Multiplicity*, see: Tully, 1995, 99, 164.

Tully goes onto say that ultimately imperial rule is 'parasitic' on the manifestations of glocal citizenship, because without 'these networks of local self-reliance . . . imperialism would not survive' (Tully, 2008b, 219, 2008c, 101). This reiterates Hardt and Negri's description of the relationship between the multitude and Empire, which echoes Marx's famous imagery of capitalism sucking on the lifeblood of the productive power of the proletariat. On Tully's reading, one of the most 'astonishing examples' of this underlying pluralism is the 'survival and resurgence of 250 million indigenous peoples with their traditions of governance and Gaia-based citizenship after five hundred years of genocide, dispossession, marginalisation and relentless assimilation' (Tully, 2008b, 301). Similarly, in the 'developed' world, a 'vast repertoire of local citizenship practices have also survived' such as 'traditional working-class organisations and new and creative forms of cooperatives and networks linking rural and urban citizens . . . low-cost housing, anti-racism, organic farming, place-based pedagogy, neighbourhood security and so on' (Tully, 2008b, 302).

Indeed, Tully does not hold back in his celebration of this horizontal form of civic freedom, which he distinguishes from any kind of rule-governed activity. These relationships are based entirely on 'trust, conviviality or solidarity and civic friendship across identity-related differences and disagreements of various kinds' (Tully, 2008b, 291). This 'is the realm of civic-freedom as *isegoria*, citizens speaking to each other in equal relationships about their common concerns, rather than *parrhesia*, speaking to their governors in unequal relationships' (Tully, 2008b, 291). It is 'tempting to say' that glocal citizens:

'govern themselves' or are 'self governing', but they are not 'governing' in so far as this term entails the correlate of the 'governed'. They are neither governing and being governed in turn nor simultaneously governing others and being governed by them. They are exercising [constituent] power *together as* citizens all the way down. (Tully, 2008b, 291)

In this respect, Tully's presentation of glocal citizenship – of immanent citizen–citizen relations – is in keeping with a great deal of post-colonial, autonomist, and alternative globalisation literature, where the emphasis is on horizontal relations, directly acting otherwise, temporary autonomous zones (TAZ), and 'changing the world without taking power'.[31] However, the problem with this model of horizontal citizen–citizen relations, of what we might call demo-autonomy (rather than demo*cracy*), is that it avoids rather than challenges the problem of domination that Tully otherwise describes so effectively. In Tully's account, the constituted

---

[31] See for example: Hardt and Negri, 2001; Bey, 2003; and Holloway, 2005.

modes of violence and domination and the constituent power of the globalisation from below, have somehow found themselves in relations of basic externality. However, it is not so easy to establish this independence, either in thought or practice, and this can be illustrated with reference to the republican conception of freedom.

From the republican perspective, citizens cannot be free in a context where background conditions of domination are still in place (Skinner, 2008). This is evident for example in the case of a slave who manages to avoid being directly coerced by his master. As Skinner says:

While such slaves may as a matter of fact be able to act at will, they remain at all times in *potestate domini*, within the power of their masters. They accordingly remain subject or liable to [the possibility of] death or violence at any time. (Skinner, 1998, 41)

Under these circumstances the slave 'depends on the good will of the protector and lives, in effect, at his or her mercy' (Pettit, 1999, 165). Sadly, this model of domination as dependency describes the circumstances of subaltern peoples under conditions of globalisation, even when they do achieve a modicum of horizontal civic freedom. On Tully's own admission, the glocal citizens are vastly overshadowed by the on-going domination of European forms of imperialism. Indeed, the celebrated example of the Zapatistas remain marginalised and in conditions of poverty on the periphery of the global economy, working-class communities in the west have been utterly fragmented and undermined by neo-liberalism, squatters and urban cooperatives are routinely harassed by the police and other agents of the state, and, as Tully knows very well, the situation of aboriginal peoples is often a compound mixture of these and many other forms of misery and exploitation.

Given these circumstances, it is clear that the focus on direct, horizontal, citizen–citizen relations does not offer a credible model of freedom in the context of globalisation. This leaves untouched the neo-liberal regime that continues to pursue economic and political priorities that have a massive consequence for ordinary people all around the world, as well as for future generations. Indeed, any credible model of independence has to include a conception of how ordinary citizens can confront and interrupt the current decisions and state, supra-state, and corporate priorities around issues such as energy consumption, transportation, weapons manufacture, and many other concerns, however difficult this may prove to be, because these decisions continue to have direct and indirect consequences for the livelihood of all humankind (Castells, 2000, 132). In short, Tully moves too quickly to celebrate an idealised view of reciprocal forms of horizontal freedom, and seems to have forgotten that the present struggles must also contain a striving for liberation. In the following chapter, we will see that it is also possible to move too far in the opposite direction. This is evident in Mouffe's co-authored work with Laclau, where freedom is conceived essentially as liberation (or emancipation) and so the democratic struggle becomes fixated on the need to contest the oppressor. In Chapter 7 I offer an alternative account that seeks to strike a path between these two extremes, where the emphasis is on the priority of the constituent power, i.e. on political struggle as a source of innovation, but where we do not lose sight of the need for this also and at the same time to be a liberation movement through a clash with the dominant powers. It is not that the present forms of (relatively) egalitarian relations characteristic of the World Social Forum and the other examples of civic partnership that Tully describes are unimportant. On the contrary, as centres of creativity and experiment in the politics of diversity, they are highly significant. However, if they prove to be the location for the emergence of a new principle, which is subsequently recognised to be of wider significance and which really does start to provide an alternate set of practices in respect of issues such as climate change and global poverty, then perhaps they will turn out to have been something like the exercises in self-government in the New England town meetings that prepared the way for the American Revolution.

Conclusion

We have seen that Tully has a long-standing aspiration to help give voice to the struggles of aboriginal peoples, and that this leads him to develop a detailed and shrewd understanding of globalisation as a mode of informal imperialism. Tully's account of globalisation is meticulous and insightful, and in Chapter 7 I present a theory of militant cosmopolitanism that is intended to provide an alternative response to the same basic forms of domination that he describes. Tully's conception of agonistic democracy is built around a struggle for autonomy and the politics of recognition. Again, these are important points of emphasis, and in many respects the explicit focus on independence gives Tully the edge over the other contemporary agonists. Tully also moves beyond conventional approaches to recognition, and he makes several important observations in his theory of the politics of 'acknowledgement'. Tully's genealogies of modern constitutionalism are also integral to his approach. They help to expose the contingent circumstances of the historical formation of the currently predominant forms of modern constitutionalism, thereby opening up a sense of wider possibility. Tully's conception of agonistic dialogue similarly contains important insights, and most notably he shows how the existing structures of rule are ultimately reifications of on-going practices. This means that they can be reiterated in alternative ways, which shows that Wittgenstein's theory is not a conservative doctrine of the perpetuity of tradition through simple repetition, but rather points to the possibility of reiteration through on-going contestation. We return to a similar position in Honig's theory in Chapter 6.

However, Tully also appropriates core assumptions from Wittgenstein that effectively serve to establish a mono-typical account of the constituent power, that is in the form of an on-going augmentation, where some background assumptions *must* always be held firm whilst others are put into question. Consequently, the moment of radical innovation is inconceivable from Tully's Wittgensteinian perspective. This places certain untenable conceptual constraints on Tully's otherwise well-pronounced concern with the strategic question, which is better served by Arendt's emphasis on the qualitative distinction between augmentation and revolution. At best, Tully presents a limited conception of revolution, understood as a particularly acute form of augmentation. These conclusions represent a regression in respect of Arendt's work, and are problematic for the reasons I discussed in Chapter 2. Tully also introduces some strong normative assumptions into his theory, when he associates agonistic dialogue with the principle of reciprocity. Perhaps the combined impact of these assumptions pushes Tully inexorably in the direction of his overly drawn distinction between the realities of oppression in the era of globalisation and an idealised model of citizen–citizen relations. By way of contrast, we need to keep focused on the inevitable combination of freedom and liberation, and, in this regard, we can affirm with Deranty and Renault that to contest the rules of the (neo-) liberal-democratic-capitalist system 'is always something more radical and confrontational, more antagonistic' than Tully describes (Deranty and Renault, 2009, 54).

5   Agonism and the problem of antagonism: Chantal Mouffe

Chantal Mouffe has elaborated her conception of agonistic democracy in *The Return of the Political* (1993), *The Democratic Paradox* (2000), and *On the Political* (2005). These works were preceded by two distinct phases in the development of Mouffe's ideas: an initial Marxist period, elaborated in the edited volume *Gramsci and Marxist Theory* (1979), and a post-Marxist stage, expounded in the influential *Hegemony and Social Strategy* (1985) and co-authored with Laclau.[1] In this chapter I start with an evaluation of Mouffe's earlier work, and I stress the importance of Derridean post-structuralism in Mouffe's transition to post-Marxism, and in Laclau and Mouffe's account of the discursive formation of social 'subject positions'.[2] It is essential to consider these earlier stages in Mouffe's intellectual journey, because this helps to explain the distinctive qualities of her version of agonistic democracy and also brings to the fore certain limitations in her approach. Indeed, we will see a clear trajectory in Mouffe's work towards an increasingly narrow understanding of the ends of democratic politics.

In the initial phases Mouffe was motivated by analogous concerns to Tully, i.e. by the struggles of subaltern subjects for autonomy or self-government. The adoption of post-structuralism enabled her to move away from the conventional Marxist idea of the proletariat, understood as the historically privileged agent of progressive change, and she combined post-structuralism with Gramsci's notion of hegemony to develop a

---

[1] For the most detailed studies of Laclau and Mouffe's wider project of discourse theory, and more generally on their co-authored works, see: Smith, 1998; Torfing, 1999; Howarth, 2000.

[2] The other principal theoretical influence on *Hegemony and Socialist Strategy* was Lacanian psychoanalysis. Jacques Lacan's ideas have been central to the subsequent development of Laclau's contribution, and more generally for the radical democratic theorists that we discussed briefly in the Introduction and in Chapter 2. We will see in this chapter that Mouffe makes use of various Freudian notions, but there is no systematic application of either Freud or Lacan in her theory of agonistic democracy. For the best overall discussion of the impact of Lacanian psychoanalysis on the radical democratic tradition, see: Stavrakakis, 2007.

sophisticated account of collective action under conditions of pluralism. Laclau and Mouffe's conception of hegemony contains several problematic assumptions – primarily, as I suggested in the previous chapter, because they focused too intensely on the politics of liberation, or in Laclau and Mouffe's terms 'emancipation', and did not fully appreciate the priority of the constituent power as a source of innovation. Nevertheless, Laclau and Mouffe's co-authored works provide some excellent insights into the challenges associated with action in concert under conditions of pluralism, and her emphasis at this stage was unequivocally on the need to contest the many different modalities of oppression in order to facilitate democratic autonomy.

However, in her agonistic writings Mouffe has concentrated instead on an altogether different problem, which is the threat of antagonism in the form of the friend/enemy antithesis. As we saw in Chapters 1 and 2, Mouffe takes these ideas from Schmitt's *The Concept of the Political*. Like Schmitt, Mouffe sees antagonism as the 'essence of the political', and this means that the prospect of physical violence remains an 'ever present possibility' in human relations. We will unpack the consequences of these assumptions in the course of this chapter, and see that these formulations do enable Mouffe to develop some important insights into the current conjuncture. In particular, this concern has enabled Mouffe to advance a sophisticated critique of the drive towards consensus characteristic of much contemporary democratic theory and practice, and evident, for example, in deliberative theory and in the technocratic post-politics of the 'third way'. Mouffe levels two criticisms against the currently widespread penchant for full consensus, i.e. without remainders or exclusions. Firstly, the predominant democratic praxis is in denial about the reality of 'the political' and, secondly, and ironically perhaps, this naive renunciation actually exacerbates conflict and makes antagonism more likely, because these tendencies open the door to extremist parties who claim to offer a meaningful alternative to mainstream consensus elites. In other words, the emphasis on consensus provokes a 'return of the political' in the form of a heightened potential for antagonism, and as evidence Mouffe points to the emergence of ethnic conflict and extreme forms of nationalism in Eastern Europe after the demise of the Soviet Union, the political mobilisation of religious fundamentalism in the United States and the Middle East, the rise of far Right extremism in parts of Europe, and the various manifestations of international terrorism.

These are valuable insights, and we explore them in more detail in the second section below. However, Mouffe's turn to Schmitt has also resulted in a restricted account of the ends of agonistic politics. The goal of agonistic democracy is no longer, as with Tully, to contest imperialism in the name of independence or autonomy. Instead, the focus is primarily, if not exclusively, on the need to avoid the 'return of the political' by sublimating the irreducible potential for antagonism. Moreover, as we will see in the third section of this chapter, this leads to a model of agonistic democracy built around the need to construct order, unity, and authority, understood as prerequisites to agonistic freedom. These themes are unmistakably associated with conservatism, and there is perhaps an additional irony here because, in her attempt to draw attention to the dangers of far Right extremism, Mouffe herself ends up perilously close to adopting a neo-conservative worldview, one where politics is no longer concerned with the art of the possible but rather with the need for security from a purportedly primordial tendency towards violence.

Again, we need to explore these points carefully, and in the latter parts of this chapter we see that Mouffe is perhaps partly saved from this cruel turn of fate by two points of emphasis in her work. The first is her repeated stress on the link between the successful sublimation of antagonism and the future augmentation of liberal democracy. Indeed, Mouffe presents the institutions of liberal democracy as the horizon of possibility for contemporary political struggles, and she envisions agonistic democracy as a perpetual (re)negotiation of the paradoxical tensions between liberalism and democracy. This broadly correlates with the other thinkers examined in this book, and Mouffe sees her theory as a more plausible understanding and defence of the liberal democratic tradition than the deliberative model and the other mainstream approaches I surveyed in Chapter 2. The second aspect of Mouffe's work that perhaps places some distance between her position and the neo-conservative worldview follows from her adoption of the Roman notion of *societas* as the appropriate form of authority for agonistic democracy. Mouffe takes this idea from the work of Oakeshott, who was, of course, also a prominent conservative thinker, although Oakeshott's understanding of being conservative was very different to Schmitt's. I explore this difference, and consider why Mouffe ends up in between these two distinct strands of conservatism. However, in his retrieval of the notion of *societas*, Oakeshott also reiterated the republican idea that authority and freedom are not necessarily antonyms. This is similarly Mouffe's point of emphasis in her encounter with Oakeshott, and here we are effectively back in the terrain of the agonistic emphasis on freedom as augmentation. This aspect of Mouffe's work is nuanced and significant, and this facilitates an exploration of some of the deeper tensions inherent in the idea of augmentation, which, in turn, helps to explain points of dis/similarity between Mouffe and Tully. The chapter closes with a consideration of Mouffe's strong rejection of the idea of cosmopolitanism. Although Mouffe's critique of Kantian cosmopolitanism is valid, her rejoinder does not represent an adequate response to the challenges of globalisation, and again we see how this is linked to her overly restricted understanding of the ends of agonistic democracy.

Pluralism and Hegemony

In Chapter 1 we saw that Mouffe shares the agonistic viewpoint that pluralism, tragedy and conflict provide conditioning circumstances of politics. Like each of the thinkers examined in this book, she is critical of liberal theory for its juridical orientation and its stress on the priority of procedural mechanisms for mediating existing conceptions of the good (Mouffe, 1995a, 1535). As Mouffe puts it, pluralism does 'not involve the "coexistence" one by one, of a plurality of subject positions but [rather] the constant subversion and overdetermination of one by the others' (Mouffe, 1995b, 33). Mouffe draws attention to a wide range of traditions in twentieth-century philosophy that might contribute to this idea. She emphasises all those approaches that converge on a 'critique of rationalism and subjectivism', and she refers not only to post-structuralism but also to phenomenology, psychoanalysis, post-Heideggerian hermeneutics, Wittgenstein, and American pragmatism (Mouffe, 1993b, 20; 1996a, 1). Nevertheless, the most conspicuous influence on her iteration of pluralism is the post-structuralist philosophy of language elaborated in Derrida's early work. Indeed, Mouffe says that pluralism can only be adequately formulated from a perspective that acknowledges the Derridean notion of *différance* as a 'condition of possibility' of identity (Mouffe, 1995a, 1534). We therefore commence with an account of the Derridean strand of post-structuralism, and the way in which Laclau and Mouffe invoked Derrida to elaborate the idea of the discursive construction of social and political identity.

For Laclau and Mouffe, 'discourse' is an ontological category that provides conditions of possibility for any meaningful engagement with the world of objects (Laclau and Mouffe, 1990, 105). As they put it, in 'our interchange with the world, objects are never given to us as mere existential entities; they are always given to us within discursive articulations' (Laclau and Mouffe, 1990, 103). They likened their understanding of discourse to Wittgenstein's language games; however, their principal source of inspiration was Saussurean and post-Saussurean conceptions of language (Laclau and Mouffe, 1985, 106, 108, 112–13). In his explanation of linguistic structure, Ferdinand de Saussure showed how the meaning of any given term or signifier is dependent upon its value – as an equivalent term – in a series of purely formal differences (Saussure,

1998, 110–20). Similarly, in Laclau and Mouffe's theory, a given discourse is a sequence of relational moments temporarily structured into some kind of a meaningful whole (Laclau, 2004). Their innovation was to apply the Saussurean notion of value to the entirety of social relations, so that all social identities, or 'subject positions', are seen as intrinsically relational (Laclau and Mouffe, 1985, 107, 115; Laclau, 2005, 68). From this perspective, there is 'no identity that is self-present to itself and not constructed as difference' (Mouffe, 1993b, 141).

Structural linguistics gives priority to relations and relationality over identity. However, classical structuralism also envisaged a closed synchronic system where 'every moment is subsumed from the beginning under the principle of repetition' (Laclau and Mouffe, 1985, 106). By way of contrast, Laclau and Mouffe endorsed Derrida's post-structuralist critique of Saussure's notion of synchronic closure. Just as Derrida emphasised the excess of relationality that overflows every attempt to establish fixed synchronic structures, so too in society and politics there is an inherent 'subversion of each of the terms by a polysemy which prevents their stable articulation' (Laclau and Mouffe, 2001, 121). This theory of constitutive pluralism is perhaps best captured in Derrida's notion of *différance*. On Derrida's account, *différance* is not a transcendental principle, it is never fully present or presentable, and yet it makes possible the presentation of objects (Derrida, 1982, 3, 6). Along with a chain of associated terms in Derrida's early work (trace, *iterability*, supplement, etc.), *différance* attempts to name the ultimately unnameable *excess* (syntactic, semantic, and temporal) of relationality, which is constitutive of all signification and thus of all forms of identity (Derrida, 1982, 26; Gasché, 1994, 99). *Différance* is the 'non-full, non-simple, structured and differentiating origin of differences' that repeatedly 'dislocates itself in a chain of differing and deferring substitutions' (Derrida, 1982, 11, 26). Translated into Laclau and Mouffe's terminology, all 'discourse is subverted by a field of discursivity, which overflows it', and so 'instability and precariousness' is the 'most essential possibility' of every discourse and no 'discursive totality is absolutely self-contained' (Laclau and Mouffe, 1985, 113; Laclau, 1990, 109).

This means that discursivity becomes, paradoxically, both the condition of possibility and impossibility of (full) signification or (full) identity, and elsewhere Mouffe has reiterated this same point in terms of a 'constitutive outside' that necessarily disrupts the self-referential unity of every identity (Mouffe, 1992, 10; 1993a, 81; 1994, 109).[3] Moreover, in keeping with the other theorists examined in this book, Mouffe's Derridean

[3] See also: Staten, 1984, 17 and Derrida, 1982, 10.

rendition of pluralism implies the tragic stress on the interminable nature of conflict. She emphasises that hers is a non-dialectical conception of relationality and so there will always be conflicts and elements of 'undecidability' in political life 'for which no rational solution could be found' (Mouffe, 1992, 10; 1995b, 33; 2000a, 13; 2005a, 10, 17).[4] However, by Mouffe's account, this does not mean that human agents become passive vehicles of the silent movement of *différance*. Instead, as we explored in Chapter 1, the tragic view leads to a stress on a finite capacity for action. Indeed, Mouffe's theory involves the acknowledgement of 'the existence of power relations and the need to transform them, while renouncing the illusion that we could [ever] free ourselves completely from power' (Mouffe, 1995a, 1537). For Mouffe, therefore, politics 'becomes a dimension which is present in all fields of human activity', and 'all levels of society can be the loci of relationships of power and the terrain for political struggle' (Mouffe, 1979b, 201; 1981, 185; 1993b, 3). The main question for agonistic politics is 'not how to eliminate power but how to constitute forms of power more compatible with democratic values' (Mouffe, 2000b, 100).

For many post-structuralists, the political value of Derrida's insights into the contingent nature of signification is encapsulated in the idea that every identity or established cultural norm can be subverted through deconstructive strategies of displacement and resignification. This is in line with Tully's emphasis on the inherent capacity of situated subjects to subvert the rules that govern their social and cultural practices, and this style of politics is perhaps exemplified in Butler's account of gender performativity, which is considered in the following chapter in relation to Honig's work. However, for Laclau and Mouffe, this deconstructive manoeuvre is only a preliminary tactic in a wider project of construction. In *Hegemony and Socialist Strategy* they were primarily concerned with rethinking the possibility of a collective struggle for emancipation under conditions of discursivity, *différance*, or of constitutive pluralism. In order to understand this aspect of Mouffe's contribution we need to first look more closely at her initial engagement with Marxism and especially her adoption and reworking of the Gramscian notion of hegemony.

In her earliest writings, Mouffe invoked Gramsci's thought to challenge the strict economism and the class reductionism of classical

---

[4] Marxist critics of Laclau and Mouffe misconstrued their theory as a kind of linguistic idealism, see, for example, Osborne, 1991, 209. However, for Laclau and Mouffe discourse designates an articulation of linguistic and non-linguistic moments or practices in 'a differential and structured system of positions' (Laclau and Mouffe, 1985, 108). The emphasis on the ontological status of 'discourse' simply denotes a materialist ontology where non-dialectical relations are primary (Laclau, 2005, 68).

Marxist theory (Mouffe, 1979b, 174). In the introduction to *Gramsci and Marxist Theory*, Mouffe maintained that Gramsci provided the necessary conceptual tools to move beyond the Marxism of the Second International, where politics and state institutions are understood straightforwardly as a reflection of class interests generated at the level of the economic infrastructure (Mouffe, 1979a, 10). Gramsci's theory provided a 'non-reductionist conception of the superstructures' that did not present them in the 'single dimension of the expression of class interests', but could nonetheless account for the necessary economic determinism of political formations 'in the last instance' (Mouffe, 1979a, 10; 1979b, 171, 188; 1981, 183). Mouffe was drawn to Gramsci's theory because of his emphasis on the importance of politics conceived in terms of the strategic formation of collective action. Gramsci became increasingly interested in the strategic question in the context of the failure of the workers' insurrection in northern Italy at the end of the First World War, and the rise of Italian Fascism. These events convinced him that the Communists could not rely on the laws of dialectical materialism to deliver the proletarian revolution, and that there is no simple causal determinism between transformations in the relations of production and their reflection in the legal and political superstructures. Taking his inspiration from Lenin and the success of the revolution in St. Petersburg in October 1917, Gramsci emphasised that Marxism is a philosophy of action or *praxis*, and he pointed to the reciprocal relationship between the infrastructure and the superstructures, the latter being understood as the realm where, as Marx said, 'men become conscious of their history and fight it out' (Marx, 1983a, 160; Gramsci, 1988, 197).

More specifically, Gramsci emphasised that the success of the proletarian struggle depended upon the capacity of the working class to construct a contingent hegemonic formation, which would enlist the consent of other subordinate social sectors in the formation of a new 'historical bloc' (Gramsci, 1988, 200–9). For example, in the context of Italy in the inter-war period, the Communists would need to win over the support of the peasants and the petite bourgeoisie, to prevent these elements being won over by the Fascists. Unlike Lenin, for whom hegemony meant simply political leadership within an alliance of fixed class interests, Gramsci understood politics as a constituent power capable of transforming social identities (Lenin, 1978; Gramsci, 1988, 205; Laclau and Mouffe, 1985, 55). As Mouffe put it, the formation of hegemony entails 'the articulation of the interests of the fundamental class to those of its allies in order to form a collective will, a unified political subject' (Mouffe, 1979a, 10). To make this point she cited the following passage from Gramsci:

[the] act [of hegemony] can only be performed by 'collective man', and this presupposes the attainment of a 'cultural-social' unity through which a multiplicity
of dispersed wills, with heterogeneous aims, are welded together with a single
aim, on the basis of an equal and common conception of the world. (Gramsci
cited in Mouffe, 1979b, 191)

In the exercise of hegemony, says Gramsci, the 'dominant group
become[s] the interests of other subordinate groups' creating a genuinely
universal or 'ethical state' (Gramsci, 1988, 205, 234).

Indeed, Gramsci took much of his inspiration from the republican
tradition, and particularly from Machiavelli. Reworking Machiavelli's
account of political *virtù* in terms of a limited capacity to outmanoeu-
vre *Fortuna*, Gramsci's innovation was to rethink the efficacy and scope
of politics, conceived as the theatre of strategic action (Gramsci, 2005;
Fontana, 1993). In this respect, he shared with Schmitt and Arendt an
emphasis on the primacy of the constituent power.[5] However, Gramsci
presented the human capacity for freedom as an element located *within*
the conventional base/superstructure topography of Marxist thought and
also *within* the teleology of the Marxist theory of history. The key protagonists in Gramsci's account of politics were always ultimately 'fundamental classes' determined at the level of the relations of production. In
other words, for Gramsci, the constituent power manifests as a degree
of freedom for those who find themselves on the stage of world history, but economic relations of production always ultimately decide the
casting, i.e. who gets to go on stage. In this sense, he does not, in the
end, get beyond the conventional Marxist viewpoint. Indeed, Gramsci's
theory is still susceptible to Arendt's critique of the Marxist theory of
history which we considered in Chapter 2, where she stressed how the
moments of genuine innovation associated with particular struggles are
reduced to the status of internal parts within the overall movement of
the historical process, thereby stripping them of their dignity and their
originality. So, for example, from this perspective the emergence of new
demands from the 1960s – environmentalist struggles, feminist struggles,
civil rights campaigns, student protests, and the struggles of sexual and
ethnic minorities – could only be figured as ultimately tangential to the
'world historical tasks' of the industrial working class, and socialist strategy could only be conceived in terms of building a collective project by
winning over these 'peripheral struggles' to the interests of the proletariat.

In the earliest phase of her career this was Mouffe's position. She said,
'the Gramscian conception of hegemony is not only compatible with

[5] For a discussion see: Kalyvas, 2000.

pluralism, it implies it' (Mouffe, 1979b, 15). However, 'this is a pluralism which is always located within the hegemony of the working class' (Mouffe, 1979a, 15). Only 'the working class, whose interests coincide with the limitation of all exploitation, can be capable of successfully bringing about an expansive hegemony' (Mouffe, 1979b, 183). The working class must therefore 'try to become a "national class", representing the interests of the increasingly numerous social groups' (Mouffe, 1979b, 197). However, by the time she published 'Working-Class Hegemony and the Struggle for Socialism' in 1983, Mouffe had moved beyond this conventional Marxist standpoint. She now recognised that a 'definitive break with economism implies the abandonment of Gramsci's thesis that only the working class can [ultimately] provide the articulating principle of the totality of anti-capitalist and democratic struggles . . . and give them a socialist orientation' (Mouffe, 1983, 22). This does not mean looking for the essential elements of an alternative revolutionary subject amongst the new social movements – the 'ecology movement often being presented as the most serious candidate for this position' – because, Mouffe contends, none of the democratic struggles 'have a predetermined centrality' (Mouffe, 1983, 23). At this point, Mouffe fully embraced the constitutive circumstances of pluralism. She said, we must 'recognise the pluralism and specificity of democratic struggles and try not to reduce their diversity to the expression of a unique contradiction' either with reference to a critique of political economy or the dialectical laws of history (Mouffe, 1983, 15, 24). Indeed, from the post-Marxist perspective of *Hegemony and Socialist Strategy*, published just a few years later, the demands of the proletariat do not ground progressive politics, because class struggles only ever have meaning in a contingently articulated discursive relationship to a series of other demands, for example ethnic, counter-cultural, gender and environmentalist demands.

However, this did not mean abandoning the idea of hegemony. In fact, hegemony now becomes the centrepiece of Laclau and Mouffe's analysis, understood as a contingent strategic effort to construct a collective emancipatory project (Mouffe, 1983, 23). Indeed, Laclau and Mouffe radicalise the Gramscian emphasis on the importance of strategic action to the point where politics is understood as a constituent power capable of shaping social, cultural, and economic forms of identity (Laclau and Mouffe, 2001, 136–8). According to Laclau and Mouffe, every context of political struggle is characterised by a series of 'demands': for example, workers' demands for higher wages, feminist demands for equality in the work place, anti-racist struggles, gay struggles for public recognition of homosexual relationships and practices, and so on (Laclau, 2005, 73). These demands remain in a relationship of 'subordination' all the while that they remain blocked from forming a 'chain of equivalence' with one another (Laclau and Mouffe, 2001, 153). However, to the extent that these struggles start to identify with one another in a collective struggle against the dominant power in society, relations of 'subordination' begin to be perceived as relations of 'oppression' and a new hegemonic subjectivity begins to emerge (Laclau, 2000, 54–5; Laclau and Mouffe, 2001, 153–4). Elsewhere, Laclau has further finessed this idea, so that the emergence of a new hegemonic formation follows from a change in the kind of demands made on the present system, from 'requests' for reforms within the system to a more general mobilisation of 'claims' that cannot be accommodated by it (Laclau, 2005, 73–86).

These concepts provide significant insights into the basis of collective action under conditions of constitutive pluralism. Indeed, *Hegemony and Socialist Strategy* has been very influential, and to a considerable extent this is because Laclau and Mouffe did not associate post-structuralism with an unqualified celebration of the politics of diversity, for example in the form of single-issue politics. Instead, they emphasised the continued importance of a collective struggle for emancipation after the demise of classical Marxism. For example, their stress on the central importance of political alliance building represents a significant advance over Connolly's tendency to write as if the emergence of democratic 'assemblages' can be modelled on the self-organising qualities of natural processes. By way of contrast, Laclau and Mouffe do not lose sight of the priority of the strategic question, and, in this sense, they clearly reiterate the Gramscian and the Machiavellian legacy. As I have said, at this stage in her career the concern with domination is also central to Mouffe's approach. The main task of democratic politics under conditions of pluralism is to present the 'different forms of inequality' – economic exploitation, racism, patriarchy, imperialism, and the destruction of the environment – as 'illegitimate and anti-natural, and thus make them equivalent as forms of oppression' (Laclau and Mouffe, 1985, 155). However, in the previous chapter, we suggested that Laclau and Mouffe's approach is, nonetheless, overly focused on the struggle with the oppressor and to the point where they focus too passionately on the need for emancipation or, in Arendt's terms, liberation. This inclination is evident, for example, in their presentation of the various struggles as 'demands' made against the dominant power, rather than as primarily potential sources of innovation (*potentia*). In fact, the struggle *against* the dominant power is central to their theory, because by their account it is this relationship that makes possible the increasing correspondence between the various unmet 'demands', as they become steadily equivalent as examples of 'oppression'. Of course, Laclau and Mouffe do also stress the politics of change, in the emergence of a new hegemonic configuration, but the point is that this only ever *shadows* the democratic *mêlée*, in the sense that it is presented as an *outcome* of a collective struggle for emancipation. In this sense, their position represents the obverse of Tully's depiction of the creative power of the horizontal citizen–citizen relations between glocal citizens, which, we have seen, is also problematic because it leaves the oppressor completely untouched and so subordinate groups remain in a relation of dependence. By way of contrast, I think we need to navigate a path between these two extremes, and we should assert, with Arendt, that politics is first and foremost about action, understood as the moment of innovation, i.e. the introduction of a new mode of being in the world, but, at the same time, to the extent that a new innovation is successful it will also necessarily disrupt the dominant powers and processes. In other words, the principal task today is to combine freedom and liberation, and in this order of priority, and I seek to pursue such a possibility in my account of agonism and militant cosmopolitanism. In fact, we will see exactly this stress on the priority of the moment of innovation, rather than on a struggle for emancipation, in the original Hellenic understanding of *hegemony* as leadership. We come back to this point in Chapter 7.

From the struggle for emancipation to the problem of antagonism

In the previous chapter we saw that Tully accentuates the ceaselessly pluralistic nature of the struggles for recognition, and how, in his view, the binary opposition has no part to play in agonistic politics. This is clearly in marked contrast to Mouffe. However, it was also suggested that there are different ways to figure the binary opposition, and there is an essential difference between the struggle between the oppressed and the oppressor, which is produced by a demand for emancipation, and the conflict between friends and enemies, which generates a discourse about the need for order and security in the context of a threat of privation. My own sense is that Tully moves too fast to dispense entirely with the first kind of binary opposition, and this is tied up with his idealised account of horizontal citizen–citizen relations. However, at this point we need to examine the trajectory in Mouffe's work, which sees her move very clearly from the first to the second form of binary opposition. In this section I consider what this means for Mouffe's critique of alternative models of democracy and, in the following section, I assess the impact of this move on her own formulation of agonistic democracy, and how this brings her increasingly within the orbit of the neo-conservative view of politics.

The stress on the continued importance of binary division is a central theme in *Hegemony and Social Strategy*, and this is in keeping with Laclau

and Mouffe's emphasis on the politics of emancipation. They reject the
conventional Marxist view, elaborated so colourfully in the first part of
The Manifesto of the Communist Party, that 'society as a whole is more and
more splitting up into two great hostile camps' and that the emergence of
this division in the political sphere is a necessary effect of the underlying
contradictions in the forces and relations of production (Marx, 1983b,
204; Laclau and Mouffe, 1985, 151). On Laclau and Mouffe's reading, the Marxist schema of a simple structural division can be traced to
the French Revolution, and to the 'Jacobin imaginary' of an opposition
between the people and the *ancien régime* (Laclau and Mouffe, 1985,
152). As they see it, this basic division retained some validity in the context of French society in the late eighteenth century. However, this was, in
fact, the 'last moment in which the antagonistic limits between two forms
of society presented themselves... in the form of clear and empirically
given lines of demarcation', and the problem with conventional Marxist
analysis is that it has desperately tried to hold onto this schema despite the
ever-increasing complexity of social forms, and a corresponding proliferation of political struggles, characteristic of modern societies (Laclau and
Mouffe, 1985, 151). Importantly, however, Laclau and Mouffe do not
reject the idea of binary division as entirely outmoded. Although this division can no longer be conceived as an underlying effect of the social structure, the binary form of political conflict is still presented as the *intrinsic*
form of emancipatory politics. Indeed, by their account, radical politics:

always consists in the construction of a social identity... on the basis of the
equivalence between a set of elements or values, which expel or externalise those
others to which they are opposed. Once again, we find ourselves confronting the
division of social space. (Laclau and Mouffe, 1985, 165)

In fact, the key question of *Hegemony and Socialist Strategy* is precisely
how to construct this emancipatory form of division under conditions of
pluralism.

However, Laclau and Mouffe's book also reveals an additional way of
conceiving of the binary division and of the circumstances that provoke
the emergence of hegemony, one that is distinct from the emphasis on
the struggle between the oppressed and the oppressor. In contrast to the
struggle for emancipation, they also present hegemony as a form of order
as such, set against the backdrop of an inherent threat of social disintegration. Indeed, they maintain that social relations would rapidly become
chaotic in the absence of some explicit attempt to construct political
order. In their terminology, 'a discourse incapable of generating any fixity
of meaning is the discourse of the psychotic' (Laclau and Mouffe, 1985,
112). This emphasis on the need for unity as a remedy to social fragmentation is quite distinct from their attempt to rework the Marxist tradition

Part II

in order to situate the struggle against capitalist exploitation within a more general movement that might render exploitation, racism, marginalisation, etc. equivalent as modes of domination. Indeed, this alternative view of order as the solution to privation has no place in the Marxist tradition, and has been articulated instead by conservative thinkers – most famously, of course, by Thomas Hobbes. These two ways of framing the binary division and their associated goods, of emancipation or unity and order, are clearly in tension in *Hegemony and Socialist Strategy*. However, in the mid 1980s, and in the context of the high point of Thatcherism and of the miners' strike, it was generally the first problematic that was at the forefront of Mouffe's concerns. She said the 'central problem is to identify the discursive conditions for the emergence of a collective action, directed towards struggling against inequalities and challenging relations of subordination' (Laclau and Mouffe, 1985, 153). Nevertheless, in her explicitly agonistic writings, from the early 1990s, the second of these concerns has taken on an increasing prominence, to the point where it has more or less become her exclusive emphasis, and Schmitt has been her central resource for formulating politics in these terms.[6]

In Chapters 1 and 2 I briefly elaborated Schmitt's depiction of 'the political' in terms of the friend/enemy relationship, and we saw that, on Mouffe's own account, it is this point of emphasis that differentiates her version of agonism from the other theorists examined in this book. Like Schmitt, Mouffe sees the possible emergence of extreme forms of antagonism as inherent in human social relations, or, as she puts it, as part of our ontological condition (Mouffe, 1993b, 2, 3; 1994, 108; Schmitt, 1996, 79). This doesn't mean that human beings are incapable of

[6] In their coauthored book Laclau and Mouffe do not differentiate sufficiently between these two binary forms of opposition, and they use the term 'antagonism' interchangeably to refer to both of them. In Laclau's subsequent work the term is employed instead to designate something like the Lacanian 'real', i.e. an un-symbolisable kernel of (impossible) plenitude; which, on his account, is supposedly constitutive (as lack) of all social relations and forms of political order. In Mouffe's later work, on the other hand, the term is used exclusively to denote the Schmittean problematic of 'the political', i.e. an inherent potential for conflict between existential enemies, which according to Mouffe is an ever present possibility in social relations. These different usages of the term 'antagonism' are not equivalent (the Lacanian iteration engenders a set of reflections about the limits of symbolic representation, whereas the Schmittean model draws attention to the conservative problematic of security and the threat of physical violence) and here I reserve the term for the Mouffean/Schmittean conceptualisation. From time to time, Laclau has also been prone to lapse into this conservative account of the construction of hegemony. For example, he says: 'when people are confronted with radical *anomie*, the need for some kind of order becomes more important than the actual ontic order that brings it about. The Hobbesian universe is the extreme version of this gap: because society is faced with a situation of total disorder (the state of nature), whatever the Leviathan does is legitimate – irrespective of its content – as long as order is the result' (Laclau, 2005, 88).

generating limited forms of reciprocity. Instead, Mouffe points to the 'double bind... that brings human beings together in their common desire for the same objects [but which] is also at the origin of their antagonism' (Mouffe, 2000b, 131). Mouffe also reworks this idea in the Derridean idiom of a 'constitutive outside' (Mouffe, 2005a, 14). She says, if the element of differentiation is a condition of every identity, then in the realm of 'collective identifications' this involves the 'creation of a "we" by the delimitation of a "them"', and the 'possibility always exists that this we/them relation will turn into a relation of the friend/enemy type' (Mouffe, 1993b, 2; 2005a, 14). Indeed, we approach the moment of antagonism 'when the "other", who up until now has been considered simply as different, starts to be perceived as someone who is rejecting "my" identity and who is threatening "my" existence' (Mouffe, 1994, 108). At this point, says Mouffe, confrontations emerge over what are (mis)understood as 'essentialist identities and non-negotiable moral values' and, as I have said, Mouffe points to various examples of these belligerent forms of politics, and perhaps especially the growth of far Right extremism across parts of Europe, as evidence of this latent potential for antagonism that could 'tear up the very basis of civility' (Mouffe, 1993b, 147; 1994, 109; 2000b, 104).

In Chapter 2 we saw that Schmitt's focus on the threat of extreme antagonism is indissociable from his presentation of the constituent power in terms of the emergence of a strong sovereign 'will' capable of ensuring the basis of political unity (Schmitt, 1996, 39). Indeed, Schmitt did not envisage the possibility of agonistic conflict – which Mouffe defines as 'legitimate dissent among friends' – within the political association (Mouffe, 1999a, 5). He clearly shared Hobbes' view that the first problem of politics is always 'the problem of the political unity of a people', and for Schmitt any degree of domestic pluralism will eventually result in the 'dissolution of the unity of the political whole' (Schmitt, 1999, 202, 207). Hence, the need for the strong sovereign power that ensures that conflict between citizens will not dissociate into a 'state of extreme enmity – that is into civil war' (Schmitt, 1999, 203). Mouffe's response to the ever-present threat of antagonism is different to Schmitt's. Indeed, the central question for her is how is it possible under these Schmittean 'conditions to create and maintain a pluralist democratic order' (Mouffe, 1993b, 4)? We will look at the details of Mouffe's response to this question in a moment, but, as a prelude, we first need to consider her critique of the currently predominant modes of democratic theory and practice, i.e. for their naive disavowal of the ever-present possibility of antagonism.

Indeed, Mouffe finds in Schmitt's concept of the political the resources to develop a kind of ideology critique of mainstream contemporary democratic theory. Her analysis is different to Honig's assessment of Habermas that I elaborated in Chapter 2. Honig draws attention to the way in which Habermas' depiction of modern constitutionalism as a progressive learning process tries to subsume the constituent power (of/for open-ended moments of innovation) under teleological principles of development, and in Chapter 2 I went on to utilise Honig's idea to survey the same tendency in a range of contemporary democratic theories. By way of contrast, Mouffe claims that Schmitt's emphasis on the irreducible nature of antagonism reveals the 'blind spot' of the prevailing theories of liberal democracy, and, as has been said, on her reading this actually makes the emergence of extreme forms of conflict more likely (Mouffe, 1993b, 1; 1999a, 2). For example, she sees evidence of this disavowal of 'the political' in the instrumentalist conception of democracy characteristic of 'aggregative democracy' (Mouffe, 2000b, 96; 1995a, 1537). She says, the presentation of democratic politics in terms of a competition between interests groups fails to understand the 'need for a construction of collective identities', and, on her reading, this model is associated with a discouragement of active citizenship which has fed into the 'current disaffection with democratic institutions and . . . the rampant crisis of legitimacy affecting western democracies' (Mouffe, 1995a, 1535; 1999b, 47; 2000b, 83, 96). The aggregative model is therefore implicated in the present 'growth of religious, moral and ethnic fundamentalisms' because they flourish in a context where lack of interest in politics is widespread (Mouffe, 2000b, 93, 96). In Chapter 2 I suggested that we need to differentiate between the pluralist and the rational choice variants of aggregative democracy, and that many of the established criticisms of the pluralist model do not stand up to scrutiny. I won't reiterate those points here, but certainly Mouffe's critique captures something significant about the economic model of democracy that runs from Downs to the present centrality of rational choice models in political science, and Mouffe is right to draw attention to the way in which the emergence of more fundamentalist forms of politics is linked to the present crises in mainstream democratic institutions.

However, the principal target of Mouffe's critique has been the deliberative model, put forward by Habermas, Benhabib, Dryzek, and others, which she says has 'no real purchase on democratic politics', and she is resolute in her rejection of the idea that rational 'consensus can . . . be obtained through dialogue' (Mouffe, 2000a, 440; 2000b, 92; 2005a, 1). We also explored this model in Chapter 2 and saw how some deliberative theorists have sought to rework the idea of consensus in light of the criticisms levelled by Mouffe and others. Deliberative theorists now typically stress the principle of reciprocity and the always only temporary and fallible nature of consensus. They similarly stress the way in which deliberation is only one aspect of politics, along with bargaining and other forms of negotiation aimed at compromise rather than consensus. However, from Mouffe's perspective, these reformulated versions of deliberation still rest upon an impossible rational ideal, because they cannot get to grips with the fact that every moment of consensus, however provisional or fallible, is 'by necessity based on acts of exclusion' (Mouffe, 1993b, 69). Indeed, from her Schmittean viewpoint, it doesn't matter whether or not the deliberative ideal is predicated on the procedural principle of (full inclusive) reciprocity or on a model of rational debate oriented towards consensus; this ideal fundamentally 'goes against the democratic requisite of drawing a frontier between "us" and "them"' (Mouffe, 2000b, 48). We will look more closely at Schmitt's understanding of democracy below. However, for the moment we should simply note that, by his account, every 'actual democracy rests on the principle that not only are equals equal but unequals will not be treated equally' (Schmitt, 1988, 9).[7] We will also see, in a moment, that this view does not preclude the possibility of forms of consensus. In fact, Mouffe has repeatedly stressed the importance of consensus as a precondition of agonistic politics. However, the key point is that, from her perspective, we need to acknowledge the 'political nature' of the articulation of consensus, through moments of in/exclusion rather than treating consensus as a 'requirement of morality or rationality' (Mouffe, 2000b, 93). In Mouffe's view, every consensus appears as a contingent 'stabilisation of something essentially unstable and chaotic', and this constitutive instability should not be seen – with Hegel, Habermas, or the contemporary theorists of deliberative democracy – as a 'temporary obstacle ... on the road ... towards harmony and reconciliation' (Mouffe, 1996a, 8–9; 1996b, 138). In some ways, this is the most compelling part of Mouffe's theory, and her repeated stress on the incommensurability of the deliberative model with the tragic vision of agonistic democracy is important, and provides a valuable counterpoint to Tully's misguided attempt to bring these two viewpoints closer together.

Mouffe exposes a comparable allusion to full consensus, without exclusions or remainders, in the dominant trends in mainstream party politics. This was exemplified in Tony Blair's New Labour project in the UK, which claimed to represent a 'win-win' politics that supposedly benefited all members of society (Mouffe, 2000b, 110). In New Labour's 'third way' ideology, socialism is redefined in terms of the efficient management of market mechanisms and the utilisation of higher economic growth to

---

[7] See also: Mouffe, 2000b, 38, 43.

redistribute wealth in society. These theories are part of a broader under-standing of 'reflexive modernity' developed by Ulrich Beck and Giddens, which, in turn, can be traced to the 'end of ideology' debates in the 1960s and the theories of 'post-industrial society'.[8] From this technocratic per-spective, political conflicts are no longer expressed 'through the left/right metaphor which was typical of industrial society but are better charac-terized in terms of safe/unsafe, inside/outside and political/unpolitical' (Mouffe, 2005a, 38). The belief is that a consensus on policy priorities and the effective management of risk can be built 'between the experts, the politicians, the industrialists and the citizens' (Mouffe, 2005a, 41). Consequently:

the cycle of confrontational politics dominant in the west since the French revo-lution has come to an end. The Left–Right distinction is now irrelevant, since it was anchored in a social bipolarity that has ceased to exist. Now the majority of the people in advanced industrial societies belong to the middle classes, the dis-appearance of class identities and the end of the bipolar system of confrontation have rendered conventional politics obsolete. (Mouffe, 1999a, 3)

However, Mouffe shows how the 'third way' rhetoric of inclusion, modernisation, and 'post politics' effectively forecloses the possibility of any opposition, which can now only be conceived in pejorative terms, i.e. as irrational or backward, and much like the dominant models of democracy in the academy, this has the effect of closing down the *agon*, because it 'does not allow voters a real choice between significantly differ-ent policies' (Mouffe, 2005a, 5, 66–9). Moreover, when 'political fron-tiers become blurred' with these false ideals of consensus, 'disaffection with political parties sets in and one witnesses the growth of other types of collective identities, around nationalist, religious, or ethnic forms of identification' (Mouffe, 2005a, 30). In other words, these trends open the door to extremist parties and have the negative effect of bringing about political polarisation (Mouffe, 2005a, 62–9). As Mouffe rightly says, across Europe the far Right has moved into the vacuum created by technocratic post-politics. For example, this is evident in the electoral success of the Freedom Party in Austria and the *Front National* in France, and growing support for the British National Party in the UK. Moreover, these trends have become much more acute in the context of the present financial crisis, with an alarming rise of far-Right extremism in Greece and parts of Eastern Europe.

Mouffe has very effectively revealed the elements of denial and conceit embedded in the models of rational and technocratic consensus, and her account of how they are implicated in the current rise of far Right and other forms of extremism does help to explain important trends in the

---

[8] See: Bell, 1999, 2001; Beck, 2011; Giddens, 2012.

present conjuncture. However, we should note how these discussions take Mouffe some distance from her earlier concern with building a collective alliance of subaltern struggles in a common opposition against various forms of domination. Moreover, to gauge just how far Mouffe travels from these erstwhile objectives, we now need to turn to her own formulation of agonistic democracy, which she presents as an alterative to the deliberative and other approaches, and where the focus becomes exclusively on the need to sublimate antagonism into constructive modes of agonism.

Agonistic democracy as the sublimation of antagonism

From Mouffe's perspective, the problem with contemporary political theory is that 'few attempts have been made to elaborate the democratic project on an anthropology which acknowledges the ambivalent character of human sociability and the fact that reciprocity and hostility cannot be dissociated' (Mouffe, 2005a, 3; 2000b, 131). Agonistic democracy can fill this gap, and Mouffe presents her model as a realist counterpoint to the naive idealism of the consensus theories and the problems of far Right extremism that accompany them. By Mouffe's account, agonistic democracy artfully redirects the threat of extreme forms of conflict, firstly by getting honest about the ineradicable presence of antagonism, and secondly by finding creative ways to sublimate hostility into more constructive forms of contest. For example, Mouffe stresses the need to resuscitate the dispute between Left and Right as an antidote to Right-wing populism. Far from 'jeopardizing democracy', this is the very 'condition of its existence', because 'antagonistic conflicts are less likely to emerge as long as agonistic legitimate political channels for dissenting voices exist. Otherwise dissent tends to take violent forms' (Mouffe, 2005a, 21, 30). These ideas resonate with the Nietzschean idea of the spiritualisation of enmity that we discussed in Chapter 1, and they are significant goods associated with agonistic democracy. However, in Mouffe's theory these goals become the overriding consideration, and this leads her to stress the importance of order and unity as preconditions of agonistic politics. Mouffe has repeatedly stressed the need to establish limits on acceptable forms of diversity through a symbolic and legal exclusion of those values that are incompatible with pluralism. As she puts it, an 'extreme form of pluralism, according to which all interests, all opinions, all differences are seen as legitimate, could never provide the framework for a political regime' (Mouffe, 1992, 11, 13; 1996c, 250).[9]

---

[9] For example, this leads Mouffe to reject the multiculturalist idea of group rights and forms of legal pluralism (Mouffe, 1993b, 99; 1995a, 1535; 2002, 4). She says: 'there must be

Indeed, the main challenge of agonistic democracy is to 'keep the emergence of antagonism at bay' and the task is 'to imagine in a different way what Schmitt refers to as "homogeneity"', i.e. to 'constitute the framework of a consensus within which pluralism can exist' (Mouffe, 1992, 14; 1999b, 50; 2005a, 16). We need to 'envisage a form of commonality strong enough to institute a "demos" but nevertheless compatible with certain forms of pluralism: religious, moral, and cultural pluralism, as well as a pluralism of political parties' (Mouffe, 1999a, 5; 1999b, 50; 2000b, 53). From Mouffe's perspective, the citizens of agonistic democracy find themselves in the paradoxical position of 'adversaries' or 'friendly enemies': they are 'friends because they share a common symbolic space but also enemies because they want to organise this common symbolic space in a different way' from one another (Mouffe, 1999a, 4; 2000b, 13; 2005a, 20). There is room for conflict about the interpretations of the shared values of the political community, but, according to Mouffe, 'there must be consensus about the values we are struggling to interpret' (Mouffe, 1996c, 136). This stress on the primary importance of unity and consensus clearly sets Mouffe apart from the other theorists examined in this book, and this emphasis has led some commentators to the conclusion that Mouffe's critique of deliberative democracy is inconsistent, that her 'agonistic theory ends up mirroring those of her deliberative democratic rivals... Despite repudiating the ideal of rational deliberation... Mouffe concludes with a politics that is in its essentials distinctly deliberative' (Breen, 2009, 138–9; Knops, 2007).

However, this reading is predicated on the false idea that consensus can only be formulated from within the deliberative paradigm, and misunderstands the limited and impassioned forms of reciprocity that Mouffe associates with the constitutive exclusions of agonistic democracy. In contrast to the prevailing rationalist approaches, Mouffe brings certain psychoanalytical concepts to bear in her theorisation of democratic consensus, and, in particular, she says Freud's 'analysis of the process of identification brings out the libidinal investment at work in the creation of collective identities' (Mouffe, 2005a, 25). In *Group Psychology and the Analysis of the Ego* (1921) Freud described identification as a libidinal tie between two or more egos such that they 'mark a point of coincidence' with one another (Freud, 1991, 137). When I identify with somebody I

a consensus on what the basic institutions are in society. There cannot be pluralism at that level. So this means we should not have different legal systems according to different communities. There must be something common, but a form of commonality, which should make room for the recognition of differences in many cultural terms' (Mouffe, 1996c, 135).

do not wish to have him or her as my 'object choice', rather I want to be like him or her (Freud, 1991, 135). Freud points out that identification results 'amongst other things in a person limiting his aggressiveness towards those with whom he has identified himself' (Freud, 1991, 140). Applying this idea to the political realm, Mouffe says that in 'order to act politically people need to be able to identify with a collective identity which provides an idea of themselves they can valorise' (Mouffe, 2005a, 25). Consequently, democratic 'politics cannot be limited to establishing compromises among interests or values or to deliberation about the common good: it needs to have a real purchase on peoples' fantasies' and imaginations (Mouffe, 2005a, 6).

Connolly has also criticised Mouffe for her emphasis on consensus as a prior condition of agonism. He appreciates that her theory is distinct from deliberative approaches and that she does not imagine the possibility of a rational consensus without exclusion. However, Connolly says Mouffe 'will require a lot of (Schmittian) exclusions' to achieve her consensus, because of the number of constituencies who are today 'deeply at odds' with the values of democratic pluralism (Connolly, 1995b, 133). As we saw in Chapter 3, he appeals instead to the cultivation of civic virtue, of an ethos of agonistic respect, which he presents as the most appropriate means to address the threats associated with the politics of fundamentalism. In a previous paper I argued that Mouffe is more realist than Connolly, because he imagines the possibility of pluralism without exclusions (Wenman, 2003b). However, on reflection, their positions are not too dissimilar, and this is because Connolly and Mouffe formulate the principal challenges associated with agonistic democracy in more or less the same way. They both draw attention to the present manifestations of extreme forms of conflict, associated, for example, with religious fanaticism or the rise of the far Right; they both explain these developments in existential or anthropological terms, i.e. as a reflection of *ressentiment* or of a primordial tendency towards antagonism; and so they both see agonistic democracy as primarily contending with limits to the good society that are supposedly entrenched in the human condition. Moreover, because of this line of thought, they have been concerned respectively with the need for a politics of moderation and of constraint, i.e. with a stress on self-restraint through an inner acknowledgement and testament of contestability (Connolly), or the importance of placing limits and constraints on pluralism through the maintenance of unity and order (Mouffe). This brings them close to the liberal and conservative traditions respectively, and they each offer less compelling depictions of the underlying purpose of agonistic democracy than Tully, who, as we have seen, explains the politics of fundamentalism instead as the product of historically specific forms of imperialism, and who links the democratic *agon* primarily to struggles to overcome domination and exercise independence.

Of course, Connolly is also concerned with challenging forms of domination in the mode of normalisation, and he stresses the disruptive quality of the constituent power in the moment of the politics of enactment. We have seen that, in her earlier work, Mouffe was similarly concerned with challenging domination, but this has clearly receded into the background in her agonistic writings, to be replaced by a persistent emphasis on the underlying threat of hostility.[10] For Mouffe, it seems that the primary, or perhaps even the exclusive, good of agonistic democracy is to ensure order and security against the backdrop of the ever-present possibility of antagonism. Ironically perhaps, in her attempt to respond to the dangers of far Right extremism, Mouffe appears to duplicate a neo-conservative understanding of politics.[11] As Rancière says, for the neo-conservative, politics is 'no longer the art of advancing the energies of the world, but rather that of preventing civil war through a . . . call to unity' (Rancière, 2007, 8). The neo-conservative conjures up the 'gaping abyss, the brink of dread, from which he then [makes] himself our protector' (Rancière, 2007, 11). Here the need for unity 'relates not to the demands of the task before us', as it had in Mouffe's earlier work, but 'rather to the representation of the archaic gulf which stands always as our limit' (Rancière, 2007, 11). These formulations neatly describe the Schmittean problematic that we examined above, as well as in Chapter 2, and in the following chapter we will see that Agamben has reworked these ideas to provide an excellent account of the emergence and reproduction of the post–9/11 security state. However, it is also clear that the underlying concerns that animate Mouffe's version of agonistic democracy share a basic point of connection with this neo-conservative worldview. Indeed, Mouffe comes perilously close to reproducing the neo-conservative problematic when she draws a primary distinction between:

'the political' (which describes the dimension of antagonism and hostility between humans – an antagonism which can take many different forms and can emerge in any form of social relation) and 'politics' (which seeks to establish a certain order and to organise human co-existence in conditions that are permanently conflictual because they are affected by 'the political'). (Mouffe, 1994, 108)

---

[10] For evaluations of Mouffe's later work predicated on similar sentiments see Schaap, 2007, 63 and Breen, 2009, 138–9.

[11] Mouffe's emphasis on the primary need to secure order against the threat of anarchy or privation is close to the realisms of Williams and Philp: see Williams, 2005, 3; Philp, 2010, 471; and for a discussion of William's view, see Honig and Stears, 2011, 192–3.

This could be read as a neat summation of the Hobbesean view of politics, and it is clear at this point just how far Mouffe has travelled from her earlier (post-)Marxist concern with the politics of emancipation.[12] However, what perhaps saves Mouffe from this tragic fate, where a committed Leftist ends up embracing the neo-conservative political imaginary, is her additional claim that the formation of democratic unity through sovereign in/exclusion creates the conditions of agonistic forms of politics. In other words, by Mouffe's account, the moment of sovereign in/exclusion does not only ensure security (through the sublimation of antagonism), it also instantiates something more than this, it 'create[s] a vibrant 'agonistic' public sphere of contestation where different... political projects' are perpetually renegotiated (Mouffe, 2005a, 3). We turn now to look at this aspect of Mouffe's theory, and in particular her presentation of agonism as an open-ended augmentation of the paradoxical principles of liberalism and democracy. This is where Mouffe, like the other thinkers examined in this book, thinks we advance the energies of the world. However, in contrast to them, Mouffe does not situate this space of agonistic freedom at the very centre of her analysis. Instead, her primary and repeated point of emphasis in her later writings is on the nasty, short, and brutish circumstances that must be kept at bay in order to make legitimate expressions of diversity possible.

The liberal democratic paradox

Another pressing question for Leftist political theorists in the 1980s was whether or not socialism could be realised within the institutions and practices of liberal democracy. In line with other prominent contributors to these discussions – such as Norberto Bobbio, Paul Hirst, and C. B. Macpherson – Mouffe understood socialism as an extension and deepening of the values associated with liberal democracy, and not, as it is presented in classical Marxist theory, as entirely antithetical to liberalism or as a radical alternative to the existing system (Macpherson, 1979, 2; Hirst, 1996; Bobbio, 2005; Mouffe, 2005a, 33). From these debates, Mouffe moved towards what has become the second most prominent theme in her later work, which has been her account of liberal democracy as the basic setting for pluralism and for agonistic politics. This idea was first formulated in the final chapter of *Hegemony and Socialist*

---

[12] Mouffe's entrenched pessimism is also close to the spirit of Freud's *Civilisation and its Discontents*, where Freud depicts the fundamental socio-political situation in a manner that is close to Schmitt and Hobbes; on this view civilised society is perpetually threatened with disintegration because of the primary mutual hostility of human beings (Freud, 1961, 66).

Strategy, where Laclau and Mouffe developed a theory of 'radical and plural democracy' in terms of an expansion of the 'principle[s] of liberty and equality' to more areas of social life (Laclau and Mouffe, 1985, 155, 184). This view was further elaborated in *The Democratic Paradox*, where Mouffe describes political modernity in terms of a permanent tension between the alternative values and traditions of liberalism and democracy (Mouffe, 2000b, 3). Drawing on Macpherson, she stressed that these two traditions were only articulated together in the nineteenth century, and they are not necessarily comfortable bedfellows (Macpherson, 1979; Mouffe, 1993b, 10). Whilst 'we tend today to take the link between [them] for granted, their union, far from being a smooth process, was the result of bitter struggles' (Mouffe, 2000b, 3).

On one side we have the liberal tradition constituted by the rule of law, the defence of human rights and the respect of individual liberty; on the other the democratic tradition whose main ideas are those of equality, identity between governing and governed and popular sovereignty. (Mouffe, 2000b, 3)[13]

This dimension of Mouffe work reaffirms the idea, set out in the Introduction, that contemporary agonistic democracy is partly defined by a characteristic stress on liberal democracy as the basic horizon of agonistic politics, and of agonism as an open-ended augmentation of liberal democratic constitutionalism. In fact, these ideas are perhaps most explicitly pronounced in Mouffe's contribution, and in order to better define the tensions that she perceives at the core of liberal democracy it will be helpful to briefly consider the attitudes of two thinkers who each represent an unqualified endorsement of one or the other doctrine, that is Schmitt and Berlin.

As we saw in Chapter 2, Schmitt wrote in the context of the Weimar Republic, and in response to the crisis in parliamentary democracy engendered by mass support for extremist parties at both ends of the political spectrum. He argued that liberalism is an inherently anti-political doctrine predicated upon a desperate disavowal of antagonism and the moment of decision (Schmitt, 1988). Pre-empting Mouffe's critique of contemporary deliberative democracy, he said:

The essence of liberalism is negotiation, a cautious half-measure, in the hope that the definitive dispute, the decisive bloody battle, can be transformed into a parliamentary debate and permit the decision to be suspended forever in an everlasting discussion. (Schmitt, 2005, 63)

Indeed, Schmitt saw the modern traditions of liberal thought moving back and forth between two models of social self-regulation in an attempt

---

[13] See also: Mouffe, 1992, 14; 1993b, 122; 1994, 111.

to systematically avoid the traumatic realities of genuine politics. Liberalism 'has attempted to transform the enemy from the viewpoint of economics into a competitor and from the intellectual viewpoint into a debating partner' (Schmitt, 1996, 28). However, the liberal fantasy of converting politics into balanced forms of legal regulation is an illusion, because, in Schmitt's view, there is no escaping the primacy of the constituent power in the form of the sovereign 'will'. The liberal conception of 'the sovereignty of law' means in reality 'only the sovereignty of men who draw up and administer this law', and so any genuinely political theory must accept the irreducible element of force and decision (Schmitt, 1996, 67). In juxtaposition, Schmitt celebrates democracy as an authentically political doctrine, because the essence of democracy is, in his view, 'an identity between law and the people's will' and if this 'identity is taken seriously, then in an emergency, no other constitutional institution can withstand the sole criterion of the people's will, however it is expressed' (Schmitt, 1988, 26, 15). Given these assumptions, Schmitt concludes that 'dictatorship is not antithetical to democracy', and 'Bolshevism and Fascism . . . are, like all dictatorships, certainly antiliberal but not necessarily antidemocratic' (Schmitt, 1988, 28, 16).

By way of contrast, Isaiah Berlin's 'Two Concepts of Liberty' was written at the height of the Cold War. In this famous essay Berlin distinguished between negative and positive forms of liberty. The former is concerned with freedom as 'an area of non-interference' where the individual is free 'to do or be what he is able to be' essentially 'unobstructed by others' (Berlin, 1982, 141, 143). This is the liberal conception of freedom, and the idea of positive liberty is, in Berlin's view, at the heart of the democratic or republican concern with self-government (Berlin, 1982, 141). Berlin sees an intrinsic relationship between the democratic goal of self-government and perfectionist doctrines in the pursuit of 'happiness, fulfilment of duty, wisdom, a just society, self-fulfilment' (Berlin, 1982, 151). He was deeply sceptical of the pursuit of positive liberty, insisting that the exercise of popular self-government is 'at times, no better than a specious disguise for brutal tyranny' (Berlin, 1982, 148). No doubt, he had in mind the popular support for Fascist and Communist governments in the mid twentieth century. Conversely, he claimed that individual freedom could be enjoyed in the absence of self-government, and that negative liberty is perfectly compatible with non-democratic forms of government, as long as the government leaves you alone, for example under a 'liberal-minded despot' such as Frederick the Great of Prussia or Josef II of Austria (Berlin, 1982, 148).

Mouffe broadly agrees with Schmitt's critique of liberalism as an anti-political doctrine concerned with placing juridical limits on the expression of political power. However, she also identifies with Berlin's anxiety about democracy as potentially authoritarian, which seems to be confirmed by Schmitt's association of democracy with the decisive manifestation of executive power under conditions of emergency. Indeed, Mouffe's objective is to use Schmitt's 'critique of liberal individualism and rationalism to propose a new understanding of liberal democratic politics instead of following Schmitt in rejecting it' (Mouffe, 2005a, 14). In fact, 'the great strength of liberal democracy, pace Schmitt, is precisely that it provides the institutions that, if properly understood, can shape the element of hostility in a way that defuses its potential' (Mouffe, 1993b, 5). Like many contemporary theorists, including Rawls and Habermas, Mouffe emphasises that democracy alone does not guarantee personal freedom or respect for individual rights. Consequently, the on-going tensions between liberalism and democracy are in fact a political good, because it is 'only through its articulation with liberalism' that the expression of popular sovereignty can 'avoid becoming tyrannical' (Mouffe, 1993b, 123; 1996d, 21). Indeed, Mouffe depicts modern politics as a permanent (re)negotiation of the 'tension deriving from the workings' of liberalism and democracy, and she describes this as the 'democratic paradox' (Mouffe, 2000b, 4). This would be better formulated as the liberal-democratic paradox, because, from Mouffe's perspective, perfect 'liberty and perfect equality become impossible', and there can only be 'temporary, pragmatic, unstable and precarious' settlements between these different doctrines (Mouffe, 2000b, 5, 10). These formulations are, of course, close to Habermas' thesis about co-originality that we explored in Chapter 2. However, in contrast to Rawls and Habermas, in Mouffe's account there is no way the opposite logics of liberty and equality can be conceptually prioritised, rationally reconciled, or neatly combined in theory or practice (Mouffe, 1999b, 44).

Nevertheless, Mouffe's reading clearly implies certain constitutional constraints on the legitimate emergence of the constituent power, and one of the central themes of her later work is the idea that widespread commitment to the values and institutions of liberal democracy establishes a precondition for legitimate forms of politics (Mouffe, 1993b, 130). This means that Mouffe effectively moves beyond a more general claim that consensus through in/exclusion provides a prior condition of agonism, to a more specific assertion that a consensus built around a passionate fidelity to the liberal democratic tradition provides that necessary condition. She says, citizens can 'agree on the importance of 'liberty and equality for all', while disagreeing sharply about their meaning and the way they should be implemented' (Mouffe, 1995c, 501). In fact, Mouffe puts forward a model of agonistic democracy where political contests are staged precisely around 'conflicting interpretations' of our shared liberal democratic tradition (Mouffe, 1995c, 501; 2000b, 80). Central to her iteration of this *agon* between friends is the idea of a contest:

staged around the diverse conceptions of citizenship which corresponds to the different interpretations of the ethico-political principles [of liberal-democracy]: liberal-conservative, social democratic, neo-liberal, radical democratic, and so on. Each of them proposes its own interpretation of the 'common good', and tries to implement a different form of hegemony. (Mouffe, 2000b, 104)[14]

This presentation of agonistic democracy in terms of a contest between contending ideological viewpoints is important, and in Chapter 7 I also stress the significance of rejuvenating ideological contest as a crucial ingredient in the struggle against neo-liberal globalisation. However, in my view, Mouffe's valuable stress on the *agon* between ideological alternatives is undercut by her insistence that these protagonists always meet within the horizon of the liberal democratic tradition. Like the other thinkers examined in this book, Mouffe explicitly rejects the possibility of revolution, which she describes as 'an act of radical re-foundation that would institute a new social order from scratch', and she clearly understands agonism as an augmentation of modern liberal democratic constitutionalism (Mouffe, 2000b, 111, 122; 2005a, 33). As we have seen in previous chapters, this depiction of revolution is a caricature, and this does not capture what is at stake in the Arendtean idea of revolution, and in the final chapter we will combine the *agon* of revitalised ideological contest precisely with the idea of the on-going possibility of the emergence of a radically new principle, or set of values, but this does not imply the idea of total transformation.

Agonism and republicanism

In addition to Mouffe's 'realist' vindication of liberal democracy against the backdrop of the Schmittean/Hobbesean problematic of antagonism, she also draws explicitly on the republican tradition, and especially on

---

[14] This agonistic stress on the value of conflict does not preclude Mouffe from also backing one of the contestants in this struggle. Indeed, she has also emphasised the need for greater equality, and to rebuild the socialist project. Mouffe advocates a restoration of social democracy around the principle of an unconditional minimum income, an enhanced role for associations, and a more equal distribution of access to employment (Mouffe, 1993b, 7; 2000b, 126). However, it is important to appreciate that these socialist objectives have not at all been at the forefront in Mouffe's later work, and they have been articulated from within an overarching framework that repeatedly stresses the need for unity in response to the threat of antagonism, and so Mouffe's position appears in its most fundamental respects to be conservative in orientation.

Oakeshott's retrieval of the notion of *societas*, in order to explain the mode of authority that conditions agonistic politics. This aspect of Mouffe's contribution is thought-provoking, and this reveals important nuances inherent in the notion of augmentation. These discussions take us back to the conceptual tensions that we explored in the previous chapter, i.e. between freedom and the rule of law, and we turn now to Mouffe's appropriation of the idea of *societas*, because this also reveals subtle but important differences between her and Tully.

In *The Return of the Political* Mouffe set out her position by navigating a passage between the arguments of liberals and communitarians, which had dominated debate in normative political theory in the 1980s. In the same way that she acknowledges important values in both liberalism and democracy, in this book she sought to blend certain liberal and communitarian insights, whilst at the same time being critical of the foundationalist assumptions underpinning both approaches (Mouffe, 1993b, 62).[15] Mouffe agrees with Rawls that we must abandon the communitarian ideal of the political community structured around a 'single substantive common good' (Mouffe, 1993b, 55). She rejects any nostalgia for a conception of democracy modelled on an 'original community of the gemeinschaft type', and she stresses that the 'defence of pluralism, the idea of individual liberty, the separation of church and state, the development of civil society', are all 'crucial contribution[s] of liberalism' to modern politics (Mouffe, 1992, 5, 12; 1993b, 62). However, Mouffe also rejects the rationalist and juridical frameworks that typically underpin theoretical defences of liberalism. From Mouffe's perspective, a 'communitarian defence of political liberalism is perfectly possible', and the exercise of individual rights and principles of justice cannot exist in abstraction from a given political community and its particular understanding of the good (Mouffe, 1993b, 46–7). She says that the communitarian critics of Rawls are right to criticise the 'atomistic liberal vision of an individual that could exist' with her 'rights and interests prior to and independently of her inscription in a community' (Mouffe, 1993b, 65, 100; see also Sandel, 1992). This atomistic conception of politics has contributed to the 'devaluation of civic action, of common concern, which has caused an increasing lack of social cohesion in democratic societies' (Mouffe, 1993b, 65). Indeed, Mouffe agrees with the communitarian attempt to 'revive some aspects of the classical conception of politics' and these observations lead Mouffe to develop a distinctive conception of citizenship (Mouffe, 1993b, 65).

---

[15] For a flavour of these debates see Rawls, 1972, 2005; Walzer, 1990, Sandel, 1992; Taylor, 1997; MacIntyre, 2007; and for an overview see Mulhall and Swift, 1992.

Mouffe presents citizenship as a 'form of identification that enables the establishment of a common political identity' (Mouffe, 1993b, 6). However, the challenge is to 'formulate the ethical character' of this model of 'citizenship in a way that is compatible with moral pluralism' (Mouffe, 1993b, 65). The task is to 'make our belonging to different communities of values, languages, [and] culture . . . compatible with our common belonging to a political community whose rules we have to accept' (Mouffe, 1995b, 34). She says, citizenship is not only a legal status and a set of rights, 'important as these are', it is also 'allegiance' to a set of democratic values and practices that 'provide the consensus which is required' to make a legitimate expression of pluralism possible (Mouffe, 1992, 8; 1993b, 65, 151; 1995b, 41). The citizen of agonistic democracy is an active citizen, somebody who conceives herself as a participant in the public life of society, and on Mouffe's reading it is 'only through public service that we can ensure and maximise our personal liberty' (Mouffe, 1992, 4, 7). In this respect, her position is comparable to Benjamin Barber's account of 'strong democracy'. Mouffe and Barber share the republican insight that 'the rights we often affect to hurl impudently into the face of government are rights we enjoy only by virtue of [popular] government' (Barber, 1984, xxiii).

Indeed, Mouffe's depiction of citizenship is close in spirit to the 'neo-Roman' tradition in republican thought, which has been recovered in Skinner's historical excavations (Skinner, 1998). The neo-Roman tradition can be traced to Machiavelli, but was exemplified in seventeenth-century theorists of the English republic, such as John Milton and James Harrington. What defines these neo-Roman writers is the idea that the presence of a 'common good above our private interests is a necessary condition for enjoying individual liberty' (Skinner, 1998, 17; Mouffe, 1993b, 63). The neo-Roman tradition does not carry the weighty per-fectionist assumptions of the Aristotelian view of politics that underpins 'thick' versions of communitarianism, where we 'can only be said to be fully or genuinely at liberty . . . if we actually engage in just those activ-ities which are most conducive to *eudaimonia* or 'human flourishing', and may therefore be said to embody our deepest human purposes' (Skinner, 1990, 296). The seventeenth-century English republicans are also distinct from the ancient Roman writers, especially Sallust, accord-ing to whom 'the most important benefit of living in a *civitas libera* is that such communities are especially well adapted to attaining glory and greatness' (Skinner, 1998, 61). By way of contrast, the neo-Roman writ-ers 'begin to place their main emphasis on the capacity of such regimes to secure and promote the liberties of their own citizens' (Skinner, 1998, 65). However, in contrast also to post-Hobbesean liberal theories, with their exclusive emphasis on the ends of government in terms of the protection of private right, these writers insisted that it is 'only possible to escape from personal servitude if you live as an active citizen under a representative form of government' (Skinner, 1998, 66).

Adopting Skinner's insights, Mouffe asserts that a republican conception that draws on this tradition 'can make room for . . . pluralism' (Mouffe, 1993b, 36). From this perspective, 'if one is to exercise civic virtue and to serve the common good, it is in order to guarantee oneself a certain degree of personal liberty which permits one to pursue one's own ends' (Mouffe, 1993b, 20). This reiterates the proximity between contemporary agonistic democracy and the republican tradition. By Mouffe's account, these two traditions coalesce in a common emphasis on the need for participation, and in their shared understanding of the significance of bonds of common loyalty as a prior condition for the enjoyment of individual liberty, and as she sees it also as a precondition of agonistic forms of pluralism.

However, Mouffe's appropriation of the neo-Roman tradition also reveals another subtle, but not insignificant, distinction between the contemporary theorists of agonism. This becomes clear when we consider Tully's emphasis that, despite the stress on participation and active citizenship as a precondition of individual liberty, the neo-Roman school remains 'within the juristic tradition' in some important respects (Tully, 2003, 540). According to Tully, Skinner's work has shown that:

an entire culture of republican humanism was 'juristic' in orientation in one crucial respect. These authors . . . defined the concepts of politics in terms drawn directly from the Roman law tradition. Skinner calls their central concept of liberty 'neo-Roman' for precisely this reason. [On this model] liberty was defined in Roman law terms and in relation to the pre-existence of a legal order. A person was said to be free or to possess the status of liberty to the extent that the law restrained others from the possibility of interfering with his possible actions. (Tully, 2003, 495)

In other words, although the neo-Roman defence of liberty does not insist on the absolute priority of individual 'rights', as in liberalism, it does nonetheless understand the law as the principal mechanism for ensuring freedom. On this model the people are 'said to be justified in revolting against a ruler who violated their liberty . . . Yet, the people revolt in order to put in place (or replace) a structure of basic law that establishes and protects their negative freedom from interference' (Tully, 2003, 495). This view of the central importance of law in maintaining republican freedom has been reiterated by both thinkers at the centre of the present revival of republican theory. In Pettit's terms, the law is non-arbitrary when it *conditions* the peoples' freedom but does not *compromise* it (Pettit, 1999, 164; 2002, 342). Or, as Skinner puts it:

the law preserves our liberty not merely by coercing others, but also by directly coercing each one of us into acting in a particular way. The law is also used, that is, to force us out of our habitual patters of self-interested behaviour, to force us into discharging the full range of our civic duties, and thereby to ensure that the free state on which our own liberty depends is itself maintained free of servitude. (Skinner, 1990, 305)

In Tully's account, these assumptions differentiate the neo-Roman tradition from a genuinely civic (as opposed to civil) republicanism, where, as we saw in the previous chapter, the law comes steadily to be understood not as an external mode of authority but rather as immanent to its own perpetual renegotiation in the on-going practices of the citizens themselves.

We have also seen that Tully does not associate freedom with acts of foundation that entirely break with an existing framework of law, and so it is important to appreciate that he too remains within the Roman tradition, he too is a theorist of augmentation. Nevertheless, what is ultimately at stake in this discussion is the relative priority of the two points of emphasis inherent in the Roman notion of augmentation, i.e. the capacity on one hand for freedom and innovation through civic activity (stressed by Tully), as well as the extant forms of authority (stressed by Skinner and Pettit) that are also and at the same time reiterated and expanded upon in moments of augmentation. Moreover, these observations help to explicate important differences between Tully and Mouffe, because, in certain crucial respects, Mouffe's theory remains closer to a civil rather than a civic conception of politics. The key point in her theory is the need to situate the agonic freedom of citizens within an effective framework of 'authority'. This is in marked contrast to Tully for whom, we have seen, the moment of agonistic freedom is principally associated with the capacity of citizens to challenge and reiterate the rules of the game. This difference is especially evident when we turn to Mouffe's encounter with the ideas of another thinker who is associated with republicanism, which is Oakeshott, and, in particular, her adoption of the notion of *societas* as descriptive of the sort of authority proper to agonistic democracy (Mouffe, 1993b, 66–73).

In *On Human Conduct* (1975), Oakeshott elaborated the distinction between *societas* and *universitas*, understood as two different modes of the 'many-in-one' of human association (Oakeshott, 1975, 200). The idea of *societas* is derived from the Roman law tradition, and represents a way of relating agents one to another so that they compose a 'formal relationship in terms of rules, not a substantive relationship in terms of common action' (Oakeshott, 1975, 201).

The tie which joins [the citizens], and in respect of which each recognises himself to be socius, is not that of an engagement in an enterprise to pursue a common substantive purpose or to promote a common interest, but that of loyalty to one another. (Oakeshott, 1975, 201)

Indeed, in the Roman tradition what brings citizens together is their acknowledgement of the authority of the laws of the civil association – the *lex* or the *respublica* – understood as a commonly agreed set of conditions of conduct and 'not devices instrumental to the satisfaction of preferred wants' (Oakeshott, 1975, 200, 263). The outcome of this 'constitutive pact' – and the broader meaning of the term *societas* – is then a certain pluralistic condition, that is, the:

socii, each pursuing his own interests or even joined with some others in seeking common satisfactions, but related to one another in the continuous acknowledgement of the authority of rules of conduct indifferent to the pursuit or the achievement of any purpose. (Oakeshott, 1975, 201)

By way of contrast, *universitas* represents a 'corporate mode of association', that is 'a many united in respect of a common purpose' and examples might include churches, trades unions, interest groups, pressure groups, political parties, charities, professional associations, and so on (Oakeshott, 1975, 203, 205). The legal recognition of the status of *universitas* can be traced to the later middle ages, where a 'corporation aggregate was recognised as persons associated in respect of some identified common purpose, in the pursuit of some acknowledged substantive end, or in the promotion of some specified enduring interest' (Oakeshott, 1975, 203). In contrast to the model of civil association, the *universitas* is a monistic conception of human aggregation and, according to Oakeshott, since the sixteenth century the notion of *universitas* has steadily become the predominant way of understanding the status and character of the state itself (Oakeshott, 1975, 205, 215). The modern state is typically understood not as a civil association, but rather as a corporate entity whose 'purpose is the diligent exploitation of the resources of its territory for the satisfaction of human wants' (Oakeshott, 1975, 291).

Mouffe appropriates Oakeshott's retrieval of *societas*, which she says can explain the kind of authority that ought to condition agonistic democracy. She says the 'authority of [the] political institutions is . . . a question . . . of the continuous acknowledgement of *cives* who recognise their obligation to obey the conditions prescribed in *res publica*' (Mouffe, 2000b, 95). However, this seems to implicate Mouffe in Oakeshott's particular brand of conservatism, because, for Oakeshott, the authority of the law as *societas* is grounded in tradition. Indeed, as Arendt has stressed, in the Roman model the acknowledgement of the authority of established tradition *is* the foundation of law as *societas* (Arendt, 1977a, 104). Elsewhere, Mouffe says that 'the respublica is the product' of relations of force and that the content of the *lex* can always be challenged through political struggle (Mouffe, 1993b, 69). This appears to be more in line with Schmitt's understanding of the relationship between law and politics, where the authority of the law is ultimately grounded in sovereign decision. As Žižek says, Schmitt's neo-conservatism must be sharply distinguished from 'every kind of traditionalism: modern [Schmittean] conservatism, even more than liberalism, assumes the lesson of the dissolution of the traditional set of values and/or authorities' (Žižek, 1999b, 18–19). Ironically perhaps, in her various attempts to formulate the prior conditions of agonistic politics – respectively in terms of legal and symbolic in/exclusions, and forms of citizenship modelled on a collective identification and an acknowledgement of the authority of the liberal democratic *societas* – Mouffe appears to have ended up moving back and forth between two contrasting forms of conservatism.

Picking up on this apparent inconsistency, Connolly says that Mouffe's emphasis on the way we are implicated 'within [the authority of] the [liberal] democratic tradition is at odds with' her 'recourse to a constitutive outside that disrupts and exceeds that tradition' (Connolly, 1995b, 132). However, perhaps this is not really an inconsistency after all, because in reality both of these elements are combined in the constituted right (*potestas*) of the modern liberal democratic state. Indeed, this amalgam (of Schmitt and Oakeshott) is more or less captured in Gramsci's Machiavellian notion of the maintenance of hegemony through a combination of force plus consent. Indeed, Mouffe's difficulty is not one of inconsistency. The point is rather that, in contrast to Machiavelli and Gramsci, who both sought to challenge the constituted powers and to bring about a new hegemonic configuration, Mouffe has somehow found herself enmeshed in the conservative problematic of the maintenance of 'authority' and order, understood as a prior condition of agonistic democracy and legitimate forms of pluralism, and in an effort to defend liberal democratic institutions against the threat of antagonism.

Nevertheless, it is also important to stress that Mouffe's concern with authority is not, in the end, incompatible with the model of freedom as augmentation. As Oakeshott says, the 'conditions of even the least ambiguous duty can be fulfilled only by a "free" agent choosing what he shall do' (Oakeshott, 1975, 157; Franco, 2003, 503). Like the other theorists examined in this book, Mouffe is committed to an idea of freedom as augmentation. However, a lot hinges on where the point of emphasis is placed in the tension between authority and freedom, or between *auctoritas* and augmentation. The contrast between Tully and Mouffe here is very marked. Where Tully stresses how it is always possible to alter and amend a rule in the moment of its application, Mouffe's anxiety about the threat of antagonism leads her to repeatedly emphasise instead the priority of a common acknowledgement of the rules of civil association. Implicit in her position is the Oakeshottean emphasises on the need for a conservative disposition towards rules. As Oakeshott sees it, the 'chief virtue' of rules and routines is 'that they are fixed and familiar' and so they 'establish and satisfy certain expectations . . . they prevent extraneous collisions and they conserve human energy' (Oakeshott, 1991, 421).

They are the product of reflection and choice, there is nothing sacrosanct about them, they are susceptible to change and improvement; but if our disposition in respect of them were not, generally speaking, conservative, if we were disposed to argue about them and change them on every occasion, they would rapidly lose their value. (Oakeshott, 1991, 421–2)

Mouffe's concern with the need for authority seems to implicate her in these sentiments, and this contrast with Tully is also clear in her brief comments on Wittgenstein. Like Tully, Mouffe also acknowledges that Wittgenstein understands rules as 'abridgements of practices', and so from his perspective it is always possible to 'follow the democratic rules in a plurality of ways' (Mouffe, 2000b, 73). However, she sees in Wittgenstein the resources for an alternative model of *authority* to the currently predominant rationalist justifications of liberal constitutionalism. She says, 'liberal democratic principles can only be defended as being constitutive of our form of life and we should not try to ground our commitment to them on something supposedly safer' (Mouffe, 2001, 134). However, once again in contrast to Tully, the key objective for Mouffe is clearly to elaborate a non-foundationalist assertion of the authority of the existing rules of the game. She says the challenge is to create a space of democratic praxis in which 'the many different practices' of '*obedience* to the democratic rules can be inscribed' (Mouffe, 2000b, 73, emphasis added).[16]

---

[16] In fact, Mouffe is closer to the vision of agonism elaborated by Johan Huizinga where the agonic game is associated with ritualised contest within a clearly delimited space, the 'playground', and where the players 'must stick to the rules of the game' despite their ardent desire to win (Huizinga, 1955, 10–11). For a discussion of Huizinga's contribution to agonistic theory see: Tully, 1999a. For a comparable position to Huizinga, with a similar emphasis on the bounded nature of the rules of the game, see Caillois, 2001.

Against cosmopolitanism

Before concluding this chapter we need to briefly consider Mouffe's response to the changing nature of democracy in the context of globalisation. In line with the other contemporary agonists, Mouffe is critical of the predominant Kantian conceptions of cosmopolitanism. However, she is the only thinker examined in this book who doesn't offer an alternative conception of cosmopolitanism. Mouffe focuses instead on the continued significance of the national political arena as well as a need for greater federalism and regionalism, and once again she arrives at these conclusions primarily through her reading of Schmitt. Like Schmitt, Mouffe says there 'can never be a democracy of mankind' because democracy can only ever exist for a 'people', and, as we have seen, the identity of the people is inscribed through relations of in/exclusion (Schmitt, 1996, 53, 55; Mouffe, 1999b, 41; 2002, 4). Consequently, the idea of cosmopolitan democracy put forward by thinkers such as Held and Archibugi is inherently spurious. Indeed, 'by justifying the right for international institutions to undermine sovereignty in order to uphold cosmopolitan law' Kantian cosmopolitanism in its various manifestations would deny the 'democratic rights of self-government for the citizens of many countries' (Mouffe, 2005a, 101). Given this stress on the tension between false claims to cosmopolitan right and the principle of democratic self-determination, Schmitt concluded that any given claim to represent 'humanity' in the international arena can only ever give rise to the 'most awful expansion and a murderous imperialism' (Schmitt, 1999, 205). Indeed, Mouffe perceived precisely these tendencies at work in the recent conjuncture in global politics. Writing in the context of the Second Gulf War, she said today the key 'international organizations are more or less directly under the control of Western powers led by the United States', and, just like in the domestic sphere, there is too much emphasis on the need for consensus and a moralisation of politics by the dominant powers who claim to speak in the name of 'humanity' (Mouffe, 2005a, 51, 82). This was evident, for example, in George W. Bush's crusade of the 'civilised world' against the 'axis of evil', which inevitably aroused strong antagonisms because it is impossible under these terms and conditions to oppose American hegemony without opposing the supposedly common interests of 'humanity' (Mouffe, 2005a, 79, 81).

In other words, although the precise emphasis is different, Mouffe arrives at similar conclusions to Tully about the predominant Kantian conception of cosmopolitanism, i.e. that it is an inherently imperialist doctrine. Similarly, Mouffe says the critique of cosmopolitanism means 'breaking with the deeply entrenched conviction in western democracies that they are the embodiment of the best regime and that they have the civilizing mission of universalizing it' (Mouffe, 2005a, 83). However, for Mouffe, this aspiration towards imperium is intrinsic in the very notion of cosmopolitanism. If any 'cosmopolitan order was [ever] able to impose itself on a global level it could only be the result of some power [falsely] identifying its interests with the whole of humanity' (Mouffe, 2005a, 107). So she does not see any prospect for something like Tully's horizontal cosmopolitanism from below. Mouffe calls instead for a revival of national democracy and regional politics.[17] She says, nation-states and national allegiances are still important sites of democratic action even 'if multi-national companies operate according to strategies largely independent of them' and 'to dismiss them . . . is to leave this potential available for articulation by right-wing demagogues' (Mouffe, 2005a, 114). Moreover, Mouffe stresses the importance of the principle of federalism, and she envisions the possibility of a new multi-polar world order based on the existence of several 'autonomous regional blocks' (Mouffe, 2005a, 116–17). The objective would be to establish 'an equilibrium among regional poles whose specific concerns and traditions will be seen as valuable, and where different vernacular models of democracy will be accepted' (Mouffe, 2005a, 129).

Mouffe is right to express concern about respect for cultural differences in a world that is dominated by western interests and values. However, it does not follow from this that every form of cosmopolitanism is incompatible with the democratic principle of self-determination. Her critique of the current global hegemony is important, but her response precludes the possibility of an alternative bottom-up hegemony of cosmopolitan forces. Mouffe's picture of the global polity as comprised of multiple *demoi* and regional blocks, each forged through moments of in/exclusion and without any shared or common vision, cannot possibly offer a solution to the challenges we face today in the form of climate change, global poverty, and diminishing energy resources. Mouffe acknowledges the

---

[17] In some respects, Mouffe's position resonates with Viroli's account of 'republican patriotism', which, he says, 'differs from both ethnic and civic nationalism. In contrast with the former, it recognises no political or moral value in the unity and ethnic homogeneity of a people, while it does recognise the moral and political importance of values of citizenship, which are entirely incompatible with any form of ethnocentrism. In contrast with the latter, it proclaims allegiance not to culturally and historically neutral political principles but to the laws, constitutions, and ways of life of specific republics, each with its own history and culture' (Viroli, 2002, 89–90).

However, Viroli also stresses that republican patriotism cannot be established on the basis of fear. In fact, the republican sees the 'absence of fear and servility' as the 'distinctive features of a truly free people' (Viroli, 2008, 78). It is difficult to see how Mouffe might reconcile this sentiment with her Schmittean paradigm of the 'the political', and of a *demos* constructed in response to an irreducible threat of antagonism.

significance of developments such as the World Social Forum, but she does not appreciate the potential in the new forms of transnational social movement politics, made possible by globalisation, which we have discussed in the two previous chapters. In Chapter 7 I explore the contours of a more militant form of cosmopolitanism, one that sees in the nascent forms of transnational politics the possibility for a new mode of open-ended universality. The hope is that out of the present transnational, democratic struggles a new cosmopolitan consciousness might emerge, one that breaks radically with the priorities of the present conjuncture, and – through the many subsequent judgements of diverse publics situated at the local, national, and regional levels – that this new cosmopolitan principle might become rooted in the decisions of state and supra-state institutions, and start to provide a genuine alternative to disciplinary neo-liberalism.

Conclusion

We have seen that Mouffe's contribution represents something of an outlier in relation to the other thinkers examined in this book. Mouffe invokes the core components of the agonistic matrix; she stresses the significance of pluralism, tragedy and the value of conflict. However, her version of agonism is also demarcated by her parallel emphasis on the on-going significance of the binary form of struggle, which she presents as something like the essence of the political. More specifically, we have tracked the movement in Mouffe's work away from her earlier stress on the conflict between the oppressed and the oppressor, which makes possible a common struggle against domination, and towards the distinction between friends and enemies, which gives rise to an alternative concern about the perennial threat of antagonism. These two modalities of the binary division are not equivalent, and Mouffe's steadily increasing concern with the Schmittean problematic of the friend/enemy relation, means that at the same time she has found it necessary to draw attention to the primary need for order or unity understood as a precondition of agonism. This brings Mouffe within the orbit of a neo-conservative worldview, where the first problem of politics is always the need to provide security from the threat of privation, which is supposedly rooted in the human condition.

In fact, Mouffe has been quite explicit about her indebtedness to conservative thinkers. She says, 'because of the rationalism prevalent in liberal political discourse, it is often amongst conservative theorists that I have found crucial insights for an adequate understanding of the political' (Mouffe, 2005a, 4). However, one is left wondering why she did not turn instead to the republican or the Marxist traditions, where she would have found plenty of good clear realist thinking about the irreducible role of conflict in politics, but where this is very often tied to a more transformative vision, concerned with the struggle against historically specific forms of domination. Indeed, even within the choices available in Schmitt's body of work, Mouffe has made use of limited resources. She has repeatedly stressed the significance of *The Concept of the Political*, with its central thesis of an underlying anthropology of antagonism, but makes little or no mention of *Constitutional Theory*, with its focus instead on the absolute priority of the constituent power, i.e. with the recognition that the 'rule of law ultimately hinges on an abyssal act... which is grounded in itself' (Žižek, 1999b, 18). We saw in Chapter 2 that, for Schmitt, these two insights are indissociable, and that this leads to his depiction of the constituent power in terms of sovereign 'will', i.e. as he who decides in the crucial moment of the exception. We will come back to these ideas in the following chapter, where we look at Agamben's reworking of Schmitt to explain the emergence and reproduction of the contemporary security state, as well as Honig's thoughtful response to this predicament. However, in Chapter 2 we also saw that it is possible to dissociate the absolute priority of the constituent power from the threat of antagonism, and this is evident in Arendt's critique of sovereignty and in her depiction of revolution as a moment of radical origination that is in some sense conditioned by pluralism. We will return to these ideas in Chapter 7. However, the important point here is that Mouffe seems to miss the most interesting elements in Schmitt, which are his reflections on the miraculous capacity of the constituent power to introduce genuine novelty into the world.

Mouffe's distinctive version of agonism certainly leaves her well positioned to critique the tendencies towards consensus, rationality, and normativity, characteristic of a great deal of contemporary democratic theory. Her resolute denunciation of deliberative democracy is compelling, and this provides an important counterpoint Tully and others who pursue a basic rapprochement between agonistic and deliberative theory. Mouffe's critique of technocratic post-politics is also very pertinent, and so too is her emphasis on the need to reignite the *agon* between ideological alternatives. However, these insights are hemmed in by Mouffe's parallel insistence that these struggles must unfold within the basic horizon of liberal democratic constitutionalism. When these claims are combined with her strong critique of cosmopolitanism and her vision of global politics in terms of multiple *demoi* and region blocks, each grounded in their constitutive exclusions and without commonality, it seems clear that her theoretical framework lacks the resources to deliver a credible alternative to neo-liberalism.

In Chapter 1 we also saw that Mouffe presents her realism as an alternative to what she reads as a certain naive optimism inherent in the other contemporary theorists of agonism, and which she thinks is derived from Nietzsche and Arendt. This estimation has some validity in respect of Connolly and Tully, and we have seen that there are elements in their respective theoretical frameworks which seek to smooth over the full implications of the tragic circumstances of the democratic *agon*: these are Connolly's tendency to model the emergence of assemblages on the self-organising qualities of natural processes, and Tully's association of agonistic dialogue with the normative principle of reciprocity. Mouffe is right to draw these inclinations into question, but she is inaccurate in her estimation that these tendencies are derived from Nietzsche and Arendt, and in the following chapter we will see that these inclinations are not present in Honig's work either. Indeed, Honig manages to formulate a model of the *agon* that is every bit as realist as Mouffe. However, her contribution is not fixed on a threat of privation, understood as an anthropological constant, and so she manages to combine an unmistakeable realism with an equally unshakeable sense of the aspirational dimension of agonistic politics.

6 Agonism and the paradoxes of (re)foundation: Bonnie Honig

Bonnie Honig has developed her style of agonistic democracy in *Political Theory and the Displacement of Politics* (1993),[1] *Democracy and the Foreigner* (2001), and *Emergency Politics* (2009). She joins Connolly and Tully in diagnosing excessive claims to unity as the principal menace to the agonistic ideal of a positive contest between proximate equals, rather than the threat of antagonism. In *Political Theory* she exposes this aspiration towards homogeneity in the predominant liberal and communitarian approaches in normative political theory and deconstructs the work of Kant, Rawls, and Sandel. Despite important differences, Honig describes each of these thinkers as advocates of a politics of 'virtue', because, in their different ways, they are all exemplary theorists of political closure. The underlying impulse in each of these theories is to 'confine politics . . . to the juridical, administrative, or regulative tasks of stabilising moral and political subjects' (Honig, 1993, 2). They are, therefore, all complicit in their own petty forms of tyranny. By way of contrast, Honig develops an alternative vision of a politics of agonistic *virtù*. The presiding instinct in this agonistic view is, with Nietzsche, to 'rouse enmity towards order' and, through strategies of genealogy and deconstruction, to uncover the excesses, remainders, and resistances that the conventional theories seek to contain. In the first section of this chapter we examine Honig's account of agonism in terms of the tensions between virtue and *virtù*, and we see that she concludes her first book by stressing that both of these impulses are inevitably at play in the democratic *agon*. On her reading, politics always 'consists of practices of settlement and unsettlement, of disruption and administration, of extraordinary events . . . and [of] mundane maintenances' (Honig, 1993, 205).

Honig draws primarily on Nietzsche and Arendt for her illustration of the politics of agonistic *virtù*, with, she says, Machiavelli in only a 'minor, supporting role' (Honig, 1993, 3). In Chapter 3 we considered Nietzsche's ideas in some detail in the assessment of Connolly and Owen's

---

[1] Henceforth: *Political Theory*.

contributions and, in the course of that discussion, we also picked up on Honig's engagement with Nietzsche. Indeed, much of what Honig takes from Nietzsche resonates with Connolly and Owen, and so in this chapter I only touch very briefly on Nietzsche's ideas again. Instead, the core of this chapter is built around a detailed appraisal of Honig's reworking of Arendt. By Honig's own account, Arendt 'forms the spiritual and conceptual centre' of *Political Theory*, and so the analysis of Honig's version of agonistic democracy also presents the opportunity to further elaborate those aspects of Arendt's thought which we have already introduced in the course of this study (Honig, 1993, 10). In particular, in the second section we will examine Honig's very insightful reworking of Arendt's topographical distinction between the political and the social, and in section three we examine her problematic repudiation of Arendt's formulation of the revolutionary event. These discussions also provide an important prelude to my own discussion in the following chapter of Arendt's concepts of pluralism and reflective judgement, which constitute crucial components in my formulation of agonism and militant cosmopolitanism.

Honig's modification of the Arendtean division between the social and political is very compelling, and she is right to stress that the creative qualities that Arendt associated with political freedom can be brought to bear in the realms of necessity that Arendt associated with 'the social'. Honig illustrates this point by drawing attention to the proximity of her modified Arendtean categories and Butler's notion of gender *performativity*. I raise some concerns about how certain areas of social relations are less susceptible to these strategies than others, but overall we can pretty much endorse this aspect of Honig's theory, and indeed Honig has gone a long way towards demonstrating how Arendt's problematic understanding of the social (as a realm of pre-political violence) can be overcome, and how Arendt's theory can thus be recuperated for a contemporary model of agonism concerned with challenging domination. These are really crucial contributions. Unfortunately, however, Honig undermines her breakthrough revision of Arendt, at least in my view, by her simultaneous repudiation of the Arendtean understanding of revolution.

Honig elucidates her critique of Arendt's formulation of the *ex nihilo* event, by comparing Arendt and Derrida's readings of the American *Declaration of Independence*. Whereas Arendt celebrates the *Declaration* as a 'purely performative speech act', and wants to rid the revolutionary event of any reference to a constative moment, and especially of any grounding in the transcendent power of the deity, Derrida understands instead that some allusion to a constative moment is part of the necessary aporetic structure of every constituent (speech) act. This analysis forms part of a more general appropriation of Derrida's position, and Honig presents the movement of *différance* and the circumstances of *iterability* as conditions of all forms of political innovation, including those extraordinary moments that Arendt, following Benjamin, associated with the revolutionary *Ursprung*. Indeed, Honig seeks to convert what she sees as Arendt's overblown formulation of the moment of radical foundation into a form of agonistic politics focused on a perpetual (re)foundation in the day-to-day practices of the citizens. In other words, Honig explicitly trades in a framework that permits a qualitative distinction between alternate moments of the constituent act – revolution and augmentation – for a single framework of augmentation (or *iterability*) in the everyday circumstances of the republic, and, in this respect, it is Derrida and not Arendt who really provides the spiritual core of *Political Theory*.

This strategy of taking (only apparently) extraordinary moments and translating them into the (only apparently) ordinary circumstances of everyday politics becomes the central theme in Honig's subsequent writings. In the remainder of the chapter we explore the strengths and limitations of this approach by looking at her analyses in *Emergency Politics* and *Democracy and the Foreigner*. We explore these books in this order of priority, even though this disrupts the chronology of their respective publication, because *Emergency Politics* is a manifestly political text, which demonstrates very clearly the genuinely transformative power of agonistic augmentation, whereas the focus in *Democracy and the Foreigner* is more problematic and is indicative of just how far Honig travels from Arendt.

In *Emergency Politics* Honig brings her basic strategy to bear on Rousseau's depiction of the paradox of foundation, and on the tensions between the 'general will' and the 'will of all', as well as in response to the Schmittean notion of the 'exception' that Agamben has reworked to explain the present circumstances of the resurgent security state. Honig's approach places the consistent power decisively in the hands of situated political actors, and especially in their capacity to resist and redirect the decisions of the sovereign, for example through creative moments of administrative discretion. This provides an excellent account of the constituent power in the mode of agonistic augmentation, and how this capacity can be brought to bear even in the present context of an expanding realm of extra-judicial executive power. These are really important insights. However, with her exclusive emphasis on the politics of the *extra*-in-the-ordinary, Honig runs the risk of complicity in the status quo, in the idea that there is no genuinely extraordinary alternative to the security state and the neo-liberal capitalist regime.

The focus in *Democracy and the Foreigner* is different. This book works through a series of foreign founder myths from popular and high culture, and demonstrates that this figure is a 'fantasy construction', and one that enables the democratic polity to live with its own constitutive *aporia*. The central message of this book is the irreducibly alien quality of the law and, here again, Honig is close to Derrida, and essentially to a Hebrew conception of the law as an unfathomable moment of divine command, which, by Honig's account of agonistic politics, can be perpetually resisted and redirected, but which precludes the possibility of the *demos* ever becoming the full authors of the law. At this point, Honig really has journeyed into very different territory to Arendt whose great insight was to show how a reworked Roman conception of authority as self-foundation, without reference to the divine or the transcendent, could be made consonant with the condition of human plurality.

Agonism and the politics of *virtù*

In *Political Theory* Honig explores the inherent tension between freedom and order, which is definitive of political life, with recourse to a conceptual distinction between theories of virtue and of *virtù*. Honig's reference to 'virtue politics' has the potential to mislead, and it is important to stress that she does not employ this term, as it is usually understood, i.e. to refer specifically to virtue ethics or communitarian conceptions of the good. Instead, Honig describes any political theory that 'confine[s] politics (conceptually and territorially) to the ... regulative tasks of ... building consensus, maintaining agreements, or consolidating communities and identities' as a form of virtue politics (Honig, 1993, 2). In other words, in Honig's classification, this term applies not only to the Aristotelian view, but also to the deontological justification of liberalism put forward by Kant and Rawls (Honig, 1993, 2). Despite fundamental differences, each of these theories is characterised by the conceited view 'that the world and the self are ... completed by their favourite conceptions of order and subjectivity' (Honig, 1993, 2–3). Drawn by the 'irresistible compulsion' of their 'foundational truths', they understand the basic role of the political theorist to find ways to 'displace politics with bureaucratic administration, jurocratic rule, or communitarian consolidation' (Honig, 1993, 4, 9). In the terms of this study, these theories aim to subsume the constituent power under constituted forms of authority, either the authority of extant communities and their particular ethical traditions, or of context-transcending principles of justice presented as foundational and rationally demonstrable.

In line with Connolly's critique of normalisation and Tully's opposition to imperialism, Honig perceives this will-to-order, system, and stability, which is deeply entrenched in western traditions of political thought, as a potential threat to genuine 'diversity, plurality [and] freedom' (Honig, 1993, 10, 78). This is 'because the efforts of political and moral orders to stabilise themselves as the systematic expressions of virtue, justice, or the *telos* of community drive them to conceal, deny, or subdue resistances to their regimes' (Honig, 1993, 3). Honig's basic objective is, therefore, to safeguard diversity from the prospective despotism of foundational political theory and practice, in the name of a counter-model of the democratic *agon* where politics is understood instead as a 'practice that is disruptive, agonistic, and, most important, never over' (Honig, 1993, 9). Like Connolly and Owen, Honig sees Nietzsche's method of genealogy as an indispensable tool for challenging the always 'imperfect construction' of some 'would-be unity', and in the service of alternative 'forms of life that have . . . been lost, silenced, or concealed' (Honig, 1993, 43–4). In *Political Theory* she presents a series of detailed genealogies of the contributions of Kant, Rawls, and Sandel. I won't set out the details of Honig's genealogies here, for want of space, but her overall conclusion is that, despite the polemical exchanges of the 1980s, and the clear differences in points of emphasis, there 'is a deep and abiding agreement among liberal and communitarian thinkers' (Honig, 1993, 164). They coalesce around a displacement of politics, and they seek in various ways to 'shut down the *agon*', and, in turn, this does violence to genuine plurality, and especially towards what Honig sees as the original multiplicity of the self.

Honig's encounter with the liberal and communitarian debate is different to Mouffe's. In the previous chapter we saw that Mouffe's objective was to combine the best insights of liberalism and communitarianism in a republican theory of citizenship, whilst dispensing with the underlying philosophical assumptions of both approaches. By her account, this conception of citizenship then becomes a precondition for agonistic politics. Honig, on the other hand, points to the respective versions of unity and closure that define the liberal and communitarian approaches, and she associates agonism in part with an unruly politics that contests the remainders that are suppressed and denied in these respective theories of 'virtue' (in her extended usage of that term). Indeed, Honig's various genealogies of the systems of moral and political closures are designed to liberate the remainders and resistances that the virtue theories seek to conceal. The point is to provide 'otherness [with] a legitimate avenue of expression instead of silencing it by branding it abnormal, unnatural, or irresponsible', and in this regard she takes her direction from Nietzsche (Honig, 1993, 65). Like Connolly, Honig stresses that the ideal of unity – exemplified in Kant, Rawls, and Sandel – 'fosters self-loathing' and 'bad conscience' in the subject towards those elements of the self which remain stubbornly resistant to self-discipline (Honig, 1993, 51). By way of contrast, Nietzsche's approach is 'more generous to life' and above all provides an antidote to the politics of *ressentiment* (Honig, 1993, 42). Indeed, Nietzsche is a theorist of ethical responsibility, and through many repetitive labours the Nietzschean Overman cultivates a capacity to 'successfully... organise a small portion of an otherwise meaningless world' (Honig, 1993, 53, 60). Moreover, it is exactly these qualities she will need in the world of agonistic politics, because to affirm, in the manner of a theorist of *virtù*, the 'perpetuity of contest' requires considerable courage, for this is to 'reject the dream of displacement, the fantasy that the right laws or constitution might some day free us from the responsibility for (and, indeed, the burden of) politics' (Honig, 1993, 211).

Importantly however, Honig concludes her book with the thought that *virtù* and virtue do not represent two 'distinct and self-sufficient options but two [necessary] aspects of political life' (Honig, 1993, 201). These terms signify respectively the 'impulse to keep the contest going and the impulse to be finally freed of the burdens of contest', and, in Honig's account, these two impulses are forever played out in movements of the democratic *agon* (Honig, 1993, 14). The specificity of the political would be lost in 'the victory of either impulse over the other', because politics consists of the interminable tensions between 'settlement and unsettlement... disruption and administration... extraordinary events or foundings and mundane maintenances. It consists of the forces that decide undecidabilities and of those that resist those decisions at the same time' (Honig, 1993, 14, 205). This iteration resembles Connolly's claim that politics is composed of the endless play between pluralism and pluralisation, governance and enactment, concentric and rhizomatic forces, etc., and both of these accounts echo Nietzsche's depiction of the non-dialectical production of form from the tension between order and chaos, Apollo and Dionysius, in *The Birth of Tragedy* (Nietzsche, 1956). These delineations clearly contrast to all those theories that seek to establish a clear conceptual priority in favour of order, justice, or virtue, but, as Honig says, to 'affirm the perpetuity of contest is not to celebrate a world without points of stabilisation, it is to affirm the reality of perpetual contest, even within an ordered setting' (Honig, 1993, 15). In other words, we find ourselves again in the terrain of the constituent power as augmentation, where freedom (as contest and interruption) is understood simultaneously as a movement of innovation and as an expansion of existing forms of order. In fact, Honig puts it in precisely these Arendtean terms. She says that her theory is directly informed by 'Arendt's theorisation of authority as a practice of augmentation that is committed not to entrenchment or settlement but to a utopian possibility of a perpetual Nietzschean self-overcoming' (Honig, 1993, 157). In this initial venture into her theory, we can clearly see Honig's proximity to Connolly and Owen's uses of Nietzsche. However, we have also said that Honig sees Arendt as the central figure in her version of agonistic politics, and it is to a detailed evaluation of Honig's reworking of Arendt that we now turn.

Honig on Arendt (1) – the exercise of freedom into the social

In Chapter 1 we touched upon Arendt's account of the exercise of freedom in the ancient *polis*. In *The Human Condition*, Arendt's Hellenism defined her phenomenology of the *vita activa*, which is presented in terms of a fixed distinction between the political (the realm of freedom as innovation) and the social (the realm of necessity). We have said that Arendt's formulation is problematic. This leaves her with an inadequate conception of the social, understood as a realm of pre-political violence, and, taken literally, has the effect of placing social issues such as poverty, patriarchal forms of oppression, and racism beyond the reach of political redirection and transformation. At this point, we need to examine this distinction more carefully and, in particular, explore Honig's reworking of Arendt's theory, where she stresses the importance of political interventions into the social, rather than seeing the two realms as a fixed topography. We will see that Arendt's formulation does contain some important criticisms of modernity, despite the clear limitations of her approach, and I argue that Honig's reconstruction of Arendt's categories is largely persuasive and she shows how Arendt's theory can be recuperated for a model of agonistic democracy concerned with challenging forms of inequality and domination. However, we should also note that some areas of social life have been much more susceptible to political reworking in this way than others.

In Arendt's account of Greek antiquity the *bios politikos* is characterised by 'action (praxis) and speech (lexis), out of which rises the realm of human affairs' and 'from which everything merely necessary or useful is strictly excluded' (Arendt, 1958, 25).

To be political, to live in a polis, meant that everything was decided through words and persuasion and not through force and violence. In Greek self-understanding, to force people by violence, to command rather than to persuade, were prepolitical ways to deal with people characteristic of life outside the polis, of home and family life, where the household head ruled with uncontested, despotic powers. (Arendt, 1958, 14)

We have seen that, for Arendt, action is synonymous with the constituent power of human agents to bring something new into the world. This is 'contrasted with the tiresome repetitions of the domestic realm and of the body', i.e. with the work and labour entailed in the reproduction of life (Honig, 1993, 80–1). Indeed, 'strictly speaking', Arendtean action 'lies outside the category of means and ends' (Villa, 2006, 94). As Dana Villa says, the Greek conception of politics is, therefore, entirely incommensurate with the modern way of 'viewing the political order as an instrumentality of the social order, as *primarily* concerned with the protection of life (Hobbes), the preservation of property (Locke), or the promotion of the general welfare (Bentham, Mill)' (Villa, 2006, 91, emphasis in the original). Indeed, one of the central theses of *The Human Condition* is the idea of the steady encroachment of the social into the political under conditions of modernity, so that genuine action is made more and more difficult, as (so-called) political questions are brought under the means/ends reasoning of economic calculations (Arendt, 1958, Chapter 6).

This aspect of Arendt's argument is close to Weber's thesis about the triumph of modern instrumental reason that was reworked by the early Frankfurt School (Adorno and Horkheimer, 1979). There is also a clear convergence between Arendt, Foucault, and also Agamben in terms of a 'biopolitical diagnosis' of modern society (Duarte, 2006, 410). Although the details in their respective narratives are quite distinct, for example on the question of where these tendencies originate and on the role of sovereignty in relation to bio-politics, each of these thinkers shares the view that, under conditions of modernity, political life has more or less been reduced to the instrumental tasks of reproducing biological life. Arendt was right to draw attention to these problematic tendencies. Her critique of modernity was more profound than a great deal of contemporary academic political theory, with its limited range of questions, largely about how to address the so-called 'fact of pluralism', and her position is 'more compelling, than a complaint that we fail to live up to some dated Hellenic ideal' (Tsao, 2006, 360). Her claim that the public realm 'has almost completely receded' in the modern age is very telling, and is evidenced not only in the mid-twentieth-century experience of totalitarianism, but also in the badly diminished quality of public life under conditions of globalisation, where societies are increasingly organised around the pleasant totalitarianism of consumer capitalism. At the heart of Arendt's critique of modernity and her thesis about the 'triumph of the social' is the idea that we need to retain a sense of politics as something more than simply housekeeping, more than the effective administration of basic needs, whether that is through welfare measures or market mechanisms. On the Arendtean view, 'politics should not be subordinate to social ends, which only can corrupt it' (Canovan, 1983, 288).

Nevertheless, Arendt's bio-political diagnosis of modernity does not come without certain costs, and it is perhaps a little ironic that the difficulties associated with this Arendtean perspective are neatly summarised by Habermas, who, we have seen, is rightly criticised by the contemporary agonists for himself having an overly idealised conception of democratic politics. Habermas says that Arendt 'pays a certain price' for her preoccupation with Greek antiquity: '(a) she screens out all strategic elements, as force, out of politics; (b) she removes politics from its relations to the economic and social environment in which it is embedded through the administrative system; and (c) she is unable to grasp [the nature of] structural violence' (Habermas, 2006, 261). However, Habermas' response to Arendt's overly purified conception of the political effectively reiterates and compounds these difficulties. He elaborates a conception of 'communicative action' that ought to be brought to bear in a 'steering capacity' into the realms of economy and society with their means/ends strategic reasoning. This facilitates the important idea of political interventions into the social; however, Habermas' solution falls short, because his idealised conception of communicative action is also hermetically sealed from strategic considerations, and, to make matters worse, his theory of communicative action is established on rationalist and cognitivist foundations that are absent in Arendt and which are entirely incommensurate with the agonistic view of politics.

Honig shares the basic sentiment in this critique of Arendt's topographical approach, if not Habermas' solutions. She says, perhaps 'unduly influenced by her own reading of ancient Greek political thought, Arendt sometimes seems to assume that the political space has to be an empty site, situated in a stable space' entirely insulated from the realms of necessity (Honig, 1993, 123). The problem with this insistence on the purity of the political is that it 'seems to leave so much in place: god, capital, technology, gender, race, class, ethnicity – none of this is touched by Arendt's politics' (Honig, 1993, 118). Arendt effectively quarantines political action, or the constituent power, from the private realm and refuses 'to treat private realm identities, like gender, as potential sites of politicization' (Honig, 1995, 136). Moreover, in Greek antiquity the realm of labour in the household was associated specifically with women and slaves, and so as 'victims of both the tiresomely predicable, repetitious, and cyclical processes of nature and the despotism of the household' women are 'determined incapable of the freedom that Arendt identifies with action in the public realm' (Honig, 1995, 142). These are good reasons then why feminists, for example, would want to steer clear of Arendt's categories – at least, in their unreconstructed form. Indeed, the potentially disastrous consequences for feminism of insisting on a fixed distinction between public and private, or political and social, belie a more general problem with the Arendtean schema. As Deranty and Renault put it:

Arendt's notion that there can be no political treatment to misery and poverty has implications beyond the attempt to preserve the purity of politics from the demands of the social. It implies also that there is nothing to be done about 'necessity', that one must simply accept, as a fact of the human condition, that many will have to be devoted to its service. Indeed, this is entailed in the very logic of the ontological separation of the spheres of labour, work and action: those who engage in the space of 'appearances' cannot, by definition, be the same as those who labour and work. (Deranty and Renault, 2009, 45)

As they understand it, this elitist orientation in Arendt's thinking means that she is not an appropriate source of inspiration for a contemporary theory of democracy, especially if we see the 'struggle against the social causes of political exclusion' as one of the main dimensions of radical politics (Deranty and Renault, 2009, 52). In spite of her reverence for political action, Arendt was not concerned, as modern socialists have been for example, 'with the conditions of access to political action' (Deranty and Renault, 2009, 44). On a literal reading of Arendt, political equality for the citizens can, therefore, 'coexist with significant inequality' for those condemned to a life of labour in the *oikos* and consequently excluded from the public realm. Moreover, this is an 'inequality which...cannot itself become the object of politics' (Deranty and Renault, 2009, 51).

These are forceful criticisms, and they get to the heart of the limitations of Arendt's celebration of the Greek *polis* as a realm of reciprocal freedoms held in place by 'pre-political' violence. Moreover, as we said in Chapter 2, she demonstrated the same aristocratic distain for those who are forever bound to the constraints associated with the reproduction of life in *On Revolution,* in her insistence that social problems such as poverty are not susceptible to political intervention (Deranty and Renault, 2009, 45). However, Deranty and Renault move too quickly in their repudiation of Arendt. By way of contrast, Pitkin has identified the key question for those who understand what is valuable in Arendt's categories, and yet who seek to resist these aristocratic conclusions. She says how can we 'acknowledge the centrality of economic and social issues in public life without reducing political freedom to either mere competitive manoeuvring for private profit or a mere by-product of some inevitable social process?' (Pitkin, 2006, 228). Put slightly differently, we might ask how can we envisage the relations between the social and the political, so that the constituent power of politics (i.e. the power of genuine innovation) can be invested into the realm of social necessity, yet without subordinating political freedom to the instrumental calculations that sustain the conditions of life? To say that politics should not be fully subordinate to social ends or processes, that there is something more to political action than means/end calculations, is not the same as saying, with Arendt, that social processes are entirely unsusceptible to political intervention, or to celebrate ancient institutions because they effectively isolated the purity of politics from social necessity. As Deranty and Renault have said, this response involves focusing on precisely the realms that Arendt rejected as non-political, i.e. the 'social processes of political exclusion' (Deranty and Renault, 2009, 46). However, they do not provide any coherent reasons – logical, conceptual, practical or otherwise – why it should *necessarily* follow that Arendt's categories are beyond recuperation in this way. In fact, Honig's contribution goes a fair way to demonstrating that this recovery is possible. Honig effectively presents two responses to these complex questions. The first of these doesn't really get to the heart of the matter, and effectively reinforces Arendt's aristocratism. However, the second response is much more promising.

Honig says Arendt 'often speak[s] as if her private realm and its activities of labour and work were to be identified with particular classes of people, or bodies, or women in particular', but, as Pitkin points out, at other times the private realm and its activities of labour and work seem to represent 'particular *attitude[s]* against which the public realm must be guarded' (Honig, 1993, 82, emphasis in the original). As Pitkin puts it, 'perhaps a "labourer" is to be identified not by his manner of producing nor by his poverty but by his "process" orientated outlook; perhaps he is "driven by necessity" not objectively, but because he *regards* himself as driven, incapable of action' (Pitkin, 2006, 227, emphasis in the original). This 'reading of labour, work, and action as (rival) sensibilities . . . might point the way to a gentle subversion of Arendt's treatment of [social life and] the body as a master signifier of irresistibility, imitability, and the closure of constation' (Honig, 1995, 143). On this reading, it is 'the labouring mentality that is excluded from political action, a mentality that is taken to be characteristic of labouring as an activity but which may or may not be characteristic of the thinking of any particular labourer' (Honig, 1993, 82). Consequently, 'no determinant class of persons is excluded from political action. Instead, politics is protected from a variety of mentalities, attitudes, dispositions, and approaches all of which constitute *all* selves and subjects to some extent and all of which are incompatible with the understandings of action Arendt valorises' (Honig, 1993, 82, emphasis in the original). This corresponds with Connolly's rejoinder to the aristocratism in the Nietzschean celebration of the 'Overman'. As we saw in Chapter 3, Connolly rereads Nietzsche's distinction between the courage of the Overman and the weakness of the 'herd mentality' as competing dispositions within the self. In a way, this reading is plausible in respect of the Nietzschean categories, because the criterion that distinguishes the Nietzschean 'Over man' from the 'last man' is his relative strength in confronting the meaninglessness of existence, and this disposition really is found amongst people from all walks of life, and can be quite easily dissociated from the question of social-economic hierarchy and domination. In contrast to Connolly, we saw that Owen locates the perfectionist dimension of Nietzsche's thought not (only) in the inner dimension of the self, but rather in the centre of the democratic *agon*, understood as a collective struggle to determine a ranking of virtues and vices. But here too Owen dissociates this struggle from any socio-economic hierarchy and stresses that, in his model, all citizens would be encouraged and supported in cultivating a capacity for post-foundational autonomy. However, the Arendtean categories are more problematic and don't lend themselves to reworking in these ways. This is because, by Arendt's account, the criteria that set off the few from the rest *are* inextricable from forms of socio-economic hierarchy and domination. Indeed, the few were determined in the Hellenic *polis*, precisely by their relative success in extricating themselves from the drudgery of social work and labour, and through subjecting others who remain bound to the tasks of reproducing the necessities of life.

Consequently, Honig and Pitkin's response is too easy, and their formulations are in danger of turning a blind eye to the hard realities of life in late capitalist societies, i.e. that the distribution of degrees of necessity is severely unevenly parcelled out. Keeping with Arendt's distinction between labour and work, we might surmise that a basic distinction can be drawn between those white collar professionals whose careers include an element of making (although increasingly also an inordinate amount of labouring), and all those who predominantly labour: blue collar workers, the majority of women, as well as the poor, and especially in the developing world, where existence for many is often exclusively bound up with reproducing the necessities of life. Arendt appears to treat these hard facts with an aristocratic shrug of the shoulders, as a misfortune about which nothing can be done politically. Honig and Pitkin are right to reject this response. However, in a perverse kind of way, Arendt is more honest, because at least she acknowledges this reality, rather than trying to step over these details by translating them instead into a safer discussion about competing psychological dispositions.

However, Honig mobilises a second response to Arendt's distinction between the social and the political, which is more promising. She explains that there is no reason why the relation between the realm of social necessity and political freedom has to be formulated topographically. Indeed, if 'action is boundless and excessive, why should it respect a public–private distinction that seeks, like a law of laws, to regulate and contain it without ever allowing itself to be engaged or contested by it' (Honig, 1993, 119). 'What if we treat Arendt's notion of the public realm... as a metaphor for a variety of (agonistic) spaces, both topographical and conceptual, that might occasion action?' (Honig, 1995, 146). This facilitates the idea of political interventions into the social, and here the constituent power is refigured as 'an unstable fissure in any otherwise highly ordered and settled practice or identity' (Honig, 1993, 123). With this model of human freedom we are:

in a position to identify and proliferate sites of political action in a much broader array of constations, ranging from the self-evident truths of God, nature, technology, capital, labour, and work to those of identity, of gender, race, and ethnicity. We might then be in a position to act – in the private realm. (Honig, 1993, 121)

Indeed, on Honig's reading 'action is possible in the private realm because the social and its mechanisms of normalisation consistently fail to achieve the perfect closures [that] Arendt attributes to them' (Honig, 1993, 124). This seems to me to be a very fruitful way to proceed, and, on this reading, agonistic democracy becomes again a strategic doctrine concerned with identifying and encouraging opportunities for the expression of human freedom, which 'escape or resist administration [and] regulation', and which have the capacity to disrupt the otherwise cyclical movements of social processes within the ostensibly 'private' realms of the household and the economy (Honig, 1993, 123–124).

Perhaps the area where this approach has been most compelling is in the realm of gender relations and the politics of sexual identity, and this is evident in the proximity between Honig's reworked version of Arendt and Butler's account of the politics of gender performativity. Indeed, Arendt emphasised that the 'Greeks always used such metaphors as flute-playing, dancing, healing, and seafaring' to distinguish political from other activities, 'they drew their analogies from those arts in which virtuosity of performance is decisive' (Arendt, 1977b, 152). According to Honig, there is no reason why this same basic conception cannot be dissociated from the Hellenic pursuit of greatness and applied instead to the construction of gender identities, so that we 'de-essentialize and denaturalise the body, perhaps pluralise it, maybe even see it as performative production, a possible site of action, in Arendt's sense' (Honig, 1995, 144). In fact, Honig shows how the relations of gendered identity played out in the so called 'private' realm of the *oikos,* which Arendt associated with the 'oppressive repetition of the univocal cycles of nature', *are* in reality 'performatives that daily reproduce' relations of inequality but are nonetheless subject to the possibility of transformation through political action – and, of course, this is exactly Butler's same point of emphasis (Honig, 1993, 123). According to Butler, established gender roles and heterosexual identities are given a false naturalisation by the relations of power that reproduce the normativity associated with the nuclear family (Butler, 1990, 187). However, the gendered body really has 'no ontological status apart from the various acts which constitute it' in certain culturally circumscribed ways (Butler, 1990, 185). Indeed, the 'possibilities of gender transformation are to be found precisely in the arbitrary' status of extant roles and performatives (Butler, 1990, 192). Gender differences and sexual identities are only ever held in place by a 'stylized repetition of acts', which are intrinsically open to a politics of subversion or resignification through a performative displacement (Butler, 1990, 191). This takes the form of a 'parodic proliferation', which we have seen particularly in queer politics, and which 'deprives [the] hegemonic culture . . . of the claim to naturalised or essentialist gender identities' (Butler, 1990, 188).

This approach enables Honig to shift the Arendtean emphasis on performance away from the 'classical polis experience' centred on 'excellence and theatrical self-display', and towards instead a 'quest for individuation and distinction against backgrounds of homogenisation and normalisation' (Honig, 1995, 159). Instead of simply 'reproducing and representing "what" we are', agonistic politics 'generates "who" we are by episodically producing new identities' (Honig, 1995, 149). In this respect, her association of agonism with gender performativity is also close to Connolly's politics of enactment. Both approaches nurture a conception of the 'self that is never exhausted by the (sociological, psychological, and juridical) categories that seek to define and fix it' (Honig, 1995, 159). These conceptions of the constituent power have been exemplified in the periodic and multifarious expressions of autonomy associated with second wave feminism and the struggles for gay rights, which have culminated in massive transformations in gender relations, personal sexual identities, and the role of women in western societies from the late 1960s. Indeed, these developments testify to the power of the politics of performativity, as many different *iter*ations over a sustained period of time can bring about substantive change in the dominant norms and practices within the context of liberal democratic regimes.

However, it is also clear that these forms of political action have had very little impact in other areas of social relations. In particular, these forms of performance politics appear to be powerless to effect change in the core structures of economic inequality, rooted in the division of labour and in the global circulation of capital. Honig does not adequately address these issues, and there is no systematic analysis in her work of the structures of domination comparable to Tully's critique of imperialism. However, this doesn't nullify the basic orientation of Honig's recovery of Arendt. It means instead that, if we are going to understand political freedom as something that emerges from and can be directed back into the realms of social necessity, then we had better also appreciate that there are some areas of social life that are more resistant to this political reworking than others. Indeed, one of the key issues in contemporary politics is whether or not it is at all possible to introduce genuine innovation in the context of the neo-liberal disciplinary regime. In the following chapter I explore prospects for this eventuality, and I argue that, in order for this kind of politics to become achievable, we need to retain the idea of the kind of radical innovation that Arendt associated with the revolutionary event. By way of contrast, Honig explicitly rejects this possibility, and we move now to her critique of the Arendtean conception of revolution.

Honig on Arendt (2) – from revolution to the politics of daily (re)foundation

In addition to her perceptive reworking of Arendt's conception of the performative character of politics, Honig also repudiates Arendt's depiction of revolution, which she describes as an 'act of foundation [that] requires no appeal to a source of authority beyond itself' (Honig, 1993, 101). In essence, Honig praises Arendt's appreciation of augmentation, but criticises her naive and exaggerated picture of revolution, and so once again this brings to the fore the difference between Arendt, with her stress on augmentation and revolution as two qualitatively distinct modalities of the constituent power, and the contemporary agonistic viewpoint with its exclusive emphasis on augmentation, and represented here by Honig supported by Derrida. However, on careful examination these distinctions are more nuanced still, because it becomes clear that Honig and Arendt present different accounts of precisely what is expanded in the moment of agonistic augmentation. This is explored in the following section, where we will see that, in her own formulation of augmentation,

Honig invokes the Hebrew conception of law as command, and she envisages agonistic politics in terms of a perpetual resistance to this irresistible authority. Arendt, on the other hand, envisaged the modern experience of augmentation, as it was embodied, for example, in the doctrine of the separation of powers, as a reworking of the Roman model, where augmentation represented an on-going and open-ended expansion of the original foundations of the city. Indeed, this reflects a more deep-seated tension between Arendt on one side and Honig and Derrida on the other, between the Roman and Hebrew conceptions of law, and we need to begin to tease out this difference, because Honig's understanding of the law in the mode of command and alterity has considerable bearing on her subsequent elaboration of agonistic democracy in *Democracy and the Foreigner* and *Emergency Politics*.

Honig's critique of the Arendtean *Ursprung* focuses on Arendt's discussion of the American *Declaration of Independence*, and Honig invokes Derrida's reading of Jefferson's famous text as a counterpoint to Arendt. Honig seeks to problematise what she sees as Arendt's overstated resistance to the 'absolute', and she sees in Derrida's contribution a more nuanced understanding of political freedom, which does not completely disavow any reference to the 'absolute'. However, in the course of this discussion it turns out that Arendt and Honig are not always talking about the same thing when they refer to the question of the status of the 'absolute'. Arendt certainly repudiated the idea that political authority can ever be grounded in any kind of transcendent moment of command, and she understood modern rationalist accounts of the transcendent as essentially modelled on the Hebrew understanding of law as divine command. In contrast to Honig and Derrida, who think that some reference to the transcendent remains 'irresistible', Arendt understood that a consistently republican conception of politics really should find the courage to get by without any reference to the absolute in the mode of transcendent authority, and, importantly, this has no place in her conception of either revolution or augmentation. However, at the same time, Arendt did not entirely repudiate the idea of the 'absolute'. As we saw in Chapter 2, she fully accepts the idea of the absolute priority of the constituent power over constituted forms of authority. Indeed, in her view, it is precisely this capacity for an 'absolute beginning' that distinguished the events of the eighteenth century from the Roman experience of augmentation, with the latter moment of freedom being understood instead in terms of a relative priority of the constituent power that manifests in a moment of innovation, but one that always also refers back to an already established foundation. In other words, the differences between Honig and Arendt are nuanced and layered at this point, so we must tread carefully here, and to begin to get to grips with this discussion, we need to first return to the question of the status of authority and how it relates to the constituent power (*potentia*).

Under conditions of modernity, political institutions can no longer be grounded in established tradition or divine authorisation, and, as Arendt understood, this means that the 'most elementary predicament of all modern political bodies, [is] their profound instability, [which is] the result of some elementary lack of authority' (Arendt, 1965, 158). However, as we discussed in the Introduction and again in Chapter 2, the onset of political modernity also represents an opportunity, this is the moment when, as Arendt says, 'men began to be aware that a new beginning could be a political phenomenon', so that authority could now be established on the basis of 'what men had done and what they could consciously set out to do' (Arendt, 1965, 40). This realisation is expressed in the idea of the absolute priority of the constituent power over constituted forms of authority, which was first explicitly formulated by Sieyès, and with which Arendt is in full agreement. However, she also stressed that modern subjects have struggled to accept these radical consequences and opportunities of their thrownness into the world, and they have typically appealed instead to some imaginary foundational or transcendent referent to provide a more secure basis for authority. For example, this tendency was clearly evident in the ostensibly secular age of the Enlightenment, where political authority still remained 'unthinkable without some sort of religious sanction' (Arendt, 1965, 159). In fact:

it was precisely the revolutions, their crisis and their emergency, which drove the very 'enlightened' men of the eighteenth century to plead for some religious sanction at the very moment when they were about to emancipate the secular realm fully from the influences of the churches and to separate politics and religion once and for all. (Arendt, 1965, 186)

Moreover, the opening passages of *The Declaration* incorporate this profound equivocation, in the tension between the 'we hold' and the 'self evident' status of the unalienable Rights of Man (Jefferson, 1999a, 97).

Jefferson's famous words . . . combine in a historically unique manner the basis of agreement between those who have embarked upon revolution, an agreement necessarily relative because related to those who enter it, with an absolute, namely with a truth that needs no agreement since, because of its self evidence, it compels without argumentative demonstration or political persuasion . . . The authority of self-evident truth may be less powerful than the authority of an 'avenging god' but it certainly still bears clear signs of divine origin; such truths are, as Jefferson wrote in the original draft . . . 'sacred and undeniable'. (Arendt, 1965, 193–4)

Honig appreciates that, for Arendt, the modern 'quest for an absolute [in the form of a self-evident truth] in which to ground and legitimate the reconstitution of the political realm' is 'deeply misguided' (Honig, 1993, 98). By Arendt's account, genuine revolutionary action is 'not aided but compromised by the unnecessary and illicit reliance' on this modern rationalist surrogate for divine authority (Honig, 1993, 107). As Honig puts it:

Absolutes [in the form of self-evident truths] occlude the contingency that is the quintessential feature of the public realm, the feature in virtue of which political freedom and human innovation are possible. Moreover, they deprivilege the very human achievement of reconstitution and founding, making it dependent on something external to the human world [in other words, depriving it of its own absolute status]. And that external something, whether it be god, natural law, or self-evident truth, is untenable in the modern era. (Honig, 1993, 98)

Arendt effectively solicits modern subjects to muster the courage to embrace the full consequences of their freedom, and to find ways to 'establish lasting foundations' without having to appeal to 'gods, a foun-dationalist ground, or an absolute [truth]' (Honig, 1993, 97). Indeed, Arendt presents an alternative rendition of *The Declaration*, one that cel-ebrates this intervention as an 'authoritative exemplification of human power and worldliness' (Honig, 1993, 101). For Arendt, *The Declaration* is a uniquely political act, a miraculous moment of human innovation, of unalloyed constituent power, and 'the source of its own authority' (Honig, 1993, 101). She also thought the eighteenth-century protago-nists were, to a considerable extent, conscious of their tremendous power. Indeed:

The very fact that the men of the American revolution thought of themselves as 'founders' indicates the extent to which they must have known that it would be the act of foundation itself, rather than an Immortal Legislator or self-evident truth or any other transcendent, transmundane source, which eventually would become the fountain of authority in the new body politic. (Arendt, 1965, 205)

Despite Honig's admiration for Arendt, she is decidedly uncomfort-able with this attempt to figure the revolutionary constituent power in terms of a purely self-referential event of human freedom, and Honig turns to Derrida's alternative reading of *The Declaration* to problema-tise this Arendtean formulation (Honig, 1993, 101). Derrida's account presupposes his more general encounter with John Austin's theory of performative speech acts, and so to comprehend the difference between Derrida and Honig on one side, and Arendt on the other, we first need to briefly venture into Derrida's critique of Austin (Derrida, 1988).

In *How to Do Things With Words*, Austin provided something like a social phenomenology of the range of speech acts available to situated subjects (Austin, 2009). Austin draws a basic distinction between constative and performative speech acts. Constative statements are statements of fact that report on some given state of affairs in the world, for example when I say 'it is raining today'; whereas, in the articulation of a performative statement, the utterance is inseparable from the performance of an action that produces some social force or change in the world, for example when the groom says 'I do' in a wedding ceremony (Austin, 2009, 3, 5, 6). However, Austin attempts to bind performative statements to solid contextual boundaries, so that 'it is always necessary that the circumstances in which the words are uttered should be in some way, or ways, appropriate', and performatives that are not contextually 'appropriate' – let's say, for example, that he's not the groom, or it's not a recognised marriage ceremony, or perhaps he's a 'she' – are described as 'infelicitous', 'unhappy', or given in 'bad faith' (Austin, 2009, 11, 15). Honig acknowledges the importance of Austin's notion of the performative speech act. Performative 'utterances draw our attention' to the constitutive power of language, to its 'other-than-referential character', to its 'extra-communicative power, to its creation, in effect, of new relations and realities' (Honig, 1993, 89). However, she joins Derrida in contesting Austin's desire to confine this constituent power within an 'exhaustively determinable context' (Honig, 1993, 90; Derrida, 1988). She says, if 'speech action was only felicitous, we would be in a realm of process and predictability where calculation, but not action, would be the appropriate modus operandi' (Honig, 1993, 91).

Honig also stresses the important connection between Derrida's reworking of the performative quality of speech and Arendt's emphasis on the creative power of action. By Arendt's account, as by Derrida's, the 'possibility of infelicity is a structurally necessary possibility of action' (Honig, 1993, 91–3). Similarly, for Arendt, when 'action works, it is not in spite of but partly because of the risk, infelicity, and dissemination that are action's characteristic features' (Honig, 1993, 92). However, Derrida's deconstruction of Austin does not lead to an insistence on the absolute priority of the performative power of language. Instead, Derrida presents the basic tension between the constative and the performative moments as a structural condition of every speech act. He says the 'undecidability between, let's say, a performative structure and a constative structure, is [always] required in order to produce' any kind of meaning (Derrida, 1986, 9) From this perspective, the Arendtean account of the revolutionary event as a purely performative moment is problematic, because here the performative element is entirely disembedded from any context or any allusion to an external referent. As Honig says, this contrasts with Derrida's emphasis on the inherently paradoxical movement of all illocutionary acts, in the sense that they simultaneously break away from, and reaffirm, some constative point of reference (Honig, 1993, 109). In other words, whereas Derrida is 'careful not to deny the effects' of the constative, Arendt 'seems to do precisely this' (Honig, 1993, 93). On Honig's reading then, Arendt's 'exclusion of the ordinary from her account of [revolutionary] action leaves her open to the same sort of criticism Derrida levels at Austin for excluding the extraordinary from his' (Honig, 1993, 93).

Moreover, the political significance of this difference between Arendt and Derrida is reaffirmed when we turn to his reading of *The Declaration*. Derrida's essay on *The Declaration* focuses on the ambiguities that problematise the authorship of the document, and in particular Derrida asks how and in what ways the American people can be said to have authored the text, when prior to *The Declaration* 'this people does not exist. They do not exist as an entity, it does not exist, before this declaration, not as such. If it gives birth to itself, as a free and independent subject, as possible signer, this can hold only in the act of the signature. The signature invents the signer' (Derrida, 1986, 10). In fact the 'We hold' is indicative of an elementary ambivalence of representation, because it is unclear whether 'independence is stated or produced by this utterance', and the rhetorical force of *The Declaration* derives in large measure from this equivocation, from the fact that one 'cannot decide which sort of utterance it is, constative or performative' (Honig, 1993, 106). On Honig's account, this reading gives Derrida the edge over Arendt, and because he appreciates that 'the American *Declaration* and founding are paradigmatic instances of politics (however impure) because of this undecidability, not in spite of it' (Honig, 1993, 107). Furthermore, Derrida suggests an alternative account of the tension between the 'we hold' and the 'self-evident truths'. In contrast to Arendt, he sees the reference to an absolute (in the form of the transcendent authority) as again part of the necessary rhetorical structure that empowers the performative act. Indeed, the absolute 'comes, in effect, to guarantee the rectitude of popular intentions, the unity and goodness of the people. He founds natural laws and thus the whole game, which tends to present performative utterances as constative utterances' (Derrida, 1986, 11). In other words, on Derrida's account the revolutionary actors appealed to an absolute (in the form of self-evident truths) 'not, as Arendt would have it, because of a failure of nerve or because they underestimated the power of their own performative but because they did not overestimate its power. To guarantee that power and secure their innovation, they had to combine their performative with a constative utterance' (Honig, 1993, 105).

Honig explicitly endorses Derrida's reading of *The Declaration*, which she presents as a corrective to Arendt's extravagant account of the (absolute) power of the revolutionary event. From Honig's viewpoint, *all* moments of political action are conditioned by the 'inevitable *aporia* of founding (or signing or promising)' (Honig, 1993, 105-6, 109). These observations suggest a specific understanding of agonistic politics, one where we turn our attention away from the grand revolutionary events so admired by Arendt, and focus exclusively of the capacity of situated subjects to perpetually or periodically 'resist' the 'irresistibility' of these structural conditions of all (speech) acts in the daily freedoms and practices of democratic politics (Honig, 1993, 109). In other words, rather than associating agonistic democracy, as Arendt does, *both* with rare and extraordinary moments of radical origin *as well as* with the constituent power in the mode of augmentation, Honig focuses singularly on the 'extraordinary measures' of (re)foundation that 'reproduce ordinary life, daily' (Honig, 1993, 123). Moreover, this stress on (re)foundation forms part of Honig's more general appropriation of Derridean notion of *iterability*. For Derrida, *iterability* designates the play of change and continuity that conditions every form of repetition. In repetition we never simply produce a replica. By resignifying an antecedent moment, repetition is also a form of variation, meaning is transformed and enhanced in a creative (re)appropriation (Gasché, 1986, 212). In order to be a *re*petition, the new performance must retain a certain semblance to what is repeated (or else it's not a repetition but something wholly other) and yet it must also be distinct (otherwise it is not a repetition but a simple identity), and 'iterability' signifies this element of change and continuity which is a condition of (im)possibility of every repetition. Following Butler, Honig associates the creative power of agonism precisely with Derridean *iterability*; with a 'subversive repetition [that] might performatively produce alternative . . . identities that would proliferate and that would, in their proliferation (and strategic deployment), contest and resist the reified' forms of established power and authority (Honig, 1993, 124).

These formulations clearly correspond with the Arendtean notion of augmentation, and Honig's emphasis on *iterability* and the necessary aporetic combination of the performative and the constative moments of every (speech) act, bring her broadly in line with the other thinkers examined in this book. Once again, we see an unequivocal stress on the simultaneous double bind of innovation and continuity, which parallels, for example, the discussion of Wittgenstein in Chapter 3. In fact, in Honig's explicit denunciation of the Arendtean notion of the revolutionary *Ursprung*, we find the most perspicuous illustration of my more general claim that the contemporary agonistic theorists offer a mono-typical formulation of the constituent power in the mode of augmentation. If Derridean *iterability* strictly conditions all forms of politics – rather than, as I would have it, particular modes of freedom – then the moment of radical innovation, or 'absolute beginning', that Arendt associated with the revolutionary origin is rendered inconceivable. Of course, this is exactly Honig's objective. She says that the problem with *On Revolution* is that there is 'no undecidability' in the Arendtean conception of the revolutionary event (Honig, 1993, 107).

However, rather than being evidence of Arendt's naivety and her failure to grasp the constitutive *aporia* of every (speech) act, this is, in my view, evidence instead of her understanding, with Machiavelli, of the importance of maintaining the qualitative distinction between the absolute and relative priority of the constituent power. It is not that the forms of politics that Honig esteems are unimportant. They surely are very important, and along with the other thinkers examined in this book Honig is right to draw attention to the elements of genuine inventiveness that repeatedly emerge within the horizon of liberal democracy, and that this creative power has been most evident in various forms of social movement politics from the late 1960s. The problem is that if the revolutionary *Ursprung* is inconceivable, then these forms of politics become effectively the essential structure of the constituent power, and this is problematic for the reasons I discussed in Chapter 2. As we have said, in the present conjuncture it is especially important to retain the Arendtean idea of radical innovation. We will explore this sentiment more fully in the following chapter, and later in this chapter we consider some of the implications of Honig's disavowal of revolution, when we turn to the question of just how effectively her exclusive emphasis on augmentation measures up to the challenges associated with the current consolidation of the security state. However, before we move on to these discussions we first need to take another look at Honig's particular rendition of augmentation because, on closer inspection, we start to see some very significant differences between her and Arendt.

Honig vs. Arendt on the character of augmentation

Honig recognises that Arendt presents an alternative conception of freedom in *On Revolution*, and one that is more conducive to her own understanding of the agonism of everyday life. Arendt insists, she says:

that acts of [radical] founding can and should resist the urge to anchor themselves in an absolute [in the form of self-evident truths]. But Arendt's account of authority as a practice of augmentation and amendment does not, in my view, commit her to this insistence. It commits her only to the insistence that we treat the absolute [presumably, at this point, not as truth, but nonetheless as a transcendent moment of authority] as an invitation for intervention, that we declare ourselves resistant to it, that we refuse its claim to irresistibility by deauthorizing it. (Honig, 1993, 115)

This summation captures aspects of Arendt's notion of augmentation, but two points of emphasis that are central for Arendt are nevertheless elided in this passage. Firstly, this summary implies that Arendt's account of revolution is inconsistent with her reflections on augmentation, whereas in fact Arendt is very explicit that revolution and augmentation represent qualitatively distinct modalities of the constituent power. Secondly, what is slipping away in this passage (and more generally in Honig's discussion of augmentation in Chapter 4 of *Political Theory*) is Arendt's careful insistence on the Roman derivation of the idea of augmentation, which I explored in detail in Chapter 2. Indeed, we need to look more carefully at the status of this 'absolute' with its 'claims to irresistibility' that Honig refers to in this passage, because in the course of her discussion, Honig steadily moves from an acknowledgement of Arendt's stress on the Roman model of augmentation, to a focus instead on augmentation as a resistance to the law as command.

Indeed, Honig says that Derrida 'recognises, more deeply than does Arendt, that the law will always resist his resistance' (Honig, 1993, 110). However, here the law refers to the divine command of the Hebrew conception. This is explicit in Derrida's later writings, where he developed a theory of political struggle staged around a constitutive *aporia* between the irreducible element of force characteristic of every positive claim to justice or right, and the 'absolute alterity' of divine law or justice that is an 'infinity . . . I cannot thematize and [yet] whose hostage I [nevertheless] remain' (Derrida, 1992, 12–13, 22–3, 27, 56). This is not the place to elaborate Derrida's political thought in detail, but, in short, this leads to a form of politics built around an incessant questioning, because a political 'force that justifies itself or is justified in applying itself' can always be 'judged from elsewhere to be unjust or unjustifiable', and so the ordeal of the 'undecidable', i.e. between positive and divine law, 'remains caught' in every extant political decision or claim to justice (Derrida, 1992, 5, 24). By Derrida's account, this *agon* (of the interminable *aporia* between human and divine law) is also mediated by a moment of messianic hope, by the promise of a redemptive moment of full justice or democracy 'to come', which is 'itself' permanently deferred, but nonetheless guides us 'like the blind' through the ordeal of the undecidable (Derrida, 1994, 28, 55, 65, 89, 168). Honig doesn't share this allusion to messianism, and she resists ethical readings of deconstruction, where, for example, as Simon Critchley would have it, an inscrutable call to responsibility and justice is said to 'regulate public space' (Critchley, 1997, 36). Nevertheless, her conception of agonistic democracy is staged primarily in terms of the capacity of situated subjects to resist and redirect the law, increasingly represented in mode of command and alterity. This is only loosely formulated in *Political Theory*, but it becomes more pronounced in her subsequent writings. Nor is it her exclusive understanding of law, as we will see in a moment in her discussion of Rousseau, but Honig's discussion of Rousseau as well as of Agamben is essentially structured by this agonistic resistance to the irresistibility of the Hebrew conception of law.

In this respect, Honig's version of agonism is really quite distinct from Arendt. Arendt stressed the central role that the Hebrew conception of law has played in western reflections on the status of authority, and how this basic paradigm of the law has remained central even under conditions of secular modernity. She said:

> It is of no great relevance if . . . this God addressed his creatures through the voice of conscience or enlightened them through the light of reason rather than through the revelation of the Bible . . . the model in whose image Western mankind has constructed the quintessence of all laws . . . was Hebrew in origin and represented by the divine Commandments of the Decalogue. (Arendt, 1965, 190–1)

This conception of law 'did not change when in the seventeenth and eighteenth centuries natural law stepped into the place of divinity' (Arendt, 1965, 190). However, one of Arendt's central objectives in *On Revolution* is to challenge the hegemony of the Hebrew conception of law. Indeed, this is a big part of what is at issue in her presentation of the events of the eighteenth century as evidence of a uniquely human capacity for an 'absolute beginning', without reference to traditional (i.e. Roman) or divine (i.e. Hebrew) authority and, by Arendt's account, this was, of course, exemplified in the American Revolution. Despite the basic fudge in the opening lines of *The Declaration*, the 'course of the American Revolution tells an unforgettable story and is apt to teach a unique lesson; for this revolution did not break out but was made by men in common deliberation and [exclusively] on the strength of mutual pledges' (Arendt, 1965, 215). We should not be misled here by the reference to 'deliberation'; for Arendt this term did not carry any of the heavy normative connotations it has acquired in contemporary political theory. Her point is simply that the revolution provides an exemplary case of human freedom, of the ability for collective self-authorship through action in concert, and without reference to the past or to the 'beyond'. Indeed, more than anything, it is this sentiment which is the core of Arendt's political theory, and this reflects her existentialist understanding of the human condition, where 'insofar as man is more than a mere creature of nature, more than a mere product of divine creativity, insofar will he be called to account for the things which men do to men in the world which they themselves condition' (Arendt, 2007, 285).

Moreover, this same desire to problematise the Hebrew conception of law underpins Arendt's retrieval of the Roman notion of augmentation. Indeed, Arendt stressed that neither the 'Greek *nomos* nor the Roman *lex* was of divine origin' (Arendt, 1965, 187). What is augmented in the Roman experience of law is not a moment of authority conceived, with Honig and Derrida, as command and alterity, but rather the original authority of the founders of the city. We noted in Chapter 2 that religion was an important component in the Roman experience of augmentation, but it is important to be clear about the details of Roman religion. In contrast to Greece, 'where piety depended upon the immediate revealed presence of the gods', in Rome, religion 'literally meant *religare*: to be tied back, obligated, to the enormous, almost superhuman and hence always legendary effort to lay the foundations, to build the cornerstone, to found [the city] for eternity' (Arendt, 1977a, 121). In Chapter 2 we also saw that Arendt appreciated that the details of Roman authority could not be reproduced under conditions of modernity. Nevertheless, her objective was to rework the Roman model to explain the wisdom of the American founders, because they understood that subsequent augmentation is necessary to keep the originary power of the revolution, as it were, 'always present', through perpetual regeneration. However, in neither of these Arendtean conceptions of the constituent power, as revolution or augmentation, nor in the specific manner of their combination that she admired in the American experience, is there any reference to an 'absolute' in the form of divine sanction, command, or alterity.[2] The only thing that is absolute in this – consistently republican – understanding of politics is the revolutionary *Ursprung*, but, importantly – crucially,

---

[2] Arendt's clear prioritising of the Greek and Roman traditions over the Hebrew conception of law should not be misunderstood as some kind of bad faith in respect of her Jewishness. Indeed, Arendt wrote extensively on Jewish affairs and embraced the experience of the Jewish diaspora as a potential education in political consciousness-raising; because 'as soon as the pariah . . . translates his status into political terms, he becomes perforce a rebel' (Arendt, 2007, 284). However, Arendt embraced the experience of her Jewishness whilst rejecting Judaism, which has no presence in her political theory (Feldman, 2007, xliv).

in fact – this does not mean that the origin is omnipotent or that the subsequent expansion takes the form of an auto-genesis. Instead, as we will see in the following chapter, and in contrast to the dialecticians and the theorists of sovereignty, the moment of origin is incapable of directing the subsequent expansion. This is because the revolutionary leap into being is always conditioned by the circumstances of human plurality, and so the meaning of the revolutionary event is entirely dependent on the judgement of multifarious others, as they take up, debate upon, and live out its significance.

Honig appreciates these conditioning elements of pluralism in Arendt's theory, and she is not concerned about any potential authoritarianism in Arendt's account of the 'absolute beginning'. Her point is rather that Arendt's conception of the act of foundation and subsequent expansion – based exclusively on mutual pledges and action in concert – could never, in itself, provide sufficient stability for the republic. Hence the need for some reference to a constative moment. In fact, Honig thinks that Arendt is only able to make these extravagant claims because of her restricted account of the scope of political action, so the Arendtean republic is always already provided with a degree of stability by the realms of the social, where everything is fixed and beyond resignification and redirection. However, I wonder what adventures in democratic freedom might be possible if we were able to introduce the power of absolute initiative that Arendt associated with revolutionary politics into the realms of the social, i.e. following Honig's very pertinent deconstruction of the Arendtean topography that we explored earlier in the chapter, and where we don't lose sight of the core of Arendt's theory, which is focused on the importance and the possibility of republican autonomy, and not on resistance to the law as command. We return to these thoughts and possibilities in the following chapter, but we first consider in more detail Honig's distinctive understanding of augmentation as developed in her subsequent writings.

The proliferation of paradoxes

This strategy of taking (only apparently) exceptional circumstances in political life and translating them into paradoxes or *aporias* which are (re)negotiated daily in the augmentation of the republic, has become the defining feature of Honig's rendition of agonistic democracy. In particular, she has applied this rationale to Williams' understanding of tragedy as (only) a rare moment in moral life, to Rousseau's paradox of democratic founding and his formulations of the general will, and to the Schmittian idea of the moment of 'exception', which has recently been reworked by Agamben to explain the growth and consolidation of the post–9/11security state. Here, I focus on Honig's reworking of Rousseau and her response to Agamben, and in both cases we see that her reading is shaped by her particular understanding of agonistic augmentation as a form of on-going and open-ended resistance to, and redirection of, the law.

In *The Social Contract* Rousseau pondered the apparent mystery of the origins of the civil association. He wondered how a people existing in a pre-socialised 'state of nature', untouched by the norms of democratic government, could found a virtuous set of institutions. Rousseau famously formulated this predicament as a paradox of democratic founding. He said:

> For an emerging people to be capable of appreciating the sound maxims of politics and to follow the fundamental rules of statecraft, the effect would have to become the cause. The social spirit which ought to be the work of that institution, would have to preside over the [founding of the] institution itself. (Rousseau, 1987, 164)

Honig is intrigued by Rousseau's predicament, which she describes as the inherent 'paradox of politics'.[3] However, she also stresses that the paradox is really played out 'at every moment of political life and not just at the origins of a regime' (Honig, 2007, 3; 2009b, xvi). Rousseau's presentation of this puzzle as a 'paradox of founding' reflects his methodology, i.e. his appeal to the social contract mythology of a fully pre-political people living in a 'state of nature' who contract with one another to set up a civil state. By way of contrast, Honig emphasises that democratic citizens are never fully untouched by political institutions, and neither are they ever fully socialised into the extant norms and procedures. Consequently:

> The seeming quandary of chicken-and-egg (which comes first, good people or good law?) takes off and attaches to democratic politics more generally . . . Every day, after all, new citizens are born, and still others immigrate into established regimes. Every day, already socialized citizens mistake, depart from, or simply differ about the commitments of democratic citizenship. Every day, democracies resocialise, recapture, or reinterpellate citizens into their political institutions and culture in ways those citizens do not freely will, nor could they. The problem that Rousseau seems to cast as a problem of founding recurs daily. (Honig, 2007, 3)

Moreover, this paradox of the emergence – or rather, in Honig's view, the perpetual (re-)emergence and maintenance – of good citizens is intrinsically linked to Rousseau's core objective in *The Social Contract*, which is to find a democratic solution to the potential friction between

---

[3] Connolly also explores the paradox of founding in Rousseau's text, see: Connolly, 1988, 56.

the freedom of the individual and the legal authority of the civil state. Rousseau's goal is to find a form of authority that will enable 'each associate' to unite 'himself with all', thereby enjoying the benefits of civil society, whilst 'still [only] obey[ing] himself alone, and [therefore] remain[ing] as free as before' (Rousseau, 1987, 174). The solution to this predicament is, of course, the idea of the 'general will', understood as a form of popular or democratic sovereignty that carries the moral weight of unanimous and enlightened agreement. To illustrate the moral character of the general will, Rousseau distinguishes this from the manifestation of a merely empirical 'will of all', which doesn't carry this status, has the potential to err, and is only really 'the sum of private wills' (Rousseau, 1987, 155). As Connolly puts it: in Rousseau's theory the people 'must purify themselves of extraneous desires and impulses, until they are able and willing to establish singularity of purpose together', rather than simply calculating on the basis of self-interest (Connolly, 1988, 64).

As various commentators have stressed, the basic direction of Rousseau's argument pre-empts contemporary theories of deliberative democracy.[4] As we saw in Chapter 2, deliberative theorists such as Habermas appeal to idealised procedures, or transparent conditions of deliberation, which are meant to provide the necessary conditions for citizens to establish something like the 'general will', and to be able to differentiate between the authentic expression of the general will, based exclusively on the rational 'force of the better argument', and the pretences of a (merely aggregative) 'will of all'. These points of connection between Rousseau and contemporary deliberative theory are unmistakeable. However, Honig also draws attention to important differences between them. Most significantly, unlike the contemporary deliberative theories, Rousseau did not invoke an 'independent normative standard' to resolve the tensions between the purity of the general will and a mere 'will of all' (Honig, 2007, 7). In fact, Honig points out that he appealed instead to the benign intervention of a foreign lawgiver (in the manner of Lycurgus), and this is at the crunch point in his argument, precisely when the moral status of the general will is hanging in the balance. We will return to Honig's discussion of foreign founders in more detail below. But for the moment we should note that, for Honig, the arrival of the foreign founder in Rousseau's text marks a certain *aporia* in his argument. In short, the foreignness of the founder marks the fact that there are no 'firm criteria or ground[s] from which to distinguish with confidence the will of all and the general will'; with the consequence that all expressions of popular sovereignty are necessarily 'haunted by heteronomy', and so

---

[4] See, for example: Khan, 2012.

in contrast to deliberative theory, the democratic quest for the general will is *inherently* intertwined with traces of 'violence, multitude, the will of all, [and] decision' (Honig, 2007, 5, 8).

Interestingly, then, Honig's account of agonistic democracy includes an emphasis on the pursuit of the Rousseauean ideal of popular sovereignty, i.e. a form of law that is willed unanimously and by a virtuous people. However, the pursuit of this ideal is overladen with pluralism, tragedy, and the value of conflict, and so, on this iteration of the democratic *agon*, 'we get neither deliberation nor decision as such; we get a politics, in which plural and contending parties make claims in the name of public goods, seek support from various constituencies, and the legitimacy of outcomes is always contestable' (Honig, 2007, 14). Honig also stresses that the predicament of how to generate or identify the general will is not an occasional but an on-going concern that 'recurs daily in democratic regimes' (Honig, 2007, 3; 2009a, xvii). Democratic theorists should therefore move away from an exclusive emphasis on 'proceduralism and constitutionalism', and focus instead on the day-to-day orientations of situated subjects towards various assertions of democratic sovereignty (Honig, 2007, 5).

There is, I think, considerable value in what Honig has to say about the tragedy of the 'general will' and the 'will of all'. In particular, her iteration reinforces the core distinction between the agonistic and the deliberative approaches, which, for example, are in danger of being elided in Tully's formulations of agonistic 'dialogue', as we have seen in Chapter 4. However, it is also important to note that the sequence of Honig's argument leads ultimately to an insistence on the alien quality of the law (Honig, 2007, 8).

The general will can never be really equally in everyone's interest nor really equally willed by everyone. Even if it were so fully willed, its authors none the less experience it as alien when it becomes a source of rule, and they are no longer only its authors but also law's subjects. (Honig, 2007, 5)

The underlying intimations to the conception of law as command and as alterity are evident here, and in Honig's version of agonistic democracy, the law is 'periodically or regularly' subject to 'democratization by way of amendment, augmentation or nullification', but in the final analysis we must conclude that the 'people' are never fully the authors of the law, instead they are always 'undecidably present and absent from the scene of democracy' (Honig, 2007, 5; 2009b, xvii).

Here, the contrast not only with Rousseau but also with Arendt is again palpable. Indeed, despite crucial differences between them, Arendt shared with Rousseau a republican commitment to the idea of self-government, and a conception of legal authority as an expression of collective self-authorship.[5] Where they differ is in their respective models of how this republican freedom might become manifest. As we have seen in Chapter 2, Arendt rejected the idea of popular sovereignty and the notion that the source of authority can be modelled on the idea of a collective 'will'. These formulations carry the hubris of omnipotence, and, of course, this is exactly what we find in Rousseau's idea of the 'general will' as virtuous unanimity, which inevitably becomes suspicious of any dissent, understood in terms of residual private or particular interests. On Arendt's account, this political imaginary was one of the root causes of the violence of the French Revolution. Nevertheless, Arendt presented an alternative account of republican self-government, one that is built upon the irreducible plurality of the public sphere and so also on the need for an open-ended politics of reciprocal judgement. We will elaborate these ideas in the following chapter, but at this point we should note that, where Arendt offers an alternative model of popular government and collective self-authorship that is attuned to pluralism, Honig's approach is different. She presents 'heteronomy' as an internal point of disruption within the Rousseauean pursuit of the 'general will', and the consequence of this formulation is to leave the people forever partially displaced from their own collective self-determination.

Honig's presentation of agonism as a series of paradoxes, which, she says, are 'challenges' to be perpetually (re)negotiated in the democratic polity 'not puzzles to be solved or overcome' (Honig, 2008, 85), also clearly resonates with Mouffe's account of the (liberal) democratic paradox that we explored in the previous chapter. However, Honig thinks that Mouffe tends to reify the constitutive paradoxes of democratic life into a fixed binary (Honig, 2007, 14). By her account, the Rousseauean paradox of the 'general will' versus the 'will of all' is more edgy than the Mouffean paradox of liberal democracy. In Mouffe's version the 'tense elements' of the Rousseauean 'paradox are split into two distinct objects: the constitution represents law-rule and the people represent self-rule and these are seen as at odds' (Honig, 2007, 9). Honig stresses that 'political events and dramas exceed such hypostatised categorizations', and she says politics 'occurs in the spaces between them' (Honig, 2007, 14). I think this summary distorts Mouffe's account of the (liberal) demo-cratic paradox to a certain degree. Mouffe does not reify liberalism and democracy into a fixed binary. Instead, as we saw in the previous chap-ter, she thinks of the agonistic contest as a struggle between a series of

---

[5] For a discussion of the differences between Rousseau and Arendt see: Canovan, 1983.

ideologies that each contains dissimilar amalgams of the principles and values associated with liberalism and democracy. This produces a contest between an assortment of protagonists rather than a straightforward binary. Of course, Mouffe's position is predicated on a binary division, but this is primarily located elsewhere, i.e. between those who agree to play the liberal democratic game and the enemies of liberal democracy, who, on Mouffe's account, must be symbolically and legally excluded from the liberal democratic *agon*. Indeed, there are differences between Honig and Mouffe's respective versions of agonistic democracy, and not least that Honig retains a stress on the aspirational dimension of democratic politics. This is in danger of being lost in Mouffe's account, with her unyielding stress on the problem of antagonism, but it is important to note that they are nonetheless alike in their resolutely tragic accounts of agonistic democracy, which they both seek to figure in the modality of constitutive paradoxes. This is in contrast to deliberative theories, but also to those tendencies in Connolly and Tully which are designed to take the edge off the tragic circumstances of politics, and which we have explored in Chapters 3 and 4.

However, it is certainly true that there is a greater emphasis on the situated struggles of particular actors in Honig's theory than in Mouffe's, and this is especially evident when we turn to Honig's response to Agamben. In Chapter 2 we considered Schmitt's presentation of the constituent power in terms of the sovereign decision taken in a moment of crisis or 'exception', such as an insurrection or civil war, and orientated towards the maintenance of security and the basic order and unity of the state, and we can now turn to Agamben's celebrated reworking of Schmitt which helps to explain the tendency towards the systematic use of extra-judicial executive power in the current conjuncture. What defines the contemporary expansion of executive power is that – rather than being associated with a particular security threat, which can be delimited temporally – the new modes of sovereignty are built instead around the paradoxical notion of a 'permanent state of exception'. As Agamben has shown, this modality of governmental power was first mobilised systematically by European states during World War One, was the basic form of law in Germany during the Third Reich, and has become the 'dominant paradigm of government in contemporary politics' (Agamben, 2005, 2). The rhetorical deployment of the idea of an on-going and open-ended state of emergency – the so call 'War on Terror' – necessitates that the sovereign 'maintain the law in its very suspension' (Agamben, 2005, 59). The 'normative aspect of law can thus be obliterated and contradicted with impunity by a governmental violence that . . . nevertheless still claims to be applying the law' (Agamben, 2005, 87).

These insights get to the heart of developments in US foreign and domestic policy in response to 9/11. For example, the curtailment of civil liberties following the introduction of the Patriot Act in 2001, the use of increased surveillance, special rendition, simulated torture techniques, and of indefinite detention in the Guantanamo confinement centre. Honig recognises the significance of Agamben's contribution, which she says helps to 'explain elements of the current political landscape that liberal and deliberative democratic theorists seem only able to criticize', and *Emergency Politics* represents Honig's response to these alarming tendencies in the current conjuncture (Honig, 2009b, 87). Honig employs a number of strategies to try to open up alternatives to this 'neo-Hobbesian, emergency-reproduced notion of sovereignty as unified and top down' (Honig, 2009b, xv). Most importantly, she draws a basic analogy between the sovereign suspension of the rule of law in the moment of 'exception', and the paradoxical element of 'discretion' exercised by situated subjects in the daily operations of politics and administrative procedures within the context of constitutional government (Honig, 2009b, xv–xvii).

If we normally think of emergency politics as identified with a 'decision' that puts a stop to ordinary life under the rule of law, then it might be useful to note that ordinary democratic practices and institutions under the rule of law also feature 'decision', those forms of human discretion presupposed by the rule of law but with which the rule of law is also ill at ease. (Honig, 2009b, xv)

In Chapter 3 of *Emergency Politics,* Honig details the creative power that can emanate from the *agon* of administrative 'discretion', by retelling the experiences of Louis Freeland Post, Assistant Secretary of Labour during the Wilson Administration, and responsible for the Bureau of Immigration during the first Red Scare. Post dismissed the cases brought against hundreds of resident aliens who had been rounded up under the 'Palmer Raids', which were instigated by the Attorney General Alexander Mitchell Palmer along with J. Edgar Hoover. These persons had been selected for deportation on the grounds of being committed to violent insurrection against the US government. Many of them had only attended meetings of anarchist or communist groups, and were not members of illegal organisations. Post insisted on due process in a context of the arbitrary expression of executive power, and he is 'often lauded as a principled proceduralist who anticipated later Court rulings' on the rights of non-citizens (Honig, 2009b, 69). However, by Honig's account, Post 'did not anticipate the law', instead he used his administrative discretion to grant the resident aliens 'rights they did not have juridically', and by skilfully working the 'paradox of politics' in his direction (Honig, 2009b, 79,82). Post used his 'humour, cleverness, idealism, humanism, prerogative, and administrative discretion' to articulate a 'visionary counter-politics' that forced executive power to 'pause and be humbled' (Honig, 2009b, 79, 81). The human qualities that this committed individual 'brought to the rule of law' were its 'necessary supplements (in the sense of both supporting and undermining it)' (Honig, 2009b, 79).

Indeed, this reference to Post as an exemplar of agonistic politics demonstrates that 'within the rule of law settings that Schmitt *contrasts* with decisionism, something like the decisionism that Schmitt approvingly identifies with a dictator goes by the name of discretion and is identified (approvingly or disapprovingly) with administrators and with administrative governance' (Honig, 2009b, 67, emphasis in the original). The underlying purpose of these analyses is to take 'emergency politics out of its exceptionalist context' and to show that situated subjects always retain opportunities for 'democratic orientation, action, and renewal even in the context of emergency' (Honig, 2009b, xv, 67). Again, this is the same basic strategy that Honig worked out in her critique of Arendt's theory of revolution. She takes the seemingly extraordinary moment and renders it less remarkable by drawing attention instead to those irreducible moments of the *extra*-in-the-ordinary. This method is further reinforced by placing the current circumstances of the post–9/11 security state in connection with the Red Scares, so that the current conjuncture can be better understood 'in the context of larger struggles over governance that have marked American liberal democracy for over a century' (Honig, 2009b, 67). Honig also stresses how her agonistic understanding of administrative discretion reinforces the falsehoods of the liberal and deliberative approaches, with their characteristic yearning for a form of law that is untouched by the exercise of power. Indeed, those theorists who typically counter Schmittean-style decisionism with an insistence on the 'rule of law' falsely present the legal system as 'somehow a condition of no-rule, [thereby] disavowing its implication in institutions of governance, despite the fact that the term – *rule* of law – implies governance' (Honig, 2009b, 85, emphasis in the original). Honig's iteration of agonistic democracy draws attention instead to the 'paradoxical dependence of the rule of law on the rule of man' (Honig, 2009b, 66). Like Tully, she says the law is 'part of a larger pattern of daily, on-going vying for power, a quotidian jurisdictional jockeying among bureaucrats, administrative political appointees, judges, lawyers, civil libertarians, as well as citizens and activists from across the political spectrum' (Honig, 2009b, 68).[6]

---

[6] Honig's conception of augmentation in terms of this hand-to-hand combat of legal and political struggles is perhaps more nuanced than Connolly's, who tends to think

These are excellent insights, and Honig provides an exemplary account of the genuinely creative power of agonistic augmentation, of the capacity of situated subjects to establish moments of innovation and redirection *within* the horizon of an established framework of authority, and even in dark times. At a more general level, Honig also contests the neo-conservative (Schmittean) association of the exercise of sovereign power with the need for survival, or the maintenance of 'mere life', which supposedly comes to the fore in moments of crisis or emergency (Honig, 2009b, xviii). The example of Post shows that even in these circumstances, forms of politics are possible where people act not out of fear, but out of courage and conviction. Post embodies a form of politics orientated not only to the 'mere life to which emergency seeks to reduce us, but also [to] the more life – *sur-vivre* – of emergence' (Honig, 2009b, xviii). In this respect, Honig moves decisively beyond Mouffe, who, as we saw in the previous chapter, runs the risk of complicity in the neo-conservative emphasis on a primary need for order and against the threat of privation. However, as we have also said at several points in this study, Honig's exclusive emphasis on freedom in terms of the *extra*-in-the-ordinary is also a precarious strategy, and one that risks complicity in the status quo, in the idea that there is no *genuinely* extraordinary alternative to the present (neo-)liberal (capitalist) regime. Here, her position stands in marked contrast to Benjamin, who was the first to understand the link between the idea of a 'permanent state of emergency' and the reproduction of extra-judicial state violence, and who responded to the Fascist *pseudo* state of emergency in the 1930s, with an insistence that the Left needed to cultivate a counter politics of the *authentically* exceptional moment, one that would disrupt the present regime and create radically new social forms (Benjamin, 1999, VIII, XVI). I turn to these possibilities in the following chapter, but, as I said in the first part of the book, it is important to keep both of these moments of innovation in play in the context of the current conjuncture. Indeed, we need an appreciation not only of the Honigean *extra*-in-the-ordinary, but also the Benjaminian truly-extraordinary moment, and, as we will see in the following chapter, both of these qualitatively distinct moments of innovation are compatible

---

of the politics of enactment largely in terms of the emergence of new rights claims. As Honig says, this: 'may make him unmindful of the role of law in producing the unilinear temporality that he seeks to decentre. It is in the discourse of law that innovative actors are invariably depicted as having "anticipated" the law (rather than having made, countermanded, or hijacked it) when they call for the recognition or entrenchment of new rights' (Honig, 2008, 98).

with the agonistic circumstances of pluralism, tragedy, and the value of conflict.[7]

Democracy and the irreducible foreignness of the founder

Despite Honig's stress on the inherent *aporia* embedded in expressions of popular sovereignty, with the consequence that the people are effectively prevented from ever really becoming the authors of the law, *Emergency Politics* nonetheless has the feel of a decidedly political text. The example of the embattled Louis Post, who uses his skill and fortitude to outwit Hoover and Palmer, to shape the outcome of particular administrative decisions and to twist the paradox of politics in his favour, is reminiscent of Machiavelli's' account of the glory of figures like Cesare Borgia, Ferdinand of Spain, and the Roman emperor Septimius Severus, who used their *virtù* to shape the direction of political fortune. However, the central message of *Democracy and the Foreigner* is more ambiguous. On the face of it, the main aim of the book is to problematise the typical depiction of foreigners and foreignness as something that threatens the community by 'marking negatively what "we" are not' (Honig, 2001b, 3). Honig notes that the depiction of foreignness as a 'problem' that needs to be solved has a long lineage in democratic and republican theory. In 'classical political thought, foreignness is generally taken to signify a threat

---

[7] In *Emergency Politics* there is perhaps a moment of equivocation in Honig's otherwise exclusive stress on the *extra*-in-the-ordinary, and this is evident in her discussion of miracles. Honig acknowledges Arendt and Schmitt's use of the metaphor of a miracle to figure the moment of radical initiative, and she draws attention to a similar viewpoint in Franz Rosenzweig, a Jewish theologian and a contemporary of Schmitt. Honig stresses the particular value of Rosenzweig's 'concept of miracle . . . [because it] functions more like a sign than a [sovereign] command and so points towards the popular receptivity and interpretation upon which signs depend' (Honig, 2009a, 90). Honig's objective seems to be to find another way to undercut the claims to extra-judicial (i.e. miraculous) power of the 'sovereign', and by drawing attention instead to the 'cultural conditions under which people are open to the miraculous, to receive, perceive, and perform it' (Honig, 2009a, 92). This observation could, of course, be accommodated within her more general schema; for example, if Honig's aim is to accentuate those little moments of miracle that can emerge in everyday politics, for instance in the mode of administrative discretion. However, elsewhere Honig says that revolution, like the miracle, similarly 'depends upon observers to receive it in a non-reductionist way' (Honig, 2008, 305). This is only a passing comment, but this apparent return of the prospect of revolution seems out of step with Honig's strong critique of revolution in *Political Theory*, and more generally with her exclusive stress on the miraculous-in-the-ordinary, rather than the truly miraculous *event*. Of course, Arendt knows very well that revolution, like all forms of action, is entirely dependent on its reception to gain any endurance and expansion in the world, and this will be the central theme in my account of agonism and militant cosmopolitanism in the following chapter.

of corruption that must be kept out or contained for the sake of the stability and identity of the regime' (Honig, 2001b, 1–2). Despite these well-entrenched predispositions, one of Honig's objectives is to challenge the idea that xenophobia is in any sense rooted in human nature, and these interventions are in the service of a form of cosmopolitanism that acknowledges and celebrates various 'passionate attachments' that transcend the nation-state (Honig, 2001b, 11). These are valuable insights and I draw upon them in the following chapter. However, there is also a deeper message in this book, which is Honig's firm insistence on the alien quality of the law.

Honig's intuition is that the 'fraught relationship to foreignness' might be generated primarily by tensions within democracy itself (Honig, 2001b, 11). By her account, the paradox of politics 'generate[s] or feed[s] an ambivalence that is then projected onto the screen of foreignness' (Honig, 2001b, 13). This leads to the counterintuitive idea that the symbolic articulation of foreignness might actually solve certain problems for democratic unity (Honig, 2001b, 4). In the mode of a psychoanalyst, Honig is concerned with the 'symbolic work' that the figure of the foreigner does for the (impossible) aspiration toward unity that characterises the democratic regime. Drawing on a series of foreign founder myths from popular and high culture – including the *Wizard of Oz*, the western movie *Shane*, the myth of immigrant America, Rousseau's *The Social Contract*, Freud's *Moses and Monotheism* and the book of Ruth in the Hebrew Bible – Honig demonstrates that this figure is a 'fantasy construction', a myth, or a 'figment of the . . . cultural imagination' and one that enables the democratic polity to live with its own constitutive *aporia* (Honig, 2001b, 4).

In Book II, Chapter VII of *The Social Contract*, Rousseau notes that it 'was the custom of most Greek cities to entrust the establishment of their laws to foreigners' (Rousseau, 1987, 163). As we have said, on Honig's account, Rousseau introduces the idea of the foreign founder into his narrative of democratic self-government at precisely the point when he is unable to deliver a criterion for ensuring the integrity of the 'general will'. The foreign founder's foreignness symbolises the necessary 'distance and impartiality needed to animate and guarantee a General Will that can neither animate nor guarantee itself' (Honig, 2001b, 21). Honig also stresses that in Rousseau's text the beneficent foreigner kindly departs from the city once his work is done, and this timely departure 'prevents the foreignness of the founder from ever becoming a problem for the regime' (Honig, 2001b, 24). Indeed, this figure of a compassionate outsider who solves fundamental predicaments for a political regime is not uncommon. For example, the *Wizard of Oz* is a 'rescue fantasy' where Dorothy is able to topple the 'forces of corruption and alienation' because she has not been socialised by the 'reign of terror that has moulded the locals into servile abjection' (Honig, 2001b, 17). More generally, however, the foreign founder is a 'radically undecidable figure', whose 'foreignness operates . . . as both support of and threat to the regime in question' (Honig, 2001b, 3, 7, 25). In a lively reading of these various texts, Honig shows that it is their foreignness 'that makes outsiders necessary even if also dangerous to the regimes that receive them' (Honig, 2001b, 3). Indeed, the ambiguous images of foreignness – as 'exotic, desirable, mysterious, wise, insightful, dangerous, objective, treasured and so on' – make the foreign founder an exemplary figure for marking the inherent elements of heterogeneity that, on Honig's account, condition each moment of democratic (re)foundation (Honig, 2001b, 4, 71, 223).

It seems to me that there are potentially some underlying conservative anxieties lurking in these formulations. For example, as Žižek has pointed out:

many conservative . . . political thinkers, from Blaise Pascal to Immanuel Kant and Joseph de Maistre, elaborated the notion of the illegitimate origins of power, of the 'founding crime' on which states are based, which is why one should offer 'noble lies' to people in the guise of heroic narratives of origin. (Žižek, 2008, 98)

There are moments when Honig's argument appears to be moving in a similar direction. For example, she says that perhaps this story of the 'too-good-to-be-true arrival of the lawgiver' is just something we 'tell ourselves so we can disavow, rather than take responsibility for, those violences . . . on which the foundings and daily maintenance of our democratic polity depend' (Honig, 2001b, 36). By this account, the myth of the foreign founder operates as something like a fantasmatic screen that convers up 'the real' of foundational violence, i.e. it is an attempt to avoid the trauma of something like Mouffe's notion of constitutive 'antagonism'. Elsewhere, however, Honig moves to expose the real buried within the imaginary of the generous outsider. For example, when she shows how the myth of immigrant America covers up the more violent aspects of the founding: slavery, conquest, and imperial expansion (Honig, 2001b, 75). However, thankfully, the overall orientation of Honig's book is not in the direction of a conservative masking of the anguish of foundational violence. Rather she seeks to mobilise the symbolism of foreignness in the cause of a cosmopolitan agenda, one that seeks to 'open up the reach of democracy in late modernity, to multiply affinities with others here, in the temporal space of the nation state, and elsewhere' (Honig, 2001b, 18). The purpose of identifying the irreducible ambiguity (foreignness)

at the foundation of the democratic state is to 'make room for the generation of alternative sites of affect and identity against which states often
guard' (Honig, 2001b, 106). The point is to 'refigure our understanding
of civic attachment' in the hope that late modern citizens might come to
see that the 'nation state is just one of several sites of always ambivalent
attachment rather than the sole and central site' of identification (Honig,
2001b, 106, 122).

   These objectives are very important, and Honig is right to stress that
democratic actions can be 'generated out of a sense of solidarity that may
be located on any number of registers – local, national, or international'
(Honig, 2001b, 103). I share her concern with nurturing those 'sites of
transnational connection that bypass state apparatus in order to pursue
shared goals' (Honig, 2001b, 72). This aspect of her approach is also
in marked contrast to Mouffe, with her strong critique of cosmopolitanism that we considered in the previous chapter. However, Honig's
more specific formulations of this agonistic cosmopolitanism also reveal
the limitations of her approach. She is rightly critical of deliberative theorists such as Habermas and Benhabib for their association of cosmopolitanism with a mode of universality that is already more or less outlined
in internationally recognised norms and basic human rights, and their
presentation of political globalisation as a learning process where we
might see these universal norms progressively incorporated into democratic will-formation above, below, and at the level of the nation-state
(Benhabib, 2006; Honig, 2006). However, Honig can't get beyond a
negative critique of these deliberative conceptions of universality, and so
she envisages cosmopolitanism largely as a resistance to 'the alienness
of a universalism that seeks to subsume the new or the foreign under
categories whose fundamental character and validity are unchanged or
unaffected by this encounter' (Honig, 2006, 111). In turn, this leads to
a relatively passive understanding of the forms of politics associated with
'agonistic cosmopolitics'. For example, she says:

We might see more citizens of privileged nations marrying, instrumentally, those
who seek to live among them, in order therefore to enable their fellow world
dwellers to stay on as their neighbours and, as a nice by-product, thereby de-
romanticizing *two* institutions insistently romanticized and still claimed by most
states as their monopoly, both marriage and citizenship. (Honig, 2006, 119,
emphasis in the original)

This resembles Tully's emphasis on the capacity of situated subjects to
subvert extant practices by directly acting otherwise. Whilst these forms
of situated *i*llegality might well have dislocatory effects, Honig's iteration repeats the limitations that we considered at the end of Chapter 4.

These practices leave in place the enormous structures of domination that surely need to be confronted more directly in any plausible model of cosmopolitanism. Moreover, this relative political delicateness follows from the more profound significance of *Democracy and the Foreigner*, which is, as we have said, Honig's insistence on the alien quality of the law.

At several points in the book, Honig explicitly invokes the conception of law as 'absolute divine power', and although this can and should always be 'resisted and engaged', on this Hebrew model the people are not the authors of the law (Honig, 2001b, 6). Indeed, Honig concludes her book with the suggestion that it might be Freud 'who provides the best resources out of which to generate a model of democratic agency', one which stresses the (always partly) alien quality of the law (Honig, 2001b, 39). Freud's *Moses and Monotheism* depicts 'subjects who experience the law as a horizon of promise but also partly alien and impositional thing' (Honig, 2001b, 39). Focusing on Freud's claim that Moses was an Egyptian prince, Honig says that 'Moses' foreignness is concealed in order to signal and secure the people's identification with the law; but it is poorly concealed in order to preserve a marker of the law's alienness to the people who live by it' (Honig, 2001b, 31). As we have seen in the example of Louis Post, this facilitates a particular model of democratic activism. Indeed, the constructive element in this 'alienation' in the law 'is that it marks a gap in legitimation, a space that is held open for future refoundings, augmentation and amendment' (Honig, 2001b, 31). However, in Honig's account, the people are fundamentally not auto*nomo*us; instead, they are 'solicited as a unity *by* the lawgiver' (Honig, 2007, 7, emphasis added). Although they are never fully captured by his law, thereby opening the space for agonistic politics, the people are effectively destined to remain always partly dependent on the external source and authority of the law. Indeed, at certain low points in the text, Honig wonders if the myth of the foreign founder is 'a projection of the people's own (illicit and therefore denied) desire to submit in a very nonrepublican way to the will of the inspiring and charismatic founder' (Honig, 2001b, 23). She stresses that the foreign founder script is typically an 'infantilizing origin story in which we abdicate democratic responsibility for our common life together' (Honig, 2001b, 38). Needless to say, the contrast again with Arendt is very striking, and one is left wondering how this infantilised people could possibly gather the resources to contend with the multiple and overlapping crises that we face today. How they could possibly struggle with and overcome the resurgent security state and the new forms of imperialism that we explored in Chapter 4?

Conclusion

Honig's engagement with Arendt is sustained and important and operates on several levels. Arendt's unreconstructed Hellenism is unacceptable because it treats forms of social oppression – from the ancient practice of slavery, to the sources of modern poverty, and the oppression of women – as pre-political forms of violence, and therefore beyond the possibility of redirection through political action. Honig is right to tackle these aspects of Arendt's theory head on, and, in this respect, her approach is different from some of the more cheery renditions of Arendt's pluralism, which tend to simply ignore this aspect of her work. Crucially, however, Honig has demonstrated how Arendt's own rendition of the constituent power, in terms of a capacity for innovation, can be redirected in ways that break open her untenable topographical distinction between the social and the political. Indeed, Honig has shown how these categories are inherently unstable, and this facilitates a form of agonistic politics where actors introduce political innovation into the realms of the social. Honig figures this in terms of a politics of performance and (re)iteration that repeatedly challenges and redirects the dominant cultural norms and practices. This has been particularly evident in feminism and the politics of gender identity, whilst other areas of the 'the social' have been more resistant to these forms of politics. However, there is no reason why, in principle, this reworked understanding of the relations between the political and the social could not be brought to bear on the more entrenched forms of domination associated with neo-liberalism, imperialism, and the security state, and we turn to these possibilities in the following chapter.

Honig also repudiates the Arendtean account of revolution as 'absolute beginning'. With Derrida, she insists on the inherent *aporia* between the performative and the constative moments, as well as the circumstances of *iterability* that condition every political *event*. This means that, from Honig's perspective, the absolute priority of the constituent power that Arendt associated with revolution is exaggerated and untenable. By way of contrast, Honig translates the extraordinary capacity for creation that Arendt sees exemplified in revolution into the moments of freedom that manifest in the (only apparently) ordinary circumstances of everyday politics, in the forms of augmentation, amendment, revision, and reiteration. In this regard, Honig's contribution confirms one of the central claims of this study, i.e. that contemporary agonistic theory trades exclusively in the politics of augmentation.

Honig's strategy of taking (only ostensibly) exceptional moments and refiguring them instead as that little bit of *extra* that often emerges in the (not so) ordinary has been the abiding theme in her model of agonistic democracy, and we have seen how she has applied this idea to a series of constitutive paradoxes, and most notably the paradoxes of the 'general will' and the 'will of all', and of the sovereign 'decision' and administrative 'discretion'. Honig's encounter with Agamben is particularly significant, and her examples of agonistic augmentation draw attention to the enduring freedom of citizens to counter the machinations of sovereign power, even as their legislators are intent on governing through fear and the ideology of a permanent state of exception.

However, these points of emphasis cannot be the whole story of the agonic freedom of citizens in the context of the security state and of disciplinary neo-liberalism. It is important to remember that the ordinary that we're talking about here (even with its little *extra*) is the basic sociopolitical coordinates, or forms of life, of liberal democratic modernity, which in the end are predicated upon a basic commitment to the legal protection of forms of possessive individualism. This is a hazardous strategy, because it runs the risk of complicity in the (neo-)liberal ideology that there is no (genuine) alternative to the present system.

Indeed, like the contemporary Wittgensteinian approaches, Honig's formulation effectively collapses the qualitative distinction between the agonism of everyday politics and the truly *extraordinary* power of the revolutionary event. In my view this represents a regression vis-à-vis Arendt's theory.[8] Indeed, as we said in Chapter 2, the priority of the strategic question obliges us to retain a sense of the qualitative distinction between revolution and augmentation, and the dominant trends in the present conjuncture also suggest that we need to hold onto the

---

[8] In her most recent work Honig attempts to refigure Arendt as a theorist of the ordinary who is closer to Wittgenstein, rather than as a theorist of the revolutionary event (Honig, 2009b, xviii). In support of this view, she draws attention to Arendt's emphasis on the elements of continuity that prepared the way for the American Revolution. Indeed, she goes so far as to say that Arendt 'may have had in mind something like Aristotle's infinite relationship between finite things when she remarked that the American revolutionaries succeeded because they practiced self-governance for decades before they rebelled' (Honig, 2007, 14). This, says Honig, suggests an altogether different conception of creation in Arendt than 'the *ab initio* variety' with which she is 'usually associated' (Honig, 2007, 14). However, as I said in Chapter 2, the pivotal contention comes at the end of Chapter Five of *On Revolution* where Arendt emphasises the radical novelty of the American Revolution, and her point is that this is despite the elements of continuity that primed this unprecedented event. Indeed, Honig's initial depiction of Arendt in *Political Theory* was correct, and her attempt to invoke Derrida as an alternative to Arendt, whilst ill conceived in my view, was nonetheless more plausible than this subsequent attempt to reread *On Revolution* with the moment of absolute initiative – and all it entails – weeded out. Moreover, the idea that Arendt understood the spacio-temporal conditions of political life in terms that are comparable with Aristotle's 'infinite sequence' is very doubtful. This idea is taken from *The Physics* and denotes exactly the conceptions of natural process, necessity, and teleology that Arendt was resolutely determined to dissociate from the human capacity for origination. See: Aristotle, 1996, Book 3, Chapter 6.

possibility of radical innovation, in response to challenges such as the global climate crisis. With her explicit disavowal of the idea of revolution, Honig's theory makes these kinds of evaluation impossible, and she very explicitly presents a mono-typical account of the constituent power in the mode of augmentation. By way of contrast to Honig, we need to recognise in the Derridean infrastructures – *différance*, iterability, unde-cidability – important insights into the circumstances of signification and relationality, but at the same time we should resist the idea that these are metaphysical principles that strictly condition all forms of politics. Crucially, these Derridean insights do not take priority over the possi-bility of the revolutionary *Ursprung*, the originary leap that momentarily breaks open or suspends the play of *différance*, but which does not then become the basis of a dialectical or any other kind of process.

We have also seen that, in Honig's particular rendition of agonistic aug-mentation, the idea of law as command and alterity comes increasingly to the fore. She says, in contrast to Schmitt (and presumably also Mouffe), we need to conceive of a form of commonality that is not 'defined by its opposition to the other as enemy', but rather 'by its openness to the other as divine' (Honig, 2009b, 92). Importantly, Honig resists the reduction of politics to ethics that demarcates most theories that are informed by this Hebrew conception of law, but this paradigm nonetheless leads to a stress on the irreducibly alien quality of the law, and Honig's empha-sis is ultimately on the limits that constrain the republican model of self-government and collective autonomy. By way of contrast, in the fol-lowing chapter we return again to Arendt for inspiration for a republican model of politics that is commensurate with the agonistic circumstances of pluralism, tragedy, and the value of conflict, but nonetheless holds firm to the possibility of self-government, through radical innovation combined with augmentation, and in the hope that we might start to find solutions to the multiple and overlapping crises that define the present conjuncture.

Part III

7   Agonism and militant cosmopolitanism

We have seen that agonism is defined by an emphasis on pluralism, tragedy, and the value of particular forms of contest. Pluralism and tragedy represent intrinsic conditions of political action, and agonistic contest is said to have the potential – if crafted wisely – to dispel the threat of antagonism or fundamentalist forms of *ressentiment*, or, with more aspiration, to be a necessary constituent in the struggles of subaltern peoples for independence and against arbitrary forms of power. These points of emphasis capture core insights about political life, and represent some of the central contributions of the theorists examined in this book. The leading proponents of agonism have also skilfully exposed the conceits of the prevailing juridical and deliberative justifications of liberal democracy, they have developed careful genealogies of different elements of our existing institutions and practices, unearthing their contingent foundations, and these narratives have reinforced a vivid sense of the agonic freedom of citizens to introduce genuine novelty into those institutions and practices through periodic moments of augmentation, enactment, articulation, or Wittgensteinian iterations of prevailing rules and norms. These forms of politics are exemplified in the repeated emergence of new social movements from the mid 1960s, as well as in the determination and fortitude of situated subjects like Louis Freeland Post. However, at the same time, we have tracked and identified an assortment of ontological and theoretical assumptions which tend to essentialise these moments of political freedom, and which operate to preclude the possibility of the emergence of the constituent power as an occasion of radical innovation and rupture. In this sense, the contemporary agonistic theorists each present a mono-typical account of the relative priority of the constituent power in the mode of augmentation, and from these viewpoints the moment of the *Ursprung* is literally inconceivable. This distinguishes the contemporary agonistic theorists from Arendt, who combined an insistence on the pluralistic and open-ended conditions of political action with a keen sense of the miraculously creative power of revolution.

Indeed, contemporary agonistic democracy is perhaps best demarcated by a characteristic emphasis on both (i) genuine innovation in modern politics (i.e. moments of freedom that are not subsumed under juridical or dialectical forms of determination) and, at the same time, (ii) the basic legitimacy of liberal democratic constitutionalism, with its emphasis on the co-originality of democratic self-government and the constitutional protection of individual rights. From the contemporary agonistic perspective, this paradoxical combination of values cannot be perfected, resolved, or progressively integrated, as Habermas would have it, but only perpetually renegotiated in the cut and thrust of genuinely open-ended struggle. However, this also means that the democratic *mêlée* is not entirely open-ended, in the sense that the constituent power is not seen to enjoy the *potentia* to instigate profound new beginnings that might discontinue the basic social and political forms of modern liberal democratic constitutionalism. This is problematic, and the contemporary theorists effectively sell themselves short, because there is nothing in the agonistic matrix of pluralism, tragedy, and conflict, which determines that the constituent power must be hemmed in by the norms, values, and institutions of liberal democracy, with its central commitment to the legal protection of forms of possessive individualism.

These conclusions show themselves to be especially problematic in the present circumstances of the global economic and environmental crises and the ascendency of large corporations and the security state. These tendencies in the current conjuncture call for a more militant stance towards existing institutions and practices, and in this final chapter I present a preliminary outline of a theory of agonism and militant cosmopolitanism that seeks to contend with these developments and to find ways to instigate radically new social and political forms in response to pressing issues such as the looming climate, population, energy, and food crises. Tully's depiction of globalisation as the latest stage in European imperialism provides a basic point of departure, and this is combined with Agamben's insights into the reproduction of the security state through a permanent state of exception, which we explored in relation to Honig's work in the previous chapter. After a brief restatement of these predominant features of contemporary politics and of the background conditions of domination, and a consideration of the global movements that struggle within and against these developments and insist that 'another world' – and not just an augmentation of liberal democracy – '*is* possible', this chapter focuses on three areas of theoretical consideration which help to delineate a more militant iteration of agonistic democracy. These are: (i) the conceptual distinction between action and pluralism or action and judgement, and why the expansive power of the democratic *agon* appears in the interface between bold and decisive action and multiple open-ended judgements; (ii) the crucial importance of a politics of militant conviction in the circumstances of an increasingly post-secular society, and as a response to passive nihilism; (iii) the need to learn something from the original Hellenic idea of leadership or *hegemonia*, again understood as a vital ingredient in the emergence of a militant cosmopolitan assemblage, and as an alternative both to any kind of sovereignty and to those theories that associate cosmopolitanism with impartiality.

Each of these theoretical interventions is intended to facilitate a theory and practice of militant cosmopolitanism.[1] At the core of this idea is a belief that a moment of absolute initiative might just arise from the politics of the contemporary transnational democratic movements, and if this revolutionary *Ursprung* was combined with an ensuing augmentation, in a manner that was recommended by Machiavelli and that Arendt so admired in the American founding, then we might have the ingredients for the emergence and subsequent expansion of a new mode of cosmopolitanism. The hope is that this initiative, which introduces a new principle (or set of values) into the world, is subsequently judged to be of wider or more universal significance, so that it is picked up and carried forward in the lived experiences of multiple publics and starts to interrupt and redirect established political priorities at the local, national, and global levels. To some these claims may appear far-fetched and utopian, but, without the invention of radically new ways of being in the world and their subsequent dissemination and genuine materialisation, then all the signs are that our children can look forward to a diminished quality of life, to massive inequalities, political instability, and increasingly authoritarian and militaristic forms of rule.

Alternate globalisation

At several points in this study we have explored the key elements associated with globalisation – most notably in Chapter 4 in relation to Tully's work. I will not repeat these points in detail here, but it is necessary to briefly accentuate a few key themes as a prelude to the conceptual analyses set out in the remainder of this chapter. At the core of economic globalisation is a series of developments, made possible by the revolution in information technology, that have ensured the consolidation of neo-liberal disciplinary control across the planet. The principal political and institutional manifestation of this development has been the relative demise of the efficacy of national government, which is manifest in a

---

[1] For an earlier formulation of the idea of militant cosmopolitanism see: Wenman, 2009.

decreased capacity of/for national executives to control market mechanisms and basic social and economic processes. Until recently, this tendency has been most pronounced in the developing world, where newly emergent states have established formal independence from former colonial powers, but remain subjugated to the control of the transnational agents of neo-liberalism, for example the World Bank and the WTO, who insist that there is no alternative to 'free' trade, the deregulation of markets, and the privatisation of formerly state-run industries as a prerequisite to the all-important objective of competitiveness and economic growth. More recently, however, these same tendencies have been more pronounced in the advanced economies of the West, and most notably in those countries on the periphery of Europe in the context of the on-going financial crises after the 2008 'credit crunch'. Indeed, the incapacity of national elites – and their representatives in the G8 and the G20 – to address the financial and sovereign debt crises reinforces the idea that economic processes, and especially capital mobility and investment priorities, are now effectively beyond the control of elected officials. The fact that the financial institutions are deemed 'too big to fail' and so have to be propped up with massive amounts of public money, whilst national governments are incapable of regulating these institutions so that the livelihoods of ordinary people remain utterly exposed to the indiscriminate fluctuations of markets, driven by the speculation of hedge fund managers and the pronouncements of credit rating agencies, reaffirms the central fact that people all round the world today are effectively hostage to the arbitrary power of turbo capitalism.

It is not only Marxists who appreciate these pressing realities. Indeed, it is a standard observation in mainstream theories of globalisation, that the increased mobility of capital 'shifts the balance of power between markets and states and generates powerful pressures on states to develop market friendly policies' (Held and McGrew, 2002, 23). However, as we saw in Chapter 4, the emergence of economic globalisation represents something more than the relative ascendancy of markets vis-à-vis national executives. Indeed, Tully shares with authors such as Hardt and Negri the crucial insight that globalisation manifests as a novel form of networked imperialism, again centred in market mechanisms and made possible by information technology, that introduces new forms of discipline that 'increasingly overlap and invest one another' in a singular process of bio-political control (Hardt and Negri, 2001, xiii). As Hardt and Negri put it, Empire 'is a decentred and deteritorialising apparatus of rule that progressively incorporates the entire global realm within its open, expanding frontiers. Empire manages hybrid identities, flexible hierarchies, and plural exchanges through modulating networks of command' (Hardt and Negri, 2001, xii). Transnational corporations are in many respects the predominant nodal points in these new systems of control. They operate as the nerve centres of a networked system of social symbolic reproduction that interpolates subjects as individual passive customers of particular lifestyle identities through a relentless feasting on consumer products, at the cost of more communal forms of organisation and subjectivity. Indeed, one of the more deeply rooted causes of these developments has been the extension of basic rights of private appropriation to corporations, who have themselves effectively acquired the status of 'possessive individuals'. The activities of these organisations have a massive impact on peoples' lives, and yet in all meaningful respects they too are beyond public control.

From the republican perspective, the basic dependence of contemporary peoples all round the world on the ostensibly 'private' choices and priorities of massive corporations and financial institutions, and the capricious fluctuations of markets, means that these institutions can only be seen as contemporary forms of arbitrary power and domination. However, it is important to grasp that, whilst enormously significant, these developments only represent one element of corruption in contemporary (neo-)liberal (disciplinary) regimes. Indeed, one of Tully's most significant insights is to draw attention to the fact that, whilst globalisation should be understood as a single system of informal imperialism, this cannot be explained in mono-causal terms, with reference to a single logic of capitalist exploitation. Instead, Empire sutures together complex forms of oppression into a composite system of domination. In fact, Tully makes the crucial observation that the current system of control effectively aims to usurp three basic (and irreducible) moments of the constituent power, which in classical republican thought ought to remain with the people. These are '(i) political power or the powers of self-government; (ii) labour or productive power; and (iii) the powers to protect oneself and others, or military and police power' (Tully, 2008b, 204). The reproduction of Empire through the attempted appropriation of this irreducible trinity of the constituent power has important implications, both for how we analyse the current machinations of constituted power, as well as for conceptions of liberation and how progressive movements might find ways to challenge and overcome this goliath.

In terms of how we evaluate the present system, this means that we need to pay due attention not only to the relations between states and markets, but also to the changing character of the military and security dimensions of the state in the context of globalisation. Although Tully is mindful of these questions, Agamben's observations about the operations of new forms of 'sovereignty' through the mobilisation of a permanent state of exception become particularly significant here. Indeed, as we discussed in the previous chapter in relation to Honig's work, these insights brilliantly capture some of the principal features of the post–9/11 security state, such as the restriction of civil liberties, increased surveillance, and the principle of pre-emptive war. Agamben is mistaken when he presents these developments as indicative of a core underlying logic of western politics going back to antiquity, and orientated towards the reproduction of forms of 'bare life' that are beyond all forms of legal or symbolic status (Agamben, 1998). However, he is correct when he points to the steady consolidation of executive control in the present context, through the rhetorical deployment of a permanent state of exception. In some important respects these forms of resurgent 'sovereignty' stand in marked contrast to the basic impotency of national- level decision making in the face of the omnipotence of markets, and I return to the question of this apparent tension in the final section of this chapter below. However, for the moment it is sufficient to note that these new forms of the security state cannot be explained with reference to a single imperative of capital accumulation, and this has clear implications for how we conceptualise those movements that seek to transform the present structures of domination.

Indeed, Empire is manifest in a series of distinct but interlocking institutional forms, which operate in a combined appropriation of the three irreducible constituent capacities (for self-government, productive labour, and self-defence), and this also means that the present struggles against domination cannot be modelled exclusively on any one of these three moments of the constituent power. In other words, the autonomist notion of the 'multitude' arising spontaneously from the wellspring of productive labour doesn't represent a credible response to the current predicament. However, whilst this analysis reveals the limitations of Marxist and neo-Marxist reductions of domination to economic exploitation and freedom to emancipated labour, the complex and overlapping forms of control also demonstrate the clear limitations of Arendt's exclusive focus on the value of political freedom and institution building, and her complete disregard of social forms of oppression. Indeed, we might surmise that the displacement of corrupt 'political' institutions is relatively achievable compared to the seemingly intractable task of bringing about meaningful 'regime change' in the colossal military and corporate structures of the present system. Nevertheless, as Tully says, an analysis that focuses exclusively on political institutions, would 'be out of touch' with the 'global populist . . . *discomfort* with the existing order' (Tully, 2008b, 206, emphasis in the original). We need to find ways to bring genuine innovation into the predominant social, economic, and military forms, and not just into forms of government in the narrow sense.

We have seen throughout this book that the political consequences of globalisation are not at all straightforward. One clear trend has been the emergence of novel forms of transnational social movement. Again, these developments are made possible by digital technology, and this reveals that globalisation is an ambiguous phenomenon, which is not only manifest as a new networked form of imperialism, but also creates opportunities for the emergence of the constituent power. The compression of space through real time communication has facilitated the enormous logistical achievements associated with organising events such as the World Social Forum. This has also created new tactical opportunities for the operations of protest, for example through the use of sites such as Facebook and Twitter and services such as Blackberry Messenger. These technologies have provided the infrastructure for the mass increased volume of protest movements around the world, from the G20 summit protests to the protests against the financial crises in Athens and Madrid, to Occupy, and the Arab Spring. We have seen how each of the theorists examined in this book, with the exception of Mouffe, has linked these kinds of developments to the possibility of new forms of cosmopolitanism. Mouffe's reservations about prospects for the emergence of cosmopolitan forms of politics are not unfounded. They stem from her due concern about the hubris of the predominant liberal conceptions of cosmopolitanism, with their focus on transnational institutions and effective global governance (Held), or global civil society understood as the embodiment of the 'law of humanity', that is supposedly rationally demonstrable and equivalent to Kantian principles of moral duty (Falk). Mouffe is right to stress that these values and institutions are symptomatic of particular readings of the western tradition, and cannot claim universal validity. Moreover, these theorists do not pay sufficient attention to the on-going significance of national identity, and the fact that institutions beyond a certain scale are incompatible with democracy. The other theorists examined here also share these concerns, but they have insisted that it is nonetheless possible to formulate alternative conceptions of cosmopolitanism that do not reproduce these difficulties and might accompany a restoration of civic activity on a local and national scale. I share this view, but I don't think the alternatives we have explored so far are sufficient.

For Connolly, cosmopolitanism means little more than transnationalism, and he associates this with those forms of social movement politics that apply pressure on particular states; for Honig, cosmopolitanism is conceived in terms of forms of solidarity that are not confined to the nation-state, but which, at best, represent an incessant *resistance* to false claims to universality; whereas, for Tully, cosmopolitanism supposedly manifests directly in the present, in those 'glocal' relations between citizens, directly acting otherwise, and that apparently emerge from the gaps in the present institutions. Each of these contributions highlights necessary but insufficient conditions of cosmopolitanism. Indeed, none of them really quite hits the nail on the head, and they each overlook what is really the most fundamental point, which is that 'cosmopolitanism' must mean something more than simply transnationalism. Indeed, the militant form of cosmopolitanism elaborated here is primarily concerned with the capacity of democratic actors to generate new social and political forms that are subsequently recognised to be of wider significance, so that they are picked up and carried forward by different actors and spectators in different locales, and become the foundation of an expanding open-ended form of universality.

With the exception of Honig's deconstructive stance towards false claims to universality, the contemporary agonistic theorists have largely dodged the question of the status of the universal, and of the relationship between the particular and the universal. Again, there are good reasons why this is so, and it is important to stress that the form of cosmopolitanism elaborated in the remainder of the chapter is incompatible with any juridical conception of 'the universal' in terms of rational postulates or principles of right, nor is it equivalent to deliberative conceptions of universality in terms of trans-contextual principles of reciprocity or impartiality. Here, the emergence of the universal is figured instead in terms of an on-going, open-ended adventure that takes up a new beginning and sees it disseminated and expanded in entirely unique and unpredictable ways. In the emergence of this origin and expansion, it is also crucially important that the new cosmopolitan principle manifests as a rupture with the present order. It is not that everything has to change overnight or even in the long term, but the key point is that a radically new standard emerges that is unaccounted for in the present system and really begins to engender a wider, cosmopolitan, or universally imagined community with real material effect. Indeed, the rudimentary stirrings of just such a form of cosmopolitan consciousness have been evident in the global justice movement, and more recently in Occupy, as well as in the World Social Forum and its yearning for radical transformation.

These are instances of what Castells calls *project* identities, aimed at constructing new values in the context of the networked society, as opposed to *resistance* identities that manifest most significantly in forms of religiously motivated violence and the politics of ethnic conflict (Castells, 1997). One of the defining features of these project identities is their irreducible plurality; they are in fact comprised of many different movements, with distinct diagnoses of the current concern. This diversity partly reflects the three-part complexity of the system of constituted powers that they struggle against, and follows also from the fact that the present system manifests primarily as a sequence of distinct yet interlocking crises. Different activist groups focus on dissimilar elements of these crises, with distinct opinions about the underlying causes, and seek to bring divergent principles into being as the basis of an alternative world order. As we will see in more detail below, it is also important to note the increasing prominence of religious groups amongst these project identities, who also struggle against the dominant priorities of the contemporary global system. Indeed, challenges to the present system have been mobilised by socialists, feminists, Muslims, Christians, environmentalists, indigenous peoples, New Agers, and many more. This is where we should rework the idea of a post-secular *agon* of ideological conflict, but without the Mouffean proviso that these protagonists must declare their fidelity to the basic legitimacy of liberal democratic institutions.

We cannot predict in any way which of these struggles, or combination of struggles, might actually deliver a moment of radical innovation, and, of course, history is not on anyone's side. Indeed, the possibility of a new beginning emerges from and into a world of plurality, tragedy, and conflict and this is not cause for melancholy or regret. Nevertheless, it also remains crucial to find ways to link the struggles of particular actors to a politics of open-ended judgement about the wider significance of specific innovations. This means that the question of judgement becomes critically important in the contemporary *agon*, and the remainder of this chapter explores how a new militant cosmopolitan expansion might be forged through the interplay between resolute moments of action and the multiple judgements of many varied spectators. Here, we will also see that the two qualitatively distinct moments of the constituent power, i.e. as absolute initiative and as augmentation, both remain central, as does the need to combine them through effective leadership or *hegemonia*.

Action, pluralism, and judgement

Throughout this study we have focused on the emergence of the constituent power, understood in terms of alternate moments of action or innovation, and it might seem incongruous to introduce the additional category of judgement at this late stage in the proceedings. The emphasis on judgement is also taken from Arendt, and she brought this idea to the fore late in her career, and most notably in her *Lectures on Kant's Political Philosophy*. It is important to introduce these reflections here, partly because, as various commentators have said, the notion of reflective judgement taken from Kant's *Critique of Judgement* offers crucial insights about the formation of public opinion in the context of agonistic pluralism,[2] but also because these categories become essential after the collapse of the Hegelian/Marxist conception of World History understood as a teleological whole, where History itself was perceived as the essential arbitrator and judge of the wider significance and status of distinct actions and events (Beiner, 1992). Indeed, now that we have been liberated from the idea of History as a ground, the stress on the perpetual interplay between action and judgement becomes fundamental to a theory of agonism and militant cosmopolitanism; where the innovations of particular actors meet with agonism at the level of multiple judgements about their significance, and where an on-going and expansive universality might emerge in the interface of this heated relationship. My concerns here, then, are not with the inner workings of the faculties that come into play in the exercise of judgement, i.e. in the respective roles of the imagination and the understanding; I am interested instead in the public function of the exercise of judgement and how this relates to the innovations of the actor. However, it is also necessary to stress at this point that, although the idea of judgement was clearly explored more systematically in Arendt's later writings, this notion was not a late adjunct to her work. In fact, the idea of reflective judgement was always implicit in Arendt's conception of pluralism elaborated in *The Human Condition*, which I introduced briefly in Chapter 2, and her stress on the importance of judgement in her later work was not designed to displace or restrain her otherwise central concern with bold and decisive action. This is important, because several commentators who are influenced by Arendt mistakenly invoke her notions of judgement and/or plurality to curb or 'tame' what might be perceived as her otherwise undue preoccupation with resolute action. For example, according to Ronald Beiner, Arendt turned to the idea of judgement in search of a surrogate for action and as a kind of solace for a 'genuine public realm', because the 'possibility of acting politically' under conditions of modernity, especially following the experience of totalitarianism, had become 'more or less foreclosed' (Beiner, 1992, 153). By way of contrast, we will see that these qualities – of pluralism and judgement – provide necessary circumstances for the emergence and the endurance of new beginnings, but they do not displace the centrality of action or freedom that remained at the core of Arendt's account of the *vita activa*, as well as at the centre of the current struggles for the invention of new forms in the context of globalisation.

The central lesson of Arendtean pluralism, as well as her theory of reflective judgement, is that the actor does not have control over the consequences of her action, and this is to a considerable extent due to

---

[2] See, for example: Beiner, 1992; Villa, 1992b; Zerilli, 2005.

the rejoinders of multiple others, who inevitably respond to the innovations of the actor and evaluate (or judge) the significance of her creation.
Indeed, one of the central themes of *The Human Condition* is that the
ancient Greeks were mistaken when they imagined that the actor's 'performance as such will be enough to generate *dynamis* and not need the
transforming reification' of surrounding spectators (as recipients and
storytellers) to 'keep it in reality' (Arendt, 1958, 205). Arendt therefore
associates pluralism with unpredictability as well as with precariousness
and boundlessness (Arendt, 1958, 195, 223). Action is precarious, partly
because it is fleeting and often simply ignored or quickly forgotten, but
also because it is irreversible, and so when it is judged by the recipients
to have a wider impact, action often has boundless results over which the
actor has little or no control (Arendt, 1958, 197). Indeed, the actor always
'acts into a medium where every reaction [judgement] becomes a chain
reaction and where every process is the cause of new processes' (Arendt,
1958, 190). Most importantly, this means that the actor is unable to 'dis-
pose of the future as though it were the present', and, as we will see below,
this insight is crucially important in relation to a critique of sovereignty
(Arendt, 1958, 245). Indeed, as Canovan put it, 'nobody who engages
in public affairs can know where the repercussions of his actions and the
intervening action of others will carry them all' (Canovan, 1983, 293).
Or, as Markell says:

Because we do not act in isolation but interact with others, who we become
through action is not up to us; instead, it is the outcome of many intersecting
and unpredictable sequences of action and response [i.e. reciprocal judgements],
such that 'nobody is the author or producer of his own life story'. (Markell, 2003,
13)

In Chapter 4 we saw that Markell associates the struggle for recognition with an imprudent demand for sovereignty, and, in fact, there
is a deeper message in his book which is that action *per se* is bound up
with an impossible ambition to master the conditions of human plurality
(Markell, 2003, 65). He therefore derives from Arendt's account of the
conditioning qualities of plurality the idea that action, as an attempt
at self-mastery, is 'not only doomed to fail, but risks intensifying [our]
suffering unnecessarily, even demanding that we give our lives for
what will turn out to have been an illusion of control' (Markell, 2003,
65). Indeed, Markell's mode of agonism is built around the principal
observation of the 'impropriety of action', which, he says, should not be
read pejoratively, but rather simply as the conditioning fact that the actor
does not own or control the outcome and consequences of his actions
(Markell, 2003, 63–4). However, in the various lessons that Markell

derives from this observation, he does end up presenting bold and decisive action in disapproving terms. The central message of his theory is that we should practise instead '*not* playing at being sovereign', and this through an internalisation, i.e. an inner acknowledgement, of the limiting conditions of action and a cultivation of 'an acceptance of practical finitude' (Markell, 2003, 69, 186, 187).[3] However, this is not the central message of Arendt's political theory. As Villa has said, Arendt shared unequivocally Nietzsche's view that the slaves' revolt in morality is manifest in this association of 'goodness' with 'abstaining from action' as self-mastery (Villa, 1992a, 284). For Arendt, human striving for immortality (which is not the same as sovereignty) through the performance of great words and deeds is definitive of genuine political action, and, like Machiavelli, this is seen as the very kernel of politics. The teaching that she extracts from the pluralistic conditions of political life, and later from her theory of reflective judgement – i.e. the fragility, uniqueness, and irreversibility of action – is definitely not that the actor should internalise a sense of finitude and depreciate or censure her own actions. Her point in *The Human Condition* and elsewhere is rather simply to stress the corresponding element of reciprocal judgement and opinion, the mutual dependence of the actor (or innovator) and those who recognise and testify to the wider significance of her action, and how the public realm emerges and expands in and from this dynamic relationship between actor and recipient, actor and spectator, actor and storyteller, actor and judge (Arendt, 1992, 55).[4] It is crucial to restate this point because, in the present context, the heroic action of the engaged partisan, of, say, environmentalism, feminism, Christianity, or Islam, is really the only hope we have to interrupt the systematic reproduction of the neo-liberal disciplinary regime. Without the courageous actor, who, strictly speaking, *reveals* herself in the moment of action, there simply is no politics.

Nevertheless, before we unpack the expansive non-dialectical dynamism between action and pluralism/judgement still further, we need

---

[3] By Markell's account, this is also the core message of Greek tragedy (Markell, 2003, 21, 69).

[4] In fact, this depiction of the *agon* – emerging in the interface between action and judgement – might be close to the original Hellenic understanding of the term. As Debra Hawhee has explained, the ancient '*agon*' meant more than simply competition in the pursuit of victory: 'For outcome-driven competition, the Greeks used the term *athlios*, from the verb *athleuein*, meaning to contend for a prize. The *agon*, by contrast, is not necessarily as focused on the outcome . . . Rather, the root meaning of *agon* is "gathering" or "assembly". The Olympic Games, for example, depended on the gathering of athletes, judges, and spectators alike. Put simply, whereas *athlios* emphasises the prize and hence the victor [the principal goal of the actor], *agon* emphasises the event of the gathering itself' (Hawhee, 2002, 185–6).

to first discard one of two basic limitations of Arendt's conceptualisation of pluralism. As we have seen, Arendt derived her understanding of plurality from the relations of isonomy in the ancient *polis*, the reciprocal play of words and deeds in the assembly, and, on her account, this was conditioned by (supposedly) pre-political forms of domination in the *oikos*. This unqualified Hellenism is deeply problematic, for reasons I discussed in the previous chapter, and we can't just appropriate Arendtean plurality/judgement without a corresponding structural assessment of the way in which plurality is presently interwoven with relations of systemic violence and oppression. Indeed, both plurality (or multiple and contending judgements) *and* forms of social and political domination set conditions for human action. It is important to be explicit on this point, because, if plurality is associated above all with the judgements and opinions of recipients and spectators, then one crucial form of power currently lies in the hands of those who control the gateways to, and the framing of, spectatorship. In today's 24-hour digital-networked society we are all (potentially) both actors and spectators in a global public sphere, but one of the principal forms of domination is surely associated with the media control of spectatorship, the control of who gets to observe particular innovations, for example the protests against the WTO and the G20 summits, or the uprisings in North Africa and elsewhere, and what judgements are already built into the narration and coverage of particular events, and so on. The contest to disseminate information about significant actions and inventions around the world has become much more complex in the context of the new digital communications technology. The Internet has greatly enhanced the capacity of activists to upload and publicise concerns about specific issues, and to draw attention to particular struggles and originations. This nonlinear (cyber) space is one of the principal theatres of agonistic conflict today, i.e. the struggle to shape public opinion though a networked multi media politics of the spectacle.[5] However, this also remains a fundamentally asymmetric contest, and the large media corporations, for example Fox News, CNN, the BBC, etc., retain an enormous influence over access to and the framing of the politics of spectatorship. Moreover, as Tully has stressed, many

---

[5] As Tully says, in the era of globalisation communication is increasingly governed 'by what Guy Debord calls "the spectacle" of affects . . . whether the spectacle is Princess Diana's death, branding, election campaigns, 9/11 or the scenes of high-tech war' (Tully, 2008b, 173). My sense is that there is no need to be despondent about this development, and activists need to be in this game. This does mean that contemporary politics is increasingly built around the aura of the image, but it doesn't follow that the spectacle is entirely unmediated by conscious reflection. Although the initial impact of the spectacle is immediate and in real time, with the 9/11 atrocities providing a paradigm case, there is always subsequently more time for reflection and to form a judgement on the significance of a given event.

millions of people around the world live in abject poverty and don't have access to communications technology. These observations need to be kept in mind, and provide important clarifications and qualifications of Arendt's account of the generation of the public sphere through the interface between action and spectatorship/judgement, and, by her account, without reference to forms of domination.

Arendt stressed that there are different sets of qualities or virtues associated with acting and judging, and this is because of the different locations of the actor and the spectator, with the actor providing a new initiative and the spectator in the position of the recipient of those innovations (Arendt, 1992, 48). As Zerilli says, the actor and the spectator simply represent 'different mode[s] of relating to, or being in, the common world' (Zerilli, 2005, 179). For Arendt, action is not concerned with sovereignty, but is nonetheless bold, decisive, focused, singular, and orientated towards the present. We have seen that political action is essentially performative, and so we might think of the captain whose skilful manoeuvres bring the ship and crew safely though a great tempest, or the virtuoso playing of an orchestra who deliver a brilliant, and subsequently renowned performance of a great symphony. These illustrations express how the actor invents new forms here and now, and in the moment of the performance she is fully orientated towards the present. Indeed, Markell's suggestion that she cultivate a sense of her own finitude could only possibly corrupt her creative power. It is true that each of these examples might well pass without a trace if it were not for the subsequent exaltation of the spectators and storytellers. Nevertheless, the need for recognition is not on the actor's mind in the momentary flash of brilliance that animates her performance. Indeed, Arendt accentuates this point; for the actor, she says, the 'meaningfulness of his act is not in the story that follows. Even though stories are the inevitable results of his action' (Arendt, 1958, 193).

The circumstances of the spectator are different. The spectators' viewpoints are retrospective and inherently plural (Arendt, 1958, 192). The spectator is 'always involved with fellow spectators. He does not share the faculty of genius, originality . . . with the actor; the faculty they [the spectators] have in common is the faculty of judgement' (Arendt, 1992, 63). Moreover, by Arendt's account, in the *agon* of reciprocal judgements, the opinions of the spectators repeatedly 'collide and become entangled with one another', and the spectators 'do not easily reach agreement' (Canovan, 1983, 301). Indeed, as Villa says, the idea that Arendt champions in her discussion of the politics of judgement is a 'contentious, agonistic, and often polemical exchange of opinion' (Villa, 2006, 126). In order to finesse her conception of the exercise of judgement in politics Arendt turned specifically to Kant's *Critique of Judgement*, and to the notion of reflective judgement that Kant associated with aesthetic judgements. Arendt was emphatic that her model of 'judgement is not practical reason; practical reason . . . tells me what to do and what not to do; it lays down the law . . . it speaks in imperatives' (Arendt, 1992, 15). Indeed, she turned to Kant's notion of reflective judgement in order precisely to outsmart the predominant view that there are determinant grounds or principles that can differentiate normatively valid judgements from those that are merely arbitrary. This normative view is, of course, the assumption that runs from Kant's own reflections on moral and political philosophy to contemporary justifications of deliberative democracy or of the public use of reason. So, we need to look more closely at Arendt's appropriation of the Kant of the third critique, and we need especially to scrutinise how this faculty of political judgement is linked to the possibility of cosmopolitanism.

Reflective judgement and cosmopolitanism

In the *Critique of Judgement* Kant describes judgement as the capacity 'to think the particular as contained under the universal' (Kant, 1987, 18). For him, judgement is determinate when the 'universal (the rule, principle, law) is given' in advance and 'subsumes the particular under it' (Kant, 1987, 18). A paradigm example of this type of judgement is the activity of solving a mathematical equation (Ferrara, 1999, 5). Kant describes reflective judgement, on the other hand, as in play when 'only the particular is given and judgement has to find the universal for it' (Kant, 1987, 19). Here a paradigm example is the judgement of taste brought into effect in the assessment of the value of a work of art (Ferrara, 1999, 5). The judgement of taste is essentially subjective, and yet not entirely so. As Kant illustrated, when we deem an object to be beautiful or sublime we speak 'as if' the judgement applies with 'universal validity' (Kant, 1987, 57). Although we cannot demonstrate the truth of our judgement (as in the activity of solving an equation) we nonetheless 'always require others to agree' (Kant, 1987, 57). In other words a reflective judgement regarding essentially subjective or 'private' feelings 'still lays claim to universal assent': others will need to be persuaded (Kant, 1987, 104).

This suggests a distinctively agonistic conception of judgement, one that is different from the various models of deliberative democracy (which are ultimately grounded in the notion of determinant judgement),[6] but

---

[6] Certainly this was the ambition of Kant's moral and political philosophy. In Kant's view, the categorical imperative, if understood and applied correctly, must, like the rules of

one that, in important respects, also moves beyond the four main conceptions of agonistic democracy examined in this study. This is because these Arendtean formulations raise explicitly the question of the relationship between the particular and the universal, but they do so in a mode that retains the agonistic appreciation of the groundlessness of political life, as well as the conditioning qualities of pluralism, tragedy, and the value of conflict. Indeed, Zerilli has stressed the significance of Arendt's appropriation of the Kantian notion of reflective judgement for precisely these reasons (Zerilli, 2005, 163, 171). She says, in the 'absence of the objective necessity of an agreement reached by proofs' an agonism of reciprocal judgements unfolds where 'each judging subject makes an aesthetic claim' about the wider significance of various actions, events, values etc. 'that posits the agreement of others and attempts to persuade them of her or his view' (Zerilli, 2005, 170). Moreover, this groundless and interminable *agon* of reciprocal judgements raises the possibility of the emergence of a new kind of universality, one that rests on temporary agreement, but without epistemic foundations or normative or legislative guidance. However, it is also at exactly this point that some commentators who are inspired by Arendt shy away from the full force of this conception of judgement,[7] and where others, who are closer to deliberative theory, depict Arendt as a proto-deliberativist, who was supposedly moving in the direction of a grounded universality, and a set of principles of validation and justification.[8] In contrast to these readings, Villa stresses

---

algebra, give us one and only one correct solution for any practical problem to which it is applied (Ferrara, 1999, 7). Once demonstrated, it would be unreasonable – in Kant's view – for anyone to object to the proper application of the categorical imperative. The same ambition is more or less approximated in late-twentieth-century 'Kantian constructivism', i.e. in Rawls' formulation of 'the original position' as well as in Habermas' 'universal pragmatics' (Ferrara, 1999, 8). However, Alessandro Ferrara detects in the later work of these authors 'a mode of justifying' their respective conceptions of the right and of justice that is more attentive to context, and which appears 'to fall more on the side of reflective judgement' (Ferrara, 1999, 9). There is, perhaps, something in this general characterisation, but Rawls and Habermas' later work nonetheless retains the core juridical and normative principles of impartiality, neutrality, and reciprocity (without remainders), none of which are compatible with the tragic conception of politics that defines agonistic democracy.

[7] Whereas Markell invokes the circumstances of Arendtean plurality in order to repudiate the idea of action as self-mastery, other commentators develop formulations of the relationship between action and judgement that establish a priority of the latter category, and again this is in order to curb what is seen as the otherwise dangerous allure of action. For example, Beiner says that, by Arendt's account, action is 'ultimately justified by the stories that are told afterwards. Human action is redeemed by retrospective judgement' (Beiner, 1992, 118). Whilst it is true that the actors' innovations would be doomed to pass without a trace without the narrations of the spectators, this terminology of redemption and justification is alien to Arendt's account.

[8] See for example: Benhabib, 2003, 196, and Kalyvas, 2005, 234–6.

that at 'no point in her thought on the nature of political action does she embrace moral cognitivism or indicate a belief in theoretical criteria that could distinguish a genuine from an inauthentic consensus' (Villa, 1992b, 718).[9] Villa's defence of Arendt's anti-normativism is basically well founded, but perhaps this statement is only really half correct. There is certainly no cognitive foundationalism in Arendt's theory of reflective judgement, but in her reflections on the Kantian notion of impartiality, Arendt appears to come very close to providing something that resembles a criterion for authentic judgement, opinion, and consensus.[10] This is a second element of Arendt's thoughts on plurality/judgement that we need to jettison, and this is also especially important, because, in Kant, it is the notion of impartiality that specifically animates 'cosmopolitan' forms of judgement.

Drawing on Kant, Arendt says the viewpoint of the spectator is potentially impartial. In contrast to transcendental theories of communication (e.g. the early Habermas' 'universal pragmatics'), she also stressed that 'impartiality is [only ever] obtained by [concretely] taking the viewpoints of others into account' rather than by obtaining 'some higher standpoint that would then actually settle the dispute by being altogether above the *mêlée*' (Arendt, 1992, 42; Habermas, 1979). Nevertheless, she insisted that a 'withdrawal from direct involvement to a standpoint outside the game is a condition sine qua non of all judgement', and the cultivation of this disinterestedness in turn becomes the condition of the formation of an 'enlarged mentality' (Arendt, 1992, 55; 1977d). This 'means that one trains one's imagination to go visiting… The greater the reach – the larger the realm in which the enlightened individual is able to move from standpoint to standpoint – the more 'general' will be his thinking' (Arendt, 1992, 43).[11] Moreover, at this point Arendt seems to follow Kant in associating this capacity for broadened horizons with cosmopolitan citizenship (Kant, 1991d). The world citizen is, therefore, really a worldly citizen, or a 'world-spectator', rather than the legal subject of a world government and, as Arendt would have it following Kant, this world spectator is in the unique position to judge the wider

---

[9] Villa pictures Arendt in something like a halfway house between Habermas, with his conception of political opinions being 'gradually purified' through consensus building, and Lyotard, with his radically 'anti-foundationalist politics of opinion 'without criteria" (Villa, 1992b).

[10] It is not entirely clear what Arendt's views are in the *Lectures on Kant's Political Philosophy*, because the lectures essentially provide an exposition of Kant's work on reflective judgement, and Arendt does not present a full account of her own views. Nevertheless, the overall gist of the text is that Arendt is broadly in agreement with Kant's account of impartiality.

[11] See also: Zerilli, 2001, 40.

significance – or universality – of any given action, because she can 'render disinterested judgement on the human significance of events unfolding in the political world' (Beiner, 1992, 123).

This model of disinterested judgement is intended to draw attention to the way in which judgement is itself a form of freedom, in the sense that the exercise of judgement is not reducible to utilitarian calculation (Zerilli, 2001). This is important, and the exercise of judgement does require a relative degree of detachment from the intensity and conviction of the actor, as we will see in more detail below. However, these formulations of 'impartiality' through disinterested judgement are nonetheless problematic, and play straight into the hands of the deliberativists, normativists, and jurists. These constructions run the risk of bringing judgement back under a rule, the rule of impartiality through fair-mindedness. Even when the notion of disinterestedness and even-handedness is based upon the model of reflective as opposed to determinant judgement, and divorced from the cognitivism and foundationalism of Habermas' theory, the idea of impartiality leads inevitably to an idealised short circuit of political power, struggle, and influence. Agonistic democracy must resolutely resist the dangerous allure of the misguided association of cosmopolitanism with the notion of impartiality. The spectator is never fully detached from the actor and her innovations. Indeed, in the era of globalisation we are all bound up in a complex network of connections and of systemic decisions and consequences that span the entire planet. There is no position of impartiality on issues such as the financial crises, diminishing energy resources, climate change, nuclear proliferation, etc., and when I observe events from far away but in real time, such as the protests in Tiananmen square in 1989, the fall of the Berlin Wall, the Battle of Seattle in 1999, the September 11 attacks, the bombing of Bagdad in March 2003, the uprising in Tahrir Square in 2011, the self-immolation of Buddhist monks in Tibet, and the Occupy strategies that unfolded in many cities throughout the world, I am immediately compelled into a Janus-faced subject position of spectator/engaged partisan. I am implicated in these events and provocations, if only because they denote struggles to challenge or reproduce the dominant system of control, which has global reach and in which we are all implicated. The position of disinterested spectator is not on the agenda today, and, as we have said throughout this study, agonistic democracy must therefore refuse all normativity and repudiate the dominant juridical modes of thinking characteristic of the bulk of contemporary political theory. We must also discard the lurking normativity in Arendt's apparent association of cosmopolitanism with impartiality.

The pivotal question, then, is whether or not it is possible to formulate an alternative conception of universality, of an 'enlarged mentality', and of cosmopolitan citizenship; one that is similarly rooted in the groundlessness of reflective judgement, but which does not lose sight of the irreducible elements of pluralism and of partisanship. The first thing to stress is that the distinction between actor and spectator is not only between (fully) interested activity and (relatively) disinterested opinion, equally important is the temporal dimension of this relationship, where the spectator/judge follows the innovations of the actor, increasingly instantaneously and in real time, but nonetheless the spectatorial viewpoint is a *retro*spective. In the theory I'm proposing here, the encounter between the spectators takes the form of a dispute about the status of particular acts and deeds. Moreover, as we discussed in Chapter 4, Arendt associated action or the moment of initiative, with the introduction of a new principle or standard into the world,[12] and so the *agon* of reciprocal judgements might give rise to a broad recognition of the wider significance of a new principle, so that this basic acknowledgement starts to become the expansive force of a sprawling universality, but where this augmentation does not take the form of any kind of agreement on the exact form or status of the new standard, but rather is manifest as an open-ended and expansive disagreement about how the new principle should be spun out for posterity, how it should be lived, spoken about, practised, institutionalised, etc. in endless and multifarious ways, and where the expansion (and the principle) itself would 'disappear the very moment an exchange became superfluous' because all the spectators 'happen to be of the same opinion' (Arendt, 1965, 88). Later in the chapter, I return to this formulation and I consider what cosmopolitanism looks like when mediated by effective leadership, rather than by misguided notions of impartiality. First however, we need to take a detour into the circumstances of the actor and consider the crucial importance of her conviction in the context of post-secularism and as a response to passive nihilism.

Post-secularism and the conviction of the actor

Amidst the more general pluralism of values characteristic of late modernity, one clear trend in the context of globalisation has been the mobilisation of various forms of religious conviction in the public life of ostensibly secular societies. Indeed, in the aftermath of the Cold War, contests

---

[12] In this respect, we saw how she contrasts to Wittgenstein, for whom it is always a question of following a rule.

between proponents of 'secular' ideologies (liberalism, socialism, environmentalism, neo-conservatism, etc.), are also increasingly intermingled with the struggles of religious activists, perhaps most notably Christians and Muslims, but also exponents of the other major world religions, as well as new forms of paganism, New Ageism, etc. In response to this development, liberal theorists have reasserted the neutrality of liberal values and institutions vis-à-vis contending 'comprehensive doctrines', and stressed the forms of rationality that are supposedly embedded in political modernity, which is understood as a 'learning process' and sees these liberal values progressively realised and recognised in democratic institutions and in 'post-conventional' forms of morality (Rawls, 2005; Habermas, 2008). By way of contrast, Connolly has argued persuasively that the modern insistence on a clear distinction between reason and faith, or science and religion, cannot be sustained (Connolly, 2005, 4–5). This means that a whole range of alternative faiths, ideologies, ontologies, and philosophies essentially find themselves on an equal epistemic status as they emerge as contending claims in the public sphere, and the differences between them cannot be arbitrated though a supposedly impartial use of public reason (Connolly, 2005, 4–5). This post-secular form of politics has been implicit throughout this book, and follows from the agonistic idea that all pronouncements about a public ranking of values (including those between faith and reason) are effectively groundless; that they rest on a *radical* rather than a *rational* decision, because of the constitutive pluralism of incommensurate values that we explored in Chapter 1. However, at this point, we need to look a little more closely at the circumstances of the democratic actor in the context of the post-secular *agon*, because it is from amidst this strange place that we might hope to see the emergence of a new beginning, and here we see that it is the conviction of the motivated partisan which is crucial.

Connolly is right to establish an essential parity between (ostensibly) secular ideologies and forms of religious belief, as they emerge as protagonists in the current conjuncture, and if we take this idea seriously then it follows that the different kinds of belief that circulate in contemporary politics cannot be grounded in anything more secure than the convictions of the actors themselves. This idea is explored in more detail in a moment. However, for reasons which will become clear, Connolly's notions of agonistic respect and critical responsiveness cannot sustain the necessary conviction of the actor, which is crucial in the post-secular *agon*, and, in fact, he ends up reproducing a kind of passive nihilism that misunderstands the politics of conviction. By way of contrast, we will take some inspiration from Badiou's reflections on the ethos of the engaged militant in order to better understand the circumstances of the contemporary political actor. However, we will also introduce some vital qualifications in respect of Badiou's contribution, and the limits of his approach are adjusted with reference to important insights drawn from Weber and Foucault, who together provide an understanding of the contemporary actor and how she might seek to translate her (theistic or atheistic, religious or non-religious) conviction into a transformative force in the democratic *agon*.

This is not the place for a detailed account of post-secularism,[13] but, to briefly capture what is at stake in the present resurgence of religion in the public sphere and why the secular assertion of a clear priority of modern reason in respect of religious belief does not offer a simple or straightforward response, we need to briefly return to the Nietzschean terrain of modern nihilism that we explored in Chapter 3. We saw that, for Nietzsche, the impact of modern nihilism is felt as a trauma in the order of knowledge, which sees the status of alternative claims to truth progressively undermined, so that modern society tends to gravitate towards a condition of passive nihilism, or a 'world [potentially] rendered valueless by the collapse of absolutes and authority' (Villa, 1992b, 287). Of course, the advent of modern scientific reason played a big part in this story. The modern sciences are the principal cause of the 'death of God' and have progressively undermined traditional ecclesiastical authority and the status of all those who have declared the truth of revelation. However, Nietzsche also understood that the various forms of modern reason are themselves incapable of withstanding the force of modern nihilism. Indeed, the apostles of modern reason tend to rely on surrogates for the Deity – the priority of method, of accurate observation, of the logic of non-contradiction, as well as notions of efficient causality, of system, process, and mechanism, etc. – which, on close inspection, all turn out to be fables, nothing more than a 'mobile army of metaphors' (Nietzsche, 1976; Rorty, 1989). These observations have subsequently been reiterated in the discourse of the philosophy of science, in the movement from Thomas Kuhn to Paul Feyerabend; and in the circumstance of the intensified nihilism characteristic of late or post-modernity, the once sacrosanct status of the sciences has itself been subject to the same kind of displacement that religion underwent during the 'age of reason'. The priority of reason and of scientific status has, to a considerable extent, lost its conventional authority, and those secularists who insist on the contrary, such as Richard Dawkins or Christopher Hitchens, end up sounding just as doctrinaire as the religious dogmatists they oppose. In other words, (post-)modern nihilism undermines the status of religion

---

[13] For a more detailed discussion see: Wenman, 2013.

and reason and, as a consequence, in the present conjuncture contending values cannot be grounded in anything more secure than an ultimately groundless politics of *conviction*. Indeed, this is what is at issue in the Nietzschean thought of the 'Overman' who confronts the trauma of passive nihilism, accepts the groundlessness of all belief, and yet who still finds the courage to 'posit' for himself 'productively, a goal, a why, a faith', for 'there is much one can achieve only by means of a conviction' (Nietzsche, 1968, 17, 18; 2003, 134, 184).

As we have said, Connolly shares this broad diagnosis of the circumstances of post-secularism. However, we also saw in Chapter 3 that he develops a theory of agonistic democracy that is largely predicated upon an anxiety about the politics of conviction. Indeed, at the core of Connolly's ethos of agonistic respect is the idea that the actor must 'sacrifice the demand for the unquestioned hegemony' of her conviction, and come to appreciate the extent to which her beliefs 'must appear profoundly contestable to others inducted into different practices' (Connolly, 2005, 32–3). The ethos of agonistic respect requires political actors to:

exercise presumptive receptivity towards others when drawing... [their] faith, creed, or philosophy into the public realm. You love your creed... But you appreciate how it appears opaque and profoundly contestable to many who do not participate in it; and you struggle against the tendency to resent this state of affairs. (Connolly, 2005, 4–5)

Indeed, if we read these formulations in light of the dynamic relationship between action and judgement, which we have said is at the heart of the democratic *agon*, we see that Connolly effectively folds the element of judgement – which ought to belong to the protagonists with whom the actor struggles in the public sphere – into the actor's internal self-relation. The actor is expected to exercise this presumptive judgement as a form of self-censoring, acknowledging the contestability of her convictions, and as a prerequisite for entering into properly agonistic relations with diverse others. Indeed, at the core of Connolly's approach is a similar set of apprehensions to Markell, that is, an anxiety about the basic immodesty of resolute action and conviction, and a corresponding emphasis on the need for the actor to cultivate a sense of her own finitude.[14]

Of course, Connolly develops these ideas precisely because of his concerns about the threat of religious and other forms of fundamentalism. On Connolly's account the religious fanatic treats his conviction

[14] Honig promotes a similar view; she says we need to find the courage to 'live life without the assurance that ours is the right, good, holy, or rational way to live' (Honig, 1993, 194). This is the key to the maintenance of a political life characterised by 'undecidability and proliferation' (Honig, 1993, 195).

as 'absolutely authoritative' and this is effectively a displacement for an underlying anxiety about the human condition, and one which gives rise to an aggressive and uncompromising politics of *ressentiment* (Connolly, 2005, 18). However, in the course of this study we have considered an alternative explanation of religious fundamentalism, one which links this phenomenon more to social and cultural factors, i.e. as a response to Euro-American imperialism rather than a reflection of underlying existential anxiety; and so, in short, Connolly overestimates the role of *ressentiment* in political life, and worries too much about the politics of conviction. Indeed, Connolly's approach is ill equipped to deliver a politics of confident self-belief, because as Vazquez-Arroyo has said, from Connolly's perspective 'conviction becomes a synonym for authoritarianism' (Vazquez-Arroyo, 2004, 14). In the end, his ethic of critical self-relation reproduces a passive kind of nihilism, where buoyant self-assertion is compelled to kneel in the presence of inner doubt and reservation. Moreover, the question of the correct diagnoses of the root causes of fundamentalist violence is crucial, because more than anything today we need the politics of the devout Christian, Hindu, and Muslim, the committed socialist, the engaged feminist, and the champion of environmentalism. These are really the only hope for the generation of new values and forms of life under circumstances of passive nihilism, and these bold innovations simply won't emerge through Connollian style self-testimonies of inherent contestability. The conviction of the democratic actor needs to be at the centre of the post-secular *agon*, this idea needs a more adequate formulation, and here Badiou's short book on St. Paul offers some pointers in the right direction.

Badiou derives a model of militant conviction from the enthusiasm and self-confidence of first century Christianity, from an assessment of Paul and his testament of universal love. Badiou also shows how an ethics of conviction is definitive not only of religious faith, but also of 'secular' forms of militancy, as expressed for example in the Marxist tradition (Badiou, 2003, 2, 31). His affirmative appropriation of Paul stands in clear distinction to Connolly's fashioning of an ethos of agonistic respect as a defence-reaction against Augustine's confrontational doctrine, which is in turn grounded in existential *ressentiment*.[15] Badiou derives from Paul a conception of truth that is distinct from the truths of philosophy. As Badiou says, the militant Paul is not a philosopher because he knows that the universal cannot take the form of a 'set of conceptual generalities' (Badiou, 2003, 108). Instead, Paul testifies to the universality of a

---

[15] Ironically perhaps, for a self-styled Nietzschean, this leaves Connolly's ethos of agonistic respect as a kind of double reactivity.

'singular event', the truth of Christ's divinity and resurrection (Badiou, 2003, 108). Indeed, here Badiou defines truth as *conviction*, the militant is an engaged actor or partisan who is marked out by her fidelity to the universal status of a singular event (Badiou, 2001, 42). This kind of truth is sustained by faith and cannot be refuted through empirical falsification or syllogistic reasoning (Badiou, 2003, 106). Indeed, in contrast to Nietzsche's own assessment of the slavishness of the teachings of the Apostle, Badiou sees in Paul all the ingredients of the Overman. Paul exemplifies a mode of conviction as 'self-legitimating subjective declaration', a commitment to 'grand politics', and an affirmation of life over death and servitude (Badiou, 2003, 61).

Badiou's emphasis on the conviction of the engaged partisan stands in contrast to the apprehensions about resolute action that characterise so much contemporary political thought, including agonistic theorists like Connolly and Markell. However, Badiou's theory also carries several implications that are incompatible with the agonistic circumstances of pluralism, tragedy, and the value of conflict. This is clear when Badiou insists on a clear priority of Truth (here as conviction rather than *episteme*) over opinions (Badiou, 2003, 49, 70, 100). Indeed, Badiou labours under the false and utterly contemptible idea that the actor is the bearer of a Truth that has the capacity to reorder the opinions of others, without any interchange and persuasion, and through a kind of Grace (Badiou, 2001, 82).[16] Badiou's contempt for 'mere opinions' is in complete contradistinction to Arendt, and he lacks the core Arendtean understanding that pluralism, i.e. the realm of reciprocal judgements, always conditions the circumstances of the actor.[17] This means that the question of the status of the universal remains with those who judge the significance of particular actions, and no form of universality will ever emerge directly from the convictions of the actor. One key issue, then, from the perspective of the democratic actor, is how she might try to translate her (theistic

---

[16] As Marchart has stressed, Badiou's contempt for opinions and disregard for questions of strategy and mediation leaves his militant actor 'remote . . . from our actually existing political world of compromise and alliance building' (Marchart, 2007a, 131, 132).

[17] Indeed, in some of his more recent writings, Badiou abandons the idea of truth as conviction, which he elaborated in the book on St. Paul, and adopts instead the position of the Platonic philosopher. Here, Badiou indulges in the worse kind of archipolitics where, for example, the idea of communism is said to represent a Platonic *eidos*, which is effectively personified in a series of 'concrete, time specific sequences' throughout the course of history (Badiou, 2010, 231–5). In these formulations, Badiou leaves behind what was most valuable in his account of truth as conviction, i.e. the stress on the 'self-legitimating subjective declaration' of the militant, and instead he further compounds his contempt for the opinions of diverse others, because here all political agents, including the militant, effectively become empty vessels for the embodiment of a 'trans-temporal' idea (Badiou, 2012, 60).

or atheistic, religious or non-religious) conviction into a transformative force in democratic politics, in the absence of Badiou's loathsome idea about the clear priority of Truth over opinions and in the light instead of Arendt's understanding that politics is always an inherently 'drawn-out wearisome process of persuasion, negotiation, and compromise', i.e. of winning over diverse opinions (Arendt, 1965, 83), and, importantly, also without having to introduce Connollian style self-doubt (contestability) into her pride, her self-confidence, and her convictions, in order to obtain a boarding pass into the democratic *agon*. Here, we can pick up a few valuable tips from Weber and Foucault.

Although the precise formulation is a little different, Badiou's depiction of the committed militant more or less corresponds to Weber's account of the advocate of an 'ethic of ultimate ends', who doesn't give consideration to consequences, and whom Weber similarly associates with the religious 'crusader' and the modern revolutionary temperament (Weber, 1993a, 122, 125). By Weber's account, this disposition represents one basic personality in political life, and one which he contrasts with the equally significant advocate of an 'ethic of responsibility' defined in terms of a concern with consequences. In his view, these 'are not absolute contrasts but rather supplements, which only in unison constitute a genuine man... who can have the "calling for politics"' (Weber, 1993a, 127). Or, as Viroli puts it, the 'true political leader is a person who is able to imagine new and better worlds and manners of living, and to work, with determination and prudence, to make them real' (Viroli, 2008, 27). These formulations are altogether better suited to a post-secular agonistic politics of contending beliefs than either Badiou's ethic of militant conviction without the need for persuasion, or Connolly's ethic of professed self-contestability. Instead, the main suggestion here is for the actor to combine her sense of conviction with an equally important recognition of the public virtues associated with the art of persuasion.

Foucault also offers important insights into how the actor might seek to translate her 'conviction' into an effective public engagement with carriers of alternate 'opinions', in his discussion of *parrhesia*. Foucault derived his account of *parrhesia* (speaking freely or with *libertas*) from late Roman antiquity, and the term refers to a form of self-artistry, that was practised by public officials, and designed to cultivate a capacity to speak candidly. *Parrhesia* is a mode of speech that enables 'one to say what one has to say, as one wishes to say it, when one wishes to say it, and in the form one thinks is necessary for saying it' (Foucault, 2005, 372). The virtue at the heart of the practice of *parrhesia* is for the actor to establish a kind of congruence between her speech and her conduct (Foucault, 2005, 402). The crucial objective is to cultivate an ethics of confident self-assertion, so that I become a living example of my own convictions (Foucault, 2005, 406–7).[18] Mahatma Gandhi, Martin Luther King Junior, and Che Guevara might all provide historical examples of this kind of lived ethos of self-assured engagement, and it seems to me that this particular gloss on the techniques-of-the-self might prove highly appropriate for the actor in the contemporary democratic *agon*, where various sets of convictions (theistic and atheistic, religious and 'secular') contend with one another, and where these contests are overlaced with the dispute between multiple spectators about the status and wider significance of particular acts and deeds. As we have said, it is in this interface between the actors and judges that we might see the emergence of a new militant form of cosmopolitanism. So, having explored the circumstances of the actor, the importance of her convictions, and her attempts to persuade others of the sincerity of her public assertion of her beliefs, we can now return to the dynamic interface between action and judgement, and examine what this relationship looks like when mediated by effective leadership rather than by misguided notions of impartiality.

Agonism, cosmopolitanism, and post-sovereign leadership

We have seen that one of the main consequences of globalisation has been the relative demise of the capacity of the nation-state to make effective decisions in the context of the devastating supremacy of capital mobility and the impact of uncontrollable market fluctuations. This tendency has been widely represented as an underlying crisis in the Westphalian order of 'sovereign' states. However, at the same the time, we have also noted the resurgence of an alternate mode of 'sovereignty' in the form of the security state, with its rhetorical deployment of a 'permanent state of exception'. Here, I explore this ambiguity more closely and examine the current machinations of sovereignty. I then consider how and in what ways the emergence and expansion of a militant form of cosmopolitanism relates to, but is also importantly different from, a mode of transnational 'popular sovereignty'. To tease out these nuances, I look

---

[18] Foucault explained how various ancient writers differentiated *parrhesia* from rhetoric. However, this distinction is not the same as the philosopher's contrast of arid Truth to all forms of eloquence. Rather, the distinction is between those public speakers who obtain eloquence 'naturally and at slight cost', through the successful practice of *parrhesia*, and those who only get there through a deliberate mastery and execution of the rules of rhetoric (Foucault, 2005, 372, 402–3). Indeed, in contrast to the deconstructionist's anxieties about essential distancing and deferral, Foucault insists, quite candidly, that the 'crucial element in this conception' of *parrhesia* is that the 'presence of the person speaking must be really perceptible in what he actually says' (Foucault, 2005, 405).

back for inspiration to earlier formulations of sovereignty and of leadership in the tradition of western political thought. Indeed, I offer two brief genealogies of these ideas. In the first of these excursions I draw on Skinner's account of popular sovereignty, as it was understood in the Italian Renaissance, and before the consolidation of the modern notion of sovereignty as embodied in the abstract person' of the state, which was formulated most notably by Hobbes. In the Renaissance republican tradition we see that sovereignty was located instead in the dynamic relationship between the *populus* and the person of the prince, and ultimately in the peoples' *judgements* about his on-going *status* as the principal citizen. These insights reinforce what we have already said about the possible emergence of an expansive and open-ended form of universality located in the dispute between the spectators about the wider significance of particular actors and actions. However, to really appreciate the potential in this dynamic relationship we need to travel back even further, to the notion of leadership (or *hegemonia*) as it was understood in Greek antiquity. Again, the focus here is on the capacity of the *leader*, understood literally as the citizen or the state who invokes a new initiative, to carry others with him, through persuasion and the on-going demonstration of his *areté*. Once again, the decisive point in this formulation is that the expansive power of the leader, or of the new inception, lies not with the actor, but rather in the judgements of those who pick up upon and expand the new initiative.

The emphasis on absolutism and omnipotence is at the heart of the notion of sovereignty, as it was formulated in early modern Europe, most notably by Jean Bodin and Hobbes, and in the context of the crises of ecclesiastical and temporal authorities that followed the European Reformation. In effect, these theories sought to transfer the power of the deity that underpinned medieval notions of divine right to modern secular institutions. In some important respects, Hobbes was a theorist of the constituent power, i.e. in his presentation of sovereign authority as originally bottom-up, as a compound of the 'Powers of most men, united by consent in one person' (Hobbes, 1994, 47). However, his story is one of a single decisive transfer of the constituent power to a constituted authority, in the creation of the abstract person of the state. After this decisive moment of initiation, the multitude 'cannot lawfully make a new Covenant, amongst themselves, to be obedient to any other, in any thing whatsoever, without his permission' (Hobbes, 1994, 101). Indeed, one of the key features of early modern theories of sovereignty was to insist on the permanence of the sovereign power: once constituted, the sovereign remains in perpetuity. As Bodin put it, 'sovereignty is the absolute and perpetual power of a commonwealth' and is in no sense limited 'either in power, or in function, or length of time' (Bodin, 1992, 3). In Hobbes, the only alternative to the perpetuity of the sovereign is to return to the state of nature, figured as absolute privation and therefore not really an option at all. As we saw in Chapter 2, Arendt rejected the idea that anything like the omnipotence of the divine 'will', might ever find a place in the public realm between men. Perhaps most significantly, these early modern theories are predicated on the fantasy that the secular power has a God-like capacity to render the future like the present, and this presupposes that he can control the consequences and subsequent reception of his actions. This fantasy of omnipotence and omnipresence can only possibly be sustained through a violation of human plurality, and so the idea of sovereignty is, therefore, inherently despotic.[19] Given these observations, it follows that any conception of cosmopolitan action in concert, that seeks to tackle the problems that define the present conjuncture, must be something essentially distinct from 'sovereignty'.

I return to this in a moment. First, however, we must reiterate the distinctive features of the contemporary security state as Agamben has explained it. This is because although this mode of resurgent 'sovereignty' is clearly not conducive to human plurality, the most disconcerting thing about this contemporary mode of government is that it does appear to have found ways to circumvent the conditioning circumstances of temporal finitude, i.e. through the rhetorical strategy of a 'permanent state of exception'. In Chapter 2 we saw that Schmitt shared the basic Hobbesean paradigm of the state as concerned above all with ensuring security and order. However, he departed from Hobbes in his acknowledgement that sovereignty cannot be established in perpetuity. For Schmitt, the durability of the power that holds together the unity of the state remains in place unless and until it is annihilated by another sovereign power. In contrast to the early modern theories, this introduces the prospect of certain temporal limitations on the reproduction of sovereignty. Indeed, in Schmitt's account the sovereign slumbers in normal times and only reveals his real identity, i.e. in the form of a 'decision in absolute purity', in times of crisis or exception, such as a civil war or violent insurrection, and precisely when everything is at stake (Schmitt, 2005, 13). However, the contemporary security state has managed to derive from these Schmittean formulations of the temporal circumstances of the exercise of sovereign power, a new modality of perpetuity, i.e. in the oxymoron of a

---

[19] Crick, who was influenced by Arendt, likewise insisted that sovereignty (even popular sovereignty) is incompatible with plurality. He said, the 'democratic doctrine of sovereignty of the people threatens . . . the essential perception that all known advanced societies are inherently pluralistic and diverse, which is the seed and root of politics' (Crick, 1964, 62).

'permanent state of exception'. As Agamben says, the state of the exception is 'not the chaos that precedes order but rather the situation that results from its suspension', and in 'our age, the state of the exception comes more and more to the foreground as the fundamental political structure and ultimately begins to become the rule' (Agamben, 1998, 18, 20). Indeed, in the context of globalisation this system of rule has gradually extended 'itself over the entire planet' (Agamben, 1998, 38). It is important to acknowledge how, in these formulations, the contemporary security state appears to find a solution to the ordeal of its own impermanence. This is especially disconcerting because we appear to be confronting a form of tyranny that has learnt how to endure and expand without rooting itself in the people. Instead, this power expands through keeping the people disorganised and permanently fearful for their security.

However, we have also noted how this consolidation of the security state seems to be at odds with the predominant view that state sovereignty is in crisis, in the context of economic globalisation. According to Wendy Brown, for example, the idea of sovereignty is tied to a basic 'fiction about the autonomy of the political', and it is ironic that this idea re-emerges at the moment when the political is being 'overwhelmed by the economic' (Brown, 2008, 251). She says the current talk of sovereignty operates as 'a kind of Viagra for the political' at the point when 'capital . . . becomes godlike: almighty, limitless, and uncontrollable' (Brown, 2008, 251, 263). Indeed, Brown sees the move towards security, demonstrated for example in the proclivity for building and reinforcing border controls and security walls, as evidence not of a renewed effectiveness of state power, but rather of an underlying weakness and anxiety (Brown, 2010, 24). In some respects, these are pertinent observations, and there can be no doubt about the overwhelming power of capital in the context of globalisation, and the fundamental weakening of executive power in relation to markets. This erosion of national autonomy, vis-à-vis the transnational agents of capital, such as the World Bank and the WTO, is one of the principal drivers of the new-networked form of imperialism that we explored in detail in Chapter 4. However, I don't think it follows that the emergence of the security state can be explained entirely as an object displacement for an otherwise impotent state power, overwhelmed by a loss of control of economic processes. Indeed, as we have already said, the idea of the permanent exception, as formulated by Agamben, needs to be understood in its own terms, as a distinct modality of control. This is important, not only because contemporary movements need to generate alternatives to *both* turbo capitalism *and* the security state, but also because we need to keep the distinctive modality of the security state in mind, when we consider what a post-sovereign form of democratic agency and cosmopolitanism might look like.

One thing is clear, which is that we cannot respond to this paradoxical mix of declining national government and the resurgence of the 'sovereign' security state by resurrecting a conception of popular sovereignty modelled on the Rousseauean notion of the 'general will', at least not if we want to construct forms of action in concert that are compatible with pluralism. As Brown says, 'it is nearly impossible to reconcile the classical features of sovereignty – power that is not only foundational and unimpeachable, but enduring and indivisible, magisterial and awe-inducing, decisive and supralegal – with the requisites of rule by the *demos*' (Brown, 2010, 49). In Chapter 6 we considered Honig's rejoinder to Rousseau and also to Agamben and we saw that she figures agonistic politics as a perpetual displacement of the location of sovereign power, or of the 'general will', through forms of iteration, augmentation, and administrative discretion etc. She says, what is 'most decisive is not, contra Schmitt, the decision, but our orientation to it, and most important of all, our (non-)complicity in it' (Honig, 2009b, 111). However, this represents an essentially negative posture towards the demands of the sovereign and his claims to omnipotence, whereas what we really need is an alternate model of collective power and agency that is congruent with pluralism, and can rival and displace the claims of the sovereign, and it is in this regard that we now turn first to the Renaissance republican tradition and then to Greek antiquity.

For Renaissance writers, 'popular sovereignty' was the marker of a republican form of government, as opposed to tyranny and arbitrary forms of power. On this model, the community must retain 'ultimate sovereignty, [and partly by] assigning its rulers and magistrates a [legal] status no higher than that of an elected functionary' (Skinner, 2002, 380). More importantly, however, for our present discussion, Skinner also stresses that for pre-Hobbsean writers the 'bearer of sovereignty is always the [concrete] *persona* constituted by the corporate body of the people, never the impersonal body of the *civitas* or *respublica* itself' (Skinner, 2002, 394). One of the defining features of the transition to modern forms of government was consequently the move from this personalised conception of sovereignty located in the body politic to the impersonal sovereignty of the great leviathan. The Hobbesian moment represents the crystallisation of this movement towards an association of sovereignty with the abstract person of the state (Skinner, 2002, 404). Post-Hobbesean political theory is therefore characterised by the 'claim that it is the state itself, rather than the community over which it holds sway, that constitutes the seat of sovereignty', and the etymology of the word state, neatly illustrates this transition (Skinner, 2002, 386). In Renaissance writers, the Latin term *status* – together with vernacular equivalents such as *estat*, *stato*, and *state* – 'were predominantly employed to refer to the state or standing of rulers themselves' (Skinner, 2002, 369). This suggests a certain model of political legitimacy. Indeed, when 'the question of the ruler's status was raised, the reason for doing so was generally to emphasise that it ought to be viewed [or judged] as a state of majesty, a high estate, a condition of stateliness' and the on-going status of the sovereign was dependent on the peoples' judgement that he remained capable of preserving the 'city in a happy, advantageous, honourable and prosperous state' (Skinner, 2002, 369, 371). In other words, a crucial feature of this tradition was to stress the dynamic relationship between the *populus* and the person of the prince, i.e. the person who enjoys a *principal status* on account of his *virtù*, which ensures that the commonwealth remains in a good *state* or condition (Skinner, 2002, 372).

It is important to stress that this Renaissance tradition does not place the seat of sovereignty in the hands of the prince, but rather it resides with the *populus* and in their on-going judgements regarding his identity and *status* as the principal actor. In this respect, these pre-Hobbesian conceptions of popular sovereignty provide important insights for a contemporary theory of agonistic democracy, and they reinforce the idea that a new mode of expansive cosmopolitanism might be driven by the multiple judgements of diverse publics about the status and significance of a new principle. Moreover, in important respects this Renaissance conception of sovereignty is essentially analogous to the Hellenic conception of leadership (or *hegemonia*).[20] Indeed, in *The Human Condition* and elsewhere Arendt presented the original notion of *hegemonia* as an inherent factor in action in concert. Arendt derived this idea from the Hellenic notion of kingship, which, she emphasised, was not synonymous with ruling, but rather with leadership. And here leadership needs to be understood literally; the leader is the actor who takes the lead or starts something new. However, as we have seen, the actor/leader does not have control over the reception of his initiation, and it is because action is always action in concert that the leader can only ever 'carry through whatever he had started' with the 'help of others' (Arendt, 1977b, 164). Indeed, the Greek king was only ever '*primus inter pares*' and this idea was predicated on 'the original interdependence of action, the dependence of the beginner and leader upon others for help and the dependence of his followers upon him for an occasion to act themselves' (Arendt, 1958, 189). Only later

---

[20] For discussions of the Hellenic notion of *hegemonia*, see also: Ehrenberg, 1960; Lebow, 2003, 122, 126; Lentner, 2005.

was this dynamic relationship, which on Arendt's account is at the very heart of the public realm, 'split into two altogether different functions: the function of giving commands, which became the prerogative of the ruler, and the function of executing them, which became the duty of his subjects' (Arendt, 1958, 189).[21]

We can see how the Renaissance conception of popular sovereignty and the Hellenic notion of leadership share a common emphasis on the dynamic relationship between the prince/*populus* and leader/followers or fellow travellers. However, the earlier formulation is more original, because it renders perspicuous the central point that the prince/leader is not sovereign. Her position is entirely dependent on the judgements of others, regarding her on-going status as *primus inter pares*. Moreover, as we have said, the actor introduces a new principle or standard into the world, and so, on this Hellenic model of leadership, we see that the endurance and expansion of the new principle is entirely dependent on it being picked up and carried forward by others, who both judge the significance of the principle and use it as an occasion for action (or new initiatives) themselves. Indeed, 'the principle inspires the deeds that are to follow and remains apparent [only] as long as the [collective] action lasts' (Arendt, 1965, 214). Again, it is this dynamic that enables us to understand the conditions of the emergence and augmentation of a militant form of cosmopolitanism. The idea is that an act of radical initiative emerging from within the transnational social movements might deliver an original principle that is subsequently judged to be of broader importance by a wide range of spectators, who then carry the new standard as a lived experience and as a set of values to multiple institutional settings, above, below, and at the level of the nation-state. This is how we might figure an expansive form of universality, where the new standard becomes a real material force in the world, as it is judged, debated upon, redirected, reiterated, and augmented in multiple, open-ended, and unpredictable ways. This means that the actors who initiate the new beginning have no control over its subsequent direction, and the principle only remains present in the world as long as it is manifest in the practices of the many subsequent travellers who convey and rework its values.

Moreover, this suggests an altogether different way of linking the faculty of judgement to cosmopolitanism than the misguided Kantian idea

---

[21] Benedetto Fontana stresses that Machiavelli and Gramsci need to be understood as part of this tradition going back to the Greeks, see: Fontana, 2000. In the Gramscian tradition, the reproduction of hegemony rests on a mixture of coercion and consent, but is not equivalent to domination, and ultimately requires skill and persuasion, and implies an on-going autonomy on the part of the persuaded (Fontana, 2000; Lentner, 2005).

that it is possible to develop a cosmopolitan standpoint by extricating oneself from the passionate attachments of the actors, and cultivating a capacity to see the world from a disinterested and impartial viewpoint. Here, instead, the identity of the cosmopolitan citizen follows from her acknowledgement of the wider significance or universality of a particular principle that has emerged from within the democratic *mêlée*, and in fact, on closer examination, among the resources for this alternative model of cosmopolitan judgement can also be found Kant's notion of reflective judgement, in his discussion of the role of the exemplar. Indeed, as Arendt says, in the exercise of reflective judgement, we inevitably make use of examples to illustrate our judgement, because, unlike in the application of determinant judgement, we cannot appeal to an abstract principle or schema (Arendt, 1992, 84). So, for example, when the Greeks thought and spoke about courageous acts, they would say that courage is *like* Achilles, or when Christians speak about goodness, they say that good-ness is *like* Saint Francis or Jesus of Nazareth, etc. (Arendt, 1992, 84). However, in contrast to the status of the universal concept or schema in the determinant judgement, the example that comes to be the refer-ent of a more universal moment in the exercise of reflective judgement, nonetheless also remains indissociable from its own particularity. Indeed, the word 'example' comes from *eximere*, 'to single out some particular' and this 'exemplar is and remains a particular that in its very particular-ity reveals the generality that otherwise could not be defined' (Arendt, 1992, 77). Again, these formulations suggest a democratic contest staged around a struggle to determine or judge which particular innovation might be, as Rado Riha puts it, elevated 'to the dignity of a "case of the universal"' (Riha, 2004, 83).[22] From the viewpoint of the actor (the proponent of environmentalism, feminism, Christianity, Islam, etc.) ago-nistic politics is a struggle for leadership (*hegemonia*), i.e. to become the

---

[22] Riha and Zerilli both liken Laclau's conception of hegemonic universality to Kant's notion of reflective judgement (Riha, 2004; Zerilli, 2004, 92). Laclau's 'universalism is not One: it is not a pre-existing something (essence or form) to which individuals accede but, rather, the fragile, shifting, and always incomplete achievement of political action' (Zerilli, 2004, 102). There is considerable validity in this analogy, but ultimately Laclau's formulations are incompatible with the idea of an open-ended expansive universalism, rooted in the on-going judgements of multiple publics about the status and significance of a new beginning. This is because Laclau variously figures hegemony as a reworking of the Hobbesean idea of sovereignty and of the Rousseauean 'general will', and, perhaps most importantly, because the Arendtean model is entirely incommensurate with the presentation of the hegemonic moment as the embodiment of an 'impossible Totality', or, with Lacan, as the personification of the lost object of an original plenitude, etc. The point here is not that a part comes to function as the Whole. These categories don't come into play in the Arendtean universe, where there is no Whole, only ever an on-going and unpredictable expansion of a precarious foundation.

innovator of a new principle, and through a demonstration of her conviction, or by speaking freely and frankly in the public realm and practising the art of persuasion. And from the viewpoint of the judge the dispute is to determine which of these struggles might become the *exemplar* for a new form of 'enlarged mentality'.[23]

Conclusion

We have seen that there is a basic homology between the Renaissance conception of popular sovereignty, the Greek conception of *hegemonia*, and the role of the exemplar in the Kantian conception of reflective judgement. The crucial element in each of these formulations is the dynamic relationship between the actors and the spectators/judges, and this is a complex and ambiguous relationship. On the one hand, the leader is clearly *principus*: where leadership is successful, as Philp says, it involves setting a 'pattern of action for others' (Philp, 2007, 78). Indeed, as Alan Keenan has stressed, Arendt's theory of leadership has this same implication. He says, 'to the extent that the freedom of the political realm is founded on a specific project, it cannot be entirely free: the "space" for action opened up' by the emergence of a new principle 'will necessarily form boundaries to and limits on the possibility of new action that follows this founding moment and founding principle' (Keenan, 1994, 309). This demonstrates why the alternative to the current neo-liberal modes of governance cannot take the form of a strict egalitarianism. To the extent that a new principle emerges to counter neo-liberalism, and is widely acknowledged to represent a new beginning so that it starts to shape the practices of diverse actors in multiple publics around the world, this origin sets certain horizons for any subsequent augmentation. In other words, these conclusions are out of step with a great deal of contemporary activist literature, where the emphasis tends to be precisely on horizontalism and on a ceaseless multiplicity – for example Tully's 'glocal

---

[23] Aletta Norval has also emphasised the importance of the exemplar as a constituting moment in the emergence of a 'form of hegemonic universalisation' (Norval, 2007, 196). Norval avoids the problematic notion of impartiality. However, she moves in the direction of an ethical rather than a properly political encounter with the exemplar. She says, the exemplar – Nelson Mandela, say, or Desmond Tutu – 'demands of us a response and responsibility', the 'exemplar acts as a *call*, as a reminder' of the 'ways in which our societies fall short' (Norval, 2007, 179, 209). This formulation passes over the question of the struggle to determine the identity of the exemplar (indeed, Norval's examples are not uncontroversial), and her ethical tone runs the risk of establishing yet another form of detachment. The exemplar does not install in us a *general* sense that things could be otherwise, but rather a particular sense that things could be greener, or more feminine, or more Christian, etc., and agonistic politics is to a large extent a struggle to determine which of these claims has a wider or more universal significance.

citizens' who supposedly enjoy unbounded freedom in their temporary autonomous zones. However, at the same time, as we have said, the actor or originator is entirely unable to control the subsequent reception of her innovation, and for the endurance and expansion of her invention she remains wholly dependent on the judgements of others, who recognise its significance and continue to carry it forward and rework it daily in their lived experience of the world, so that the principle becomes transformed and disseminated in multiple and unpredictable ways.

Indeed, these formulations also reiterate the reasons why the exclusive emphasis on augmentation characteristic of Connolly, Tully, Mouffe, and Honig leaves them forever hemmed in within the horizons of possibility established in the revolutions of the eighteenth century and their founding principles. The only way to move beyond this horizon will be in the form of a new origin and subsequent expansion. Such a possibility is really our only prospect to find long-term solutions to the present multiple and overlapping crises. The transnational movements and the World Social Forum are great cauldrons of experimentation and innovation, but it is striking how little originality and genuine leadership there is currently in more mainstream political institutions and parties. In the wake of the financial crisis, and as we hover on the precipice of a global economic slump, the talk is to a very large extent about how much of the debt we have to service in order to pretty much go on as before. The biggest challenge today is, therefore, to translate the radical capacity for innovation associated with the transnational social movements into a genuine material force in the world; and the only way this is going to happen is if a new principle or standard emerges which becomes embedded in the lived practices of the citizens, who carry the new standard into the arenas of governmental and trans-governmental decision making and debate, so that is begins to operate as a genuine rival to the utterly discredited system of disciplinary neo-liberalism, and in turn provides the foundation for a new organising code for the networked global system. Without this kind of movement, we will continue to muddle on as before, but the destructive consequences of the present system will be more and more acutely felt.

Conclusion: Agonism after the end of history

In the introduction I suggested that the contemporary agonists run the risk of complicity in the idea that we have reached the 'end of history'. Indeed, we have seen that the contemporary theorists find themselves hemmed in within the basic horizon of liberal democracy for two principal reasons: firstly, because of their explicit commitment to the legitimacy of liberal democratic institutions and practices, and especially to the idea of the co-originality of public and private autonomy; and, secondly, because of the tendency, which we have seen repeated throughout this study, to associate agonistic freedom exclusively with the constituent power in the mode of augmentation. The idea of augmentation captures the sense of interruption *and* tradition, or innovation *and* continuity, and if these forms of politics (as enactment, articulation, aversion, *iterability*, etc.) represent the essential structure of the constituent power, then this means that all new innovations that emerge in the current conjuncture will at the same time be bound back to the eighteenth-century origins of our present institutions and practices. The referent of this expansion is the authority of the liberal democratic (capitalist) regimes that were founded in the age of Enlightenment. By Arendt's account, these systems were themselves created in a moment of radical rupture with the pre-modern Roman past. However, if the notion of the absolute beginning is now exhausted, or was always an illusion, as the contemporary agonists would have it, then we no longer possess the resources to move beyond the legacy of these elementary foundations. By way of concluding this study, I'd like to return to these assertions, and to offer some brief comments on the complicated question of the relationship between agonistic democracy and the possibility of historical transformation.

Of course, none of the agonistic theorists we have examined in this book share Fukuyama's claim that the collapse of the Soviet Union could be read in Hegelian terms, i.e. as evidence that western liberal democratic capitalism represents the final historical form of state, one that lacks any serious contenders, and which therefore ensures the full realisation of freedom (through the free-market economy) and mutual recognition (through universal rights of citizenship) (Fukuyama, 1992). Instead, as Derrida emphasised, the discourse of the end of history really signalled the end of the dialectical conception of History, because the nineteenth-century idea, invoked by Fukuyama like Alexandre Kojève before him, i.e. that historical change could be grasped retrospectively in its Totality, is now widely discredited (Derrida, 1994). The demise of the dialectical understanding of World History as a teleological Whole has been in no small measure down to the contributions of post-structuralism, and we have seen that the anti-dialectical mode of thought is one of the defining features of contemporary agonistic democracy. We have also seen that Schmitt, Benjamin, and Arendt were similarly fierce critics of the Hegelian/Marxist conception of history in the first half of the twentieth century, from the 1920s to the 1950s, and, in this sense at least, they pre-empted the general orientation of post-structuralism. By Arendt's account, modern conceptions of history – whether they are derived from Hegel, Marx, Comte, or Durkheim – effectively degrade particular actions and events, which become 'accidental by products' or 'functions of an over-all process' (Arendt, 1977c, 57, 63). If the purpose of history is realised in an inner *telos*, then the end effectively cancels out and makes unimportant what went before, so that 'single events and deeds and sufferings have no more meaning here than hammer and nails have with respect to the finished table' (Arendt, 1977c, 80).

Again, we have seen these same sentiments expressed in the contemporary agonistic theorists, perhaps especially in the critique of Habermas' account of liberal democracy as an on-going learning process, oriented towards a progressive reconciliation of popular sovereignty and constitutional rights. As the contemporary agonists have shown, these ideas effectively subsume the politics of genuine open-ended innovation under the direction of an overall process. The Habermasian dialectic might not be as grandiose as Fukuyama or as deterministic as the Marxism of the Second International, but the tendency to incorporate freedom into the overall movement of a teleological process is inherent in all forms of modernity represented as process or progress. As Arendt flatly put it, it 'is against human dignity to believe in progress' (Arendt, 1992, 77). When Benjamin and Arendt developed their critiques of the dialectic they were somewhat lonely figures. However, today we find widespread incredulity towards the dialectic and also more generally towards the idea of progress, and not just in the academy but also more generally in popular culture and throughout society. This represents liberation, and this liberation goes hand in hand with the agonistic stress on freedom and with the restoration of the idea of the priority of politics and of the constituent power.

However, in the Introduction we also said that the withering away of the discourse of World History as Totality has not produced an alternative conception of the temporality of the post-modern republic that is conducive to human flourishing. Instead, we seem to find ourselves trapped in a destructive apparition that there is no alternative to the present system of free-market capitalism, and this is all the more remarkable in the context of the present financial crisis, which by all accounts is on the scale of the underlying problems of the 1930s, and yet, as we have said, mainstream political debate and political leadership is bereft of new ideas. In the course of this study we have seen that the neo-liberal discourse of the perpetuity of free-market capitalism is further compounded by the machinations of the security state, which also claims to have discovered the secret of eternal youth by mobilising society around the idea of a permanent state of exception. The combined effect of these two claims to perpetuity leaves contemporary citizens caught in a nightmare scenario of being progressively administered through various mechanisms of governance that are designed to constantly regenerate economic growth and to protect them from unknown and yet recurrent security threats. The contemporary agonists are mindful of these developments, and they offer poignant and often compelling accounts of the ways in which situated subjects seek to contest and redirect these tendencies. However, this is also the point where the contemporary theorists find themselves exposed to the risk of complicity in the reproduction of the present system, and for the two reasons mentioned above.

The explicit commitment to the basic legitimacy of liberal democracy is not the most decisive factor. This reflects the choices and commitments of the individual thinkers and doesn't imply anything fundamental about the relationship between agonism and liberal democracy. In fact, if we consider some of the most recent publications we can perhaps detect the stirrings of a different attitude. The second volume of Tully's *Public Philosophy* (2008) represents one of the best diagnoses of the pathologies of neo-liberalism, and Tully's analyses call for a more radical response to the machinations of imperial power than he himself delivers; Connolly's *A World of Becoming* (2010) has a much more militant tone than his earlier writings, and Honig's *Emergency Politics* (2011) is similarly very edgy and captures what is at stake in the murky and dangerous world of an expanding extra-judicial sovereign power. Perhaps, if the present trends continue, these theorists will be pulled further away from their explicit fidelity to the traditions and practices of liberal democracy. However, it is the second point that is more intrinsic, i.e. the fact that these theorists work with theoretical and ontological frameworks that cannot grasp the qualitative distinction between augmentation and

revolution, and which establish augmentation, i.e. the moment of transformation and continuity, as the essential structure of the constituent
power. In the end, it is for this reason that the contemporary agonistic
theorists lack an adequate conception of the possibility of historical
transformation.

The contemporary theorists are mindful of the importance of history,
and we have seen that they have made extensive use of the Nietzschean/
Foucauldean idea of genealogy. This is a retrospective procedure, which
is designed to reveal the arbitrary foundations of existing institutions and
practices that have become naturalised by bringing back into view past
alternatives that have been suppressed or inhibited. Genealogy is a powerful tool that helps to open up possibilities for change, i.e. by exposing the
contingency of norms and practices that are currently taken as given, and
by demonstrating how things have been otherwise. Tully describes this
as a form of context-*transgressing* critique, which he contrasts favourably
to the context-*transcending* forms of critical theory modelled on Habermas' juridical mode of thought, i.e. where the idea is to establish critical
purchase on existing practices from a kind of God's eye view (of idealised
communication) that is arrived at by abstracting from the normative content of each and every historical form of society (Tully, 1999b). Again,
these are important differences, and Tully is right to stress the priority
of the situated critique of the genealogist, over the overblown claims to
transcendence characteristic of Habermasian critical theory. However, at
the same time, the agonistic emphasis on genealogy strongly reinforces
the idea that augmentation represents the essential structure of the constituent power. This is because genealogy involves drawing existing institutions into question one at a time, and this helps to create possibilities
for change, but only ever in the form of partial moments of transgres-
sion, i.e. those moments of *il*legality that we explored in Chapter 4.
Thankfully, we don't have to choose between the incomplete transgressions of the genealogist and the Archimedean form of transcendence
characteristic of Habermasian critical theory, and this becomes clear
when we get back behind post-structuralism, where we find the possibility of the revolutionary *Ursprung* as it was formulated by Arendt and
Benjamin.

Indeed, the contributions of these two thinkers remain remarkably
fresh and pertinent, and precisely because they both linked the democratic *agon* to the possible emergence of a moment of radical origin. As
we saw in Chapter 2, this idea was at the centre of Arendt's *On Revolution*,
where she reiterated Benjamin's conception of revolution which he had
set out in his 'Theses on the Philosophy of History' written early in
1940, shortly before his untimely death. For Benjamin, revolution is an

insurgent 'now time', or a moment of rupture that radically interrupts the historical continuum, or which breaks open history conceived as any kind of evolutionary or dialectical process. Brown, who is mindful of the ahistorical tendencies in a great deal of contemporary political theory, says that, in Benjamin's view, history is occasionally interrupted by a 'fecund political moment', one that 'sets history's sails in a new [and unexpected] direction', but which 'comes with no guarantees, with no lack of struggle and no certainty about the outcome' (Brown, 2001, 157–8). In other words, the Benjaminian conception of revolution facilitates a more dramatic model of the possibility of/for historical transformation than the only ever partial transgressions of the genealogist, but, importantly, this is not a dialectical conception of change. Indeed, in the course of this study we have seen that the *Ursprung* is not sovereign, nor is it capable of giving rise to any kind of autogenesis. In other words, this is not the model of origin as full presence or as the 'transcendental signified' that is the object of the post-structuralist critique. The Benjaminian idea is more nuanced; the *Ursprung* represents a momentary leap into being that emerges from what Althusser calls the 'vacuum of the conjuncture'. This breaks open the historical continuum, and really represents nothing more than a moment of radical possibility, one which announces the prospect of an absolute beginning (Althusser, 1999, 64). Moreover, as we have seen, in the Arendtean version, this moment of innovation would be doomed to pass without a trace unless it was picked up and carried forward in multiple and unpredictable ways, and the initiators have no control or direction over this subsequent expansion.

In Benjamin, the revolutionary 'now time' is also associated with messianism. In the absolute contingency of the revolutionary moment we glimpse the possibility of redemption for past sufferings and the opportunity to reactivate previous possibilities that were foreclosed in the consolidation of the present system (Benjamin, 1999). Again, there are certain parallels here (but only up to a point) with the genealogist, in the sense that both approaches draw attention to the fact that aspects of the past are never entirely beyond the possibility of retrieval. However, my sense is that we should avoid this association of the *Ursprung* with any notion of redemption for past sufferings. This reading lends itself to an ethical rather than a properly political understanding of the ruptural moment. Indeed, it is just such a reading that we find in Derrida, who is also influenced by Benjamin, and for whom the messianic redemption, i.e. the promise of a moment of plenitude or justice 'to come', is shorn of its capacity to create historical transformation, and becomes instead an ethical dimension of my relations with the other, so that 'the moment I open my mouth I am in the promise', understood as a commitment to a non-violent and on non-instrumental 'relation to the other' (Derrida, 1997, 82–3). By way of contrast, Arendt did not incorporate these messianic qualities into her account of the *Ursprung*. In Arendt's iteration, revolution simply denotes the human capacity for radical innovation, it signifies the absolute priority of the constituent power, and is associated with the prospect of a moment of profound creativity, one that might contain sufficient *potentia* 'in itself to begin a new historical process' (Arendt, 1977c, 81).

In addition, as we have seen throughout this study, Arendt had learnt, from the great wisdom of Machiavelli and from the experience of the American founding, the crucial importance of combining the moment of initiative with a subsequent augmentation. As we saw especially in the previous chapter, the new beginning will only endure and expand if it is subsequently judged to be of wider significance, so that it starts to be spun out for posterity in the lived experiences of many diverse publics. In fact, Arendt stressed that this element of pluralism and judgement was (almost) coterminous with the new beginning. In this respect, she drew attention to the role of the revolutionary councils, which, she emphasised, have emerged around all of the major revolutionary events of modern times: from the ward system in the New England townships, to the Paris commune, the Russian Soviets, and the people's councils in Budapest in 1956 (Arendt, 1965, 275). Each 'time they appeared, they sprang up as the spontaneous organs of the people, not only outside of all revolutionary parties but entirely unexpected by them and their leaders' (Arendt, 1965, 252). Once again, we find the dynamic relationship between the new revolutionary principle and a wide plurality of judgement and differences of opinion emerging from the epicentre of what Althusser calls the 'aleatory void' (Althusser, 1999, 79).

My sense is that these formulations remain highly pertinent for thinking about the continued relevance of the idea of revolution today. In the aftermath of the 2008 financial crisis, and in the context of Occupy and the Arab Spring, these formulations not only suggest that the prospect of historical transformation remains a real possibility, but they also reiterate how and why this idea is commensurate with the agonistic circumstances of pluralism, tragedy, and the value of conflict. In contrast to Kant, who observed in the enthusiasm of the spectators of the French revolution a sign that history is providential, and moving – however haphazardly – in the overall direction of the Enlightened moral order (Kant, 1991e), perhaps we might see instead, in the current upsurge in activism all around the planet, a sign that the transnational social movements might just have the *potentia* to take us beyond the corrupt remnants of the (neo-)liberal ideal and to deliver a miraculous new beginning. This would dislocate the historical continuum and, through its subsequent augmentation, move the historical journey in new and uncharted directions.

Bibliography

Ackerman, B. (1991) *We the People. Vol. 1: Foundations.* Cambridge, MA: Belknap Press of Harvard University Press.

(1992) *The Future of Liberal Revolution.* New Haven and London: Yale University Press.

Adorno, T. W. and Horkheimer, M. (1979) *Dialectic of Enlightenment.* London and New York: Verso.

Adorno, T. W. and Scholem, G. (eds.) (1994) *The Correspondence of Walter Benjamin, 1910–1940.* Chicago and London: University of Chicago Press.

Agamben, G. (1998) *Homo Sacer: Sovereign Power and Bare Life.* Stanford, CA: Stanford University Press.

(2005) *State of Exception.* Chicago: University of Chicago Press.

Althusser, L. (1999) *Machiavelli and Us.* London and New York: Verso.

Archibugi, D. (1998) 'Principles of Cosmopolitan Democracy' in Daniele Archibugi, David Held, and Martin Kohler (eds.) *Re-imagining Political Community: Studies in Cosmopolitan Democracy.* Cambridge: Polity.

Arditi, B. (2008) *Politics on the Edges of Liberalism: Difference, Populism, Revolution, Agitation.* Edinburgh: Edinburgh University Press.

Arendt, H. (1958) *The Human Condition.* Chicago and London: The University of Chicago Press.

(1965) *On Revolution.* New York: The Viking Press.

(1970) *On Violence.* London: Allen Lane, Penguin.

(1972) 'Civil Disobedience' in *Crises of the Republic.* San Diego, New York and London: Harcourt, Brace, and Company.

(1977a) 'What is Authority?' in *Between Past and Future.* New York: Penguin.

(1977b) 'What is Freedom?' in *Between Past and Future.* New York: Penguin.

(1977c) 'The Concept of History: Ancient and Modern' in *Between Past and Future.* New York: Penguin.

(1977d) 'Truth and Politics' in *Between Past and Future.* New York: Penguin.

(1978) *The Life of the Mind.* San Diego, New York and London: Harcourt, Inc.

(1992) *Lectures on Kant's Political Philosophy.* Chicago: University of Chicago Press.

(2005) *The Promise of Politics.* New York: Schocken Books.

(2007) 'The Jew as Pariah: A Hidden Tradition' in *The Jewish Writings.* New York: Schocken Books.

Aristotle (1982) *Poetics.* New York and London: W.W. Norton and Company.

(1996) *The Physics.* Oxford: Oxford University Press.

Asman, C. L. (1992) 'Theatre and Agon/Agon and Theatre: Walter Benjamin and Florence Christian Rang' in *Modern Language Notes* 107(3): 606–24.

Augustine (1983) *The Confessions*. London: Hodder and Stoughton.

(1998) *The City of God: Against the Pagans*. Cambridge: Cambridge University Press.

Austin, J. L. (2009) *How to do Things with Words*. Oxford: Oxford University Press.

Bachrach, P. (1969) *The Theory of Democratic Elitism: A Critique*. London: University of London Press.

Bachrach, P. and Baratz, M. (1962) 'Two Faces of Power' in *American Political Science Review* 56(4): 947–52.

Badiou, A. (2000) *Deleuze: The Clamour of Being*. Minneapolis: University of Minnesota Press.

(2001) *Ethics: An Essay on the Understanding of Evil*. London and New York: Verso.

(2003) *Saint Paul: The Foundation of Universalism*. Stanford, CA: Stanford University Press.

(2010) *The Communist Hypothesis*. London and New York: Verso.

(2012) *The Rebirth of History: Times of Riots and Uprisings*. London and New York: Verso.

Barber, B. (1984) *Strong Democracy*. Los Angeles and London: University of California Press.

Barker, D. (2009) *Tragedy and Citizenship: Conflict, Reconciliation, and Democracy from Haemon to Hegel*. Albany: SUNY Press.

Barry, B. (2001) *Culture and Equality*. Cambridge: Polity.

Beck, U. (2011) *Risk Society: Towards a New Modernity*. London: Sage.

Beetham, D. (1998) 'Human Rights as a Model for Cosmopolitan Democracy' in Daniele Archibugi, David Held, and Martin Kohler (eds.) *Re-imagining Political Community: Studies in Cosmopolitan Democracy*. Cambridge: Polity.

Beiner, R. (1992) 'Hannah Arendt on Judging' in Hannah Arendt *Lectures on Kant's Political Philosophy*. Chicago: University of Chicago Press.

Beistegui, M. (2000) 'Hegel or the Tragedy of Thinking' in Miguel de Beistegui and Simon Sparks (eds.) *Philosophy and Tragedy*. London and New York: Routledge.

Bell, D. (1999) *The Coming of Post-Industrial Society: A Venture in Social Forecasting*. New York: Basic Books.

(2001) *The End of Ideology: On the Exhaustion of Political Ideas in the Fifties*. Cambridge, MA and London: Harvard University Press.

Bellamy, R. (1999) *Liberalism and Pluralism: Towards a Politics of Compromise*. London: Routledge.

Benhabib, S. (1996) 'Toward a Deliberative Model of Democratic Legitimacy' in Seyla Benhabib (ed.) *Democracy and Difference: Contesting the Boundaries of the Political*. Princeton: Princeton University Press.

(2003) *The Reluctant Modernism of Hannah Arendt*. Lanham, MD: Rowman and Littlefield.

(2006) 'Another Cosmopolitanism' in Robert Frost (ed.) *Another Cosmopolitanism*. Oxford and New York: Oxford University Press.

Benjamin, W. (1988) *The Origin of German Tragic Drama*. London: Verso.

(1999) 'Theses on the Philosophy of History' in *Illuminations*. London: Pimlico.

Bennett, J. (2010a) *Vibrant Matter: A Political Ecology of Things*. Durham, NC and London: Duke University Press.

(2010b) 'A Vitalist Stopover on the Way to a New Materialism' in Dianna Coole and Samantha Frost (eds.) *New Materialisms: Ontology, Agency, and Politics*. Durham, NC and London: Duke University Press.

Bentley, A. (1908) *The Process of Government*. Chicago: The University of Chicago Press.

Bergson, H. (1960) *Creative Evolution*. London: Macmillan.

Berlin, I. (1982) 'Two Concepts of Liberty' in Anthony Quinton (ed.) *Oxford Readings in Philosophy: Political Philosophy*. Oxford: Oxford University Press.

(1997) 'The Originality of Machiavelli' in *Against the Current: Essays in the History of Ideas*. London: Pimlico.

(1998) 'The Pursuit of the Ideal' in *The Proper Study of Mankind: An Anthology of Essays*. London: Pimlico.

Bey, H. (2003) *The Temporary Autonomous Zone: Ontological Anarchy, Poetic Terrorism*. 2nd edn. Autonomedia.

Blake, M. (2005) 'Liberal Foundationalism and Agonistic Democracy' in Melissa S. Williams and Stephen Macedo (eds.) *Political Exclusion and Domination*. New York and London: New York University Press.

Bobbio, N. (2005) *Liberalism and Democracy*. London: Verso.

Bock, G. (1990) 'Civil discord in Machiavelli's Istorie Fiorentine' in Gisela Bock, Quentin Skinner, and Maurizio Viroli (eds.) *Machiavelli and Republicanism*. Cambridge: Cambridge University Press.

Bodin, J. (1992) *On Sovereignty*. Cambridge: Cambridge University Press.

Bohman, J. (1998) 'The Coming of Age of Deliberative Democracy' in *Journal of Political Philosophy* 6(4): 399–425.

Brady, J. S. (2004) 'No Contest? Assessing the Agonistic Critiques of Jürgen Habermas' Theory of the Public Sphere' in *Philosophy and Social Criticism* 30(3): 331–54.

Breen, K. (2009) 'Agonism, Antagonism, and the Necessity of Care' in Andrew Schaap (ed.) *Law and Agonistic Politics*. Aldershot: Ashgate.

Brown, W. (2001) *Politics out of History*. Princeton: Princeton University Press.

(2008) 'Sovereignty and the Return of the Repressed' in David Campbell and Morton Schoolman (eds.) *The New Pluralism: William Connolly and the Contemporary Global Condition*. Durham, NC and London: Duke University Press.

(2010) *Walled States, Waning Sovereignty*. New York: Zone Books.

Buchanan, I. and Thoburn, N. (2008) *Deleuze and Politics*. Edinburgh: Edinburgh University Press.

Burckhardt, J. (1998) *The Greeks and Greek Civilisation*. London: Harper Collins.

Butler, J. (1990) *Gender Trouble*. London and New York: Routledge.

(2000) *Antigone's Claim: Kinship between Life and Death*. New York and Chichester, West Sussex: Columbia University Press.

Caillois, R. (2001) *Man, Play and Games*. Urbana and Chicago: University of Illinois Press.

Campbell, D. and Schoolman, M. (2008) 'Introduction: Pluralism "Old" and "New"' in David Campbell and Morton Schoolman (eds.) *The New Pluralism: William Connolly and the Contemporary Global Condition.* London: Duke University Press.

Caney, S. (2005) *Justice beyond Borders: A Global Political Theory.* Oxford: Oxford University Press.

Canovan, M. (1983) 'Arendt, Rousseau, and Human Plurality in Politics' in *The Journal of Politics* 45(2): 286–302.

(1995) *Hannah Arendt: A Reinterpretation of her Political Thought.* Cambridge: Cambridge University Press.

Carver, T. and Chambers, S. (2008) 'Introduction: Politics, Theory, and Innovation: the Writings of William E. Connolly' in Terrell Carver and Samuel Chambers (eds.) *William Connolly: Democracy, Pluralism, and Political Theory.* London and New York: Routledge.

Castells, M. (1997) *The Information Age: Economy, Society, Culture. Vol. 2: The Power of Identity.* Malden: Blackwell.

(2000) *The Information Age: Economy, Society, Culture. Vol. 1: The Rise of the Network Society.* 2nd edn. Malden: Blackwell.

Cerbone, D. R. (2003) 'The Limits of Conservatism: Wittgenstein on "Our Life" and "Our Concepts"' in Cressida J. Heyes (ed.) *The Grammar of Politics: Wittgenstein and Political Philosophy.* Ithaca and London: Cornell University Press.

Clausewitz, C. von (2007) *On War.* Oxford: Oxford University Press.

Cohen, J. (1991) 'Institutional argument... is diminished by the limited examination of the issues of principle' Review of Robert Dahl's Democracy and its Critics in *The Journal of Politics* 53(1): 221–5.

(1997) 'Deliberation and Democratic legitimacy' in James Bohman and William Rehg (eds.) *Deliberative Democracy: Essays on Reason and Politics.* Cambridge, MA: MIT Press.

Coles, R. (2005) 'The Wild Patience of Radical Democracy: Beyond Žižek's Lack' in Lars Tønder and Lasse Thomassen (eds.) *Radical Democracy: Politics Between Abundance and Lack.* Manchester and New York: Manchester University Press.

Connolly, W. E. (1969) 'The Challenge of Pluralist Theory' in William Connolly (ed.) *The Bias of Pluralism.* New York: Atherton.

(1984) 'The Dilemma of Legitimacy' in William Connolly (ed.) *Legitimacy and the State.* Oxford: Basil Blackwell.

(1988) *Political Theory and Modernity.* 2nd edn. Oxford and New York: Basil Blackwell.

(1991) *Identity/Difference: Democratic Negotiations of Political Paradox.* Ithaca and London: Cornell University Press.

(1993a) *The Augustinian Imperative.* London: Sage.

(1993b) 'Beyond Good and Evil: The Ethical Sensibility of Michel Foucault' in *Political Theory* 21(3): 365–89.

(1993c) *Political Theory and Modernity.* Ithaca and London: Cornell University Press.

(1993d) *The Terms of Political Discourse.* 3rd edn. Oxford: Blackwell.

(1995a) *The Ethos of Pluralization*. Minneapolis: University of Minnesota Press.

(1995b) 'Twilight of the Idols' in *Philosophy and Social Criticism* 21(3): 127–37.

(1999a) 'Brain Waves, Transcendental Fields and Techniques of Thought' in *Radical Philosophy* 94 (March/April): 19–28.

(1999b) *Why I Am Not a Secularist*. Minneapolis: University of Minnesota Press.

(1999c) 'Assembling the Left' in *Boundary 2* 26(3): 47–54.

(2000a) 'Speed, Concentric Cultures and Cosmopolitanism' in *Political Theory* 28 (5): 596–618.

(2000b) 'The Liberal Image of the Nation' in Duncan Ivison, Paul Patton, and Will Sanders (eds.) *Political Theory and the Rights of Indigenous Peoples*. Cambridge: Cambridge University Press.

(2001) 'Spinoza and Us' in *Political Theory* 29(4): 583–94.

(2002) *Neuropolitics: Thinking, Culture, Speed*. Minneapolis and London: University of Minnesota Press.

(2005) *Pluralism*. Durham, NC and London: Duke University Press.

(2006) *Political Science and Ideology*. New Brunswick and London: Transaction Publishers.

(2008) *Capitalism and Christianity, American style*. Durham, NC and London: Duke University Press.

(2010) 'A World of Becoming' in Alan Finlayson (ed.) *Democracy and Pluralism: The Political Thought of William E. Connolly*. London: Routledge.

(2011) *A World of Becoming*. Durham, NC and London: Duke University Press.

Coole, D. and Frost, S. (eds.) (2010) *New Materialisms: Ontology, Agency, and Politics*. Durham, NC and London: Duke University Press.

Copjec, J. (2002) *Imagine There's No Woman: Ethics and Sublimation*. Cambridge MA: MIT Press.

Crick, B. (1964) *In Defence of Politics*. Harmondsworth: Penguin.

Critchley, S. (1997) 'Deconstruction and Pragmatism – Is Derrida a Private Ironist or a Public Liberal?' in Chantal Mouffe (ed.) *Deconstruction and Pragmatism*. London: Routledge.

Dahl, R. A. (1956) *A Preface to Democratic Theory*. Chicago and London: The University of Chicago Press.

(1961) *Who Governs?* New Haven: Yale University Press.

(1982) *Dilemmas of Pluralist Democracy: Autonomy vs. control*. New Haven and London: Yale University Press.

Dahl, R. A. and Lindblom, C. E. (1976) *Politics Economics and Welfare*. Chicago and London: The University of Chicago Press.

Deleuze, G. (1983) *Nietzsche and Philosophy*. London: Althlone.

(1988) *Spinoza: Practical Philosophy*. San Francisco: City Lights Books.

(2001) *Pure Immanence: Essays on Life*. New York: Zone Books.

Deranty, J-P. and Renault, E. (2009) 'Democratic Agon: Striving for Distinction or Struggle against Domination and Injustice?' in Andrew Schaap (ed.) *Law and Agonistic Politics*. Aldershot: Ashgate.

Derrida, J. (1982) *Margins of Philosophy*. Chicago: University of Chicago Press.

(1986) 'Declarations of Independence' in *New Political Science* 7(1): 7–15.

(1988) 'Signature Event Context' in *Limited INC*. Evanston, IL: Northwestern University Press.

(1992) 'Force of Law: the Mystical Foundations of Authority' in David Gray Carlson, Drusilla Cornell, and Micheal. Rosenfeld (eds.) *Deconstruction and the Possibility of Justice*. New York: Routledge.

(1994) *Spectres of Marx*. New York and London: Routledge.

(1997) 'Remarks on Deconstruction and Pragmatism' in Chantal Mouffe (ed.) *Deconstruction and Pragmatism*. London: Routledge.

Descartes, R. (1986) *Meditations on First Philosophy*. Cambridge: Cambridge University Press.

Deveaux, M. (1999) 'Agonism and Pluralism' in *Philosophy and Social Criticism* 25(4): 1–22.

Dewey, J. (1977) 'The Public and its Problems' in *John Dewey: The Essential Writings*. New York: Harper and Row.

Downs, A. (1985) *An Economic Theory of Democracy*. Boston: Addison Wesley.

Dryzek, J. S. (2002) *Deliberative Democracy and Beyond: Liberals, Critics, Contestations*. Oxford: Oxford University Press.

(2006) *Deliberative Global Politics: Discourse and Democracy in a Divided World*. Cambridge: Polity.

Duarte, A. (2006) 'Biopolitics and the Dissemination of Violence: The Arendtian Critique of the Present' in Garrath Williams (ed.) *Hannah Arendt: Critical Assessments of Leading Political Philosophers. Vol. III*. London and New York: Routledge.

Duncan, G. and Lukes, S. (1963) 'The New Democracy' in *Political Studies* XI (2): 156–77.

Dworkin, R. (1978) 'Liberalism' in Stuart Hampshire (ed.) *Public and Private Morality*. Cambridge: Cambridge University Press.

(2005) *Taking Rights Seriously*. London: Duckworth.

Dyzenhaus, D. (ed.) (1998) *Law as Politics: Carl Schmitt's Critique of Liberalism*. Durham, NC and London: Duke University Press.

Edyvane, D. (2008) 'Justice as Conflict: The Question of Stuart Hampshire' in *Contemporary Political Theory* 7(3): 317–340.

Ehrenberg, V. (1960) *The Greek State*. Oxford: Basil Blackwell.

Eisenberg, A. I. (1995) *Reconstructing Political Pluralism*. Albany, NY: SUNY Press.

Elster, J. (1997) 'The Market and the Forum' in James Bohman and William Rehg (eds.) *Deliberative Democracy: Essays on Reason and Politics*. Cambridge, MA: MIT Press.

Elstub, S. (2010) 'The Third Generation of Deliberative Democracy' in *Political Studies Review* 8(3): 291–307.

Euben, P. (1990) *The Tragedy of Political Theory: The Road not Taken*. Princeton: Princeton University Press.

Falk, R. (1995) 'The World Order Between Inter-State Law and the Law of Humanity: The Role of Civil Society Institutions' in Daniele Archibugi and David Held (eds.) *Cosmopolitan Democracy: An Agenda for a New World Order*. Cambridge: Polity.

(1999) *Predatory Globalisation: A Critique*. Cambridge: Polity.

Feldman, R. H. (2007) 'Introduction' in Hannah Arendt *The Jewish Writings*. New York: Schocken Books.

Ferrara, A. (1999) *Justice and Judgment*. London: Sage.

Fishkin J. S. (1991) *Democracy and Deliberation: New Directions for Democratic Reform*. New Haven and London: Yale University Press.

Fontana, B. (1993) *Hegemony and Power: On the Relation between Gramsci and Machiavelli*. Minneapolis and London: University of Minnesota Press.

(2000) 'Logos and Kratos: Gramsci and the Ancients on Hegemony' in *Journal of the History of Ideas* 61(2): 305–26.

Forst, R. (2011) 'The Power of Critique' in *Political Theory* 39(1): 118–23.

Fossen, T. (2008) 'Agonistic Critiques of Liberalism: Perfectionism and Emancipation' in *Contemporary Political Theory* 7(4): 376–94.

Foucault, M. (1977) *Discipline and Punish: The Birth of the Prison*. London: Allen Lane, Penguin.

(1980a) 'Two Lectures' in Colin Gordon (ed.) *Michel Foucault: Power/Knowledge*. Brighton: Harvester.

(1980b) 'Truth and Power' in Colin Gordon (ed.) *Michel Foucault: Power/Knowledge*. Brighton: Harvester.

(1980c) 'The Eye of Power' in Colin Gordon (ed.) *Michel Foucault: Power/Knowledge*. Brighton: Harvester.

(1988) *The History of Sexuality. Vol. 3: The Care of the Self*. London: Allen Lane, Penguin.

(1989) *Madness and Civilisation*. London: Routledge.

(1991a) *Discipline and Punish: The Birth of the Prison*. London: Penguin.

(1991b) 'Governmentality' in Graham Burchell, Collin Gordon, and Peter Miller, (eds.) *The Foucault Effect: Studies in Governmental Rationality*. Hemel Hempstead: Harvester Wheatscheaf.

(2002) 'The Subject and Power' in James Faubion (ed.) *Michel Foucault: Power. Essential Works of Foucault 1954–1984. Vol. 3*. London: Penguin.

(2005) *The Hermeneutics of the Subject: Lectures at the Collège de France 1981–1982*. New York: Picador.

(2009) *Security, Territory, Population: Lectures at the Collège de France 1977–1978*. Basingstoke: Palgrave.

Franco, P. (2003) 'Oakeshott, Berlin, and Liberalism' in *Political Theory* 31(4): 484–507.

Fraser, N. (1997) *Justice Interruptus: Critical Reflections on the 'Postsocialist' Condition*. New York and London: Routledge.

(2008) *Scales of Justice: Reimagining Political Space in a Globalising World*. Cambridge: Polity.

Freud, S. (1961) *Civilisation and Its Discontents*. New York and London: W. W. Norton and Company.

(1991) 'Group Psychology and the Analysis of the Ego' in Albert Dickson (ed.) *The Penguin Freud Library. Vol. 12: Civilisation, Society and Religion*. London: Penguin.

Fukuyama, F. (1992) *The End of History and the Last Man*. London: Penguin.

Gabardi, W. (2001) 'Contemporary Models of Democracy' in *Polity* 33(4): 547–68.

Galston, W. A. (2010) 'Realism in Political Theory' in *European Journal of Political Theory* 9(4): 385–411.

Gasché, R. (1986) *The Tain of the Mirror*. Cambridge, MA: Harvard University Press.

(1994) 'Yes Absolutely: Unlike Any Writing Pen' in Ernesto Laclau (ed.) *The Making of Political Identities*. London: Verso.

Gay, V. P. (1997) 'Interpretation Interminable: Agonistics in Psychoanalysis' in Janet Lungstrum and Elizabeth Sauer (eds.) *Agonistics: Arenas of Creative Contest*. New York: SUNY Press.

Geuss, R. (2008) *Philosophy and Real Politics*. Princeton and Oxford: Princeton University Press.

Giddens, A. (1999) *Runaway World: How Globalization Is Shaping Our Lives*. London: Profile Books.

(2012) *The Consequences of Modernity*. Cambridge: Polity.

Gramsci, A. (1988) 'Prison Writings: 1929–1935' in David Forgacs (ed.) *A Gramsci Reader*. London: Lawrence and Wishart.

(2005) 'The Modern Prince' in Antonio Gramsci *Selections from the Prison Notebooks*. London: Lawrence and Wishart.

Gray, J. (2007) *Enlightenment's Wake*. Abingdon: Routledge.

Gursozlu F. (2009) 'Debate: Agonism and Deliberation – Recognising the Difference' in *The Journal of Political Philosophy* 17(3): 356–68.

Gutmann, A. and Thompson, D. (1996) *Democracy and Disagreement*. Cambridge, MA: Belknap Press of Harvard University Press.

(2004) *Why Deliberative Democracy?* Princeton: Princeton University Press.

Habermas, J. (1979) *Communication and the Evolution of Society*. London: Heinemann.

(1988) 'Reconciliation through the Public Use of Reason' in *The Inclusion of the Other*. Cambridge, MA: MIT Press.

(1997) 'Popular Sovereignty as Procedure' in James Bohman and William Rehg (eds.) *Deliberative Democracy: Essays on Reason and Politics*. Cambridge, MA: MIT Press.

(2001) 'Constitutional Democracy: A Paradoxical Union of Contradictory Principles?' in *Political Theory* 29(6): 766–81.

(2006) 'Hannah Arendt's Communications Concept of Power' in Garrath Williams (ed.) *Hannah Arendt: Critical Assessments of Leading Political Philosophers*. Vol. III. London and New York: Routledge.

(2008) *Between Naturalism and Religion*. Cambridge: Polity.

Hamilton, A., Jay, J. and Madison, J. (1987) *The Federalist Papers*. London: Penguin.

Hampshire, S. (1999) *Justice is Conflict*. London: Gerald Duckworth and Co.

(2005) *Spinoza and Spinozism*. Oxford: Oxford University Press.

Handel, M. (2001) *Masters of War: Classical Strategic Thought*. 3rd edn. London: Routledge.

Hardt, M. and Negri, A. (2001) *Empire*. Cambridge, MA: Harvard University Press.

Harvey, D. (2003) *Spaces of Global Capitalism: Towards a Theory of Uneven Geographical Development*. London: Verso.

(2006) *The New Imperialism*. Oxford: Oxford University Press.

Hawhee, D. (2002) 'Agonism and Arete' in *Philosophy and Rhetoric* 35(3): 185–206.

Hegel, G. W. F. (1956) *The Philosophy of History*. New York: Dover.

(1967) *The Philosophy of Right*. London: Oxford University Press.

(1977) *Phenomenology of Spirit*. Oxford: Oxford University Press.

(1991) *Elements of the Philosophy of Right*. Cambridge: Cambridge University Press.

Held, D. (1993) 'Democracy: From City-States to a Cosmopolitan Order?' in David Held (ed.) *Prospects for Democracy: North, South, East, West*. Cambridge: Polity.

(1995) *Democracy and the Global Order: From the Modern State to Cosmopolitan Governance*. Cambridge: Polity.

(2006) *Models of Democracy*. 3rd Edn. Cambridge: Polity.

Held, D. and McGrew A. (2002) *Globalisation/Anti-Gloalisation*. Cambridge: Polity.

Hirst, P. Q. (1996) *Associative Democracy: New Forms of Economic and Social Governance*. Cambridge: Polity.

Hobbes, T. (1994) *Leviathan*. London: Everyman.

Holloway, J. (2005) *Change the World without Taking Power: The Meaning of Revolution Today*. 2nd edn. London: Pluto Press.

Honig, B. (1993) *Political Theory and the Displacement of Politics*. Ithaca and London: Cornell University Press.

(1995) 'Toward an Agonistic Feminism: Hannah Arendt and the Politics of Identity' in Bonnie Honig (ed.) *Feminist Interpretations of Hannah Arendt*. University Park: The Pennsylvania State University Press.

(1996) 'Difference, Dilemmas, and the Politics of Home' in Seyla Benhabib (ed.) *Democracy and Difference: Contesting the Boundaries of the Political*. Princeton: Princeton University Press.

(2001a) 'Dead Right, Live Futures: A Reply to Habermas's 'Constitutional Democracy'' in *Political Theory* 29(6): 792–805.

(2001b) *Democracy and the Foreigner*. Princeton: Princeton University Press.

(2006) 'Another Cosmopolitanism? Law and Politics in the New Europe' in Robert Frost (ed.) *Another Cosmopolitanism*. Oxford and New York: Oxford University Press.

(2007) 'Between Decision and Deliberation: Political Paradox in Democratic Theory' in *The American Political Science Review* 101(1): 1–17.

(2008) 'The Time of Rights: Emergency Thoughts in an Emergency Setting' in David Campbell and Morton Schoolman (eds.) *The New Pluralism: William Connolly and the Contemporary Global Condition*. Durham, NC and London: Duke University Press.

(2009a) 'Antigone's Laments, Creon's Grief: Mourning, Membership, and the Politics of Exception' in *Political Theory* 37(1): 5–43.

(2009b) *Emergency Politics: Paradox, Law, Democracy*. Princeton: Princeton University Press.

(2010) 'Antigone's Two Laws: Greek Tragedy and the Politics of Humanism' in *New Literary History* 41(1): 1–33.

(2011) "[Un]Dazzled by the Ideal?': Tully's Politics and Humanism in Tragic Perspective' in *Political Theory* 39(1): 138–44.

Honig, B. and Stears, M. (2011) 'The New Realism: from Modus Vivendi to Justice' in Jonathon Floyed and Marc Stears (eds.) *Political Philosophy Versus History? Contextualism and Real Politics in Contemporary Political Thought.* Cambridge: Cambridge University Press.

Honneth, A. (1995) *The Struggle for Recognition: The Moral Grammar of Social Conflicts.* Cambridge: Polity.

Hornqvist, M. (2004) *Machiavelli and Empire.* Cambridge: Cambridge University Press.

Howard, M. (2002) *Clausewitz: A Very Short Introduction.* Oxford: Oxford University Press.

Howarth, D. (2000) *Discourse.* Buckingham: Open University Press.

Huizinga, J. (1955) *Homo Ludens: A Study of the Play Element in Culture.* Boston: The Beacon Press.

Ivison, D. (2011) '"Another World is Actual": Between Imperialism and Freedom' in *Political Theory* 39(1): 131–7.

James, W. (1909) *A Pluralistic Universe.* London: Longmans, Green and Co.

Jay, M. (1986) *Permanent Exiles: Essays on the Intellectual Migration from Germany to America.* New York: Columbia University Press.

Jefferson, T. (1999a) 'The Declaration of Independence' in Joyce Appleby and Terence Ball (eds.) *Jefferson: Political Writings.* Cambridge: Cambridge University Press.

(1999b) 'To James Madison' in Joyce Appleby and Terence Ball (eds.) *Jefferson: Political Writings.* Cambridge: Cambridge University Press.

Kaldor, M. (1998) 'Reconceptualising Organised Violence' in Daniele Archibugi, David Held, and Martin Kohler (eds.) *Re-imagining Political Community: Studies in Cosmopolitan Democracy.* Cambridge: Polity.

(2003) *Global Civil Society: An Answer to War.* Cambridge: Polity.

Kalyvas, A. (2000) 'Hegemonic Sovereignty: Carl Schmitt, Antonio Gramsci and the Constituent Prince' in *Journal of Political Ideologies* 5(3): 343–67.

(2005) 'Popular Sovereignty, Democracy, and the Constituent Power' in *Constellations* 12(2): 223–44.

(2008) *Democracy and the Politics of the Extraordinary: Max Weber, Carl Schmitt, and Hannah Arendt.* Cambridge and New York: Cambridge University Press.

(2009) 'The Democratic Narcissus: The Agonism of the Ancients Compared to that of the (Post)Moderns' in Andrew Schaap (ed.) *Law and Agonistic Politics.* Aldershot: Ashgate.

Kant, I. (1987) *Critique of Judgement.* Indianapolis: Hackett.

(1991a) 'Idea for a Universal History with a Cosmopolitan Intent' in Hans Reiss (ed.) *Kant Political Writings.* Cambridge: Cambridge University Press.

(1991b) 'Perpetual Peace: A Philosophical Sketch' in Hans Reiss (ed.) *Kant Political Writings.* Cambridge: Cambridge University Press.

(1991c) 'The Metaphysics of Morals' in Hans Reiss (ed.) *Kant Political Writings.* Cambridge: Cambridge University Press.

(1991d) 'What is Enlightenment?' in Hans Reiss (ed.) *Kant Political Writings.* Cambridge: Cambridge University Press.

(1991e) 'The Contest of Faculties' in Hans Reiss (ed.) *Kant Political Writings*. Cambridge: Cambridge University Press.

Kaufmannn, W. (1992) *Tragedy and Philosophy*. Princeton: Princeton University Press.

Keenan, A. (1994) 'The Abyss of Freedom and the loss of the Political in the work of Hannah Arendt' in *Political Theory* 22(2): 297–322.

Khan, G. (2012) 'Politics and Morality in Habermas' Discourse Ethics' in *Philosophy and Social Criticism* 38: 149–68.

(2013) 'Critical Republicanism: Habermas and Mouffe' in *Contemporary Political Theory*. DOI: 10.1057/cpt.2013.3.

Knops, A. (2007) 'Agonism as Deliberation – On Mouffe's Theory of Democracy' in *Journal of Political Philosophy* 15(1): 115–26.

Kohler, M. (1998) 'From the National to the Cosmopolitan Public Sphere' in Daniele Archibugi, David Held, and M. Kohler (eds.) *Re-imagining Political Community: Studies in Cosmopolitan Democracy*. Cambridge: Polity.

Kuhn, T. (1996) *The Structure of Scientific Revolutions*. 3rd edn. Chicago and London: University of Chicago Press.

Kymlicka, W. (1995) *Multicultural Citizenship*. Oxford: Oxford University Press.

(1996) 'Three Forms of Group Differentiated Citizenship', in Seyla Benhabib (ed.) *Democracy and Difference: Contesting the Boundaries of the Political*. Princeton: Princeton University Press.

(2002) *Contemporary Political Philosophy: An Introduction*. 2nd edn. Oxford: Oxford University Press.

(2007) 'The New Debate on Minority Rights (and Postscript)' in Anthony Simon Laden and David Owen (eds.) *Multiculturalism and Political Theory*. Cambridge: Cambridge University Press.

Laborde, C. and Maynor, J. (2008) 'The Republican Contribution to Contemporary Political Theory' in Cecile Laborde and John Maynor (eds.) *Republicanism and Political Theory*. Oxford: Blackwell.

Lacan, J. (1992) *The Ethics of Psychoanalysis. The Seminar of Jacques Lacan: Book VII*. London and New York: Routledge.

Laclau, E. (1990) *New Reflections on the Revolutions of Our Time*. London: Verso.

(2000) 'Identity and Hegemony: The Role of Universality in the Constitution of Political Logics' in Judith Butler, Ernesto Laclau, and Slavoz Žižek *Contingency, Hegemony, Universality*. London: Verso.

(2001) 'Democracy and the Question of Power' in *Constellations* 8(1): 3–14.

(2004) 'Glimpsing the Future' in Simon Critchley and Oliver Marchart (eds.) *Laclau: A Critical Reader*. London: Routledge.

(2005) *On Populist Reason*. London: Verso.

(2006) 'Why Constructing a People Is the Main Task of Radical Politics' in *Critical Inquiry* 32 (Summer): 646–80.

Laclau, E. and Mouffe, C. (1985) *Hegemony and Socialist Strategy*. London: Verso.

(1990) 'Post-Marxism without Apologies' in Ernesto Laclau *New Reflections on the Revolutions of Our Time*. London: Verso.

(2001) *Hegemony and Socialist Strategy*. 2nd edn. London: Verso.

Laugier, S. (2006) 'Wittgenstein and Cavell: Anthropology, Scepticism, and Politics' in Andrew Norris (ed.) *The Claim to Community: Essays on Stanley Cavell and Political Philosophy*. Stanford, CA: Stanford University Press.

Lebow, R. N. (2003) *The Tragic Vision of Politics: Ethics, Interests and Orders* Cambridge: Cambridge University Press.

Lefort, C. (1988) *Democracy and Political Theory*. Cambridge: Polity.

Leif, W. (2005) 'Exclusion and Assimilation: Two Forms of Domination in Relation to Freedom' in Melissa S. Williams and Stephen Macedo (eds.) *Political Exclusion and Domination*. New York and London: New York University Press.

Lenin, V. I. (1943) *State and Revolution*. New York: International Publishers Co.

(1978) *What Is To Be Done?* Peking: Foreign Languages Press.

(2002) 'Letters from Afar' in Slavoj Žižek (ed.) *Žižek on Lenin: The 1917 Writings*. London and New York: Verso.

Lentner, H. H. (2005) 'Hegemony and Autonomy' in *Political Studies* 53(4): 735–52.

Leonard, M. (2005) *Athens in Paris: Ancient Greece and the Political in Post-War French Thought*. Oxford: Oxford University Press.

Lindahl, H. (2007) 'Constituent Power and Reflexive Identity: Towards an Ontology of Collective Selfhood' in Martin Loughlin and Neil Walker (eds.) *The Paradox of Constitutionalism: Constituent Power and Constitutional Form*. Oxford: Oxford University Press.

(2008) 'Democracy, Political Reflexivity and Bounded Dialogues: Reconsidering the Monism-Pluralism Debate' in Emilios Christodoulidis and Stephen Tierney (eds.) *Public Law and Politics: The Scope and Limits of Constitutionalism*. Aldershot: Ashgate.

(2009) 'The Opening: Alegality and Political Agonism' in Andrew Schaap (ed.) *Law and Agonistic Politics*. Aldershot, Ashgate.

Lindblom, C. E. (1965) *The Intelligence of Democracy: Decision making through mutual adjustment*. New York: The Free Press.

Linklater, A. (1998a) 'Citizenship and Sovereignty in the post-Westphalia European State' in Daniele Archibugi, David Held, and Martin Kohler (eds.) *Re-imagining Political Community: Studies in Cosmopolitan Democracy*. Cambridge: Polity.

(1998b) *The Transformation of Political Community: Ethical Foundations of the Post-Westphalian Era*. Cambridge: Polity.

Loughlin, M. and Walker, N. (eds.) (2007) *The Paradox of Constitutionalism: Constituent Power and Constitutional Form*. Oxford: Oxford University Press.

Lukes, S. (1974) *Power: A Radical View*. London: Macmillan.

(1991) *Moral Conflicts and Politics*. Oxford: Oxford University Press.

Luxemburg, R. (2008) 'Reform or Revolution' in Helen Scott (ed.) *The Essential Rosa Luxemburg*. Chicago: Haymarket books.

Lyotard, J.-F. (1986) *The Postmodern Condition: A Report on Knowledge*. Manchester: Manchester University Press.

(1988) *The Differend: Phrases in Dispute*. Minneapolis: University of Minnesota Press.

Machiavelli, N. (1947) *The Prince*. Illinois: Crofts Classics.

(1970) *The Discourses*. Harmondsworth: Penguin.

MacIntyre, A. (2007) *After Virtue*. 3rd Edn. London: Duckworth.

Macpherson, C. B. (1962) *The Political Theory of Possessive Individualism: Hobbes to Locke*. Oxford: Oxford University Press.

(1979) *The Life and Times of Liberal Democracy*. Oxford: Oxford Univesity Press.

Mansbridge, J. (1983) *Beyond Adversary Democracy*. Chicago and London: The University of Chicago Press.

Marchart, O. (2007a)*Post-Foundational Political Thought: Political Difference in Nancy, Lefort, Badiou and Laclau*. Edinburgh: Edinburgh University Press.

(2007b) 'Acting and the Act: On Slavoj Žižek's Political Ontology' in Paul Bowman and Richard Stamp (eds.) *The Truth of Žižek*. London: Continuum.

Marcuse, H. (1966) *Eros and Civilisation: A Philosophical Enquiry into Freud*. Boston: Beacon Press.

Markell, P. (1997) 'Contesting Consensus: Rereading Habermas on the Public Sphere' in *Constellations* 3(3): 377–400.

(2003) *Bound by Recognition*. Princeton: Princeton University Press.

Marx, K. (1983a) 'A Contribution to the Critique of Political Economy' in Eugene Kamenka (ed.) *The Portable Karl Marx*. Harmondsworth: Penguin.

(1983c) 'The Eighteenth Brumaire of Louis Bonaparte' in Eugene Kamenka (ed.) *The Portable Karl Marx*. Harmondsworth: Penguin.

(1983b) 'Manifesto of the Communist Party' in Eugene Kamenka (ed.) *The Portable Karl Marx*. Harmondsworth: Penguin.

Mathiowetz, D. (2008) '"Interest" Is a Verb: Arthur Bentley and the Language of Interest' in *Political Research Quarterly* 61(4): 622–35.

McCormick, J. P. (2001) 'Machiavellian Democracy: Controlling Elites with Ferocious Populism' in *The American Political Science Review* 95(2): 297–313.

Michelman, F. (1995) 'Always Under the Law?' in *Constitutional Commentary* 12(2): 227–47.

Mill, J. S. (1978) *On Liberty*. Indianapolis: Hackett Publishing Company.

Miller, D. (2008) 'Republicanism, National Identity, and Europe' in Cecile Laborde and John Maynor (eds.) *Republicanism and Political Theory*. Oxford: Blackwell.

Miller, N. R. (1983) 'Pluralism and Social Choice' in *The American Political Science Review* 77(3): 734–47.

Moller Okin, S. (1999) *Is Multiculturalism Bad for Women?* Princeton: Princeton University Press.

Montesquieu (1989) *The Spirit of the Laws*. Cambridge: Cambridge University Press.

Moon, D. J. (1998) 'Engaging Plurality: Reflection on *The Ethos of Pluralisation*' in *Philosophy and Social Criticism* 24(1): 63–71.

Mouffe, C. (1979a) 'Introduction: Gramsci Today' in Chantal Mouffe (ed.) *Gramsci and Marxist Theory*. London: Routledge.

(1979b) 'Hegemony and Ideology in Gramsci' in Chantal Mouffe (ed.) *Gramsci and Marxist Theory*. London: Routledge.

(1981) 'Hegemony and the Integral State in Gramsci: Towards a New Concept of Politics' in George Bridges and Rosalind Brunt (eds.) *Silver Linings: Some Strategies for the Eighties*. London: Lawrence and Wishart.

(1983) 'Working Class Hegemony and the Struggle for Socialism' in *Studies in Political Economy* 12 (Fall): 7–26.

(1992) 'Preface: Democratic Politics Today' in C. Mouffe (ed.) *Dimensions of Radical Democracy*. London: Verso.

(1993a) 'Liberal Socialism and Pluralism. Which Citizenship?' in Judith Squires (ed.) *Principled Positions*. London: Lawrence and Wishart.

(1993b) *The Return of the Political*. London: Verso.

(1994) 'For a Politics of Nomadic Identity' in George Robertson, Melinda Mash, Lisa Tickner *et al.* (eds.) *Travellers' Tales: Narratives of Home and Displacement*. London: Routledge.

(1995a) 'Democracy and Pluralism: A Critique of the Rationalist Approach' in *The Cardozo Law Review* 16(5): 1533–45.

(1995b) 'Democratic Politics and the Question of Identity' in John Rajchman (ed.) *The Identity in Question*. London: Routledge.

(1995c) 'The End of Politics and the Rise of the Radical Right' in *Dissent* (Fall): 498–502.

(1996a) 'Deconstruction, Pragmatism and the Politics of Democracy' in Chantal Mouffe (ed.) *Deconstruction and Pragmatism*. London: Routledge.

(1996b) 'Democracy, Power, and the "Political"' in Seyla Benhabib (ed.) *Democracy and Difference: Contesting the Boundaries of the Political*. Princeton: Princeton University Press.

(1996c) 'On the Itineraries of Democracy: An Interview with Chantal Mouffe' in *Studies in Political Economy* 49 Spring: 131–48.

(1996d) 'Radical Democracy or Liberal Democracy?' in David Trend (ed.) *Radical Democracy: Identity, Citizenship, and the State*. New York: Routledge.

(1999a) 'Introduction: Schmitt's Challenge' in Chantal Mouffe (ed.) *The Challenge of Carl Schmitt*. London: Verso.

(1999b) 'Carl Schmitt and the Paradox of Liberal Democracy' in Chantal Mouffe (ed.) *The Challenge of Carl Schmitt*. London: Verso.

(2000a) 'Rorty's Pragmatist Politics' in *Economy and Society* 29(3): 439–453.

(2000b) *The Democratic Paradox*. London: Verso.

(2001) 'Wittgenstein and the Ethos of Democracy' in Ludwig Nagl and Chantal Mouffe (eds.) *The Legacy of Wittgenstein: Pragmatism or Deconstruction*. Frankfurt am Maim: Peter Lang.

(2002) 'Democracy: Radical and Plural. CSD Interview' in *Centre for the Study of Democracy Bulletin* 9(1) Winter 2001–2002: 1–7.

(2005a) *On the Political*. London and New York: Routledge.

(2005b) 'For an Agonistic Public Sphere' in Lars Tønder and Lasse Thomassen (eds.) *Radical Democracy: Politics Between Abundance and Lack*. Manchester and New York: Manchester University Press.

Mulhall, S. and Swift, A. (1992) *Liberals and Communitarians*. Oxford: Blackwell.

Negri, A. (1999) *Insurgencies: Constituent Power and the Modern State*. Minneapolis and London: University of Minnesota Press.

Newey, G. (2001) *After Politics: The Rejection of Politics in Contemporary Liberal Philosophy*. Basingstoke: Palgrave.

Nietzsche, F. (1956) 'The Birth of Tragedy' in *The Birth of Tragedy and The Genealogy of Morals*. New York: Anchor Books.

(1968) *The Will To Power*. New York: Vintage.

(1976) 'On Truth and Lie in an Extra-Moral Sense' in Walter Kaufmann (ed.) *The Portable Nietzsche*. Harmondsworth: Penguin.

(1989) 'On the Genealogy of Morals' in *On the Genealogy of Morals and Ecco Homo*. New York: Vintage Books.

(1990) *Beyond Good and Evil*. London: Penguin.

(1994a) 'Homer on Competition' in *On the Genealogy of Morality*. Cambridge: Cambridge University Press.

(1994b) *On the Genealogy of Morality*. Cambridge: Cambridge University Press.

(1998a) *Twilight of the Idols*. Oxford and New York: Oxford University Press.

(1998b) *Philosophy in the Tragic Age of the Greeks*. Washington: Regnery Publishing.

(2003) 'The Anti-Christ' in *Twilight of the Idols and The Anti-Christ*. London: Penguin.

Norval, A. (2006) 'Democratic Identification: A Wittgensteinian Approach' in *Political Theory* 34(2): 229–55.

(2007) *Aversive Democracy: Inheritance and Originality in the Democratic Tradition*. Cambridge: Cambridge University Press.

Nyíri, J. C. (1982) 'Wittgenstein's Later Work in Relation to Conservatism' in Brian McGuinness (ed.) *Wittgenstein and His Time*. Oxford: Basil Blackwell.

Oakeshott, M. (1975) *On Human Conduct*. Oxford: Clarendon.

(1991) 'On Being Conservative' in *Rationalism in Politics and Other Essays*. Indianapolis: Liberty Fund.

Olson, M. (1977) *The Logic of Collective Action*. Cambridge, MA: Harvard University Press.

Osborne, P. (1991) 'Radicalism without Limit? Discourse, Democracy, and the Politics of Identity' in Osborne, P. (ed.), *Socialism and the Limits of Liberalism*, London: Verso.

Owen, D. (1994) *Maturity and Modernity: Nietzsche, Weber, Foucault and the Ambivalence of Reason*. London: Routledge.

(1995) *Nietzsche, Politics and Modernity*. London: Sage.

(2002) 'Equality, Democracy, and Self-Respect: Reflections on Nietzsche's Agonal Perfectionism' in *Journal of Nietzsche Studies* 24(Fall): 113–31.

(2003) 'Genealogy as Perspicuous Representation' in Cressida J. Heyes (ed.) *The Grammar of Politics: Wittgenstein and Political Philosophy*. Ithaca and London: Cornell University Press.

(2008) 'Pluralism and the Pathos of Distance (or How To Relax with Style): Connolly, Agonistic Respect and the Limits of Political Theory' in *The British Journal of Politics and International Relations* 10(2): 210–26.

(2009) 'The Expressive Agon: On Political Agency in a Constitutional Democratic Polity' in Andrew Schaap (ed.) *Law and Agonistic Politics*. Aldershot: Ashgate.

Owen, D. and Tully, J. (2007) 'Redistribution and Recognition: Two Approaches' in Anthony Simon Laden and David Owen (eds.) *Multiculturalism and Political Theory*. Cambridge: Cambridge University Press.

Paine, T. (1986) *Common Sense*. London: Penguin.

Parekh, B. (2006) *Rethinking Multiculturalism: Cultural Diversity and Political Theory*. Basingstoke: Palgrave.

Pateman, C. (1970) *Participation and Democratic Theory*. Cambridge: Cambridge University Press.

Patton, P. (2000) *Deleuze and the Political*. London and New York: Routledge.

Pettit, P. (1997) *Republicanism: A Theory of Freedom and Government*. Oxford: Oxford University Press.

(1999) 'Republican Freedom and Contestatory Democratisation' in Ian Shapiro and Casiano Hacker-Cordón (eds.) *Democracy's Value*. Cambridge: Cambridge University Press.

(2002) 'Keeping Republican Freedom Simple: On a Difference with Quentin Skinner' in *Political Theory* 30(3): 339–356.

Philp, M. (2007) *Political Conduct*. Cambridge, MA, and London: Harvard University Press.

(2010) 'What is to be Done? Political Theory and Political Realism' in *European Journal of Political Theory* 9(4): 466–84.

Pitkin, H. F. (1999) *Fortune is a Woman. Gender and Politics in the Thought of Niccolo Machiavelli*. Chicago and London: University of Chicago Press.

(2006) 'Justice: On Relating Private and Public' in Garrath Williams (ed.) *Hannah Arendt: Critical Assessments of Leading Political Philosophers. Vol. III*. London and New York: Routledge.

Pizer, J. (1995) *Toward a Theory of Radical Origin: Essays on Modern German Thought*. Lincoln and London: University of Nebraska Press.

Pocock, J. G. A. (1975) *The Machiavellian Moment: Florentine Political Thought and the Atlantic Republican Tradition*. Princeton and Oxford: Princeton University Press.

Pohlhaus, G. and Wright, J. R. (2002) 'Using Wittgenstein Critically: A Political Approach to Philosophy' in *Political Theory* 30(6): 800–27.

Prigogine, I. and Stengers, I. (1984) *Order out of Chaos: Man's New Dialogue with Nature*. New York: Bantam Books.

Rancière, J. (1999) *Disagreement: Politics and Philosophy*. Minneapolis and London: University of Minnesota Press.

(2007) *On the Shores of Politics*. London: Verso.

Raskin, M. (1984) 'Morgenthau: The Idealism of a Realist' in Kenneth Thompson and Robert J. Myers (eds.) *Truth and Tragedy: A Tribute to Hans J. Morgenthau*. New Brunswick and London: Transaction Books.

Rawls, J. (1972) *A Theory of Justice*. London: Oxford University Press.

(2005) *Political Liberalism*. New York: Columbia University Press.

Riha, R. (2004) 'Politics as the Real of Philosophy' in Simon Critchley and Oliver Marchart (eds.) *Laclau: A Critical Reader*. Abingdon: Routledge.

Riker, W. (1984) *The Theory of Political Coalitions*. Westport: Greenwood Press.

Rorty, R. (1989) *Contingency, Irony, and Solidarity*. Cambridge: Cambridge University Press.

(1999) *Philosophy and Social Hope*. London: Penguin.

Rousseau, J. J. (1987) 'On the Social Contract' in *Jean-Jacques Rousseau: The Basic Political Writings*. Indianapolis and Cambridge: Hackett.

Said, E. W. (1994) *Culture and Imperialism*. London: Vintage Books.

Sandel, M. (1992) 'The Procedural Republic and the Unencumbered Self' in Tracy B. Strong (ed.) *The Self and the Political Order*. Oxford: Blackwell.

Sanders, L. (1997) 'Against Deliberation' in *Political Theory* 25(3): 347–76.

Saussure, F. de (1998) *Course in General Linguistics*. London: Gerald Duckworth.

Schaap, A. (2006) 'Agonism in Divided Societies' in *Philosophy and Social Criticism* 32(2): 255–77.

(2007) 'Political Theory and the Agony of Politics' in *Political Studies Review* 5(1): 56–74.

(2009) 'Introduction' in Andrew Schaap (ed.) *Law and Agonistic Politics*. Aldershot: Ashgate.

Scheuerman, W. E. (1996) 'Carl Schmitt's Critique of Liberal Constitutionalism' in *The Review of Politics* 58(2): 299–322.

Schmitt, C. (1988) *The Crisis of Parliamentary Democracy*. Cambridge, MA: MIT Press.

(1996) *The Concept of the Political*. Chicago: The University of Chicago Press.

(1999) 'Ethic of State and Pluralist State' in Chantal Mouffe (ed.) *The Challenge of Carl Schmitt*. London: Verso.

(2005) *Political Theology: Four Chapters on the Concept of Sovereignty*. Chicago and London: The University of Chicago Press.

(2008) *Constitutional Theory*. Durham, NC and London: Duke University Press.

Schoolman, M. (2008) 'A Pluralist Mind: Agonistic Respect and the Problem of Violence Towards Difference' in David Campbell and Morton Schoolman (eds.) *The New Pluralism: William Connolly and the Contemporary Global Condition*. Durham, NC and London: Duke University Press.

Schumpeter, J. A. (1970) *Capitalism, Socialism and Democracy*. London: Allen and Unwin.

Sieyès, E. (2003a) 'What is the Third Estate' in Michael Sonenscher (ed.) *Sieyès: Political Writings*. Indianapolis and Cambridge: Hackett.

(2003b) 'Views of the Executive Means Available to the Representaives of France in 1789' in Michael Sonenscher (ed.) *Sieyès: Political Writings*. Indianapolis and Cambridge: Hackett.

Simons, J. (1995) *Foucault and the Political*. London: Routledge.

Skinner, Q. (1973) 'The Empirical Theorists of Democracy and their Critics: A Plague on both their Houses' in *Political Theory* 1(3): 287–306.

(1990) 'The Republican Ideal of Political Liberty' in Gisela Bock, Quentin Skinner, and Maurizio Viroli (eds.) *Machiavelli and Republicanism*. Cambridge: Cambridge University Press.

(1998) *Liberty before Liberalism*. Cambridge: Cambridge University Press.

(2000) *Machiavelli: A Very Short Introduction*. Oxford: Oxford University Press.

(2002) 'From the State of Princes to the Person of the State' in *Visions of Politics. Vol. II: Renaissance Virtues*. Cambridge: Cambridge University Press.

(2008) 'Freedom as the Absence of Arbitrary Power' in Cecile Laborde and John Maynor (eds.) *Republicanism and Political Theory*. Oxford: Blackwell.

Smith, A. M. (1998) *Laclau and Mouffe: The Radical Democratic Imaginary*, London and New York: Routledge.

Spinoza, B. de (1955) 'The Ethics' in *On the Improvement of the Understanding, The Ethics, Correspondence*. New York: Dover.

Staten, H. (1984) *Wittgenstein and Derrida*. Lincoln: University of Nebraska Press.

Stavrakakis, Y. (2005) 'Negativity and Democratic Politics: Radical Democracy Beyond Reoccupation and Conformism' in Lars Tønder and Lasse Thomassen (eds.) *Radical Democracy: Politics Between Abundance and Lack*. Manchester and New York: Manchester University Press.

(2007) *The Lacanian Left: Psychoanalysis, Theory, Politics*. Albany, NY: SUNY Press.

Stears, M. (2007) 'Review Article: Liberalism and the Politics of Compulsion' in *British Journal of Political Science* 37(3): 533–53.

Strassler, R. B. (2008) *The Landmark Thucydides: A Comprehensive Guide to the Peloponnesian War*. New York: Free Press.

Sun Tzu (2008) 'The Art of War' in Thomas G. Mahnken and Joseph A. Maiolo (eds.) *Strategic Studies: A Reader*. London and New York: Routledge.

Tan, K.-C. (2004) *Justice Without Borders: Cosmopolitanism, Nationalism and Patriotism*. Cambridge: Cambridge University Press.

Taylor, C. (1992a) *Multiculturalism and the 'Politics of Recognition'*. Princeton: Princeton University Press.

(1992b) 'To Follow a Rule' in Mette Hjort (ed.) *Rules and Conventions*. Baltimore, MD: Johns Hopkins University Press.

(1997) 'What's Wrong with Negative Liberty' in Robert E. Goodin and Philip Pettit (eds.) *Contemporary Political Philosophy: An Anthology*. Oxford: Blackwell.

Thiele, L. P. (1990) 'The Agony of Politics: The Nietzschean Roots of Foucault's Thought' in *The American Political Science Review* 84(3): 907–25.

Torfing, J. (1999) *New Theories of Discourse: Laclau, Mouffe, Žižek*. Oxford: Blackwell.

Trotsky, L. (2007) *The Permanent Revolution* in Leon Trotsky *The Permanent Revolution and Results and Prospects*. London: Socialist Resistance.

Truman, D. (1962) *The Governmental Process*. New York: Alfred A. Knopf.

Tsao, R. T. (2006) 'Arendt against Athens: Rereading the Human Condition' in Garrath Williams (ed.) *Hannah Arendt: Critical Assessments of Leading Political Philosophers. Vol. III*. London and New York: Routledge.

Tully, J. (1989) 'Wittgenstein and Political Philosophy: Understanding Practices of Critical Reflection' in *Political Theory* 17(2): 172–204.

(1990) 'Political Freedom' in *The Journal of Philosophy* 87(10): 517–23.

(1993) *An Approach to Political Philosophy: Locke in Contexts*. Cambridge: Cambridge University Press.

(1995) *Strange Multiplicity: Constitutionalism in an Age of Diversity*. Cambridge: Cambridge University Press.

(1998) 'The Pen is a Mighty Sword: Quentin Skinner's Analysis' in James Tully (ed.) *Meaning and Context: Quentin Skinner and his Critics*. Princeton: Princeton University Press.

(1999a) 'The Agonic Freedom of Citizens' in *Economy and Society* 28(2): 161–82.

(1999b) 'To Think and Act Differently: Foucault's Four Reciprocal Objections to Habermas' Theory' in Samantha Ashenden and David Owen (eds.) *Foucault contra Habermas: Recasting the Dialogue between Genealogy and Critical Theory*. London: Sage.

(2000a) 'Struggles over Recognition and Distribution' in *Constellations* 7(4): 469–82.

(2000b) 'The Struggles of Indigenous Peoples for and of Freedom' in Duncan Ivison, Paul Patton, and Will Sanders (eds.) *Political Theory and the Rights of Indigenous Peoples*. Cambridge: Cambridge University Press.

(2002a) 'Political Philosophy as Critical Activity' in *Political Theory* 30(4): 533–55.

(2002b) 'The Unfreedom of the Moderns in Comparison to Their Ideals of Constitutional Democracy' in *The Modern Law Review* 65(2): 204–28.

(2003) 'Diverse Enlightenments' in *Economy and Society* 32(3): 485–505.

(2005) 'Exclusion and Assimilation: Two Forms of Domination in Relation to Freedom' in Melissa S. Williams and Stephen Macedo (eds.) *Political Exclusion and Domination*. New York and London: New York University Press.

(2008a) *Public Philosophy in a New Key. Vol. I: Democracy and Civic Freedom*. Cambridge: Cambridge University Press.

(2008b) *Public Philosophy in a New Key. Vol. II: Imperialism and Civic Freedom*. Cambridge: Cambridge University Press.

(2008c) 'On Law, Democracy and Imperialism' in Emilios Christodoulidis and Stephen Tierney (eds.) *Public Law and Politics: The Scope and Limits of Constitutionalism*. Aldershot: Ashgate.

(2011) 'Dialogue' in *Political Theory* 39(1): 145–60.

Vatter, M. (2005) 'Pettit and Modern Republican Political Thought' in Melissa S. Williams and Stephen Macedo (eds.) *Political Exclusion and Domination*. New York and London: New York University Press.

Vazquez-Arroyo, A. Y. (2004) 'Agonised Liberalism: the Liberal Theory of William E. Connolly' in *Radical Philosophy* 127(Sept/Oct): 8–19.

Villa, D. R. (1992a) 'Beyond Good and Evil: Arendt, Nietzsche, and the Aestheticization of Political Action' in *Political Theory* 20 (2): 274–308.

(1992b) 'Post Modernism and the Public Sphere' in *The American Political Science Review* 86 (3): 712–21.

(2006) 'Arendt, Aristotle and Action' in Garrath Williams (ed.) *Hannah Arendt: Critical Assessments of Leading Political Philosophers. Vol. III*. London and New York: Routledge.

Virilio, P. (1991) *Desert Screen: War at the Speed of Light*. London and New York: Continuum.

(2006) *Speed and Politics: An Essay on Dromology*. Los Angeles: Semiotext(e).

Viroli, M. (2002) *Republicanism*. New York: Hill and Wang.

(2008) *How to Read Machiavelli*. London: Granta.

Walker, J. T. (1966) 'A Critique of the Elitist Theory of Democracy' *The American Political Science Review* 60(2): 285–95.

Walzer, M. (1990) 'The Communitarian Critique of Liberalism' in *Political Theory* 18(1): 6–23.

Warren, M. (1992) 'Democratic Theory and Self-Transformation' in *The American Political Science Review* 86(1): 8–23.

Weber, M. (1993a) 'Politics as Vocation' in Hans Heinrich Gerth and Charles Wright Mills (eds.) *From Max Weber: Essays in Sociology*. London: Routledge.

(1993b) 'Science as Vocation' in Hans Heinrich Gerth and Charles Wright Mills (eds.) *From Max Weber: Essays in Sociology*. London: Routledge.

Weber, S. (1985) 'Afterword: Literature – Just Making it' in Jean-Francois Lyotard and Jean-Loup Thebaud *Just Gaming*. Minneapolis: University of Minnesota Press.

Wenman, M. A. (2003a) 'What is Politics? The Approach of Radical Pluralism' in *Politics* 23(1): 57–65.

(2003b) '"Agonistic Pluralism" and Three Archetypal Forms of Politics' in *Contemporary Political Theory* 2(2): 165–86

(2003c) 'Laclau or Mouffe? Splitting the Difference' in *Philosophy and Social Criticism* 29(5): 581–606.

(2009) 'Hegemony and Globalist Strategy' in Adrian Little and Moya Lloyd (eds.) *The Politics of Radical Democracy*. Edinburgh: Edinburgh University Press.

(2014) 'Secularism, Agonism and the Politics of Conviction' in Brian Black, Gavin Hyman and Graham Smith (eds.) *Confronting Secularism in Europe and India: Legitimacy and Disenchantment in Contemporary Times*. London: Bloomsbury Academic.

(forthcoming) 'William E. Connolly: Resuming the Pluralist Tradition in American Political Science' in *Political Theory*.

White, S. K. (1998) '"Critical Responsiveness" and Justice' in *Philosophy and Social Criticism* 24(1): 73–81.

(2000) *Sustaining Affirmation: The Strength of Weak Ontology*. Princeton and Oxford: Princeton University Press.

(2002) 'Pluralism, Platitudes, and Paradoxes: Fifty Years of Western Political Thought' in *Political Theory* 30(4): 472–81.

Widder, N. (2002) *Genealogies of Difference*. Urbana and Chicago: University of Illinois Press.

Williams, B. (2005) *In the Beginning Was the Deed: Realism and Moralism in Political Argument*. Princeton and Oxford: Princeton University Press.

Winch, P. (1973) *The Idea of a Social Science and Its Relation to Philosophy*. London: Routledge and Kegan Paul.

Wingenbach, E. (2011) *Institutionalising Agonistic Democracy: Post-Foundationalism and Political Liberalism*. Farnham: Ashgate.

Wittgenstein, L. (1967) *Philosophical Investigations*. 3rd edn. Oxford: Blackwell.

(1974) *Tractatus Logico-Philosophicus*. London and New York: Routledge.

(1975) *On Certainty*. Oxford: Blackwell.

Wolin, S. (1992) 'What Revolutionary Action Means Today' in Chantal Mouffe (ed.) *Dimensions of Radical Democracy*. London: Verso.

(2004) *Politics and Vision: Continuity and Innovation in Western Political Thought*. Expanded edn. Princeton and Oxford: Princeton University Press.

Young, I. M. (1990) *Justice and the Politics of Difference*. Princeton: Princeton University Press.

(1995) 'Together in Difference: Transforming the Logic of Group Political conflict' in Will Kymlicka (ed.) *The Rights of Minority Cultures*. Oxford: Oxford University Press.

(2000) *Inclusion and Democracy*. Oxford: Oxford University Press.

(2007) 'Structural Injustice and the Politics of Difference' in Anthony Simon Laden and David Owen (eds.) *Multiculturalism and Political Theory*. Cambridge: Cambridge University Press.

Zerilli, L. M. G. (2001) 'Wittgenstein: Between Pragmatism and Deconstruction' in Ludwig Nagl and Chantal Mouffe (eds.) *The Legacy of Wittgenstein: Pragmatism or Deconstruction*. Frankfurt am Main: Peter Lang.

(2003) 'Doing without Knowing: Feminism's Politics of the Ordinary' in Cressida J. Heyes (ed.) *The Grammar of Politics: Wittgenstein and Political Philosophy*. Ithaca and London: Cornell University Press.

(2004) 'The Universalism Which Is Not One' in Simon Critchley and Oliver Marchart (eds.) *Laclau: A Critical Reader*. Abingdon: Routledge.

(2005) '"We feel our Freedom": Imagination and Judgement in the thought of Hannah Arendt' in *Political Theory* 33(2): 158–88.

Žižek, S. (1999a) *The Ticklish Subject*. London: Verso.

(1999b) 'Carl Schmitt in the Age of Post-Politics' in Chantal Mouffe (ed.) *The Challenge of Carl Schmitt*. London: Verso.

(2001) *Did Somebody Say Totalitarianism?* London: Verso.

(2002) 'Introduction: Between the Two Revolutions' in Slavoj Žižek (ed.) *Žižek on Lenin: The 1917 Writings*. London and New York: Verso.

(2006a) *The Universal Exception*. London and New York: Continuum.

(2006b) 'Against the Populist Temptation' in *Critical Inquiry* 32 (Spring): 551–74.

(2008) *Violence*. London: Profile Books.

Index

Printed in Great Britain
by Amazon